Readers tell us that EATER'S CHOICE really works . . .

"Using the 10% saturated fat diet in your book I lowered my lipids from 347 mg/dL to 204 mg/dL. . . . The magnitude of the results was both rewarding and surprising."

Joe D. Burek, D.V.M., Doylestown, Pennsylvania

"I started on the 3% saturated fat regime and lowered my cholesterol from 249 to 145 without exercise and lost the 20 pounds I wanted to lose in the process. . . . Thank you for writing such a simple, easy-to-understand book."

Cary Lichtenstein, Chicago, Illinois

"Thank you for your wonderful book. . . . I have had a cholesterol problem for 3 years and have been unable to decrease it. After only 2 weeks on your food plan, my cholesterol dove from 220 to 199."

Mildred Kani, Kenner, Louisiana

"Thought you'd like to know that between your great recipes and sat-fat/cholesterol information and my husband's will power, he went from 340 to 220 in 4 months. We couldn't have done it without you!"

Adrienne Breen, Chicago, Illinois

and gives them the facts they need . . .

"Bravo! Your book provides everything one should know in order to outwit the heart attacker."

Mundy Torok, Dover, New Jersey

"Your book is a revelation — what I've been looking for for years. Now for the first time I have facts and figures, and it's simple for me to stay within our fat budget. It's very exciting to know what to do."

Bernadette Stubbs, San Jose, California

"I am proud to say that after 3 weeks and 5 days my total cholesterol went from 301 to 209. Thank you for your book, which made counting the sat-fats easy and fun."

Gary Crouch, San Antonio, Texas

EATER'S CHOICE is recommended by experts . . .

"I've recommended your book to all my patients needing cholesterol-control diets. I've given it numerous times as a gift — even since Christmas."

Mary H. Belenky, R.D., Arnold, Maryland

"Among all the cholesterol books from the technical/professional point of view, yours is the best."

Richard N. Podell, M.D., M.P.H., New Providence, New Jersey

"I loved your book! I am a nurse and work for a cardiologist. We have recommended your book to many of our patients."

Debbie Ouillette, Pinconning, Michigan

"I am the Health Educator for our Health Department. I have found your book to be an excellent, clear, and *practical* resource."

Eric Triffin, West Haven, Connecticut

and provides delicious eating!

"My compliments to the chef!"

Marcia Dunn, Pittsburgh, Pennsylvania

"A whole new way of living with food."

Carol Beatty, Montpelier, Vermont

"One of our patients came in for a check-up — cholesterol 301. I suggested *Eater's Choice*. Last week his cholesterol was 171. . . . He and his wife feel like they are eating gourmet meals all the time."

Naomi Shaiken, New York, New York

"The recipes are fantastic! No boredom here. I have not tried one that we haven't liked. Yours is the first book I turn to when trying to decide what to cook for company."

Debbie Bailey, Pittsburgh, Pennsylvania

"My husband had a 410 cholesterol count, and the diet sheets his doctor gave him totally confused me. I got *Eater's Choice*, and at the end of 6 weeks his chol was 198! . . . As an Iowa farm girl I learned to cook using all the 'good' things — lots of butter, eggs, cream, and meat. This gives you an idea of what a total change it has been for me. . . . Best of all, my husband tells anyone who listens how well he eats, how good the meals are, and how pleased he is."

Jean M. Gray, Scottsdale, Arizona

EATER'S CHOICE

A FOOD LOVER'S GUIDE TO LOWER CHOLESTEROL

Dr. Ron Goor and
Nancy Goor

Illustrations by Nancy Goor

Revised Edition

HOUGHTON MIFFLIN COMPANY
Boston

Library of Congress Cataloging-in-Publication Data
Goor, Ron.
    Eater's choice.
    Bibliography: p.
    Includes index.
    1. Low-cholesterol diet.   2. Low-cholesterol
diet — Recipes.   I. Goor, Nancy.   II. Title.
RM237.75.G66   1989   613.2'6   88-13675
ISBN 0-395-50082-6

Printed in the United States of America

Q 10 9 8 7 6 5 4 3 2 1

Book design by Joyce C. Weston

*To the staff and participants of the
Coronary Primary Prevention Trial, whose
dedication and perseverance helped prove
that lowering blood cholesterol reduces
the risk of heart attack.*

*And to Charles Suther
whose encouragement helped make
this book possible.*

Acknowledgments

The authors wish to thank the many people who have contributed to the development of this book: Annette Arbel, Kathy Boyd, Buffie Brownstein, Judy Chiostri, Karen Feinstein, Leslie Goodman-Malamuth, Charles and Jeanette Goor, Alex and Dan Goor, Ilene Gutman, Nancy Hallsted, Anita Hamel, Mary Hanke, Barbara Hilberg, Arlene Howard, Dr. Donald Hunninghake, Eleanor Iverson, Sally and Carl Jones, Ann Jons, Esther Krashes, Dr. John LaRosa, Suzanne Lieblich, Bonnie Liebman, Morton Liftin, Eva MacLowry, Berengere and Jean-François Maquet, Sherri McKissick, Joy Mara, Alyssa Mezebish, Martin and Helen Miller, Dr. James and Ruth Phang, Muriel Rabin, Isabelle Schoenfeld, Dr. Helmut Schrott, Judith Sheard, and Lian Tsao.

CONTENTS

A NOTE ON THE REVISED EDITION

IN THE TWO years since *Eater's Choice* was first published, new cholesterol guidelines have been announced and new scientific evidence supporting the benefit of lowering cholesterol has been published. New drugs and food products that lower blood cholesterol levels are now on the market. In addition, we have learned what issues need more clarification from the questions asked by readers as well as by people who have attended our lectures.

To keep *Eater's Choice* up to date and responsive to your needs, we have added discussions of the following topics to the revised edition: the new Adult Treatment Panel Guidelines on Detection and Treatment of High Blood Cholesterol; a recent scientific study, which shows that reducing elevated blood cholesterol can lead to plaque reversal; a new class of cholesterol-lowering drugs; and timely information on fish oil tablets, olive oil, snack foods, desserts, and commercial foods.

We have also added 30 new heart-healthy recipes to satisfy requests from readers for more. A few were favorites contributed by our readers themselves. (If you have any great recipes, please send them to us at *Eater's Choice,* P.O. Box 2053, Rockville, MD 20852; we are always looking for delicious new dishes to try out and include in a future edition.)

Our goals for this edition have not changed: we want you to understand how foods affect blood cholesterol and the risk of heart disease and, more specifically, to evaluate your own diet and learn how to make heart-healthy food choices. The 230 delicious (and mostly easy to make) heart-healthy recipes will help you follow the *Eater's Choice* method and will quickly convince you that heart-healthy eating can be a great pleasure.

— Dr. Ron Goor and
Nancy Goor

FOREWORD

MODERN MEDICINE deserves much credit for improving the health and longevity of Americans by reducing the incidence of many infectious diseases and other causes of death of the past. However, as Americans live longer, diseases of a somewhat different nature — chronic diseases — are taking a relatively larger toll. Just when many people reach the peaks of their careers or a much deserved retirement, their lives may be devastated by heart disease or cancer. Heart disease alone accounts for 50 percent of the deaths in the United States. It is a major cause of disability and a major drain on our emotional and financial resources, both national and personal.

Heart disease is the result of multiple risk factors associated with our high living standard: rich foods, smoking, lack of exercise. In other words, the American way of life may be dangerous to our health. But I am convinced that lifestyles can be changed; in fact, they are changing. Scientific evidence has proven that quitting smoking reduces the incidence of lung cancer and heart disease. Lowering blood pressure reduces the incidence of stroke and heart disease. It is gratifying to see the decline of these diseases in the segments of the population that have made changes. As a consequence, mortality from heart disease has declined by 30 percent and that from stroke by 45 percent in the past twenty years.

While an individual cannot be given a guarantee, these trends show that the adoption of a sensible lifestyle can prevent the development of diseases that threaten both the length and quality of life.

Now a major national public health campaign is being launched against a third, equally potent risk factor for heart disease: high blood cholesterol. Recent evidence has shown that lowering high levels of blood cholesterol will indeed reduce the risk of heart disease. Blood cholesterol levels can be lowered by eating less saturated fat and cholesterol.

The first step is consciousness raising. We need to become aware of the hazards of elevated blood cholesterol levels. To discover if you are at increased risk for heart disease, know your blood cholesterol number. High blood cholesterol is a silent killer. There are no symptoms to warn you until the disease is fully developed, and by then it is often too late. Sudden death can be the first symptom.

If your blood cholesterol is too high, take steps to lower it with the help of your physician. It is up to you, however, to take control over this risk factor. Learn what can be done about it, make the necessary changes, and stick to them.

One of the changes to lower blood cholesterol recommended by the American Heart Association is to reduce total fat intake to 30 percent of daily caloric intake, saturated fat intake to 10 percent, and cholesterol intake to no more than 300 mg per day. Many people find this advice hard to apply. What does it mean in practical terms? How much of which foods should you eat to consume 10 percent of calories from saturated fat?

I have found that *Eater's Choice* addresses these questions in an easy, effective way. *Eater's Choice* discusses the saturated fat content of foods along with a comprehensive discussion of various risk factors of heart disease. Armed with this knowledge, you can figure out exactly what you should be eating to follow the American Heart Association guidelines. The *Eater's Choice* approach to lowering blood cholesterol works because *you* choose the foods you eat.

Eater's Choice is a valuable tool for physicians and other health professionals. Because it uses a quantitative assessment, both you and your physician know exactly what changes you must make in your eating pattern to achieve a healthy blood cholesterol level. Most important, *Eater's Choice* gives those at risk the facts and skills they need to modify their own diet in order to lower their cholesterol. I have found that people who assume responsibility for their own problems are more likely to devise solutions they can live with and thus achieve results that will be lasting.

Eater's Choice will help you discover that a healthy way of eating can also be delicious and satisfying. Far from being a sacrifice, eating heart-healthy foods makes the good life worth living. This book should become a handbook for the making of a modern public health campaign designed to improve the quality of life for all Americans.

Julius Richmond, M.D.
Former Surgeon General of the United States and
Assistant Secretary of Health,
Department of Health and Human Services

Professor of Health Policy Research and Education
Harvard University

INTRODUCTION

LIKE MILLIONS of other Americans, I come from a family with a history of heart disease. My father had his first of three heart attacks when he was only thirty-one. I was three years old at the time. I grew up with heart disease. It was there, but I didn't take it too seriously.

When I was thirty-one, my blood cholesterol level was measured for the first time. It was 311 mg/dL, the doctor told me — an abnormally high level that put me at very high risk for heart disease, especially with my family history. He sent me to the National Institutes of Health (NIH) to be screened for participation in a clinical trial. The trial was designed to test the effect of lowering blood cholesterol on the risk of heart disease.

At NIH, physicians explained the degree of risk associated with my blood cholesterol level and the nature of the experiment. The experiment included coronary angiography. This test involves inserting a tube through a leg artery up to the heart. A dye is injected so that the amount of blockage of the coronary arteries can be visualized. The mortality rate for the test was only 1 in 100, I was assured.

Learning about the risks of the experiment as well as the risk associated with my elevated blood cholesterol level scared the hell out of me. Although I was excluded from participating in the study (my blood cholesterol level dropped below the cut-off point for entry into the study when I went on the mild study diet), this experience may well have saved my life.

For the first time, I began to realize the seriousness of high blood cholesterol. I was a heart attack just waiting to happen. But equally important, I got a taste of what it is like to be a patient, to have tests done on me and to think of myself as sick. This was hard to take. After all, I was a young man of thirty-one, and I felt great.

This experience taught me two lifesaving lessons. First, although I felt fit and vigorous, I was actually at high risk for heart disease because of my high blood cholesterol level. And with my family history, it could not be ignored. Second, I could lower my blood cholesterol level simply by changing what I ate.

It was too bad it took me all those years to realize the wisdom of my parents' advice about the foods I ate. They were always recommending a low-cholesterol, low-fat diet. I resented their insistence when there seemed to be little relevance to my health. My father was the one who was sick, not I.

How foolish I was. Coronary heart disease is a slow, insidious disease that begins in childhood and develops without symptoms over decades. Then, all of a sudden, boom — a heart attack that may be fatal and, if not, will certainly change your life.

My NIH experience changed my life. I wanted to do something professionally about cholesterol and heart disease. I took my wife and young sons to Boston and added a master of public health degree to my Ph.D. in biochemistry. I then returned to Bethesda, where I got a job as the National Coordinator of the Coronary Primary Prevention Trial at the National Heart, Lung, and Blood Institute of the National Institutes of Health. As I will explain later, this trial was developed to test the hypothesis that lowering your blood cholesterol really does lower your risk of heart disease.

I was involved with this trial for seven years, from its beginning to its end. After it was successfully completed, I took a new job in the Heart Institute as Coordinator of the National Cholesterol Education Program. I wanted to get the word out to the public, physicians, and dietitians about blood cholesterol, diet, and heart disease.

After a year and a half, I became convinced that the way to reach the public was to write a book — this book, which is filled with the information I have gained as a professional in this field. This is not just an academic subject for me. I have lowered my blood cholesterol from 311 mg/dL to 200 mg/dL merely by changing the foods I eat. My two young sons consider heart-healthy eating the natural way to eat. They are not even aware that they are reducing their risk of coronary heart disease and developing healthy habits for the future; they just enjoy eating good food.

Changing my eating habits has been an easy, inexpensive, and pleasant way for me to lower my risk of heart disease. That is what this book is all about. I want to tell *you* how to do it.

— Dr. Ron Goor

ONE

EATER'S CHOICE

FOR YOU

I

THIS BOOK was written for you, whether you are an average, healthy American, a recipient of a triple coronary bypass, or a survivor of four heart attacks. If you are in good health, it will give you the knowledge and skills to help you stay healthy and improve your chances of avoiding heart disease and possibly some common forms of cancer. And if you already have heart disease, this book will give you the tools to help you slow down further progression of your condition.

THE INSIDIOUS DISEASE

It may be difficult for you to worry about heart disease if you are healthy, active, and in the prime of life. But here are some alarming statistics that should jar you out of your complacency.

- Fifty percent of Americans die of heart disease.
- Heart disease is the leading cause of death in the United States, outnumbering deaths from cancer and accidents combined.
- Three Americans suffer heart attacks every minute.
- One American dies from a heart attack every minute.
- The first symptom for half the victims of heart disease is death.
- More than 500,000 Americans die from heart attacks each year.
- More than 650,000 Americans are hospitalized for heart attacks each year.
- More than 5 million Americans have angina or other symptoms of heart disease. Many of these people lead highly restricted, painful, and fearful lives.

Choose Not to Be a Part of These Grim Statistics: These statistics are a national shame. They need not be true. Heart disease is not a natural consequence of aging. The epidemic of heart disease is a product of the way we live. By changing our lifestyles, we can make an impact on our health.

In fact, it is already happening. Coronary heart disease has declined by 30 percent in the past twenty years and stroke has decreased even more. Many experts believe that the lifestyle changes Americans are making are reducing the incidence of heart disease. Americans are consuming less cholesterol and saturated fat and have lower blood cholesterol levels. They are smoking fewer cigarettes. They have lowered their blood pressure. They are exercising more.

The lifestyle changes you and your family make can also make a difference. You can increase the chances that you and your family will escape coronary heart disease by the way you choose to live.

But you must act now. The first symptom of half of those who die of heart attacks is death itself. All the improvements in emergency coronary care are of no help in such cases. This high rate of sudden death places an important premium on *prevention*. No one but you can make the necessary decisions that affect your heart disease risk.

Three Major Risks

How do you know if you are at increased risk for coronary heart disease? You are at increased risk if you

- smoke,
- have high blood pressure (over 140/90),
- have elevated blood cholesterol (over 200 mg/dL).*

These are the three major risk factors for coronary heart disease that you can control.

One Plus One Equals Four: The presence of any one of the risk factors (high blood cholesterol, cigarette smoking, or high blood pressure) *doubles* your risk of coronary heart disease. Having two of these risk factors *quadruples* the risk. Thus, if you smoke and have high blood pressure, your risk is enhanced fourfold. And if you smoke, have high blood cholesterol, and have high blood pressure, your risk increases *eightfold* (see Figure 1). It certainly makes you think. We hope it will make you stop smoking, seek advice on con-

---

*Milligrams of cholesterol per deciliter of blood

Risk of Coronary Heart Disease Increases with Additional Risk Factors

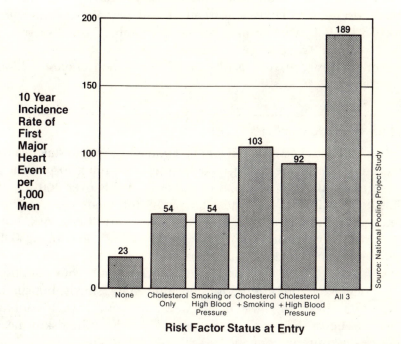

10 Year Incidence Rate of First Major Heart Event per 1,000 Men

Source: National Pooling Project Study

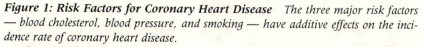

Risk Factor Status at Entry

Figure 1: Risk Factors for Coronary Heart Disease   *The three major risk factors — blood cholesterol, blood pressure, and smoking — have additive effects on the incidence rate of coronary heart disease.*

Adapted with permission from the Journal of Chronic Diseases, *vol. 31, Pooling Project Research Group, "Relationship of Blood Pressure, Serum Cholesterol, Smoking Habit, Relative Weight, and ECG Abnormalities to Incidence of Major Coronary Events: Final Report of the Pooling Project." Copyright 1978, Pergamon Press, Ltd., and with permission of the American Heart Association, Inc.*

trolling your high blood pressure, and continue reading this book to find out how to lower your blood cholesterol.

What do all these risks mean and how do they apply to you and your life decisions? Perhaps this analogy will help you understand: Suppose that life is like playing Russian roulette. In this game of Russian roulette, you have a partially loaded gun pointed at your head. Obviously, the more chambers that contain bullets, the higher the chance that you will die.

Think of risk factors as the bullets in the chamber of the gun. The more risk factors for coronary heart disease you have, the greater are the chances you will have a heart attack and, perhaps, die. The question is: Do you want to play with one chamber loaded or two or three or four? **The choice is yours!**

(For more about risk factors other than blood cholesterol, see Chapter 9.)

THIS BOOK IS FOR YOU

This book has been written for all of you who want to stay healthy and enjoy life to the fullest, and for the more than 50 percent of American adults whose blood cholesterol level is over 200 mg/dL. This book will help you understand how the foods you eat affect your blood cholesterol level and thus your heart disease risk. Most important, it will teach you the necessary eating and cooking skills to reduce your chance of suffering a heart attack.

Act Now: Don't wait for a heart attack to grab your attention. The clogging of your arteries is happening NOW, slowly, but surely, and it won't wait for you to decide to change your ways. It's not too late (and never too soon) to take action to reduce the risk of heart disease for yourself, your spouse, and your children.

A Special Note to Those Who Already Have Heart Disease

Especially if you already have angina or have had a coronary by-pass operation or a heart attack, you can benefit from this book. As we will explain in Chapter 3, you can slow or stop the progression of the life-threatening blockage of the coronary arteries and, in some cases, even reverse it.

A Special Note to the Total Population

This book is for everyone. The *Eater's Choice* low-fat eating plan and recipes are not just for people who are worried about coronary heart disease. The National Cancer Institute recommends a diet low in fat and high in fiber to help prevent some common cancers, such as colon and breast cancers. A similar low-fat diet is also recommended for diabetics. For those concerned with their looks as well as their health, eating foods low in fat is one of the best ways to lose weight and stay trim. You'll feel better, too. As Dr. Richmond points out in the Foreword, "Far from being a sacrifice, eating heart-healthy foods makes the good life worth living." So, no matter who you are, take this book to heart.

Remember:

1. Heart disease is the leading cause of death in the United States.
2. Three major risk factors for coronary heart disease are high blood cholesterol, high blood pressure, and cigarette smoking.
3. *You* can control the three major risk factors of heart disease.

2 IT'S YOUR HEART — KEEP IT TICKING

YOU GO to the doctor for a physical. You're feeling great. You're not *too* heavy — well, just a few pounds; a bit soft and blubbery around the middle. But, you've never felt better. You get a little breathless walking up steps, but other than that, you feel like a twenty-year-old. Your doctor sits you down. His expression is serious. "You are in good physical condition," he tells you, "but your blood cholesterol is 245." "So?" you ask. "So," he answers, "you're a good candidate for a heart attack. The higher your blood cholesterol, the higher your risk of heart disease."

You feel a queasy sensation in your stomach. Your head begins to spin. "What is blood cholesterol?" you ask. "How does it affect my heart?" You've read about cholesterol in the newspapers. You remember something about HDL, or good cholesterol, and triglycerides, but it never really sank in. Now you're ready to listen. You *need* to understand it. It's *your* heart. It's *your* life.

THE HEART AND HEART DISEASE

The heart is a muscle that pumps blood throughout the body to deliver nutrients to all the body's cells and to remove waste materials. Just how much work the heart does is mind-boggling. Even while you rest or sleep, the heart beats between 70 and 80 times each minute and pumps nearly 5 quarts of blood. That adds up to about 100,000 beats and about 1800 gallons of blood pumped each day.

During vigorous exercise, the heart can increase its output nearly fivefold. Blood is kept moving through the extensive network of arteries, capillaries, and veins by the pumping heart at such a rate that

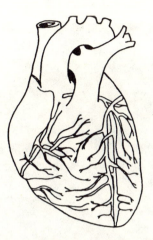

Figure 2: The Heart and Coronary Arteries The coronary arteries and the network of vessels branching off from them come down over the top of the heart like a crown (corona) and supply the heart muscle with oxygenated blood. Drawing by Judy Beavers.

blood can make the trip from the heart to the big toe and back in less than one minute.

In order to do all this work, the heart muscle needs a constant supply of nutrient-rich, oxygenated blood. This is supplied by the coronary arteries that branch off from the aorta (see Figure 2).

What Is Atherosclerosis? The underlying cause of coronary heart disease is a process called atherosclerosis. Atherosclerosis is the clogging of the coronary arteries with fatty, fibrous, cholesterol-laden deposits (called atheromata or plaques). These deposits thicken the artery wall, thus narrowing the channel through which the blood flows. Plaques are caused by an excess of cholesterol in the blood (see Figure 3).

When Does Atherosclerosis Begin? In countries where people eat foods high in saturated fat, plaques begin to develop in childhood. Plaque formation progresses at different rates in different people, depending on their ability to metabolize fat. (Both high blood pressure and smoking speed up the rate of atherosclerosis.) Over the course of the first three to four decades of life, plaque deposits gradually increase and the openings of the coronary arteries gradually narrow (see Figure 4).

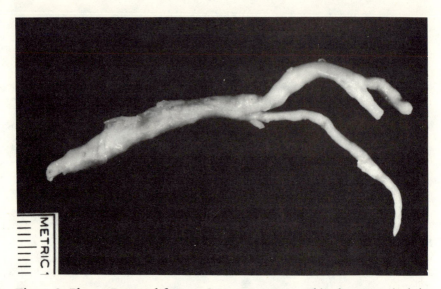

Figure 3: Plaque Removed from a Coronary Artery This plaque acquired the shape of the coronary artery that it completely blocked. Photo by Maggie Moore, laboratory of Dr. William C. Roberts, NHLBI.

Figure 4: Progression of Blocking of a Coronary Artery The progressive blocking of a coronary artery by the accumulation of plaque is shown in these three cross-sections.

During this time there are usually no symptoms. You feel good. You are active, in your prime, enjoying the good life. Then suddenly, or so it seems, the inevitable occurs. An artery that feeds blood to the heart muscle becomes 75 percent or more blocked with plaque.

What Is Angina? If you are lucky, the first symptom of coronary heart disease may be angina pectoris. This mildest and earliest symptom is brief chest pain, usually experienced upon exertion. Angina occurs because not enough blood can get through the blocked arteries to supply oxygen to the heart muscle cells. Cells deprived of oxy-

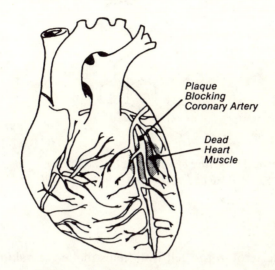

Figure 5: Damage to the Heart Muscle After a Heart Attack *The shaded area shows the extent of dead heart muscle resulting from the blockage of a coronary artery. Drawing by Judy Beavers.*

gen for only a few minutes can recover if you rest, thereby reducing the demand on the heart. If the oxygen supply is cut off for longer periods, permanent damage to the heart may result.

The First Symptom May Be Your Last: If you are not so lucky, a small blood clot may become lodged in the narrowed artery and completely block the flow of blood to part of the heart. This part of the heart muscle dies. Result: **heart attack or sudden death** (see Figure 5).

WHAT IS CHOLESTEROL AND WHY DO WE HAVE IT?

Let's backtrack. The doctor says your blood cholesterol is too high. What does heart disease have to do with cholesterol?

Cholesterol is an odorless, white, powdery substance (see Figure 6). It is like a fat in that it does not mix with water. We are concerned with cholesterol because in excess it forms plaque, which clogs the coronary arteries and causes heart disease.

Cholesterol also has many beneficial and vital functions. It is a necessary ingredient of the cell walls of *all* animals, including hu-

Cholesterol

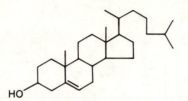

HO

Figure 6: Chemical Structure of Cholesterol *Cholesterol is a fatlike substance with a sterol ring structure. It is found in foods and in the VLDL, LDL, and HDL lipoproteins in the blood.*

mans. Cholesterol in the cell wall helps make your skin waterproof and also slows down water loss by evaporation from the body. Cholesterol is also used in the formation of the steroid and sex hormones. Cholesterol acts as an insulator in the myelin sheath that surrounds nerves and allows normal transmission of nerve impulses.

Cholesterol is transported in the blood stream together with fats. It is in this capacity that cholesterol becomes implicated in heart disease.

FAT FACTS

In your blood right now are various kinds of particles carrying fat around to do useful work or get stored for later use. Everyone has his or her own balance of the various kinds of particles, depending on diet, heredity, and physical activity. Because we now know one kind of particle is good and another bad, it is worth knowing which is which.

Lipoproteins

Fats* in your body (and in foods) generally occur as *triglycerides*. They are transported in blood, which consists mainly of water. They are broken down and their energy released by enzymes,** which

---

*Fats are one of the five major classes of nutrients; the other four are proteins, carbohydrates, minerals, and vitamins.
**Enzymes are proteins that speed up chemical reactions without themselves being changed.

function in a water medium. However, fats do not mix with water. So fats are packaged into particles to keep them from separating out from the water in the blood. These particles, which also contain proteins and cholesterol, are called *lipoproteins* (*lipo* means fat). Three of the major types of lipoproteins are very low density lipoproteins (VLDL), low density lipoproteins (LDL), and high density lipoproteins (HDL).

VLDL Lipoproteins: The liver uses excess carbohydrates and fats from the foods you eat to make triglycerides (fats). These triglycerides are packaged into VLDL (very low density lipoprotein) particles for distribution from the liver to the rest of the body. VLDL particles contain large amounts of triglycerides and lesser amounts of cholesterol, protein, and other fats. VLDL particles are produced and released into the blood stream in large quantities after meals.

LDL Lipoproteins: The Bad Cholesterol: As the VLDL particles circulate through the blood stream, triglycerides are removed from the particles and enter cells, where they are used as a source of energy. The fat-depleted VLDL particles are called LDL (low density lipoprotein) particles. The cholesterol and protein that remain constitute a large part of the LDL particles.

LDL particles remain in the blood stream for different periods of time in different people. The longer the cholesterol-rich LDL particles remain in the blood stream, the more likely it is that some of their cholesterol will be added to the plaque that is building up in the coronary artery walls. As more and more cholesterol deposits are added to the plaque, the artery channel becomes more and more narrow. You know the result. When blood can no longer flow through a coronary artery, the part of the heart supplied by that artery dies. Result: heart attack.

Thus, the higher the LDL level in the blood, the more cholesterol is available to clog the coronary arteries and the higher is the risk of developing atherosclerosis and coronary heart disease. The cholesterol in LDL deserves its name of "bad cholesterol."

In some people, LDL particles are quickly removed from the blood stream by special LDL receptors on cell surfaces. Once inside the cells, cholesterol from the LDL particles is broken down. When these fortunate people with a normal or high number of LDL receptors have their blood cholesterol measured, their LDL is very low.

Other people have reduced numbers of fully functioning LDL receptors (the genetic constitution of the individual determines the number and activity of the LDL receptors). In these people, LDL particles remain in the blood stream longer, producing a higher LDL level in the blood. Since LDL particles are so rich in cholesterol, a high LDL level results in a high blood cholesterol level.

HDL Lipoproteins: The Good Cholesterol: HDL (high density lipoprotein) particles are the smallest of the lipoprotein particles. HDL removes cholesterol from LDL particles and cells and transports it to the liver. Here most of the cholesterol is broken down into bile acids and excreted into the small intestine. Some of the cholesterol is reprocessed into new VLDL particles.

By removing cholesterol from LDL, HDL prevents cholesterol from accumulating in the coronary arteries and thus protects against the development of heart disease. The higher the HDL level, the more cholesterol is removed from the blood stream and the lower is the risk of heart attack. The lower the HDL level, the less cholesterol is removed from the blood stream, and the greater is the risk of heart disease.

Cholesterol: While cholesterol is not a lipoprotein, it is contained in all the lipoproteins. It is of particular interest because it is a major culprit in the formation of plaque.

Cholesterol in the blood is derived partly from cholesterol in the foods you eat and partly from cholesterol made in the liver and the intestine. Because cholesterol is so vital to the normal functioning of the body, all of the body's cholesterol needs can be met by cholesterol made in the liver. In addition, each cell in the body can make cholesterol. Even if you consumed no cholesterol at all (i.e., if you were a strict vegetarian), your body would manufacture enough cholesterol for proper growth and development. However, consumption of too much cholesterol can overload your system and end up as plaque in your coronary arteries.

Note: Cholesterol in foods is not the only, or even the most important, nutrient that affects your blood cholesterol level. The amount of saturated fat in foods is a more important factor in raising blood cholesterol levels, as we will see in Chapter 5.

What *Your* Cholesterol and Lipoprotein Values Mean

All this talk about lipoproteins and cholesterol is very abstract. You want to know about *your* lipoproteins and *your* cholesterol. What do the numbers that you receive from your doctor or from a blood cholesterol screening mean? Do your levels put you at increased risk for heart disease?

First, the total blood cholesterol reading is the sum of the cholesterol in your VLDL, LDL, and HDL particles. Thus, if your total blood cholesterol level is 250, the breakdown may look like this:

$$
\begin{array}{r}
45 \text{ mg/dL of HDL-cholesterol} \\
+ \quad 20 \text{ mg/dL of VLDL-cholesterol} \\
+ \quad 185 \text{ mg/dL of LDL-cholesterol} \\
\hline
250 \text{ mg/dL of total cholesterol}
\end{array}
$$

HDL: Average HDL-cholesterol levels for adult males are about 45 mg/dL and about 55 mg/dL for adult females. Levels lower than average place you at increased risk. The lower they are, the greater your risk. Levels below 35 mg/dL should be a cause for concern. Levels above the average decrease your risk. The higher they are, the lower your risk.

If your HDL is low, you can raise it, but only within narrow limits. Regular aerobic exercise and losing weight if you are overweight will increase your HDL levels. On average, nonsmokers have higher HDL levels than smokers.

A low HDL level, especially in combination with other heart disease risk factors such as high blood pressure, smoking, or a family history of heart disease, is an especially dangerous combination. If your HDL is low, you should see your physician and take vigorous steps to reduce as many of these other risk factors as possible. You should lower your blood pressure, stop smoking, exercise regularly, lose weight if overweight, and lower your LDL if it is too high.

Because of their sex hormones, most premenopausal women have higher levels of HDL than do men of the same age. During the thirty or so years that women are protected from developing atherosclerosis by high levels of HDL, many men are accumulating plaque at a fast rate. As a result, many men begin to experience heart disease at early ages (as early as their forties). This is not to imply that women are immune to heart disease. Once women reach menopause and lose their protective hormones, they too begin to develop plaque at a fast rate. In fact, heart disease is the leading cause of death in women, occurring fifteen to twenty years later than in men.

VLDL and Triglycerides: VLDL is not measured directly. It is calculated from your triglyceride level as follows:

$$VLDL = triglycerides \div 5.$$

Triglycerides can be measured only after a twelve-hour fast.

Average values of triglycerides are about 140–150 mg/dL for men and about 100–120 mg/dL for women. Triglycerides are considered a risk factor for heart disease only at levels above 250 mg/dL. If your triglycerides are too high, restrict your intake of simple sugars (sweets) and alcohol (an important factor in raising triglycerides), exercise regularly, and lose weight if you are overweight. Eating less simple sugar, less saturated fat, and more complex carbohydrates (grains, vegetables, and fruits) will help you lose weight and thus lower your triglycerides.

LDL: Average levels of LDL-cholesterol are about 135–145 mg/dL for men and about 120–135 mg/dL for women. About half of American adults have levels higher than these. Such levels are too high for long-term health and are the major reason heart disease is the leading cause of death in this country.

You can lower your LDL-cholesterol levels by changing the foods you eat and by losing weight. Specifically, eating foods low in saturated fats and cholesterol lowers your LDL. Eating less saturated fat increases the number of LDL receptors, thus allowing for increased removal of LDL (bad) cholesterol from the blood. Eating less cholesterol reduces the amount of cholesterol available to be made into lipoproteins in the liver and released into the blood.

LIPOPROTEINS AND YOUR RISK OF HEART DISEASE

LIPOPROTEIN	RISK INCREASES IF:	TO REDUCE YOUR RISK:
HDL	Low	Exercise regularly Stop smoking Lose weight if overweight
VLDL (Triglycerides)	High	Restrict alcohol Exercise regularly Lose weight if overweight Eat less simple sugar (sweets) Eat less saturated fat
LDL	High	Eat less saturated fat Eat less cholesterol Lose weight if overweight

The majority of total blood cholesterol is carried in the LDL. Since the total blood cholesterol level is a reflection of the LDL level, it is usually sufficient to monitor only total blood cholesterol. In the rest of this book, we will refer only to total blood cholesterol. But you should know that when you reduce your total blood cholesterol by changing the foods you eat, you are primarily lowering your LDL level and thus your risk of heart disease.

YOU CAN CHOOSE TO LOWER YOUR RISKS

This chapter makes it clear that the most dramatic reduction of coronary heart disease risk can be achieved by lowering your LDL-cholesterol level. And you have an effective, inexpensive, safe, and palatable way to lower your LDL: **change the foods you eat.** YOU can stop clogging up your arteries by eating the right foods. YOU can make a difference in your heart's destiny. And that is what this book is all about. *Eater's Choice* gives you a way to lower your LDL by lowering the amount of saturated fat you eat without depriving you of your favorite foods.

By the time you finish Chapter 10, you should be convinced that it really does matter what foods you pour into your body. If you bought a new car and wanted to keep it in tiptop operating condition, you would never fill it with dirty gas oozing big globs of junk that could collect in the pipelines and clog the fuel line. You would make sure you fed it the best gas available. Why not treat yourself as well as you treat your car?

Remember:

1. The heart is a living pump that must be constantly supplied with oxygen and nutrients via the coronary arteries.
2. Atherosclerosis is the process by which the coronary arteries are progressively blocked by cholesterol-rich deposits.
3. Heart attacks occur when a coronary artery becomes 75 percent or more blocked. A heart attack involves death of the part of the heart muscle normally supplied by the blocked coronary artery.
4. Cholesterol in the blood is found in the lipoprotein particles involved in fat transport: VLDL, LDL, and HDL. Total blood

cholesterol is the sum of the cholesterol in VLDL + LDL + HDL.

5. High levels of HDL cholesterol ("good" cholesterol) lower the risk of heart disease. You can raise your HDL by exercising regularly, losing weight if you are overweight, and stopping smoking.

6. High levels of LDL cholesterol ("bad" cholesterol) raise the risk of heart disease. You can lower your LDL and your risk of coronary heart disease by eating less saturated fat and cholesterol.

THE EVIDENCE 3

AT THE END of the last chapter, we categorically stated that you could lower your blood cholesterol and thus stop clogging your arteries by changing your eating habits. Before you consider a major revamping of your old eating style, you may want proof that the change will indeed lower your blood cholesterol level and that lowering your blood cholesterol will reduce your risk of coronary heart disease.

Without drowning you in a sea of scientific data, we will merely touch on a few of the more important studies that show that:

1. elevated blood cholesterol is a risk factor for coronary heart disease;
2. blood cholesterol levels can be raised or lowered by the foods you eat;
3. lowering blood cholesterol reduces the risk of coronary heart disease.

EVIDENCE PART I: ELEVATED BLOOD CHOLESTEROL IS A RISK FACTOR FOR CORONARY HEART DISEASE

The Framingham Study

For almost forty years, investigators have been studying the health of the population of Framingham, Massachusetts, paying particular attention to risk factors for heart disease. Blood cholesterol levels have been measured and remeasured, heart attacks have been recorded. Even today, data on the original participants and their chil-

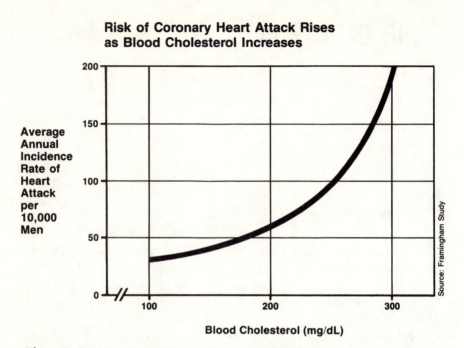

Risk of Coronary Heart Attack Rises as Blood Cholesterol Increases

Average Annual Incidence Rate of Heart Attack per 10,000 Men

Blood Cholesterol (mg/dL)

Source: Framingham Study

Figure 7: Coronary Heart Disease Risk and Blood Cholesterol Risk of coronary *heart disease rises with increasing blood cholesterol levels. Risk increases rapidly as blood cholesterol levels rise above 200 mg/dL.*

dren are being collected and analyzed. The results of this long-term population study are conclusive: **blood cholesterol levels predict the future incidence of heart attacks.**

The relationship between blood cholesterol levels and heart attacks is shown in a curve popularly known as the "Framingham risk curve" (see Figure 7). This curve is smooth and continuous. As blood cholesterol levels go up, risk of heart attack rises. At blood cholesterol levels above 200 mg/dL, risk rises rapidly. The risk is four times greater at a blood cholesterol level of 300 mg/dL than at a blood cholesterol level of about 200 mg/dL. (The Framingham risk curve could just as accurately be expressed in terms of LDL-cholesterol level instead of total blood cholesterol.) Although even the lowest blood cholesterol levels carry some risk of coronary heart disease, Dr. William Castelli, director of the Framingham Study, has stated that no one with a blood cholesterol level below 150 mg/dL has ever had a heart attack in Framingham.

EVIDENCE PART II: BLOOD CHOLESTEROL LEVELS CAN BE LOWERED (OR RAISED) BY DIET

Blood cholesterol levels are not set in concrete. They can be changed. To a large extent YOU can lower (or raise) your blood cholesterol level by what you eat. Here's the evidence to prove it.

International Comparisons

Comparing diets of countries with low and high coronary heart disease rates reveals a direct correlation between the amount of saturated fat in the diet and the blood cholesterol level and incidence of heart disease among the different populations.

The rates of coronary heart disease among countries varies almost tenfold from a low of 100 per 100,000 in Japan to a high of 900 per 100,000 in Finland. The Japanese eat little beef (a food high in saturated fat) and much fish (a food low in saturated fat and rich in polyunsaturated fat). The Finns, on the other hand, eat large amounts of cheese and whole milk products — foods high in saturated fat.

Countries with high average blood cholesterol levels and high rates of coronary heart disease have diets in which saturated fat accounts for over 15 percent of total calories. This includes the United States, Scotland, England, Finland, and Holland. Countries with very low blood cholesterol levels and very low coronary heart disease rates have diets in which saturated fats contribute less than 10 percent of total calories. Such countries include Japan and Greece.

Is the Evidence Valid? How can we be sure that these differences in coronary heart disease rates among countries are really due to dietary differences and not to genetic differences?

Japan to Hawaii: Changing Dietary Habits. An interesting study of Japanese migrants to Hawaii and San Francisco sheds light on this question. Japanese in Japan have one of the lowest rates of coronary heart disease. They have low blood cholesterol levels (the average blood cholesterol level was found to be less than 170 mg/dL) and eat a diet in which fat contributes only about 10 percent of total calories and saturated fat only about 3 percent. By Western standards, this is a very low fat diet.

The Japanese who have migrated to Hawaii have adopted some Western dietary habits. They eat a diet higher in fat and saturated fat than the typical Japanese diet but not as high as a typical American diet. The Japanese in Hawaii have higher blood cholesterol levels and higher rates of coronary heart disease than those in Japan but not as high as those in San Francisco.

Japan to Hawaii to San Francisco: Accumulating Bad Dietary Habits and Plaques. The Japanese who have migrated to San Francisco have gone even further in adopting American dietary habits, have blood cholesterol levels similar to native Americans, and, alas, have rates of coronary heart disease similar to Americans. Clearly, it is diet, and not genetics, that is raising the blood cholesterol levels and consequently the coronary heart disease rates of the migrants.

Vegetarians Provide Evidence. Most Seventh-Day Adventists are ovo-lacto vegetarians and thus eat some eggs and dairy products. Some, however, are strict vegetarians and eat no animal products at all. Others eat meat.

In general, those who are strict vegetarians have the lowest blood cholesterol levels. Ovo-lacto vegetarians (the majority of Adventists) have slightly higher blood cholesterol levels. Those who eat meat have the highest levels. *The vegetarian Adventists (including ovo-lacto vegetarians) have significantly lower heart disease rates than other Americans of the same age and sex.* It should be kept in mind that Adventists also do not drink coffee or alcohol or smoke tobacco.

Dietary Studies in Normal Volunteers. The strongest and most direct evidence that diet affects blood cholesterol levels comes from studies of normal volunteers whose intakes of saturated, polyunsaturated, and monounsaturated fats and cholesterol are varied under tightly controlled conditions on special hospital wards. These studies show that LDL cholesterol levels decrease when dietary saturated fat and cholesterol are decreased and when dietary polyunsaturated fat is increased. Removing saturated fat from the diet has two times the blood cholesterol–lowering impact as does adding an equal amount of polyunsaturated fat.

How Your Heredity Fits In

At this point a question always seems to pop up. If blood cholesterol levels are affected by diet, why do people who eat exactly the same diet have different blood cholesterol levels?

Your blood cholesterol level is determined by how your genetic constitution affects the metabolism of the fats and cholesterol you eat. In other words, blood cholesterol level depends on an interaction between genetics and diet — that is, how sensitive you are to the amounts of saturated fats and cholesterol you eat.

We are a population with a great range of genetic constitutions affecting the control of blood cholesterol levels. Upon exposure to the typical high-fat, high-cholesterol American diet, these different genetic constitutions are expressed as widely divergent blood cholesterol levels. Thus, some people can eat large amounts of saturated fat and cholesterol and maintain a blood cholesterol level of 150 mg/dL. Other people on the same fatty diet maintain a blood cholesterol level of 350 mg/dL.

The Japanese in Japan show much less variability in blood cholesterol levels. However, the fact that there is much genetic variability in the Japanese population is revealed when they are exposed to a typical American diet of high saturated fat and cholesterol. Thus, one person with a blood cholesterol of 170 mg/dL in Japan may find it rise to 230 mg/dL on a San Francisco diet, while another may find it rise to 280 mg/dL, while yet another may find it rise only to 180 mg/dL.

EVIDENCE PART III: LOWERING BLOOD CHOLESTEROL REDUCES YOUR RISK OF CORONARY HEART DISEASE

The big question that remains is: Does lowering elevated blood cholesterol levels in humans reduce the risk of coronary heart disease? The answer is a resounding and definite YES.

The Coronary Primary Prevention Trial Gets Results

In 1973, the National Heart, Lung, and Blood Institute (one of the National Institutes of Health) began a ten-year study, the Coronary Primary Prevention Trial (CPPT), to test the lipid hypothesis: lowering blood cholesterol levels reduces the incidence of coronary heart disease.

The basic plan of the study was as follows. To test the lipid hypothesis, two groups of men with identical risks of coronary heart disease were selected. At the outset, both groups had identical average blood cholesterol levels of almost 300 mg/dL. Both groups followed a mild cholesterol-lowering diet. In addition, one group received a drug (cholestyramine) that lowered their blood cholesterol levels while the other group received a placebo that looked and tasted like the real drug but had no blood cholesterol–lowering effect. During the study, the only risk factor difference between the two groups was the lower blood cholesterol level of the drug-treated group.

CPPT Results: Lowering Blood Cholesterol Cuts Risk: At the end of the ten years, there was a definite difference in the incidence of coronary heart disease between the two groups. The group treated with the active drug had a lower average blood cholesterol level and a lower incidence of fatal and nonfatal heart attacks than the group that was not drug-treated.

Blood cholesterol levels in the drug-treated group were, on average, 9 percent lower than those in the placebo group. The incidence of fatal and nonfatal heart attacks in the treated group was 19 percent lower than in the placebo group. (There were reductions of a similar magnitude in new cases of angina, coronary bypass surgery, and electrocardiographic abnormalities in the treated group.)

This figures out to a fantastic ratio: for every 1 percent reduction in blood cholesterol, there was a 2 percent reduction in risk. Thus, participants who achieved a 25 percent reduction in blood cholesterol reduced their risk of heart attack by 50 percent.

These results may be applicable to you. For every 1 percent you reduce your blood cholesterol, your risk may be reduced by as much as 2 percent. Pretty good odds.

Another NIH Study Confirms CPPT Results: Another NIH study, which was conducted at the same time, also tested the lipid hypothesis. It produced results that could actually be seen in the coronary arteries. In this study, men and women were chosen with elevated blood cholesterol levels and atherosclerotic narrowing of their coronary arteries. They were randomly divided into two groups. Both groups followed a mild cholesterol-lowering diet. One treatment group received a blood cholesterol–lowering drug (cholestyramine) and the other a placebo.

At the beginning of the study, both groups underwent coronary angiography to evaluate the extent of atherosclerosis or narrowing of their coronary arteries. (Coronary angiography is a technique that uses an iodine-containing dye and x-ray pictures to allow visualization of the coronary arteries.) At the end of the study, five years later, the severity of atherosclerosis of the coronary arteries of both groups was once more assessed by coronary angiography.

The results were dramatic. Investigators could actually *see* that lowering LDL-cholesterol levels in the drug treatment group prevented the further narrowing of the coronary arteries.

In 1987 these results were confirmed. The Cholesterol-Lowering Atherosclerosis Study (CLAS) was an angiographic study of middle-aged men who had undergone coronary bypass surgery. Those men who were treated with a combination of drugs (colestipol and niacin) and diet had lower LDL levels, higher HDL levels, and, as a result of these changes, significantly less accumulation of atherosclerotic plaque than those not treated with a combination of drugs and diet. More exciting, 16.2 percent of the drug-and-diet-treated group experienced regression of atherosclerotic plaque.

Diet Versus Drug: You may wonder how we can assume that lowering blood cholesterol levels by diet is effective in reducing risk of coronary heart disease when the CPPT and the NIH and CLAS studies were drug studies.

Participants in the placebo group in the CPPT showed a range of reduction of LDL-cholesterol levels. These reductions were achieved by diet alone since these men received no active drug. Just as in the drug group, the greater the reduction in LDL-cholesterol by diet, the greater was the reduction in the incidence of coronary heart disease.

Remember:

1. The higher the blood cholesterol, the greater is the risk of developing coronary heart disease.
2. Blood cholesterol levels are determined in part by genetic factors and in part by the foods you eat.
3. Reductions of up to 33 percent in blood cholesterol level can be achieved by diet alone.
4. Reducing blood cholesterol levels lowers risk of fatal and nonfatal heart attack.

4 IS YOUR BLOOD CHOLESTEROL TOO HIGH?

THE CORONARY Primary Prevention Trial (CPPT) results were positive. **Lowering blood cholesterol (and LDL) prevented heart attacks.** The lipid hypothesis was proven.

What do these results mean to you personally? How high is *your* risk? How much do *you* have to lower your blood cholesterol to reduce your risk?

NATIONAL INSTITUTES OF HEALTH RECOMMENDATIONS

To provide guidelines to physicians and the public, the National Cholesterol Education Program of the National Institutes of Health (NIH) convened an Adult Treatment Panel. This distinguished panel of scientists and physicians reviewed all of the available scientific and medical data and, on October 5, 1987, made the following recommendations (see Appendices for a more complete summary of the Adult Treatment Guidelines):

- Know your blood cholesterol number.
- Keep your blood cholesterol below 200 mg/dL by diet (and drugs, if necessary).

NATIONAL INSTITUTES OF HEALTH RECOMMENDATIONS

BLOOD CHOLESTEROL LEVELS, MG/DL

AGE	RECOMMENDED	BORDERLINE-HIGH RISK	HIGH RISK
20+	under 200	200–239	240+

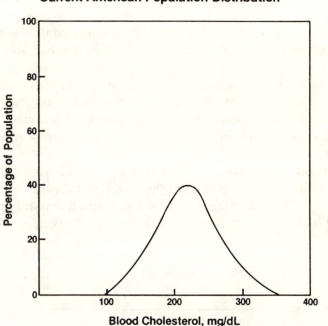

Current American Population Distribution

Figure 8: Current U.S. Distribution of Blood Cholesterol   *The average blood cho-lesterol level for adult Americans is about 215–220 mg/dL. Over 50 percent of American adults have blood cholesterol levels above 200 mg/dL.*

- Diet is the first line of treatment to reduce blood cholesterol be-low 200 mg/dL and should be given a fair and rigorous trial for at least 6 months before even considering drugs. In fact, most adults can expect to lower their blood cholesterol below 200 mg/dL by diet alone.
- The presence of coronary heart disease or other risk factors for heart disease, such as male sex, family history of premature heart attack (before age 55), cigarette smoking, high blood pressure, low HDL (below 35 mg/dL), diabetes, cerebrovascular or periph-eral vascular disease, and severe obesity (30 percent or more overweight) indicate the need for more vigorous therapy.

What Is Normal Blood Cholesterol?

The NIH recommendations are very definite: keep your blood cho-lesterol level below 200 mg/dL. However, you may be (or may al-

ready have been) told by health professionals that a blood cholesterol much higher than 200 mg/dL is *normal.* These advisers are not
trying to dig you an early grave. They are just confusing the two
meanings of normal — normal in a statistical sense and normal
meaning disease-free.

But you must understand what normal means in reference to your
blood cholesterol so you will not be lulled into a false sense of se-
curity about your blood cholesterol level. Ask for numbers. Blindly
accepting your blood cholesterol level as "normal" may be injurious
to your long-term health.

"Normal" Statistically Speaking: Here's what "normal"
means in a statistical sense. You begin with a curve (see Figure 8)
which plots the percentages of Americans with different blood cholesterol levels. This curve looks like many other curves, for example,

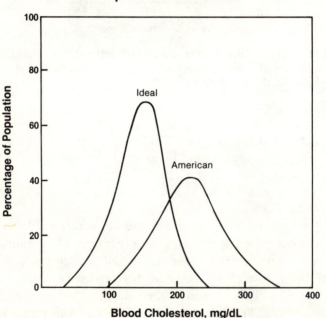

*Figure 9: Comparison of Current U.S. Blood Cholesterol Distribution with an
Ideal Distribution* *The ideal distribution of blood cholesterol levels exhibits lower
levels than the current U.S. distribution and has an average of about 150 mg/dL. Only
a small percentage of the ideal population has blood cholesterol levels above 200 mg/dL.*

curves that plot the distributions of weights, heights, or blood pressures in a population. In all such curves, persons with normal values in a statistical sense are found in the middle 95 percent of the curve. In Figure 8, normal blood cholesterol would include values that range from about 150 mg/dL to about 300 mg/dL.

Normal Is Not Necessarily Healthy: Just because values occur *often* in a population, this does not make them normal in the healthy sense. Blood cholesterol levels in the statistically normal range of 200 to 300 mg/dL are too high for long-term health. That is why there is an epidemic of heart disease in this country, why 550,000 people die of heart disease each year — one each minute — and why 5.4 million people have been diagnosed as having coronary heart disease.

As one physician so wisely explained, "We confuse normal with optimal. Normal in America is to have a heart attack in middle age, and we don't think that is good. We need new optimal levels. Somewhere around 180 to 200."

A Truly Normal Distribution: If the current distribution of blood cholesterol levels in the United States is not normal, what would a distribution of truly normal blood cholesterol levels (i.e., levels not associated with disease) look like? In Figure 9, an "ideal" distribution of normal blood cholesterol levels (i.e., levels associated with little or no heart disease) is shown together with the distribution of current levels in the United States.

You can see that the entire ideal curve of normal blood cholesterol levels is shifted to lower levels. It has an average level of 150 mg/dL instead of 215–220 mg/dL. Only a small percentage of the ideal population has blood cholesterol levels above 200 mg/dL. In this idealized population, a blood cholesterol level of 230 mg/dL is highly elevated rather than normal. Where does your blood cholesterol fit on this curve?

Relating Risk to Blood Cholesterol Levels in Different Populations

In Figure 10, shading indicates cholesterol levels (above 200 mg/dL) associated with increased risk of heart attack. You can see several interesting facts.

First, very few people in the ideal population are at increased risk of heart attack due to elevated blood cholesterol levels. Heart disease would be relatively rare in this population. Those few people at

Average is *Not* "Normal"

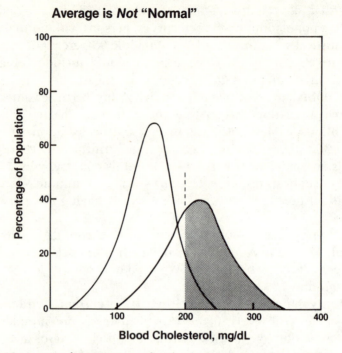

*Figure 10: Average is **NOT Normal*** *The shading indicates blood cholesterol levels associated with increased risk of heart attack.*

highest risk have cholesterol levels slightly above 200 mg/dL, levels currently considered normal in the United States. A real-life example proves the point. The distribution of blood cholesterol levels in Japan is essentially identical to the ideal distribution. Heart disease in Japan is indeed rare: one-tenth the rate in the United States.

Second, a study of these curves makes it clear that a large percentage of the current population of the United States is at increased risk of heart disease due to elevated blood cholesterol levels. Alas, heart disease is not at all rare in the United States. Over 50 percent of the population has blood cholesterol levels above 200 mg/dL, a level at which the risk curve begins to rise steeply. It is no coincidence that the NIH Adult Treatment Panel recommends that people with elevated blood cholesterol levels take action to reduce them to below 200 mg/dL.

While those people with very high blood cholesterol levels (say, above 280 mg/dL) are clearly at very high risk, they account for only

---

BYPASS PATIENTS — TAKE HEED

Bypass operations may eliminate the symptoms of heart disease, such as angina; but they do not cure the underlying atherosclerotic process, which goes on depositing fat in your coronary arteries. Bypass artery grafts have been found to accumulate plaque at a faster rate the higher the blood cholesterol level. It is common for such grafts to close completely within three to five years. *This need not happen.* You can slow or even reverse the clogging of your bypass artery graft by changing what you eat and thereby lowering your blood cholesterol level.

---

a small percentage of the total population and thus for only a small percentage of the number of heart attacks. There are many more people with "normal" levels of about 230–240 mg/dL and they account for the great bulk of heart disease.

Now you can see why we recommend that you should insist on knowing your blood cholesterol level. Know your numbers. Don't settle for a statement that your cholesterol is normal.

AVERAGE BLOOD CHOLESTEROL OF HEART ATTACK PATIENTS

In fact, the average blood cholesterol level of patients admitted to coronary care units with heart attacks is about 230–240 mg/dL. The average blood cholesterol level of persons receiving coronary artery bypass grafts is also about 230–240 mg/dL. These levels are mistakenly considered normal by many health professionals. Pretty scary news, yes?

Because many of these patients do not have high blood pressure, do not smoke, and have no family history of premature heart disease, until recently they were considered to have no risk factors for heart disease. But today their blood cholesterol of, say, 230–240 mg/dL is understood to be a prime factor in the development of their disease.

AN ACTION PLAN FOR ALL AMERICANS: EAT LESS FAT

No matter whether you have been told that your blood cholesterol level is normal or that you are at borderline-high or high risk, if you want to reduce your risk of coronary heart disease you must get your blood cholesterol level down to below 200 mg/dL. The recommended method is to change the foods you eat.

The National Institutes of Health (NIH) and the American Heart Association (AHA) recommend that all Americans over the age of two years adopt a diet that reduces total dietary fat intake. (More information about dietary fats and their effects on blood cholesterol levels is in the next chapter.) Total fat should be reduced to no more than 30 percent of total calories. The fat calories should be evenly distributed among the three types of fat as follows:

	FATS (% OF TOTAL CALORIES)				CHOLESTEROL (MG PER DAY)
	TOTAL	SAT.	MONO.	POLY.	
AHA and NIH recommend no more than	30	10	10	10	200–300
current U.S. intake	40	17	16	7	470

In addition, intake of total calories should be reduced, if necessary, to correct obesity and to maintain desired body weight.

You may find these recommendations complicated and difficult to follow. That is why we developed *Eater's Choice*. As we explain in the next chapter, *Eater's Choice* not only simplifies the AHA recommendations by focusing only on reducing saturated fat intake, but also provides a method for translating the abstract guidelines into actual food choices.

Eat Right and Your Blood Cholesterol Will Show It

Do not be discouraged if your blood cholesterol level is too high. The picture is not bleak. Most people can lower their blood cholesterol simply by changing the foods they eat. In fact, it takes only about three weeks to see a change in your blood cholesterol level. Of course, you must make enough changes in the foods you eat and stick with them for your blood cholesterol level to fall below the danger zone and stay there.

You may expect to achieve dramatic reductions of your blood cholesterol — reductions up to 30 percent, depending on your responsiveness to diet and how much you change the foods you eat. Reductions of 10 to 15 percent are common. Thus, if your starting blood cholesterol level is 270 mg/dL, you might be able to lower it by about 80 mg/dL (about a 30 percent decrease) to 190 mg/dL. If your starting blood cholesterol level is 240 mg/dL, you might be able to lower it by about 70 mg/dL (about a 30 percent decrease) to 170 mg/dL.

How much you can lower your blood cholesterol by changes in the foods you eat depends on the following factors:

- your original eating pattern;
- your heredity, which determines how responsive your blood cholesterol is to changes in your diet;
- how much you change the foods you eat.

The higher the amount of saturated fat and cholesterol in your original eating pattern and the higher your resulting blood cholesterol, the greater will be the fall in your blood cholesterol with a decreased intake of saturated fat and cholesterol.

Those Who Need It the Most Benefit the Most: As you can see from the above, although the percentage decrease is the same for both, the person with the higher blood cholesterol level achieved a greater reduction (80 mg/dL decrease) in response to a blood cholesterol–lowering eating plan than did the person with a lower starting level (70 mg/dL decrease). Both will benefit from changes in what they eat, but persons with the highest risk can expect a larger absolute reduction. This should motivate those most in need of reducing their coronary heart disease risk.

Your Own Private Statistics: Enough of official edicts. You are already on your way to eradicating heart disease — even if it's only your own. The next chapters will help you apply all you have learned about blood cholesterol, foods, and heart disease to your own life. You will set personal blood cholesterol–lowering goals and learn how to meet those goals.

Remember:

1. A blood cholesterol level considered to be "normal" in the United States may be too high for long-term health. Over 50

percent of the adult American population has blood cholesterol levels above 200 mg/dL, the point at which risk begins to rise sharply.

2. All adults are advised to reduce their blood cholesterol below 200 mg/dL by adopting a diet that reduces total dietary fat intake.

EATER'S CHOICE: EATING FOR LIFE

5

YOU HAVE BEEN inundated with statistics, biochemical explanations, and evidence. Enough! Let's get started with practical advice to improve and lengthen your life. Let's get started with the *Eater's Choice* plan for lowering your blood cholesterol level.

Eater's Choice is the name given to this plan because it is an eating plan with choice — your choice. *Eater's Choice* gives you the knowledge to decide your own personal blood cholesterol goals and tailor your food choices to meet these goals.

Eater's Choice focuses on the saturated fat content of foods as the basis for making food choices. You determine the amount of saturated fat you should eat to lower your blood cholesterol and you keep track of how much saturated fat you are eating.

FATS

Total fat in a food is the sum of three kinds of fat: saturated fat, monounsaturated fat, and polyunsaturated fat. Each has a different effect on the blood cholesterol level. Foods contain mixtures of these different types of fat in different proportions. No food contains pure saturated, monounsaturated, or polyunsaturated fat.

Saturated Fat: Saturated fat is called saturated because all the carbon atoms in the long fat molecule carry the maximum possible number of hydrogen atoms; that is, the carbon atoms are *saturated* with hydrogen atoms (see Figure 11). Saturated fat is generally solid at room temperature. Foods high in saturated fats are red meats, and whole milk dairy products, including butter and cheese. Five kinds of vegetable fats are saturated: coconut oil, palm oil, palm kernel oil,

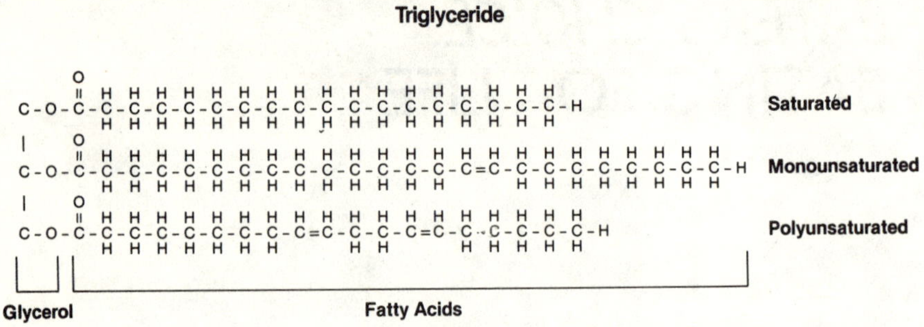

Triglyceride

Saturated

Monounsaturated

Polyunsaturated

Glycerol   Fatty Acids

Figure 11: Chemical Structures of the Fats   *Triglycerides are composed of three fatty acids attached to a glycerol molecule: In saturated fats all the carbon atoms (C) in the molecule carry the maximum possible number of hydrogen atoms (H). Monounsaturated fat has one point of unsaturation and thus can absorb two additional hydrogen atoms. Polyunsaturated fat has two or more points of unsaturation and thus can absorb four or more additional hydrogen atoms.*

cocoa butter (in chocolate), and hydrogenated vegetable oil. In general, animal fats are high in saturated fats and plant fats are low. **Saturated fat raises LDL-cholesterol and total blood cholesterol levels.**

Monounsaturated Fat: Monounsaturated fat has one point of unsaturation; that is, there are two fewer hydrogen atoms than in a fully saturated fat (see Figure 11). The richest source of monounsaturated fat is olive oil. Recent scientific evidence indicates that monounsaturated fat lowers total blood cholesterol by lowering LDL-cholesterol without lowering HDL-cholesterol.

Polyunsaturated Fat: Polyunsaturated fat has two or more points of unsaturation; that is, there are four or more fewer hydrogen atoms than in a fully saturated fat (see Figure 11). Polyunsaturated fats are generally liquid at room temperature. In general, vegetable oils, except coconut and palm oils, are high in polyunsaturated fat. Polyunsaturated fat lowers blood LDL-cholesterol levels and, to a much lesser extent, HDL-cholesterol levels.

Dietary Cholesterol: Dietary cholesterol raises LDL-cholesterol. Cholesterol is found *only* in animal products, such as beef, pork, poultry, fish, cheese and other whole milk dairy products, and eggs. Especially rich sources of cholesterol are egg yolks and organ meats, such as liver, pancreas, and brain. Cholesterol is *not* found in foods made from plants, such as vegetables, fruits, nuts, or seeds.

CHOLESTEROL CONTENTS OF SELECTED FOODS*

(The American Heart Association recommends that your intake of cholesterol should not exceed 200–300 mg each day.)

FOOD	PORTION	CHOLESTEROL, MG
Dairy		
Butter, regular	1 pat	11
Cheeses		
cottage, creamed	1 cup	31
2%	1 cup	19
low-fat	1 cup	10
natural and processed	1 oz	16–35
Egg yolk	1 large	274
Milk		
whole	1 cup	33
2%	1 cup	18
skim	1 cup	5
Yogurt		
low-fat	8 oz	10–14
nonfat	8 oz	0–1
Meat, Fish, Poultry		
Cooked beef, veal, pork, chicken, turkey, fish	1 oz	18–25
Crab, cooked	1 oz	28
Kidney, beef, cooked	1 oz	200
Liver		
beef, cooked	1 oz	126
chicken, simmered	1 oz	180
Scallops, cooked	1 oz	15
Shrimp, cooked	1 oz	43
Plant Products		
Fruits		0
Grains		0
Vegetables		0
Vegetable oils		0

*Adapted from *Composition of Foods*, Handbook Number 8, U.S. Department of Agriculture.

FOCUS ON SATURATED FAT, NOT CHOLESTEROL

Eater's Choice focuses on the saturated fat content of foods because, of the four dietary constituents that influence blood cholesterol levels (saturated fat, monounsaturated fat, polyunsaturated fat, and cholesterol), saturated fat is the most potent determinant of blood cholesterol levels. It is twice as effective in raising blood cholesterol as polyunsaturated fat is in lowering it. The more saturated fat you remove from your daily consumption, the more your LDL-cholesterol level will fall.

This does *not* mean you can eat as much saturated fat as you want as long as you eat twice as much polyunsaturated fat. Fats have more calories per unit weight than either proteins or carbohydrates. Fats contain 9 calories per gram while proteins and carbohydrates each have only 4 calories per gram. **Fats make you fat.** In addition, fats have been implicated as a risk factor in developing certain cancers, such as breast and colon cancers.

Eater's Choice focuses on the saturated fat and *not the cholesterol content of the foods you eat* for the following reasons. First, with only a few easy to remember exceptions, saturated fat and cholesterol occur in the same foods; they are fellow travelers. So, by avoiding foods high in saturated fat, you are also avoiding foods high in cholesterol. The exceptions are: egg yolks and organ meats (brain, pancreas, liver, kidneys), which are high in cholesterol but have only moderate amounts of saturated fat. On the other hand, coconut oil, palm oil, palm kernel oil, hydrogenated vegetable oil, and cocoa butter (in chocolate) are very high in saturated fat but have no cholesterol.

Second, the cholesterol you eat has much less effect on raising blood cholesterol levels than does saturated fat. Many people assume that all you have to do to lower your blood cholesterol level is to eat less cholesterol. Eggs are loaded with cholesterol. Eat fewer eggs and your blood cholesterol problem is licked, so the argument goes. However, contrary to popular belief, the amount of fats, especially *saturated fats,* that you eat has a much greater effect on your blood cholesterol level than does the amount of cholesterol you consume.

Of course, this does not mean that you should eat unlimited numbers of eggs or other high-cholesterol foods. Remember that the American Heart Association and the Adult Treatment Panel recommend a daily cholesterol intake of no more than 200–300 mg (one large egg yolk contains 274 mg). Avoid foods high in cholesterol. Think before you eat.

Third, keeping track of only saturated fat makes *Eater's Choice* a simple yet effective plan to follow. The simpler a plan is to follow, the more likely you are to follow it and the more likely you are to succeed in lowering your blood cholesterol level.

HOW TO REDUCE YOUR SATURATED FAT INTAKE

You can reduce your saturated fat intake in two ways:

1. Reduce the amount of fat you eat by substituting foods high in complex carbohydrates (starches) and fiber (such as rice, whole-grain pastas, breads, and cereals, vegetables, and fruits) for foods high in saturated fat. And replace high-fat foods with low-fat or nonfat foods, such as sour cream with low-fat yogurt. (See the food tables at the end of the book for the saturated fat contents of common foods.)
2. Substitute foods high in polyunsaturated fat (such as margarine and vegetable oils other than coconut or palm oil) for foods high in saturated fat (such as butter, lard, and beef tallow). However, be sure polyunsaturated fat contributes no more than 10 percent of total calories.

The Total Diet Counts

As you establish your new eating plan, you must remember that to lower your blood cholesterol you will have to make changes in what you eat. **You will have to make enough changes to make a difference.** What is important are the amounts and types of fats you eat and not the actual foods that supply them. Individual foods either raise or lower your blood cholesterol level by the way they contribute to the daily total of total fat, saturated fat, polyunsaturated fat, and cholesterol.

But how many changes do you have to make to make a difference? How much is enough? *Eater's Choice* is a plan that allows you to determine how much is enough by keeping track of your saturated fat intake. How you set your daily saturated fat budget will depend on how much you want to reduce your blood cholesterol level. Periodic monitoring of your blood cholesterol level will tell you if your change in food choices has made a sufficient difference in lowering it or if you must make more changes in your eating pattern.

You need not wait months to see if your heart-smart eating behavior has lowered your blood cholesterol level. It takes only about three weeks to achieve up to 30 percent lowering of your blood cholesterol if you have made the right food choices.

While the types and amounts of fats and not the foods that contain them are important to the health of your body, which foods contain the fats you eat are of utmost importance to you. Thus, 30 calories of saturated fat from bacon or from cheesecake may have identical effects on your blood cholesterol level but undoubtedly quite different effects on your palate and psyche. And that is why *Eater's Choice* is useful for you. You tailor your food choices to fit your saturated fat budget *and* your taste buds.

Cold Turkey: A Dish for Some: Before we delve into *Eater's Choice* we realize some of you may not want to take the trouble to monitor your sat-fat (saturated fat) intake. You may wish to restrict your diet totally to foods low in saturated fat: fish, white meat turkey or chicken without skin, loads of vegetables and fruits, bread (made without hydrogenated oils), oatmeal, rice, pasta, skim milk, low-fat yogurt and cottage cheese, tub margarine and olive, safflower, sunflower, or corn oil, etc.

Going cold turkey means completely eliminating all foods high in saturated fat. This includes red meats, such as beef, veal, pork, ham, and cold cuts, as well as whole dairy milk products, such as cheese, sour cream, cream, whole milk, 2% milk, butter, and ice cream, in addition to most commercial snacks and baked goods and other products made with palm oil, palm kernel oil, coconut oil, hydrogenated vegetable oil, cocoa butter, or lard.

If you want to try this approach, all the recipes in this cookbook are dishes you can eat with complete freedom. They are designed to be low in saturated fat *and* delicious.

Take It Easy: A Strategy for Others: If you feel there are too many foods that you cannot give up without sinking into a deep depression, that life would not be worth living without brie and crackers, *Eater's Choice* gives *you* control over your choices of food and still allows you to lower your blood cholesterol level.

Of course, you will not be able to eat *everything* you want in the amounts and as often as you want, but you will be able to eat that brie if you make enough low-fat choices in your diet to compensate for the added saturated fat. This is a flexible plan that you will change and modify until you reach your target low blood cholesterol level.

A STEP-BY-STEP GUIDE TO *EATER'S CHOICE*

First, if you have not already done so, have your physician measure your total blood cholesterol. (New technology is now available to measure blood cholesterol in mere minutes from a drop of blood taken from your finger. This revolutionary advance in blood analysis will make it possible to have your blood cholesterol measured at your work place, health clinic, even shopping malls, as well as at your physician's office.) If your total blood cholesterol level is elevated, you should also know your levels of HDL, triglycerides, and LDL. (Remember: a twelve-hour fast is required before your blood is drawn to measure triglycerides and LDL.) See Chapter 2 for a discussion of all the lipoproteins in the blood.

Ask for numerical values. Make sure you know both your HDL and your LDL levels in addition to your total blood cholesterol. Remember, the lower your HDL level, the higher your risk and the greater the incentive to lower your LDL level.

NOTE: Cholesterol levels measured within three months after a heart attack, surgery, or other physical trauma may be abnormally low.

If your blood cholesterol is low (below 200 mg/dl), you may decide to stop reading this book — unless you want some great recipes that bring pleasure to diners regardless of their blood cholesterol level. Continue to have your blood cholesterol checked every three years to be sure it does not rise with age. If it becomes elevated, you should take steps to lower it. (Now aren't you glad you bought this book three years ago, after all?)

Set Your Blood Cholesterol Target

Set your own personal blood cholesterol goals. You know what your blood cholesterol level is. You know that you want it to be below 200 mg/dL. Recall from the Framingham risk curve (Chapter

3) that the lower your blood cholesterol level, the lower your risk of coronary heart disease.

Perhaps you want to lower your blood cholesterol level in stages. Perhaps it is now 260 mg/dL and you want to take it down to 230 mg/dL as the first step. Fine. You just have to tailor your eating to meet this goal. After a month, have your blood cholesterol level measured again. When you have achieved your goal of 230 mg/dL and feel comfortable with your new eating pattern, you are ready to make additional diet changes to lower your blood cholesterol to 200 mg/dL.

Know Your Desirable Body Weight

Because the amount of saturated fat allowed on the *Eater's Choice* plan is based on the number of calories you eat each day, you need to know how many calories you consume or should consume. If you are overweight, you should choose your desirable weight as a goal. Table 1 on page 43 lists desirable weights for men and women of different heights and body frame sizes.

To help keep your weight down, you should also be exercising. (Be sure to consult your doctor about what exercise you can do safely.) Even just taking a vigorous walk for thirty minutes each day will help you lose weight. (And you'll feel better too!) Losing weight if you are overweight will contribute to reducing your blood cholesterol and LDL levels, raising your HDL level, and will reduce your risk of coronary heart disease morbidity and mortality.

Determine Your Frame

In order to use the table of desirable weights (Table 1) you need to know if your body frame is small, medium, or large. You can determine this by placing your left thumb and middle finger around your right wrist. Squeeze your fingers as tightly as possible. If the thumb and finger overlap, you have a small frame. If they just touch, your frame size is medium. If they do not touch, then you have a large frame. This method is a bit crude, but accurate enough for our purpose. Find your desirable weight by sex, height, and frame size on the chart.

Know Your Ideal Daily Caloric Intake

In order to determine your daily caloric intake, you must know your approximate daily level of activity (daily energy expenditure)

Table 1: Desirable Weights for Adults Age 25 and Over*
(weight in pounds without clothing)

HEIGHT WITHOUT SHOES		FRAME		
(FEET)	(INCHES)	SMALL	MEDIUM	LARGE
Men				
5	2	112–120	118–129	126–141
5	3	115–123	121–133	129–144
5	4	118–126	124–136	132–148
5	5	121–129	127–139	135–152
5	6	124–133	130–143	138–156
5	7	128–137	134–147	142–161
5	8	132–141	138–152	147–166
5	9	136–145	142–156	151–170
5	10	140–150	146–160	155–174
5	11	144–154	150–165	159–179
6	0	148–158	154–170	164–184
6	1	152–162	158–175	168–189
6	2	156–167	162–180	173–194
6	3	160–171	167–185	178–199
6	4	164–175	172–190	182–204
Women				
4	10	92–98	96–107	104–119
4	11	94–101	98–110	106–122
5	0	96–104	101–113	109–125
5	1	99–107	104–116	112–128
5	2	102–110	107–119	115–131
5	3	105–113	110–122	118–134
5	4	108–116	113–126	121–138
5	5	111–119	116–130	125–142
5	6	114–123	120–135	129–146
5	7	118–127	124–139	133–150
5	8	122–131	128–143	137–154
5	9	126–135	132–147	141–158
5	10	130–140	136–151	145–163
5	11	134–144	140–155	149–168
6	0	138–148	144–159	153–173

*Courtesy of Metropolitan Life Insurance Company, New York, N.Y., 1959
For persons between 18 and 25 years of age, subtract 1 pound for each year under 25.

in addition to your desirable weight. To determine your level of activity, try to identify which of the following five descriptions most accurately describes your level of activity during the preceding week. Choose a lower level of activity if you are not sure which of two levels best describes your activity.

ON EXERCISE AND LOSING WEIGHT

A pound of body fat contains about 3500 calories. To lose 1 pound of fat, you must burn 3500 calories more than you eat. If you burn 500 calories more a day than you eat, you will lose 1 pound of fat a week. Thus, if you normally burn 1700 calories a day, you can theoretically expect to lose a pound of fat each week if you stick to a 1200-calorie-per-day diet. When you begin a weight-reduction diet, you may at first lose weight somewhat faster, primarily because of loss of water.

Alternatively, you may continue to eat the same number of calories (1700 calories in the example given above) and burn 500 calories more a day by increasing your exercise. Or, better yet, you may lose weight by combining both exercise and reduced caloric intake.

Activity Levels*

Very Sedentary: Limited activity, confined to a few rooms or a house. Slow walking, no running. Most major activities involve sitting.

Sedentary: Activities involve mostly walking or some sporadic slow running at a jogging speed of approximately ten minutes per mile. Recreational activities include bowling, fishing, target shooting, horseback riding, motorboating, snowmobiling, or other similar activities. Less than ten minutes of continuous running (faster than a jog) per week.

Moderately Active: Activities include golf (eighteen holes), doubles tennis, sailing, pleasure swimming or skating, aerobic dancing, Jazzercise, downhill skiing, or other similar activities. Between ten and twenty minutes of continuous running at least three times per week.

Active: More than twenty minutes of sustained activity, such as jogging, swimming, competitive tennis, or cross-country skiing, more than three times per week or more than forty-five minutes of

---

*From *The DINE System* by Dr. Darwin Dennison

Table 2: Ideal Caloric Level Based on Goal Weight, Activity Level, and Sex

DESIRABLE WEIGHT	SEX	ACTIVITY LEVEL				
		VERY SEDENTARY	SEDENTARY	MODERATELY ACTIVE	ACTIVE	SUPER ACTIVE
90	M	1170	1260	1350	1440	1530
	F	1053	1134	1215	1296	1377
95	M	1235	1330	1425	1520	1615
	F	1111	1197	1282	1368	1453
100	M	1300	1400	1500	1600	1700
	F	1170	1260	1350	1440	1530
105	M	1365	1470	1575	1680	1785
	F	1228	1323	1417	1512	1606
110	M	1430	1540	1650	1760	1870
	F	1287	1386	1485	1584	1683
115	M	1495	1610	1725	1840	1955
	F	1345	1449	1552	1656	1759
120	M	1560	1680	1800	1920	2040
	F	1404	1512	1620	1728	1836
125	M	1625	1750	1875	2000	2125
	F	1462	1575	1687	1800	1912
130	M	1690	1820	1950	2080	2210
	F	1521	1638	1755	1872	1989
135	M	1755	1890	2025	2160	2295
	F	1579	1701	1822	1944	2065
140	M	1820	1960	2100	2240	2380
	F	1638	1764	1890	2016	2142
145	M	1885	2030	2175	2320	2465
	F	1696	1827	1957	2088	2218
150	M	1950	2100	2250	2400	2550
	F	1755	1890	2025	2160	2295
155	M	2015	2170	2325	2480	2635
	F	1813	1953	2092	2232	2371
160	M	2080	2240	2400	2560	2720
	F	1872	2016	2160	2304	2448
165	M	2145	2310	2475	2640	2805
	F	1930	2079	2227	2376	2524
170	M	2210	2380	2550	2720	2890
	F	1989	2142	2295	2448	2601
175	M	2275	2450	2625	2800	2975
	F	2047	2205	2362	2520	2677
180	M	2340	2520	2700	2880	3060
	F	2106	2268	2430	2592	2754
185	M	2405	2590	2775	2960	3145
	F	2164	2331	2497	2664	2830

DESIRABLE WEIGHT	SEX	ACTIVITY LEVEL				
		VERY SEDENTARY	SEDENTARY	MODERATELY ACTIVE	ACTIVE	SUPER ACTIVE
190	M	2470	2660	2850	3040	3230
	F	2223	2394	2565	2736	2907
195	M	2535	2730	2925	3120	3315
	F	2281	2457	2632	2808	2983
200	M	2600	2800	3000	3200	3400
	F	2340	2520	2700	2880	3060
205	M	2665	2870	3075	3280	3485
	F	2398	2583	2767	2952	3136
210	M	2730	2940	3150	3360	3570
	F	2457	2646	2835	3024	3213
215	M	2795	3010	3225	3440	3655
	F	2515	2709	2905	3096	3289
220	M	2860	3080	3300	3520	3740
	F	2574	2772	2970	3168	3366

recreational tennis, paddle ball, or other activities at least three times per week.

Super Active: At least one and a half hours of vigorous activity (training for competitive athletics, full-court basketball, mountain climbing, weight training, football, wrestling, or other similar activity) four days per week or more than two and a half hours of recreational activity four or more times per week.

Your Daily Caloric Needs

Use Table 2 to determine the number of calories you should consume each day. First, locate your desirable weight along the left-hand column. Making sure you use the correct row for your sex, find the number of calories under the column for your activity level.

This is the calorie level that will maintain your desirable weight based on your activity level. If your activity level changes, as it might with changes in season, you should determine your level of caloric intake anew. If you want to lose weight and you are not doing so after two or three weeks, determine your caloric intake using a lower activity level.

The following example will help you understand how to determine your desirable caloric level.

WORKSHEET TO DETERMINE
YOUR DAILY SAT-FAT BUDGET

Name _George_   Date _3/27/88_

STEP 1: DETERMINE YOUR DESIRABLE WEIGHT

    A. Sex: Male _X_   Female _____

    B. Height: _5_ feet _10_ inches

    C. Frame (wrist method):

        Small _____   Medium _X_   Large _____

    D. Weight Range (Table 1): _146-160_

    E. Desirable Weight: _150_

STEP 2: DETERMINE YOUR DAILY CALORIC INTAKE

    A. Activity Level   Very Sedentary _____
        (see text):

                     Sedentary _____

                     Moderately Active _____

                     Active _X_____

                     Super Active _____

    B. Daily caloric intake (use Table 2): _2400_

STEP 3: DETERMINE YOUR DAILY SAT-FAT BUDGET

    DAILY SAT-FAT BUDGET:

    _10_% of daily caloric intake = _240_

George is 5 feet 10 inches tall. He determines by the wrist test that he is of medium frame. To find how much he should weigh, he locates his height in the left-hand column of Table 1. Looking across the row for 5 feet 10 inches, he finds his weight range under the frame column labeled Medium. His weight range is 146–160. George actually weighs 160 pounds but wants to lose 10 pounds and weigh 150 pounds.

George jogs for thirty minutes five times a week. After reading the descriptions of various activity levels above, he determines that his activity level is Active. He finds his desirable weight (150) in the left-hand column of Table 2. Looking across the row for 150 for males (M), he finds his ideal caloric intake level under the Active column. George's ideal daily caloric intake is 2400 calories.

Reduce Saturated Fat to 10 Percent of Total Calories or Less

Now that you have determined *your* calorie level, you can figure out how much saturated fat you should eat each day. Your daily allotment of saturated fat will ultimately depend on the initial level of your blood cholesterol and how much your blood cholesterol drops in response to a lower saturated fat intake.

The first step for everyone, no matter how high your initial blood cholesterol level, is to reduce your saturated fat intake to no more than 10 percent of your total calories. We call this the *Eater's Choice* 10 Percent Plan. (Those with high-risk blood cholesterol levels — see National Institutes of Health recommendations in Chapter 4 — should consider starting directly with the *Eater's Choice* 6 Percent Plan discussed on page 50.)

In practical terms, what does that mean? Here is George again. George should consume 2400 calories a day to maintain his desirable weight. His blood cholesterol level is 250 mg/dL. To lower his blood cholesterol below 200 mg/dL, he must reduce his saturated fat intake to 10 percent or less of his daily calories. Ten percent of 2400 calories is 240 calories of saturated fat. George should eat no more than 240 calories of saturated fat each day.

To help you visualize what 240 calories of saturated fat means in terms of foods, there are:

• 45 calories of saturated fat in 1 cup of whole milk;

WORKSHEET TO DETERMINE YOUR DAILY SAT-FAT BUDGET

Name _____   Date _____

STEP 1: DETERMINE YOUR DESIRABLE WEIGHT

     A. Sex: Male _____   Female _____

     B. Height: _____ feet _____ inches

     C. Frame (wrist method):

        Small _____   Medium _____   Large _____

     D. Weight Range (Table 1): _____

     E. Desirable Weight: _____

STEP 2: DETERMINE YOUR DAILY CALORIC INTAKE

     A. Activity Level   Very Sedentary _____
        (see text):   Sedentary _____

                    Moderately Active _____

                    Active _____

                    Super Active _____

     B. Daily caloric intake (use Table 2): _____

STEP 3: DETERMINE YOUR DAILY SAT-FAT BUDGET

     DAILY SAT-FAT BUDGET:

        _____% of daily caloric intake = _____

- 100 calories of saturated fat in 4 ounces of lean, broiled ground beef;
- 12 calories of saturated fat in 4 ounces of roasted chicken breast without skin;
- 155 calories of saturated fat in a Big Mac.

You can use the blank worksheet on page 49 to determine *your* daily sat-fat budget. Use George's worksheet as a guide.

Once you go on the *Eater's Choice* plan, you will want to monitor your blood cholesterol levels periodically to see how you are doing. Remember, it only takes two to three weeks for blood cholesterol levels to respond to changes in eating patterns. At first you should check at more frequent intervals — six weeks, six weeks, three months, six months — until your blood cholesterol stabilizes at its new lower level. Then have it checked every twelve months. Do not get upset if your blood cholesterol level fluctuates slightly — this is normal.

To prevent your blood cholesterol from rising, you must continue to follow the *Eater's Choice* plan, to keep your sat-fat intake at 10 percent or less of your calories. Your blood cholesterol level is affected by what you eat and will jump right back to its previously high level if you return to your old eating habits.

Eater's Choice 6 Percent Plan

If after about six months your blood cholesterol has not fallen below 200 mg/dL, you will need to switch to the *Eater's Choice* 6 Percent Plan. As you might guess, on the 6 Percent Plan you reduce your sat-fat intake to no more than 6 percent of your total calories. In George's case, he would eat no more than 144 (6 percent of 2400) calories of saturated fat a day on the *Eater's Choice* 6 Percent Plan.

Again, once you have brought your blood cholesterol below 200 mg/dL you must continue to follow the *Eater's Choice* 6 Percent Plan. As described above, monitor your blood cholesterol periodically — six weeks, six weeks, three months, six months — and then once a year after you are sure your blood cholesterol has stabilized below 200 mg/dL.

For some, moving to a 3 percent plan may be necessary if strict adherence to a 6 percent plan has failed to reduce their blood cholesterol to below 200 mg/dL.

The Appeal of *Eater's Choice*

The main goal of *Eater's Choice* is to help you lower your risk of heart disease. What you may find just as important is that it allows enough personal choice to keep both your psyche and taste buds happy. You will still be able to eat the fatty foods you love, but perhaps less often or in smaller quantities.

The menu plans in Part II will give you some idea of how well you can eat on an *Eater's Choice* 10 Percent or 6 Percent (or even 3 Percent) Plan. The recipes at the end of the book will satisfy your palate without overloading your sat-fat budget and will give you tips on how to modify high-fat recipes from other cookbooks to create low-fat dishes.

A Balanced Diet

Eater's Choice emphasizes eating less saturated fat to lower your blood cholesterol level, but you must remember that your diet has to be balanced. In your zeal to reduce your intake of fats, you must not forget that you need vitamins, minerals, proteins, fiber, and bulk. (The meal plans in Chapter 11 will give you examples of balanced low-fat meals.)

As you remove saturated fat from your diet, you will have to replace it with something else. Most health experts today recommend replacing the saturated fat calories you eliminate with calories from complex carbohydrates. Complex carbohydrates are found in whole-grain breads and pastas, fruits, and vegetables. Enriching your diet with these foods has the additional advantages of increasing your intake of vitamins, minerals, and fiber.

Insoluble fiber, such as in whole wheat, may help prevent certain cancers, such as colon cancer. Soluble fiber, such as in oat bran products, has been found to lower blood cholesterol levels.

ADDED BENEFITS OF *EATER'S CHOICE*

Weight Loss

One of the loveliest benefits of *Eater's Choice* is a natural loss of weight. Many people report losing 10–15 pounds, and some as much as 40. You will be eating less fat and thus fewer calories without necessarily eating less food.

"But," you ask in disbelief, "if I replace saturated fat with complex carbohydrates, won't I turn into a tub? Everyone knows carbohydrates are fattening." If this is what you think, get this myth out of your head.

All fats — saturated, polyunsaturated, and monounsaturated — contain 9 calories per gram. Proteins and carbohydrates, on the other hand, contain only 4 calories per gram. Carbohydrates have less than half the calories per unit weight than fats (4 versus 9) and thus twice the bulk per calorie. Carbohydrates fill you up at half the caloric cost. Carbohydrate calories, even in excess, are not stored as fat tissue. Excess fat calories are stored as fat tissue. Fat makes fat!

It is not the potato that makes you fat, it is what you do to it. A medium baked potato has 105 calories. You glob 3 tablespoons of sour cream (26 calories per tablespoon) on top and the innocent potato becomes 183 calories. A piece of bread has 80 calories per slice. When you slather it with butter at 100 calories per tablespoon, it becomes 180 calories per slice. It is the large amount of fat in the American diet that leads to overweight and obesity.

Dr. William Castelli, director of the Framingham Heart Study, aptly concurs:

> If you take the lowly potato, it's about 100 calories, let's say. If you chop it up and cook it in fat, you're up to 275 to 300 calories from that original hundred calories. If you slice it up real fine and make potato chips, you're up to 400 calories over that original potato. Now what's the difference? Just fat. What kind of fat? Well, frequently it's totally saturated fat. Why? Well, someone learned that if you cook potato chips in a totally saturated fat, they stay crispier longer. The shelf life, you know, of the potato chip goes on and on and on and on. The shelf life of the person who eats it doesn't. That's our problem.

Expanding Your Palette

A whole new world of foods will be open to you as you replace your saturated fats with complex carbohydrates. Both your food palette and taste palate will be expanded as you explore new recipes that fit into your sat-fat budget. For starters, try Indian Vegetables (Chapter 18) or Chicken with Green Beans (Chapter 15) or Low-Fat Calzone (Chapter 19).

LAST RESORT: DRUGS

If diet does not reduce your blood cholesterol adequately and *you are really following your eating plan to the letter,* you may need to take drugs prescribed by a physician. The preferred drugs are bile acid sequestrants — either cholestyramine (Questran)* or colestipol (Colestid) and nicotinic acid (niacin).

The bile acid sequestrants bind bile acids in the intestine and prevent their reabsorption and return to the liver. The bile acids are excreted in the feces. To compensate for the loss of bile acids, the liver removes large amounts of LDL-cholesterol from the blood. The cholesterol is converted into bile acids, which are then secreted into the intestine, where they help emulsify dietary fats.

Niacin lowers blood cholesterol levels by reducing the formation of VLDL, thereby blocking the formation of LDL. In small amounts (about 100 mg per day), niacin is a vitamin and has no effect on blood cholesterol. In doses large enough to lower blood cholesterol (1000–3000 mg per day), niacin is a potent drug with side effects (such as flushing, an itching rash, gastric upset, and/or blurred vision) and potential toxicities. It is recommended that people taking large doses should be under a physician's supervision and should have their liver function, blood glucose, and blood uric acid monitored periodically. Large amounts of niacin should not be taken by people with the following conditions: peptic ulcers, liver disease, gouty arthritis, or some types of heart rhythm disturbances.

Lovastatin is the first of a new class of potent blood cholesterol–lowering drugs: HMG CoA reductase inhibitors. These drugs work by blocking the synthesis of cholesterol in the liver. To compensate, the liver increases the amount of cholesterol, mainly LDL-cholesterol, that it removes from the blood. At this writing, lovastatin holds much promise but long-term safety has not yet been established.

If this discussion produces a vision of a banana split with four scoops of ice cream covered with chocolate sauce and whipped cream in one hand and a glass of bile acid sequestrant in the other, you will be sorely disappointed. All the drugs have side effects or toxicities and, with the exception of niacin, cost between $800 and $2200 a year, depending on drug and dose. In addition, drug therapy does not make up for eating a high-fat diet. Drugs complement a blood cholesterol–lowering diet. In fact, the more you lower your blood cholesterol by diet, the more effective will be your use of drugs. And remember, a low-fat, cholesterol-lowering diet has additional benefits that drugs do not have, such as weight control, reduced risk of some common cancers, low cost, no unpleasant side effects, and great taste.

---

*Questran was the drug used in the Coronary Primary Prevention Trial to lower blood cholesterol levels and incidence of heart attacks.

Regularity

An added benefit of removing fat from your diet and increasing fiber, particularly whole grains, fruits, and vegetables, is the increased regularity of your excretory system.

Remember:

1. *Eater's Choice* is a simple method for lowering blood cholesterol by limiting the amount of saturated fat you eat while giving you control over your food choices.
2. Step-by-Step Guide to *Eater's Choice:*
   a. Have your total blood cholesterol measured; if it is above 200 mg/dL, have all your lipoproteins measured — total cholesterol, LDL, HDL, and triglycerides.
   b. Set your blood cholesterol goal (not to exceed 200 mg/dL).
   c. Determine how much you should weigh.
   d. Determine how many calories you must eat to maintain that weight. Calorie requirements depend on your sex, frame size, and activity level.
   e. Multiply your total daily calorie allotment by 10 percent (or 6 percent) to determine your maximum daily saturated fat budget; follow eating plan and monitor blood cholesterol levels in three months.
   f. If blood cholesterol is still above 200 mg/dL after six months, begin the 6 Percent (or 3 Percent) eating plan.

MAKING THE RIGHT CHOICES

6

Now THAT YOU or your physician have figured out how many calories of saturated fat you should eat each day, you are probably eager to put *Eater's Choice* into action.

Obviously, since you are setting limits on the saturated fats you consume, you will have to know the saturated fat contents of foods that you eat. The food tables at the end of the book list foods, their caloric value, and the number of calories of saturated fat they contain. After you determine the number of calories of saturated fat in a given portion of food, you can budget it into your daily food intake in one of two ways.

If planning is impractical or not in your nature, you can keep a running total of what you eat for the day. When you reach your daily allotment of saturated fat, that is it — no more saturated fat until tomorrow.

If you are a planner type, you can determine what your meals will be for the day or a week and add up the saturated fat calories in advance. You can make choices before you eat. "Hmmm," you think, "I'll spend ——— calories on ——— and ——— calories on ———." Planning ahead also makes you a more efficient grocery shopper.

If you plan ahead, you can save up sat-fat calories for a particular day or special occasion. Perhaps you are going out to dinner Saturday night and want to splurge on a big steak and a rich dessert. By not spending your total saturated fat budget each day, you may be able to save enough sat-fat calories to eat a 6-ounce lean and trimmed porterhouse steak (78 sat-fat calories), 2 tablespoons of sour cream (28 sat-fat calories) on your baked potato, and a piece of cheesecake (89 sat-fat calories).

Likewise, even if you have spent your sat-fat budget for the day and your Aunt May insists that you try the strawberry whipped cream cake she has made *just for you,* you may take a piece without dropping dead on the spot. Blood cholesterol levels do not respond to a single day's food intake; they reflect the sum of the fats you have eaten over the past several weeks. To make up for the splurge, eat fewer sat-fat calories than allowed on your budget for the next few days. But try to limit overdrawing your sat-fat budget in emergency situations or your arteries will pay the penalty.

You may think adding up sat-fat calories will take all the spontaneity out of eating. However, you probably eat a limited number of foods and a limited number of dishes (whether you cook them or eat them out). Sooner than you think, you will know their sat-fat values as well as you know the telephone numbers of your friends. Within a short time, you will learn which combinations and amounts of your favorite foods will fit into your sat-fat budget. For example, you will learn that if you want to have cheese on a bagel for breakfast, you might choose a turkey sandwich for lunch. If you want ice cream for dessert, you might choose scallops for dinner.

To help you keep track of your sat-fat intake, you may want to use the order form at the end of the book to send away for a handy, pocket-sized Sat-fat Estimator and/or a Passbook.

Another approach to determining the sat-fat content of the foods you eat is to use a computer nutrient-analysis program. Many such programs are available. *Take Control! of Cholesterol,* for one, is a user-friendly, menu-driven software program based on the *Eater's Choice* approach. It helps you determine your sat-fat budget, plan suitable menus using the *Eater's Choice* recipes and tables of sat-fat contents of foods, track your actual daily intake of saturated fat, find satisfying alternative foods to fit into your sat-fat budget, and adjust recipe proportions to meet your personal needs. (Order information is at the end of the book.) The DINE System is a more nutritionally comprehensive system. With a database of 3500 food items, this user-friendly program will analyze the saturated fat content in the foods you eat and in recipes. It will also provide the amounts of fourteen other nutrients: monounsaturated and polyunsaturated fats, protein, complex carbohydrates, sugar, cholesterol, and key vitamins and minerals, including sodium, potassium, and calcium. The analysis compares your diet with current dietary guidelines. The DINE System is available for Apple and IBM computers. You can get more information by writing to: DINE Systems, Inc., 724 Robin Road, West Amherst, New York 14228.

Monitor Your Sat-Fat Intake Every Six Months: Just as you should have your blood cholesterol level measured periodically to make sure you are maintaining a level below 200 mg/dL, you should monitor your sat-fat calories for one or two days every six months. This will help you know you are still eating within your sat-fat budget.

FOOD TABLES

The food tables at the end of the book can help you see how much saturated fat lurks in the foods you eat. This information gives you the power to take control and make your own food choices — choices that allow you to lower your blood cholesterol and enjoy eating at the same time.

The food tables are arranged in the following groups: beverages; dairy; fast foods; fats and oils; fish and seafood; fruits and fruit juices; grain products; meats; mixed dishes; nuts and seeds; poultry; sauces and gravies; sausages and luncheon meats; soups; sugars and sweets; vegetables; miscellaneous items. Within each group, items are arranged in alphabetical order.

Data for meats, fish, and poultry are usually given in 1-ounce portion sizes, to help you compare the fat contents of foods, and sometimes also in a measure commonly used for cooking or eating. For instance, if you eat 7 ounces of chicken, you would multiply the sat-fat content by 7 to determine the amount of saturated fat you actually ate.

Be careful. These food tables make meats look like low-fat foods because the fat values are given for 1-ounce portions. Rarely does anyone eat only 1 ounce of meat.

Measuring

In order to use the food tables, you will need to measure the actual amounts of the foods you eat. In addition to measuring spoons and measuring cups, you might find an inexpensive kitchen scale useful.

Use these measuring tools to determine the size of the serving you actually eat and see how many times larger or smaller it is than the listed portion. Then calculate the actual numbers of calories you are consuming. For example, if 1 ounce of cheddar cheese contains 54 calories of saturated fat and you eat ½ ounce, then you are consuming 54 × ½ calories or 27 calories of saturated fat.

How the Food Tables Help You

By focusing on fats rather than foods, the food tables allow you to choose, based on your own preferences, combinations of foods that can fit into your daily sat-fat budget.

You may be able to eat less of a certain food rather than eliminate it entirely. Since the cup of ice cream you long for contains 80 sat-fat calories, then ½ cup has only 40 sat-fat calories. Maybe your sat-fat budget can accommodate the smaller helping.

Using the food tables, you may be able to find a low sat-fat substitute for a food you normally eat. For example, during the course of a day, you may eat a total of six pats of butter — on toast, sandwiches, and a baked potato. Since each pat of butter contains 23 calories of sat-fat, butter is contributing 23 × 6 or 138 calories of sat-fat to your daily sat-fat budget. In place of butter, substitute margarine at 6 calories of sat-fat per teaspoon (equivalent to a pat). The margarine will contribute only 6 × 6 or 36 calories of sat-fat to your daily sat-fat budget at a savings of 102 sat-fat calories.

Here are some other benefits of using the food tables:

1. Hidden sources of saturated fat will jump out at you. "Wow! My nondairy, cholesterol-free coffee whitener has 26 calories of sat-fat per ounce. My daily 3 cups of coffee with 3 ounces of whitener equals 78 calories of sat-fat — that's a third of my sat-fat budget for the whole day, and I haven't even eaten anything!" You can determine if it is really worth eating those fatty foods once you know their sat-fat content.

2. You can check to see if foods that you always considered low-fat are truly low in fat. Take veal, for one: a fiction has developed that veal is less fatty than other beef. Check out the food tables and see how false this assumption is.

3. You can use the food tables to check and modify recipes. For example, a pie recipe uses 1 cup of sour cream, or 270 calories of saturated fat. Replace the sour cream with an equivalent amount of low-fat yogurt, and you only add 3 calories of saturated fat to the pie.

Choices

A list of "Choices" that shows different foods all containing about the same amount of saturated fat can be found in Chapter 12. This list makes it easy to plan your menu. Perhaps you have 200 calories of saturated fat budgeted on your *Eater's Choice* 10 Percent Plan. You have "spent" all but 50 calories. You can check the column with the heading 41–50 calories of saturated fat and find something you feel like eating. Of course, you need not feel compelled to spend all of your daily sat-fat budget each day.

You may wish to add some of your favorite foods to the list of choices.

And Coming in the Next Chapter . . .

Hold on to your seats: the next chapter will tell you all the juicy gossip about the fats in the foods you eat.

Remember:

1. Budget saturated fat into your daily food intake by keeping a running total for each day or planning ahead for the week.
2. The food tables list saturated fat contents of common foods. They help you:
   a. keep track of your saturated fat intake;
   b. choose a variety of foods you like with different sat-fat values to fit into your sat-fat budget;
   c. check and modify recipes.

7 WHERE'S THE FAT?

THE FOCUS of *Eater's Choice* is on limiting saturated fat in your diet while still allowing you to make food choices that reflect your food preferences. There is no large source of saturated fat concentrated in just one food. Nearly every food contains some fat, and most of the fat is hidden. Fats added at the table, such as spreads and salad dressings, account for only about one-fourth of the fat intake, while three-quarters of the fat is invisible or hidden in foods such as red meat, dairy products, baked goods, frozen dinners, and fat used in food preparation.

To help you analyze and change your daily meal plan, the list below will focus your attention on the high sat-fat foods you may have been eating — often without realizing they are high sat-fat foods. For example, do you think of beef as full of fat, or do you think of beef as protein? Is milk on your list of high-fat foods? Do you know how much fat is in a glass of whole milk?

The Top 50 Percent: The following food items contributed about 50 percent of the total saturated fat consumed by Americans during the time period 1976–1980. In descending order of importance, they were: hamburgers, cheeseburgers, meat loaf; whole milk and whole-milk beverages; cheeses, excluding cottage cheese; beef steaks and roasts; hot dogs, ham, and luncheon meats; doughnuts, cookies, and cake; eggs.*

The Next 28 Percent: Another 28 percent (for a cumulative total of 78 percent) of the saturated fat intake was contributed by, in descending order: pork, including chops and roasts; butter; white bread,* rolls,* and crackers; ice cream and frozen desserts; marga-

---

*These foods are relatively low in saturated fat, but the large amounts consumed contribute substantial saturated fat calories to the American diet.

rine; 2% milk; mayonnaise and salad dressings; French fries and fried potatoes; salty snacks; bacon; nondairy coffee creamers; sausage.

Do these foods sound familiar? Do they contribute heavily to your saturated fat intake? Check the food tables to see how much saturated fat these and other foods actually contain. You might be surprised — even shocked. Your immediate reaction might be that you must eliminate these foods, *now,* if not sooner.

Not a Bare-Bones Eating Plan: Relax. Any food can be fitted into *Eater's Choice.* No food need be completely eliminated. The food tables will help you determine *how much* and *how often* you can eat certain foods. Of course, the higher the saturated fat content of a food, the less often or the smaller the amount you will be able to fit into your personalized daily saturated fat budget.

Use Food Tables as You Read This Chapter: As we discuss the fat contents of common foods in this chapter, check back to the food tables to compare foods. Soon, you will have learned the sat-fat contents of the foods you commonly eat and will find you no longer need to look up every food in the tables.

MEATS

Since ground beef is number one on the saturated fat hit parade, let us look at the meat category. All the meat, poultry, and fish entries in the food tables are given in 1-ounce portions to help you compare the different meats. You can easily calculate the sat-fat content by multiplying the number of ounces of meat you eat times the saturated fat contained in 1 ounce. For instance, 1 ounce of braised lean flank steak has 16 calories of saturated fat per ounce. If you eat 6 ounces of flank steak, you are consuming 6 × 16 or 96 calories of saturated fat.

Hamburger — Three Times Fattier: You're thinking about dinner. The refrigerator is bare. Should you buy round steak or ground beef? You look at the beef section of the food tables. Trimmed, lean, round steak happens to be the leanest cut of red meat. It contains 7 calories of saturated fat per ounce. Check out the broiled lean ground beef: 25 calories of saturated fat for the same portion size. If you eat 6 ounces of either meat, the round steak will contribute 7 × 6 or 42 sat-fat calories, while the ground beef will contribute 25 × 6 or 150 sat-fat calories. The round steak has less than one-third the calories of saturated fat found in the broiled lean ground beef. Would this comparison help you decide?

Admittedly, hamburger is a convenience food. It's fast and tasty. However, it is so chock full of saturated fat your arteries shudder when a mere whiff of hamburger floats under your nose. If you need to prepare a delicious meal in a hurry, sauté scallops with garlic and ginger (5 minutes), cover a white fish with lemon yogurt and bake for 5–10 minutes, or cut round steak thin and sauté with onions and green peppers (15 minutes). Or try Soybean Vegeburgers (Chapter 22), a healthy substitute for hamburgers.

For those of you who would rather give up your right arm than give up hamburgers, here are several hints to make your hamburger healthier. Broil rather than pan-fry hamburgers so some of the fat drips away. Immediately after cooking, place hamburgers between paper towels to absorb excess fat. Mix ground beef with bread crumbs or soybean protein (GranBurger, available from Worthington Foods) to make your hamburger half as fatty.

The Veal Story: Lean veal is often recommended as an acceptable meat for a heart-healthy eating pattern. However, you can see that 1 ounce of the leanest veal, broiled lean veal round, contains 14 calories of saturated fat, considerably more saturated fat than 1 ounce of the leanest beef, round steak (7 sat-fat calories per ounce). Braised lean veal breast contains 156 calories of saturated fat per 6 ounces — more than three-quarters the daily allotment of saturated fat on a 2000 calorie per day *Eater's Choice* 10 Percent Plan. Think before you eat veal.

Under the Wool, a Lot of Fat: The saturated fat content of lamb

---

RED MEATS — BIG SATURATED FAT DONORS

In general, the higher the grade of meat, the more fat and saturated fat it contains. Take note: regardless of the grade or cut, the fat of all red meats is predominantly saturated (about 45 percent of the fat) and very little polyunsaturated fat (2 percent of the fat). Although some fat is lost through broiling and some fat can be trimmed, much of the fat is marbled throughout the meat and remains in it even after cooking.

is comparable to all but the fattiest cuts of beef. Even the leanest cuts of lamb — lamb leg and lamb loin — are moderately high in saturated fat, containing about 60 calories of saturated fat per 6 ounces. Lamb shoulder and rib chops contain about 84 calories per 6 ounces.

Pork, Both High and Low: Pork has a reputation as a high-fat food. But the amount of fat (sat-fat) in pork dishes depends on the cut and the way you prepare it. For example, some pork dishes are relatively low in saturated fat, such as roasted lean tenderloin (24 sat-fat calories per 6 ounces) or broiled lean center loin (54 sat-fat calories per 6 ounces), while other dishes are high in sat-fat, such as roasted center rib loin with fat (132 sat-fat calories per 6 ounces) and pan-fried loin blade with fat (204 sat-fat calories per 6 ounces).

TAKE NOTE: Trim the fat from pork before cooking and you remove half the sat-fat calories. Save another 3 to 5 calories of sat-fat per ounce of meat by braising, broiling, or roasting instead of pan-frying.

By far the worst pork product in terms of saturated fat content is bacon. Three medium slices of cooked bacon contain 30 calories of saturated fat. A healthier alternative to bacon is Canadian bacon, which has about one-sixth as much saturated fat. Thus, an amount of Canadian bacon equivalent to 3 slices of regular bacon contributes only 5 calories of saturated fat.

What If You Still Want Red Meat?

You can see that all red meat contains too much saturated fat to be healthy for your coronary arteries. But can red meats fit into your *Eater's Choice* budget? The answer is yes — a yes that depends on the cut of meat, the amount, and how it is prepared. And because red meats are so high in saturated fat, you may have to adjust your saturated fat intake from other sources.

For example, if you consume 2000 calories per day, the *Eater's Choice* 10 Percent Plan allows 200 calories of saturated fat, and the *Eater's Choice* 6 Percent Plan allows 120 calories of saturated fat. One 4-ounce lean hamburger provides 100 sat-fat calories, 50 percent of the daily saturated fat allotment on the *Eater's Choice* 10 Percent Plan and 83 percent on the *Eater's Choice* 6 Percent Plan. That leaves 100 (10 Percent Plan) or 20 (6 Percent Plan) sat-fat calories for the rest of the day. Maybe every once in a while you have to have red meat or you will bite a passing stranger. Fine, have the red meat. On the other hand, you have other choices.

Meat Leaves Center Stage

If red meats are to be eaten on the *Eater's Choice* plan, you have two choices: either you limit the rest of your saturated fat intake for that day, or you use meat as a condiment. Eventually you will stop thinking of meat as the centerpiece of the meal — a 12-ounce steak with a vegetable on the side. Instead, you will use a meat such as thinly sliced flank steak to provide taste and texture to, say, a rice-based or a vegetable-based dish or a pasta. Chinese recipes provide many good examples of combining small amounts of meats with a variety of vegetables to create mouth-watering dishes.

Good Meat: Chicken

Chicken is very low in sat-fat compared to other meats. Six ounces of roasted chicken breast without skin contain 18 calories of saturated fat, versus 42 for round steak and 150 for ground beef.

Chicken breast is the part of the bird lowest in fat and thus your best choice.

CHICKEN PART (WITHOUT SKIN)	SAT-FAT CALORIES PER 6 OZ
breast	18
drumstick	24
leg	36
wing	36
thigh	48
back	54

In addition, chicken breast is one of the most versatile of meats and can be substituted for beef or pork in many recipes. Lemon Chicken, Phyllo Chicken with Rice, Artichokes, and Cream Sauce, and Sesame Chicken Brochettes (all found in Chapter 15) are but a few of the millions of interesting, delicious, and often quick and easy recipes using chicken breasts without skin.

Skin the Beast: Chicken breast scores high as a heart-healthy food as long as it is prepared properly. Bake half a breast without skin for 8 calories of sat-fat. Bake it with the skin on, and your sat-fat calories climb to 19. Batter-dip and fry it with the skin on, and your sat-fat calories soar to 44. TAKE NOTE: skin must be removed *before* cooking or the fat from the skin will be absorbed by the meat.

Better Meat: Turkey

The leanest poultry meat is roasted turkey breast without skin (see box below) which contains only 6 calories of saturated fat per 6 ounces. Dark meat turkey, such as the leg, contains three times as much saturated fat (18 calories), but compared to even the leanest red meats, it is low in saturated fat.

Turkey breast or cutlets ground in a food processor or meat grinder make an excellent low sat-fat ground beef substitute for making burgers, adding to spaghetti sauces and chilis, etc. However, be aware that ground turkey purchased at the grocery store may be loaded with large amounts of turkey fat and skin, and thus may not be a low-fat choice. For example, one commercially ground turkey product contains 36 calories of fat per ounce. Considering that plain white turkey meat contains less than 2½ calories of fat per ounce, the food manufacturer must be adding 33½ calories of fat and skin per ounce to the ground turkey. That's a lot of fat. At about 11 calories of sat-fat per ounce (44 sat-fat calories per 4 ounces), this brand of ground turkey is a better choice than lean ground beef at 25 sat-fat calories per ounce (100 sat-fat calories per 4 ounces). However, it is a choice that should not be eaten with abandon. To make matters worse, the fat content of commercially ground turkey is often not given. To ensure that your ground turkey is low in fat, grind it yourself.

WARNING: Pay attention to turkey labels. Do not buy Butterball turkeys or turkeys that have been shot up with coconut or other hydrogenated oils. Buy plain ol' natural unadulterated turkeys. Cook them breast down and they will still be juicy.

Best Meat: Fish

All animals that live in the water — shellfish, fish, and even marine mammals — contain a special kind of fat called omega-3 polyunsaturated fat. Omega-3 polyunsaturated fats are especially potent in lowering blood triglyceride levels. So, if high blood triglycerides are your problem, eating plenty of fish may be your salvation. Omega-3 polyunsaturated fats also reduce blood clotting. It is the small clots floating through the blood stream that often get caught in clogged arteries, causing heart attacks. The fewer clots that are formed the better.

Not only do fish contain the risk-reducing omega-3 polyunsaturated fats; they also are low in saturated fat. Lean fish such as flounder and sole contain only about 1 calorie of saturated fat per ounce. Even fatty fish such as red salmon have only about 5 calories of saturated fat per ounce — and the fattier the fish the more omega-3 polyunsaturated fat they contain. However, be advised — deep-frying fish or cooking them in cream or butter sauces turns a heart-healthy food into a heart-risky one.

Eat the Fish, Not the Capsule: The best way to get omega-3 polyunsaturated fats is by eating fish. Fish oil capsules are not the answer.

- Fish oil capsules are not regulated by the Food and Drug Administration, and thus may contain either very little or a lot of omega-3 polyunsaturated fat. You have no way of judging the potency of different brands.
- All the fat-soluble contaminants found in fish are concentrated in the fish oil in the capsules.
- Fish oil capsules add unnecessary fat and calories to your diet.
- Fish oil capsules are expensive.

A TIP: tuna packed in water tastes delicious and has 12 fewer calories of saturated fat per 3½-ounce can than tuna packed in oil. The oil used is soybean oil and not fish oil. If you are only able to purchase tuna packed in oil, wash the tuna with water to remove excess oil before eating. This will remove unwanted fat and calories.

Ruining Chicken, Turkey, and Fish

We often hear protests: "I eat only chicken, fish, and turkey, and yet my cholesterol is pushing 280 mg/dL. Am I one of those people whose cholesterol isn't affected by diet?" No! Even heart-healthy foods can be made heart-risky by the way they are prepared.

Nutritious and low in fat, chicken, turkey, and fish are often transformed into cholesterol-raising high-fat foods when they are processed into frozen dinners. This is how it works: pollock is a fish with trace saturated fat — that means a tiny bit more than 0 calories of saturated fat. A food processing company takes the pollock, cuts it into fish sticks, breads it, fries it in partially hydrogenated palm oil, and packages it. Now, according to the label the serving size of 4 pollock fish sticks contains 10 grams or 90 calories of fat and 45 calories of saturated fat (calculated by the Sat-fat Estimator,* which helps you estimate the sat-fat calories from the grams of fat on a label). The food processing company took an almost totally fat-free, heart-healthy food and increased its fat content by more than 9000 percent.

Fast-food restaurants commit similar crimes when preparing chicken and fish. Foods with negligible saturated fat become sat-fat gold mines when breaded and deep-fried in saturated oils. Remember — just because it's chicken, turkey, or fish does not mean it's heart-healthy.

Cholesterol in Meats

All the meats — fish, poultry, and red meats — contain approximately equal amounts of cholesterol, about 25 mg per ounce or about 150 mg per 6 ounces. But take a look at the differences in calories of saturated fat. (Remember, these amounts are for only 1

CHOLESTEROL AND SATURATED FAT VALUES OF MEAT, POULTRY, FISH, AND SEAFOOD

	CHOLESTEROL MG/OZ	SATURATED FAT CALORIES/OZ
Veal breast	36	26
Lamb loin chop, broiled	26	23
Pork chop, broiled	28	21
Sirloin steak, broiled	26	19
Chicken breast, no skin	24	3
Turkey breast, no skin	20	1
Flounder, baked	20	1
Shrimp	43*	1

*Shrimp has slightly more cholesterol than other meats, but is extremely low in saturated fat (1 calorie per ounce) and contains risk-reducing omega-3 polyunsaturated fats. How much shrimp can you eat? As much as you can afford — unless you are a shrimp fisherman or very wealthy.

*See order form on the last page of the book.

ounce of meat.) Thus, decisions about choosing meats are best made on the basis of saturated fat content and not cholesterol content.

Fish and white meat turkey or chicken without skin are so low in saturated fat that large quantities could be fitted into any heart-healthy eating plan if it were not for their cholesterol contents. However, if you are going to stay within the American Heart Association guideline of 200–300 mg of cholesterol per day (see Chapter 5), you should not exceed 10–12 ounces per day of even the leanest fish or poultry. If your physician or dietitian has recommended a limit of 100 mg of cholesterol per day, then you should not eat more than about 4 ounces of even the leanest fish or poultry. Don't worry — you won't starve eating even this amount.

Sausages and Luncheon Meats

Sausages and luncheon meats are extremely high in saturated fat as well as extremely high in sodium. They are poor choices to fit into your eating budget.

Consider the sausage. One Polish sausage contributes over 200 calories of saturated fat to your sat-fat budget, more than is allowed for the whole day on the *Eater's Choice* 10 Percent Plan for a 2000 calorie per day intake level.

Smoked link sausages are also very high in saturated fat. Although they are small, each 2.4-ounce sausage link contains about 70 calories of saturated fat, which represents approximately 35 percent of the 200 sat-fat calories allowed on the *Eater's Choice* 10 Percent Plan and 58 percent of the 120 sat-fat calories allowed on the *Eater's Choice* 6 Percent Plan. Thus, eating only one sausage link may mean making severe restrictions in your saturated fat intake for the rest of the day. Two links would completely use up your saturated fat allowance on the *Eater's Choice* 6 Percent Plan.

What's a baseball game or cookout without a hot dog nestled in a warm bun and covered with ketchup or mustard and pickle relish? What about two or three? Beware! A two-ounce all-beef frankfurter contains 61 calories of sat-fat. If that hot dog is in addition to your regular meals, you may be in great danger of having overspent your sat-fat budget — unless you planned ahead.

MILK AND MILK PRODUCTS

Milk — A High-Fat Food

Milk is characterized by its fat content. Thus, whole milk is generally about 3.3 percent fat. This means that 3.3 percent of the total weight is contributed by fat. (This system of rating milk was established many years ago to insure a minimum fat content as a way of protecting consumers from watered-down milk.)

The amount of fat in whole milk — 3.3 percent — seems so trivial, hardly worth counting. False — do not be fooled. Most of the weight of milk is accounted for by water. In terms of calories, fat accounts for 72 of the total 150 calories in a cup of whole milk, or 48 percent of the total calories. A cup of whole milk contains 45 calories of saturated fat.

Thus, whole milk is a high-fat food. On a 2000 calorie per day eating pattern, 4.4 cups of whole milk would provide 200 calories of saturated fat and would thus account for the entire saturated fat allotment on the *Eater's Choice* 10 Percent Plan. A mere 2.7 cups of whole milk would provide 120 calories of saturated fat, accounting for the entire saturated fat allotment on the *Eater's Choice* 6 Percent Plan.

Most (about 64 percent) of the fat in milk products is saturated fat regardless of whether it is whole, 2%, or 1% milk. This is true of all milk products, including yogurt, cream, ice cream, and cheese. **Think before you eat.**

Move Toward Skim Milk

Low-fat milk (2%) tastes pretty similar to whole milk. If you are a whole milk drinker, start by changing to 2% milk. Although 2% milk contains less fat than whole milk, it still contains 27 calories of saturated fat per cup. After a few weeks, try 1% milk. It contains only 14 calories of saturated fat per cup.

However, the best favor you can do your heart is to drink skim milk. "Yuk," you say, "it looks like blue water." We say, "If you don't love it now, you will. It just takes getting used to. Our kids are revolted by whole milk."

And what great benefits. Skim milk is essentially fat-free, containing at most 3 calories of saturated fat per cup. Look at these statistics:

	WHOLE MILK PER CUP	SKIM MILK PER CUP
Total calories	150	86
Sat-fat calories	45	3
Cholesterol, mg	33	4
Calcium, mg	291	302

It may take time, but it is worth working your way toward skim milk.

More Calcium in Skim Milk Than Whole Milk: Milk is an important source of calcium. Calcium is vital for developing and maintaining strong bones and preventing osteoporosis in later life. Skim milk contains more calcium than whole milk: 302 mg of calcium per cup of skim milk versus 291 mg per cup of whole milk. Most skim milk available today has been fortified with vitamins and thus contains just as many vitamins as whole milk. Skim milk is just as nutritious as whole milk *and* is heart-healthy.

Butter

The creamy sweet taste of butter is irreplaceable, but its saturated fat content is so high you must either use it sparingly or find a suitable substitute. The food industry has invested heavily in producing such substitutes. They range from whipped butter, which has about 25 percent less saturated fat than regular butter, to butter-margarine blends, with about 50 percent less saturated fat, margarines, with about 70 percent less saturated fat, and diet margarines, with about 86 percent less saturated fat.

Cream

Coffee drinkers, did you realize that adding 1 tablespoon of light cream to a cup of coffee uses 18 calories of saturated fat of your sat-fat budget? Three cups of coffee with cream provide 54 calories of saturated fat, about one-quarter of the daily allotment of saturated fat under the *Eater's Choice* 10 Percent Plan for 2000 total calories and almost half of the daily allotment under the *Eater's Choice* 6 Percent Plan. And all that for three dinky little tablespoons of cream. Mind-boggling.

Half-and-half contains half as much saturated fat as light cream while 2% milk provides about a tenth the amount of saturated fat as light cream. How about using 1% or skim milk, or drinking your coffee black?

You must be careful when using nondairy coffee whiteners. Read the label. Nondairy coffee whiteners have vastly different saturated fat contents, depending on the type of fat used. The more common coconut oil coffee whiteners contain 13 calories of saturated fat per ½ ounce (equivalent to a tablespoon). Coffee whiteners made with soybean oil contain only 3 calories of saturated fat per ½ ounce, about the same amount as whole milk.

Cheese, Wonderful Cheese, Why Are You Almost All Fat?

The sad story about cheese is that whole milk cheeses derive 80 to 90 percent of their calories from fat. Thus, 1 ounce of cheddar cheese provides 114 calories, of which 81 are from fat. One ounce of cream cheese contains 90 calories of fat and a total of 99 calories. Over half of the fat calories are contributed by saturated fat.

You can include cheese in your *Eater's Choice* eating plan, but you will have to sacrifice other sources of sat-fat in your diet. Just plan ahead. Keep your daily sat-fat budget low and you will be able to sneak in a piece of cheese without sinking your heart-healthy diet boat. However, before you devote your entire sat-fat budget to cheese, be aware that most cheeses are extremely high in sodium.

HINT: Satisfy your cheese hunger with minimal sat-fat calories by using a cheese slicer to shave yourself a thin piece of cheese. Remember: many thin slices make one big fat slice.

Lower-Fat Cheeses: The only real low-fat cheese is 1% cottage cheese. One percent cottage cheese contains one-quarter the saturated fat calories of creamed cottage cheese and tastes just as good. Mix cottage cheese with cut-up fruit for a refreshing low-fat lunch. Cover Honey Whole-Wheat Bread (Chapter 23) with sliced bananas and 1% cottage cheese for a filling, scrumptious breakfast. One percent cottage cheese can be used in cooking as a creamy substitute for higher-fat cheeses, as in Creamy Chicken Pot Pie (Chapter 15), Spinach Quiche (Chapter 19), and Calzone (Chapter 19).

Part skim milk ricotta and mozzarella are lower in saturated fat than their whole milk counterparts. One-half cup of part skim milk ricotta contains about half the saturated fat calories of whole milk ricotta: 55 versus 93. One ounce of part skim milk mozzarella contains 28 sat-fat calories versus 40 sat-fat calories for whole milk mozzarella. These cheeses may be lower in saturated fat, but they are still high enough that you need to monitor them carefully as part of your sat-fat budget.

Yogurt

Several different varieties of yogurt, with vastly different saturated fat contents, are available. They include nonfat, low-fat, and regular high-fat yogurt. Some yogurts are loaded with eggs and cream. Read the label of the yogurt you choose to make certain it has a low saturated fat content.

Nonfat or low-fat yogurt makes a good substitute for sour cream in many recipes (even in a sweet dessert such as Deep-Dish Pear Pie, page 336). Whole milk plain yogurt contains about a sixth as much saturated fat as sour cream, while skim milk plain yogurt contains almost 1/100.

Do Not Skimp on Low-Fat Dairy Foods

Let us say it again: to stay healthy and to keep your bones and teeth strong, you need the calcium that dairy foods provide. Women especially need calcium to prevent osteoporosis. Children need calcium for strong bones and teeth and for growth. Eat dairy products, but eat low-fat dairy products, such as skim milk, 1% cottage cheese (creamy and good), and low-fat or nonfat yogurt.

Fit cheeses, cream, sour cream, whole milk, and whole milk yogurt into your sat-fat budget as a splurge. Cook with low-fat products. Substitute low-fat yogurt or buttermilk for cream or sour cream. We even substitute skim milk for cream (see Potato Soup with Leeks and Broccoli, Chapter 14, or Mushroom Sauce, Chapter 17) with excellent gustatory results.

FATS AND OILS

Two of the most important and widespread changes made by the American public to lower blood cholesterol levels are the substitution of margarine for butter and the substitution of polyunsaturated vegetable oils for saturated animal fats such as lard or beef tallow.

Margarine

Margarines vary in their ratio of heart-healthy polyunsaturated fat to heart-risky saturated fat (P/S ratio). The more polyunsaturated fat in relation to saturated fat, the less heart-risky is the food; the smaller the proportion of polyunsaturates, the more heart-risky. In general, a P/S ratio greater than or equal to 1:1 is considered good, and a ratio less than 1:1 is bad.

For example, a margarine made with sunflower oil that has 5 grams of polyunsaturated fat and 2 grams of saturated fat has a P/S ratio of 5:2 or 2.5:1. A margarine made with soybean oil with 4 grams of polyunsaturated fat and 2 grams of saturated fat has a P/S ratio of 2:1. Choose the margarine made with sunflower oil. Most soft or tub margarines have higher P/S ratios than stick or hard margarines. Check the label.

For comparison, butter has a P/S ratio of 0.09:1.

Olive Oil: Number-One Choice in the Vegetable Oil Contest

Olive oil contains mainly monounsaturated fat and little polyunsaturated fat. As a result, its P/S ratio — 0.6:1 — looks mediocre. However, it turns out that olive oil is the most heart-healthy of all the oils. Recent research indicates that olive oil lowers LDL-cholesterol without lowering HDL-cholesterol. Epidemiological studies show that populations (such as Greeks and Italians) who use olive oil as the predominant source of fat in their diet have very low rates of heart disease. Choose olive oil even for baking. (Like olive oil, peanut oil is predominantly monounsaturated. However, scientific research has shown that peanut oil causes clogging of coronary arteries in some animals. Why take a chance?)

Second choice are vegetable oils with the lowest saturated fat content and the highest polyunsaturated fat content. Safflower oil has a P/S ratio of 8.3:1. Sunflower oil has a P/S ratio almost as good as that of safflower oil: 6.4:1. Other oils with good P/S ratios are corn (4.6:1) and soybean (4:1).

Vegetable oils used in commercial food products are often hydro-genated. This means that polyunsaturated oils are converted chemically to saturated oils. Even safflower oil that has been hydrogenated loses some (or all) of its heart-healthy properties.

Coconut Oil: The Pits

Coconut oil is given to lab rats and other animals normally resistant to developing elevated blood cholesterol levels to produce atherosclerotic plaques and heart disease. With a P/S ratio of 0.02:1 and 106 sat-fat calories per tablespoon it is the most heart-risky fat known. If you are smarter than a rat, you will avoid coconut oil at all costs. Following close is palm kernel oil (100 sat-fat calories/tablespoon) and palm oil (60 sat-fat calories/tablespoon). All of these oils should be avoided. This may be more difficult than you would imagine because coconut, palm kernel, and palm oils are commonly used in commercial baked products and candies. *Read those labels!*

All Oils Have Equal Calories

You will note that all the oils are really mixtures of polyunsaturated, monounsaturated, and saturated fats. None contains only one type of fat. We refer to an oil as polyunsaturated or monounsaturated or saturated because it contains predominantly that type of fat. Regardless of the type of oil, they all contain the same number of calories because they are 100 percent fat, and all fats contain 9 calories per gram. All are high in calories and should be avoided as much as possible, especially by people trying to maintain their desirable weight.

Lard, Chicken Fat, and Other Animal Fats

All animal fats contain large amounts of monounsaturated fat, relatively small amounts of polyunsaturated fat, moderate to large amounts of saturated fat, and moderate amounts of cholesterol. Of the animal fats, chicken fat is the least heart-risky and beef tallow is the most heart-risky. *But no animal fats can be recommended for persons trying to lower their blood cholesterol levels.* The heart-healthy alternatives are olive oil, polyunsaturated vegetable oils, and tub margarines with high P/S ratios.

Keep Short on Shortening

Many baked products contain either plant or animal shortening. Choose these products selectively because in either case the fats are predominantly saturated. Notice in the food tables the relatively high amounts of saturated fats and the low P/S ratio of the various types of shortening.

Mayonnaise

You will be happy to find something you know and love but do not have to avoid completely: mayonnaise. While mayonnaise contains egg yolks and therefore cholesterol, it also contains predominantly polyunsaturated fat (the P/S ratio of some brands may be as high as 3.5:1) and therefore can fit into *Eater's Choice*. For those of you watching your weight, reduced-calorie mayonnaises are available with half the total calories, slightly less sat-fat, and equally high P/S ratios as real mayonnaise.

Before you feel too happy, take heed. All mayonnaises are almost pure fat and so are high in calories. Use mayonnaise in moderation.

Salad Dressings

Many salad dressings are high in saturated fats as well as polyunsaturated fats. A tablespoon of blue cheese dressing or French dressing has 14 calories of saturated fat. Russian has 10, followed closely by Italian with 9, and Thousand Island with 8. One problem with using salad dressing is that one never delicately sprinkles only a tablespoon of salad dressing on one's salad. Another problem is that salad dressings are often high in sodium. Do not ruin the health value of your salad by drowning it in highly fattening and fatty salad dressing.

A more heart-healthy alternative is to use commercial low-fat, low-sodium dressings. Or make your own: in a jar, combine olive oil, vinegar, minced garlic, some herbs (oregano, thyme, or basil, for example), a little Dijon mustard, salt, and pepper — and shake.

DESSERTS

Many Americans enjoy having a sweet, rich dessert to top off their dinner and often their lunch, too. Unfortunately, many of our favorite desserts are rich in saturated fat. A cup of ordinary vanilla ice cream contains 80 calories of saturated fat. Compare this with a cup of vanilla ice milk (32 calories of saturated fat), a cup of orange sherbet (21 sat-fat calories), and a cup of low-fat frozen yogurt (12 sat-fat calories). The low-fat frozen yogurt has less than one-sixth as much saturated fat as the ice cream. Even better are the new nonfat frozen yogurts (such as Colombo Lite) that eliminate all sat-fat calories while retaining the creamy texture and delicious taste.

Fortunately frozen yogurt is becoming increasingly more available in ice cream parlors, restaurants, and grocery stores. But be advised. *Yogurt* is not a synonym for *low-fat*. Ask about the fat content and the ingredients. Many yogurt vendors can provide nutritional information. For example, one popular brand contains 2 grams of fat per 4 ounces. The primary fat is butterfat. This works out to 18 calories of total fat and about 12 sat-fat calories. Another brand contains 0.9 grams of butterfat per ounce. If you eat 4 ounces (about half a cup), you will be eating (4 × .9) 3.6 grams of total fat or about 32 fat calories and about 22 sat-fat calories.

A new type of nondairy frozen dessert called Tofutti has arrived on the scene. *Beware!* Although it is a nondairy product and relatively low in saturated fat, it should *not* be considered a healthy substitute for ice cream. Tofutti contains little soy. It is extremely high in total calories and total fat calories. A cup of chocolate Tofutti has 420 calories of which 234 come from fat. This is more calories than in all but the richest ice creams. Too much of any fat — even polyunsaturated — is unhealthy and may contribute to girth growth.

The Fat Impact of Desserts

A single cake-type doughnut contains 24 calories of saturated fat. A piece of chocolate devil's food cake made with butter and iced with chocolate contains 56 calories of saturated fat. Coconut custard pie contributes about 51 calories of saturated fat per slice. Apple pie made with vegetable shortening, lemon meringue pie, and cherry pie each contain about 30 calories of saturated fat per slice. A piece of Boston cream pie made with butter contains 27 calories of saturated fat, but only 18 calories if made with vegetable shortening instead of butter.

Commercial cookies are the downfall of many sat-fat counters. Like crackers and nuts, cookie consumption is a miraculous occurrence. Somehow, scores of cookies get from the plate or the box into the mouth without the cookie consumer having put them there. Cookie eaters must pay attention. Because most cookie brands have no nutritional labeling, consumers have no way of knowing how much fat each cookie contains. They must make fat judgments by reading the ingredients on the label. Labels that list coconut, palm kernel, palm, or hydrogenated vegetable oil; butter; or lard should be left on the grocery shelf.

Being on a low sat-fat diet does not mean you must give up delicious desserts. Why not bake your own? Try the desserts beginning on page 316. Nothing could be simpler or more delicious than Cinnamon Sweet Cakes (page 338) at 8 sat-fat calories per square. What about Deep-Dish Pear Pie (page 336) at 12 sat-fat calories per slice, or Tante Nancy's Apple Crumb Cake (page 330) at 15 sat-fat calories for a trip to the sublime?

Just a note of caution: even desserts that are low in saturated fat are generally more caloric and fat-filled than other parts of your meal. You are not going to stay thin by eating baked or frozen desserts at every meal. How about fruit?

Read labels for hidden coconut, palm kernel, palm, or hydrogenated vegetable oil in commercial desserts.

The Good Guys

Many Europeans finish their large meal of the day with a piece of fruit. How about a delicious (and heart-healthy) dessert of sliced fruit mixed with low-fat yogurt? You will see the advantages fruits offer when you consider the saturated fat content of most fruits. An apple contains less than 1 calorie of saturated fat, 3 apricots less than 0.2, a banana about 2, 1 cup of cherries about 0.7, an orange about 0.4, a peach less than 0.1, a pear about 0.3.

Substituting fruits for rich, sweet desserts will allow you much greater freedom in choosing meats, dairy products, and other foods that contain saturated fats. The choices are yours to make . . . as long as you stay within your own saturated fat budget.

SNACKS

Snacks can be the downfall of any healthy eating plan — but they do not have to be.

Popcorn

One of the greatest snacks known to mankind since some ancient American Indian threw dried corn kernels into a fire is popcorn. Low in calories, high in fiber, popcorn is truly a treat. It is filling without being fattening (if you do not drench it in butter or margarine). Be sure to make your own popcorn because even the simplest butter-free commercial popcorn is usually made with coconut oil and is extraordinarily high in saturated fat.

Microwave popcorn has become increasingly popular. But before popping it into your microwave and then into your mouth, read the label. One brand lists 13 grams of fat per 3 cups. Since hydrogenated coconut oil is the fat used (wouldn't coconut oil be bad enough?) and it is 100 percent saturated fat, 3 cups of popcorn, once fiber-rich and fat-free, now contain 13×9 or 117 sat-fat calories per serving. Other microwave popcorns made with partially hydrogenated cottonseed and soybean oil list 13 grams of fat per 3 cups on their labels. They also contain at least 13×9 or 117 fat calories, but since the oils are less saturated, there are 35 calories of saturated fat per 3 cups instead of 117. While 35 sat-fat calories is better, it's not great. And who stops at 3 cups?

The most heart-healthy of the microwave popcorns use partially hydrogenated soy oil and range from 6–8 grams of fat for 3 cups. This works out to at least 54–72 calories of fat and 16–22 sat-fat calories for 3 cups. This is a little better, but considering the added expense and high sodium content of microwave popcorn, why not buy ordinary popcorn and pop it in a hot-air popper or saucepan? It takes no time to pop and will be much healthier.

For the lowest calorie popcorn, pop your own in an air popper. Alternatively, pop it in a popcorn popper or saucepan with a poly-unsaturated oil. The 1-quart saucepan made by Farberware is a perfect popcorn maker. Cover the bottom of the saucepan with 1 table-spoon of sunflower oil. Set the burner to high. Pour about ¼ cup popcorn evenly over the bottom of the pan. Cover the saucepan. Soon the corn will begin to pop. When popping starts to slow down, raise the pot 1 to 2 inches above the burner. When popping stops, pour the popcorn into a big bowl, salt lightly, and enjoy, enjoy. You will make about 4½ cups of popcorn.

HINT: Store popcorn kernels in the refrigerator to keep them fresh and pop-worthy.

Crackers

Crackers are so small, you hardly notice that you have eaten ten in one sitting. But even though they are small in size, they aren't small in sat-fat calories. And, of course, the sat-fat calories add up, as one cracker after another disappears into your mouth. A typical brand of hearty wheat crackers has 8 sat-fat calories each. Eight calories is not much, but 8 × 10 equals 80 calories, which is probably almost half your sat-fat budget.

Most cracker containers list ingredients but not the amount of fat. Avoid crackers that contain coconut, palm kernel, palm, or hydrogenated oil, butter, or lard.

Nuts

Nuts are a popular snack choice. The trouble with nuts is that they are very high in total fat and thus high in calories: about 160 to 190 calories per ounce. (Only 40 shelled peanuts, a small handful, weigh an ounce.) Nuts are also addictive. Who ever heard of eating one peanut? A couple of handfuls disappears without notice — but you and everyone else will notice soon enough if you overdose on nuts. Eat nuts sparingly.

If you must eat nuts, the ones with the least amount of saturated fat are walnuts, pecans, almonds, pistachios, and hazelnuts (about 13 to 17 sat-fat calories per ounce of dry-roasted shelled nuts).

The Bad Guys

Cashews, macadamia nuts, brazil nuts, and coconut contain, in increasing order, greater amounts of saturated fat. Coconut is almost purely saturated fat and should be avoided like the plague.

Peanut Butter

Pure, unadulterated peanut butter is a high-protein food, composed mainly of monounsaturated fats and a relatively small amount of saturated fat (12 sat-fat calories per tablespoon). All-natural peanut butters made from peanuts only, no salt added, are often ground and packaged in your local grocery stores. That is the good news. The bad news is that peanut butter is a high-fat and high-calorie food. It derives 72 of its 95 total calories (per tablespoon) from fat. And, in addition, experiments implicate peanut oil in clogging the arteries of some animals. Beware of familiar brands of processed peanut butters, which are filled with added salt, sugar, and partially hydrogenated vegetable fats. Eat peanut butter in moderation.

Veggies

Tasty, healthy, and filling, but often overlooked as snacks, are cut-up vegetables. Carrots, cauliflower, broccoli, celery, and cucumbers may be eaten raw or with a low-fat yogurt dip.

Yogurt

A carton of yogurt is a refreshing snack. (See page 72.) Choose nonfat, flavored yogurts. They give you gustatory pleasure without adding a single sat-fat calorie to your sat-fat budget. (Ron says eating Colombo Lite Vanilla is like eating ice cream.)

Muffins, Bagels, Etc.

An Oat Bran Muffin (pages 308–311) with coffee, a slice of Honey Whole-Wheat Bread (page 303) with a glass of skim or low-fat milk, or half a bagel with margarine make excellent snacks. Of course, you know any snack should be eaten in moderation — even healthy ones.

FAST FOODS

You lead a busy life. Fast-food restaurants offer the chance to pop in and get a filling and tasty meal at a moderate price. But is it healthy for your heart?

It is possible at some fast-food restaurants to order a meal that is not horrendously high in saturated fat. Filet of sole at the Ponderosa contains only about 24 calories of saturated fat, a McDonald's hamburger about 40, a Kentucky Fried Chicken thigh about 27, a Roy Rogers roast beef sandwich about 29, and a bowl of Wendy's chili about 38 calories of saturated fat. Many of these restaurants now offer salad bars. If you stick to vegetables and a minimal amount of dressing, you will not break your sat-fat bank.

However, if you are going to be tempted by a Big Mac, which contains 155 calories of saturated fat, or a Hardee's double cheese-burger, with about 117, or a Dairy Queen Super Brazier hot dog with cheese containing about 134 calories of saturated fat, then do not step inside these restaurants. The fat in Wendy's Cheese-Stuffed Po-tato is equivalent to melting *nine pats* of butter (180 sat-fat calories) over a potato.

Go to a fast-food restaurant only after you have checked the food tables for the sat-fat values of the foods you plan to eat. Do not stray from your choice when temptation rears its ugly head.

Overdose on Sodium

In addition to containing large amounts of saturated fat, fast foods contain very large amounts of sodium: a Big Mac contains 1010 mg of sodium, a Dairy Queen Super Brazier hot dog with cheese con-tains 1986 mg of sodium, Arby's club sandwich contains 1610 mg. Your intake of sodium should be between 1100 and 3300 mg for the whole day. (See Chapter 9.) Each of these items contains more than enough sodium to catapult you over the daily minimum without any additional sources of sodium for the day. With sodium from other foods eaten that day, you are likely to exceed even the maximum allotment of sodium. This is especially a problem if you have high blood pressure.

THE JOYS OF REAL FOOD

Perhaps you have to go to a fast-food restaurant every once in a blue moon. But, on the whole, why not eat real food? Every recipe need not be time-consuming. Try the starred recipes in this book, for starters. They are quick and easy. Sitting down with your family in relaxed surroundings is more heart-healthy than spending ten sec-onds at a fast-food joint, stuffing your mouth with a highly saturated piece of rubbery, salty meat surrounded by airy white bread.

This sentiment needs repeating: take time to make real food. One hour a day to prepare dinner is a small amount of time to devote to an activity that will lengthen and improve the quality of your life.

Remember:

1. Red meats such as beef, veal, lamb, and some pork products are extremely high in saturated fat. The higher the grade of meat, the more saturated fat it contains.
2. Turkey and chicken with the skin removed and fish are all low in saturated fat. (Always remove the skin *before* you cook poultry.)
3. Dairy products are excellent sources of calcium but many are high in fat and saturated fat. Whole milk derives almost half its calories from fat. Most cheeses derive about 80 percent of their calories from fat. Choose low-fat dairy products, such as low-fat yogurt, low-fat cottage cheese, and skim milk.
4. Recent evidence indicates that olive oil, rich in monounsaturated fatty acids, may be the most heart-healthy oil. For margarines and other oils, the higher the polyunsaturated to saturated (P/S) ratio, the more heart-healthy.
5. Coconut oil, which is found in many commercial foods, is one of the most heart-risky foods you can eat. *Avoid it diligently.*
6. Most fast foods are loaded with sat-fat and sodium. Do your coronary arteries a lifelong favor by staying clear of fast-food restaurants.

FROM THEORY TO PRACTICE 8

YOU ARE NOW ready to act. You have already figured out your ideal caloric intake and your daily sat-fat budget. Now you must look at your own eating pattern to see how much saturated fat you actually eat and how to reduce it.

Keep a Record: The best way to find out what you actually eat is to write down everything you consume for two or three days. Include a typical week day and a weekend day. *Write down everything.* Be sure to include that glass of orange juice you drank in the afternoon and that handful of peanuts you grabbed before dinner. Measure everything.

Next, use the food tables to find the total calories and sat-fat calories for the foods you ate and add them up.

This very important exercise may surprise you. You may discover that the Danish pastry you usually eat for breakfast squanders 47 sat-fat calories, without giving you any nutritional value. You may find that most of the saturated fat you eat is concentrated in a few foods, which you can easily change. Analyzing your eating pattern will allow you to make the most effective and enduring changes in the way you eat.

Slow, but Enduring: Having discovered the sat-fat pitfalls in your daily food record, you may be eager to take immediate action and completely revamp your eating pattern. However, slow down! If you make too many changes too fast, you are not likely to stick with them. The changes in your eating pattern will do you and your heart good only if they are permanent.

Remember, it takes years to develop the atherosclerotic plaque that blocks the coronary arteries. Taking a few months to modify your lifelong eating patterns should not cause any harm and will result in more lasting changes.

APPROACH I

One approach to making gradual changes is to focus your attention on the worst culprits. Can you eat these less often, in smaller amounts, or even not at all? Go for the worst first. Change one or a few things at a time.

First, write down your menu for yesterday. Say it looks like this:

FOOD ITEM	CALORIES	
	TOTAL	SAT-FAT
Breakfast		
Soft-boiled egg	79	15
3 slices bacon	109	30
1 slice whole-wheat toast	60	1
1 pat butter	36	23
Coffee + 1 tbsp half-and-half	20	10
Lunch		
Big Mac	563	155
_____		
_____		
_____		
10 French fries	220	33
Pepsi Lite	1	0
Dinner		
6 oz sirloin steak	372	72
1 small baked potato	105	0
1 pat butter	72	23
_____		
_____		
_____		
_____		
1 cup ice cream	270	80
Coffee + 1 tbsp half-and-half	20	10
Snack		
_____		
1 cup whole milk	150	45
Total	2077	497

Interesting. If your total calorie intake for the day was supposed to be 2000, 497 is way over your sat-fat allotment of 200 calories allowed on the *Eater's Choice* 10 Percent Plan. You need to eliminate 297 calories of saturated fat to get down to your 200 calorie sat-fat budget.

What contributes the most saturated fat for the day? The Big Mac at 155. How about having a ham and cheese sandwich at 81, or

REPLACEMENT FOOD ITEMS	CALORIES TOTAL	SAT-FAT	SAVINGS IN SAT-FAT CALORIES
Breakfast			
1 waffle	86	6	9
2 slices Canadian bacon	86	12	18
2 slices whole-wheat toast	120	2	(1)
2 tsp margarine	60	10	13
Coffee + 1 tbsp 2% milk	8	2	8
Lunch			
Turkey sandwich			
3 oz turkey breast	114	3	
2 slices whole-wheat bread	120	2	145
1 tsp mayonnaise	33	5	
10 French fries	220	33	0
Pepsi Lite	1	0	
Dinner			
6 oz sirloin steak	372	72	0
1 medium baked potato	146	0	0
1 tsp margarine	30	5	18
Steamed broccoli w/lemon	53	1	(1)
Mixed salad	8	0	
1 tbsp Italian dressing	69	9	(9)
1 slice whole-wheat bread	60	1	(1)
1 tsp margarine	30	5	(5)
1 cup ice milk	184	32	48
Coffee + 1 tbsp 2% milk	8	2	8
Snack			
1 oz Cheerios	110	3	(3)
1 cup 2% milk	121	27	18
Total	2039	232	265

better yet tuna or turkey breast (3 ounces of either, with 1 teaspoon of mayonnaise) at 10 sat-fat calories each? Even with the ham and cheese, your total sat-fat for the day is reduced to 423. With the tuna or turkey breast, the total becomes 352. That's beginning to look a lot better.

Can you do without those fatty strips of bacon? Replace the bacon with Canadian bacon and reduce your sat-fat calories from 30 to 12. Why not eat that egg on a day when your cholesterol intake is not so high? How about eating ice milk (32 sat-fat calories) instead of ice cream (80 sat-fat calories)? And margarine instead of butter (20 sat-fat calories for the day instead of 46)? And 1 cup of 2% milk instead of whole milk, for 27 instead of 45 sat-fat calories? All these changes together bring your daily total sat-fat intake to 232 calories (see meal plans). Great! You are almost there. And there is always tomorrow to make more changes.

Great news for all you food lovers. You can see in the meal plans that by reducing your sat-fat calorie intake, you are actually eating *more* — more foods, more variety, more bulk, a more balanced and healthier menu. Reducing your sat-fat intake will not make you hungry; just the opposite — the fruits, vegetables, and grains you substitute will make you feel blissfully full.

A Few "Sacrifices" for the Old Bod'

By evaluating your eating habits and figuring out what foods you can do without or replace with less fatty substitutes, you can bring your saturated fat total down with little pain. The next stage is to make a few sacrifices. (You will find that these so-called sacrifices are not sacrifices at all. You are substituting foods that are just as satisfying or *more* satisfying than those you ate before.)

Try drinking 1% milk instead of 2%. That's a reduction of 13 calories of saturated fat per cup. How about skipping fatty desserts every day but Sunday? Wow. Watch that sat-fat total drop.

Use small amounts of beef as a condiment with rice or pasta. Choose leaner cuts of beef, such as flank steak or round. Instead of having beef four times a week, eat it only twice a week. Perhaps not at all.

Replace some or all of your red meat meals with chicken, turkey, or fish. (This book is filled with scrumptious recipes for chicken, turkey, and fish. Try them.) Notice how much impact the substitution of fish or poultry for beef has on your daily saturated fat intake. Also notice how eliminating sat-fat calories from meat frees up calories that you can spend on a wide variety of foods — foods that are tasty, nutritious, and low or moderate in fat content.

REMEMBER: as you reduce your fat intake, increase your complex carbohydrate intake. Eat more whole-grain cereals and breads, rice, and pasta. Eat more fruits and vegetables. You will feel less lethargic after meals, you will be more regular, you will undoubtedly lose weight, and, who knows, you might have a better sex life.

APPROACH 2

An alternative approach to changing your eating habits is to focus on changing one meal at a time. For example, for the first few weeks only make changes in your breakfast menu. Get rid of that bacon and sausage. Eliminate those doughnuts at 24 calories of saturated fat each, not to mention all that sugar. Avoid granola: it is billed as healthy but look how saturated it is. Notice the coconut they add. It is not worth clogging your arteries for a little crunch.

New Breakfast

How about toast and margarine? Try low-fat Cinnamon French Toast (page 315), low-fat cottage cheese in half a cantaloupe, strawberries and plain low-fat yogurt, an egg on toast (once or twice a week), oatmeal or oat bran* with raisins and cinnamon, or a carton of flavored nonfat yogurt.

Oat bran, a rich source of soluble fiber, is filling and known to lower blood cholesterol levels. Studies by Dr. James Anderson at the University of Kentucky Medical Center have shown that consumption of about 17 grams of soluble fiber a day lowers blood cholesterol levels 13 to 19 percent in only three weeks. (See the table on the following page for other sources of soluble fiber.)

Oat bran may be eaten as a hot cereal and also may be baked into a variety of tasty muffins (see Chapter 23). Apple-raisin, apricot, or

---

*Oat bran is sold in bulk in health-food stores. Mother's Oat Bran by Quaker Oats may be found in the hot-cereal section of many grocery stores.

orange oat muffins are great with coffee and are easily carried to work for a morning coffee break.

Caution: A daily sprinkle of oat bran in your juice or even five oat bran muffins a day will not save you from the cholesterol-raising effects of a diet high in saturated fat. A low sat-fat diet is the most effective way to maximize your cholesterol lowering.

WHERE TO FIND SOLUBLE FIBER*

FOOD	SERVING SIZE	SOLUBLE FIBER (G)
Grains		
Oat bran	⅓ cup dry	2.0
All-Bran	⅓ cup	1.7
Oat bran muffin	1	1.6
Oatmeal	¾ cup, cooked	1.4
Rye bread	2 slices	0.6
Whole-wheat bread	2 slices	0.5
Dried Beans and Peas		
Black-eyed peas	½ cup, cooked	3.7
Kidney beans	½ cup, cooked	2.5
Pinto beans	½ cup, cooked	2.3
Navy beans	½ cup, cooked	2.3
Lentils	½ cup, cooked	1.7
Split peas	½ cup, cooked	1.7
Vegetables		
Peas	½ cup, cooked	2.7
Corn	½ cup, cooked	1.7
Sweet potato	1 baked	1.3
Zucchini	½ cup, cooked	1.3
Cauliflower	½ cup, cooked	1.3
Broccoli	½ cup, cooked	0.9
Fruit		
Prunes	4	1.9
Pears	1	1.1
Apples	1	0.9
Bananas	1	0.8
Oranges	1	0.7

*From: Nutrition Action Healthletter, Center for Science in the Public Interest, December 1985.

NOW FOR LUNCH

After you have established new and lasting changes in your breakfast, you will be ready to make changes in lunch. If you often eat this meal out, you have an additional challenge. You will have less control over the foods available than if you bring your lunch from home. (See Chapter 10 for tips on how to eat out.)

You might want to consider these options: eating out less often and bringing lunch from home more often; choosing low-fat, low saturated fat items from the menu and passing up the high-fat, heart-risky items; choosing restaurants that offer more low-fat, low saturated fat menu choices. The last option may be especially necessary if you are used to eating lunch in a fast-food restaurant.

If you have to eat at fast-food restaurants, stick to the salad bar. Use low-calorie dressings or make your own dressing with oil and vinegar. If you must use regular salad dressings, exercise restraint.

YOUR MOTHER WAS RIGHT

Many adults have established the pattern of eating no breakfast and no lunch or a very light lunch. For some, the mistaken notion is that this is a good way to lose weight. For others, breakfast and lunch may be the casualties of life in the fast lane. In any case, it is much healthier to eat three well-balanced meals than to starve yourself all day. Stuffing into one meal all the calories and nutrients needed for functioning at peak efficiency makes for very low efficiency peaks.

The chances are that if you eat only one or two meals a day, you will get hungry and eat snacks. Most snacks are notoriously high in calories, fat, saturated fat, sodium, and/or sugar and appallingly low in vitamins, minerals, and fiber.

In addition, saving most of your calories for the end of the day, when you are least active, leads to weight gain. Try eating relatively larger breakfasts and lunches and lighter dinners. Make all your meals low-fat (see the meal plans in Chapter 11 for suggested low-fat meals) and see if you don't feel better and function better.

Lunch Options

How about a turkey breast sandwich for lunch (not on a croissant, which is loaded with butter)? Most delis and sandwich shops carry white meat turkey sandwiches. Even with mayonnaise, a turkey sandwich contains a mere 10 calories of saturated fat. How about a bowl of chili *non* carne (peas and beans are rich in protein and fiber and low in fat)? How about a big bowl of sliced fresh fruit mixed with low-fat yogurt or low-fat cottage cheese? How about a chef's salad (hold the cheese) with turkey and ham (optional) and low-fat dressing? Your coronary arteries are looking better and better.

One of the advantages of changing from a high-fat to a low-fat lunch will become evident immediately. You will not feel tired and sluggish after a low-fat meal, so you will be at your peak during the afternoon. You may be so energetic your boss will give you a raise. If you are the boss, you might give yourself a raise.

THE DINNER TACKLE

Finally, after you have both breakfast and lunch under control, you are ready to tackle dinner. Try beginning your meal with a low-fat soup, such as Cucumber Soup (page 161) at 2 sat-fat calories per bowl. Not only is it low in saturated fat, it is cooling, delicious, and one of the easiest-to-make soups known to modern man. Soups help fill you up so you are less tempted to gorge on the higher-fat foods in the main course and in dessert. If you make your own soups, you can control the amount of salt and fat you use. Make a large pot of soup and freeze part for future meals.

Why not eat a low-fat chicken or fish dish? Try Apricot Chicken Divine (page 188) or Shanghai Fish (page 233). Try Turkey Scaloppine Limone (page 216) or Kung Pao Chicken with Broccoli (page 199). There are so many delicious recipes for chicken, turkey, and fish it will take you years to try them all. Vegetable dishes should be explored. As an important part of the meal or as the main dish, vegetables offer interesting flavors and textures as well as vitamins, minerals, and fiber. When not drowned in fat, vegetables fill you up without filling you out. Pastas or rice mixed with a small amount of meat or poultry can make a tasty main dish low in sat-fat calories.

"But I must have beef, too," you cry. *Eater's Choice* allows you to fit beef into your sat-fat budget — perhaps not as often as before, perhaps in smaller portions. Perhaps rather than eating a big fat steak four nights a week, you might eat steak one night, rice mixed with small pieces of beef another, vegetarian chili yet another, and fish, chicken, and turkey the rest of the week.

If you eat dinner in restaurants, many of the same considerations that applied to lunch are relevant.

Togetherness in Health

Since dinner is often the one meal that the whole family eats together, the question arises whether the whole family should eat low-fat, low–saturated fat meals. The simple answer is a loud YES. The American Heart Association recommends that all Americans over the age of two years adopt this new low-fat eating pattern. Both the American Heart Association and the National Cancer Institute recommend it to help prevent heart disease and certain cancers.

Establish Good Eating Habits Early: If you or your spouse have high blood cholesterol levels, there is a good chance that your children will also have high blood cholesterol levels. Heart-healthy meals will benefit *everyone* in the family. The eating habits that will help you control your blood cholesterol will help your children avoid developing atherosclerosis in the first place. As you have probably already realized, it is hard to change long-established, deep-rooted eating habits. It will be much easier for your children to establish healthful eating habits when they are young than to change them halfway through life.

If everybody in the family eats the same way, you are more likely to stick to the new eating pattern. Of course, this means everyone must learn to eat new foods and recipes and gradually modify their eating pattern. It will be worth it. You will be doing your children and spouse a lifelong favor.

A BALANCED DIET; OR, MAN DOTH NOT LIVE ON LESS SATURATED FAT ALONE

Although *Eater's Choice* focuses on saturated fat, you must take care to eat foods from all four food groups: vegetables and fruits;

grains and cereals; meats, fish, and poultry; dairy. It cannot be over-emphasized that good long-term health depends on eating a variety of foods. You need about 40 different nutrients to stay healthy. These nutrients are in the foods you normally eat — as long as you eat many different types of foods.

See Chapter 13 for examples of foods in each food group and what nutrients they contain.

Tips to Keep Your Eating in Balance

Here are some important tips you should keep in mind as you change your eating habits:

1. Replace fats with filling, fiber-rich complex carbohydrates, such as whole grains, fruits, and vegetables (not sugars, which have no nutritional value beyond calories).
2. Carbohydrates have half as many calories as fats, so you are not likely to gain weight by replacing fats with carbohydrates. It is not the carbohydrates (such as potatoes or bread) but the fats (such as butter) added to them that cause weight gain.
3. Peas and beans (complex carbohydrates) are rich in protein and fiber and low in fat.
4. Choose whole-grain (such as whole-wheat bread) rather than refined-grain products (such as white bread); refining removes vitamins and fiber from the food.
5. Whole-oat products, such as oat bran, dried peas, and beans, are high in soluble fiber and have been shown to lower blood cholesterol levels.
6. Be sure to include adequate amounts of calcium in your diet. Choose low-fat milk products, such as skim milk, low-fat yogurt, and low-fat cottage cheese. They are rich in calcium and low in saturated fat.
7. Certain polyunsaturated fats are required for good health and must be obtained from the diet (just like vitamins); you should not eliminate all sources of fat from your diet.
8. Choose cooking methods that do not add fat to otherwise low-fat, low saturated fat foods. Baking, roasting, broiling, poaching, and steaming are preferred to frying (especially deep-frying). Try sautéeing in a wok to reduce fat absorption.

9. Avoid fad or crash diets. Even though you are concentrating on removing saturated fat from your diet, you must consume an adequate supply of calories to maintain your desirable weight. It is important to realize that if you consume too few calories, you may not get an adequate supply of vitamins and minerals. If you have any doubts about the adequacy of your daily dietary intake, consult a physician or registered dietitian.

Plan Ahead

As we mentioned above, you may find it helpful to develop meal plans for a whole week at a time. It will make shopping easier. But in any case, bring home a variety of foods that provide adequate amounts of vitamins, minerals, and fiber and are not overloaded with calories, refined sugars, sodium, and fats.

Heart-Healthy Storage: Today your cupboard is probably filled with all sorts of horrible, high sat-fat foods that make the new you shudder in disgust. Eventually, you will stock your larder (terrible term) with low-fat foods, herbs, spices, whole grains, and your refrigerator with fresh fruits and vegetables. (See Stocking Up, page 150, for suggestions of foods to keep on hand.)

In fact, the contents of your cupboard and refrigerator are good indicators of how seriously you are taking your cholesterol-lowering. When you are able to throw away that box of cheese crackers that you have been hoarding or that small carton of whipping cream that you just might need for a special occasion, you will know that you have really changed your lifestyle and are waltzing down the path of good living and heart-health — the ultimate goal of *Eater's Choice*.

Honesty Is the Best Heart-Healthy Policy

Eater's Choice only works if you follow it faithfully. Do not fool yourself. "Only one little bite . . . just this time" is the theme song for those who have elevated cholesterol levels. You may fool yourself, but you will not fool your blood cholesterol.

Check and Recheck Blood Cholesterol Level

You should have your blood cholesterol level checked at frequent intervals to monitor the effectiveness of the changes you have made in your eating habits, especially at the beginning.

To help you and your physician interpret your numbers, you should also keep a three-day food record some time in the two-week period before your cholesterol test. (Reread page 83 about keeping food records.)

By analyzing these records you will see how your sat-fat intake has affected your blood cholesterol level. You might find that your cholesterol dropped to 188 mg/dL because you eliminated fast-food restaurant-hopping. Or that your cholesterol rose by 50 points because you spent the last two weeks splurging and making exceptions. Or that a 10 percent sat-fat budget is too high to bring your cholesterol number below 200 mg/dL, so you lower your sat-fat budget to 6 or 7 percent. Or that you lowered your cholesterol by 30 points and are now ready to make more changes that will ensure another 30-point drop.

Each blood cholesterol check and food record review will give you insight. You might pat yourself on the back and continue to eat within your sat-fat budget. Or you might shake your head in disgust or disappointment and rethink your diet.

The frequency of blood checks will be determined by your physician. After your blood cholesterol has been stabilized below 200 mg/dL, you probably will not need to have your level checked more than once a year.

Remember:

1. Easy does it. Make changes in your eating pattern *slowly* so that they will be *permanent* changes.
2. To make gradual changes:

   Approach 1: Reduce or change the foods in your daily menu that contribute the most saturated fat. If this does not lower your blood cholesterol level to below 200 mg/dL, make more changes.

   Approach 2: Focus on one meal at a time. First eliminate those highly saturated breakfast foods you can do without and replace them with foods low in saturated fat. After you have established new and lasting changes in breakfast, make changes in lunch and then dinner.

3. Be sure to choose foods from all four food groups: vegetables and fruits, dairy, meats, and grains. Only a well-balanced diet

will provide all the essential minerals, vitamins, fiber, and calories.

4. Peas, beans, and oat bran have been shown to lower blood cholesterol levels.

5. Have your blood cholesterol measured periodically to learn if your new eating habits have actually lowered your blood cholesterol level.

9 OTHER RISK FACTORS FOR CORONARY HEART DISEASE

WE HAVE WRITTEN this book out of our zeal to see coronary heart disease go the way of diphtheria and polio, to see it become a medical curiosity of the past. Our emphasis is on one of the most important risk factors for heart disease: blood cholesterol. Of course, there are other risk factors for coronary heart disease.

Heart disease is the leading cause of death in the United States. It kills three times as many people as all forms of cancer combined. Think of the people you know. According to national statistics, on average, half of the people you know will die of coronary heart disease.

Scientists have identified the major factors that increase risk of heart attacks. You have no control over some of these risks. However, you can affect their influence by modifying those risk factors over which you do have control.

RISKS YOU CANNOT CONTROL

Family History

Heart disease tends to run in families and thus has a genetic or inherited component. If one or both of your parents had a heart attack before the age of sixty, your chances of having one are increased by twofold.

Sex

Men have a greater chance of having a heart attack than women. Fifty-year-old men have a fivefold greater risk of having a heart attack by the age of sixty than do fifty-year-old women. Women seem to be protected from heart disease before menopause by their sex hormones. At the onset of menopause, a woman's risk of heart disease begins to rise. Whereas the rate of heart attacks in men begins to rise at about age forty-five, in women comparable rates are not seen until about age sixty. Lest women feel too complacent about their low rates of heart disease in middle age, they should know that heart disease is the leading cause of death for older women.

Age
Risk of heart disease increases with age for both men and women. For men thirty-five to sixty-five years old, risk of heart attack increases twofold for each decade of life. For women forty-five to sixty-five years old, risk increases threefold for each decade of life.

While heart disease strikes beginning in middle age, it is never too early to change your lifestyle to lower your risk. Remember: the underlying disease process (clogging of the coronary arteries) begins in childhood. Don't let the lack of symptoms fool you into complacency. On the other hand, if you are already middle-aged or older, do not lose hope. It is never too late to lower your blood cholesterol and slow down, stop, or even reverse the blockage of your coronary arteries.

DON'T JOIN THE ODDS, BEAT THEM!
Do not use the fact that you have a bad family history, that you are old, or that you are a male as an excuse to die of a heart attack. Bringing down your blood cholesterol level to below 200 mg/dL by eating a diet low in saturated fat gives you the same odds as people without those risks.

RISKS YOU CAN CONTROL
The fact that you cannot change your age, sex, or parents should not discourage you. The uncontrollable risk factors account for only a part of the total risk. The rest is accounted for by three powerful risk factors over which you do have control: cigarette smoking, high blood pressure, and high blood cholesterol.

Smoking

Most people associate cigarette smoking with lung cancer. While it is true that most lung cancer is caused by smoking, cigarettes cause more coronary heart disease than lung cancer. Smoking one pack a day doubles the risk of a heart attack, while smoking more than one pack a day triples the risk. In addition to heart disease, smoking causes serious diseases of the lungs, such as emphysema and chronic obstructive lung disease, resulting in an estimated 50,000 preventable deaths each year.

If you smoke, you should realize that it is never too late to benefit from quitting. Your risk of coronary heart disease begins to decrease immediately upon stopping. If you smoke one pack a day, your risk of heart disease one to five years after stopping is only 20 percent higher than that of a person who never smoked. Ten years after stopping, you are at no higher risk for heart disease than if you had never smoked. If you smoke more than one pack a day, your risk of heart disease is three times higher than that of a person who never smoked. One year after stopping, your risk drops to one and one-half times higher than that of a person who never smoked. By twenty years after quitting, you are at no higher risk for heart disease than if you had never smoked. So take control of your life and give up the weed. Reduce your risk of heart disease, lung disease, and cancer all in one fell swoop by quitting smoking once and for all.

High Blood Pressure

Both high blood pressure (often called hypertension) and high blood cholesterol are silent killers. They are called silent because there are usually no symptoms or telltale signs. You will not know if you have these risk factors unless you have them measured. Yet they are both deadly. High blood pressure can cause strokes, aneurysms (the weakening and bursting of an artery wall, which causes massive internal bleeding and often sudden death), and coronary heart disease.

About 60 million Americans, or 1 out of every 4 adults, have high blood pressure. High blood pressure is a leading cause of the 500,000 strokes, 175,000 stroke deaths, and 550,000 heart attack deaths each year. High blood pressure is most common in blacks, the obese, diabetics, the elderly, and women taking oral contraceptives. The presence of high blood pressure doubles the risk of coronary heart disease and raises the risk of stroke by sevenfold.

The Joint National Committee of the High Blood Pressure Education Program recommends that blood pressures should be lower than 140/90 mm Hg. The lower the blood pressure, the lower are the risks of strokes, aneurysms, and heart disease.

The first line of treatment for high blood pressure is reduction of sodium in the diet to between 1100 and 3300 mg per day, regular aerobic exercise, and, when necessary, weight reduction. (For reference, 1 teaspoon of table salt contains 2132 mg of sodium.) In general, Americans consume far too much sodium. Currently, the average American consumes 4000 to 5000 mg of sodium each day. *The Sodium Content of Your Food* (*Home and Garden Bulletin* Number 233, U.S. Department of Agriculture) is a useful publication to help you keep track of your sodium intake. It is available from the Government Printing Office, Washington, D.C. 20402.

Risks Are Additive

The presence of any one of the three controllable risk factors (high blood cholesterol, high blood pressure, smoking) doubles your risk of heart disease (see Figure 1, Chapter 1). The simultaneous presence of two of these risk factors quadruples your risk. The addition of the third risk factor increases the risk yet another twofold, resulting in an eightfold higher risk of heart disease. The elimination of a risk factor has an equal but opposite effect on risk as does its addition. Thus, smokers with high blood pressure and high blood cholesterol who quit smoking and reduce their blood pressure and blood cholesterol to healthy levels can cut their risk of heart attack by up to eightfold!

OTHER RISK FACTORS

Diabetes Mellitus

Diabetics have a twofold greater rate of coronary heart disease than do normal people. Moreover, diabetics who survive a heart attack have a poor long-term prognosis. Finally, heart disease is more likely to be fatal in diabetics than in people with normal glucose tolerance. The increased risk of coronary heart disease due to diabetes is independent of the other major risk factors, high blood cholesterol and high blood pressure. But diabetics can lower their risk of coronary heart disease by lowering their blood cholesterol and blood pressure. For diabetics as well as nondiabetics, diet is the first line of treatment for lowering blood cholesterol and blood pressure.

The new dietary recommendations for diabetics are similar to those recommended in this book for persons who want to lower their blood cholesterol levels. Thus, diabetics should reduce their intake of saturated fat and cholesterol and increase their intake of complex carbohydrates and fiber. They should limit their intake of simple or refined sugars.

Obesity

Obese people suffer significantly higher rates of illness and death than people of the same age who are not overweight. Obesity is associated with higher rates of angina pectoris, stroke, and sudden death. High blood pressure and diabetes, risk factors for heart disease, are three times more common in obese people. Death rates from heart disease are 50 percent higher for obese people. In general, the risk of death increases about 2 percent for every pound over "desirable" weight (National Institutes of Health Consensus Conference on Obesity).

Obesity also increases the risk of developing arthritis, respiratory disorders, cancer of the uterus, breast, and cervix in women, and cancer of the colon, rectum, and prostate in men.

An effective way to combat obesity is to follow *Eater's Choice*. Although not designed as a weight-loss diet, responses from readers have shown us that the *Eater's Choice* system often results in weight loss (15–20 pounds is typical; more than 40 pounds has been reported). This is easy to understand. Following *Eater's Choice*, the eater learns to make choices that are heart-healthy — and coincidentally low in fat. And we know that fat makes fat. Fat has more calories (9) per gram of weight than protein (4) or carbohydrates (4). Excess fat is stored as body fat while carbohydrate and protein are more likely to be burned for energy. Thus, the reduction of saturated fat from the diet for the purposes of lowering blood cholesterol often leads to a natural reduction of excess fat from the body.

Lack of Physical Exercise

Exercise is an important part of a healthy lifestyle and is essential for cardiovascular fitness. While it may not prevent you from having a heart attack, data suggest it will increase your chances of survival. Regular exercise helps control weight and lower blood pressure.

Most experts recommend moderate aerobic exercise for the maximum cardiovascular benefit. Aerobic exercise involves continuous exertion, usually in a repetitive or rhythmic motion. Examples include running or jogging, walking, rowing, swimming, bicycling, aerobic dancing, and jumping rope. When exercise is aerobic and performed with sufficient intensity and duration, it will raise HDL-cholesterol. But before you wear yourself to a frazzle running fifteen miles a day so you can eat lardburgers at every meal, be advised that exercise does not negate the ill effects of a high-fat diet. The best way to lower your LDL-cholesterol and thus your risk of a heart attack is to reduce your intake of saturated fat.

Exercise also aids in weight control by burning calories. Increasing the amount and intensity of exercise in addition to eating less will result in weight loss. Regular vigorous exercise in many people actually curbs the appetite, with the result that fewer calories are consumed. Finally, regular aerobic exercise results in an improved feeling of well-being.

A WORD OF CAUTION: Exercise may increase the risk of sudden death in people with advanced coronary atherosclerosis. If you are forty or older and have a sedentary lifestyle, it is highly advisable to have a physical examination by a physician, including an electrocardiogram (and even an exercise electrocardiogram) before starting an exercise program. It is also helpful to get professional guidance in designing your exercise program, to ensure that the exercises you choose are not harmful or dangerous, that you start off slowly and intensify your efforts at the appropriate rate, that you vary your exercise program to prevent fatigue, boredom, and drop-out, and, finally, that you get the most cardiovascular benefit from the time and effort you invest.

Like other lifestyle changes that you might be making at this time, exercise will only benefit your cardiovascular system and your overall health if you continue to do it faithfully. It cannot be a sometime thing. Excuse the pun, but it is for life.

High Blood Triglycerides

Recently an expert panel concluded that people with triglyceride levels below 250 mg/dL after a twelve-hour fast and normal blood cholesterol levels do not have an increased risk of heart disease. However, people with triglyceride levels between 250 and 500 mg/dL after a twelve-hour fast are at modest risk of cardiovascular disease. Those with levels above 500 mg/dL are at additional risk of pancreatitis.

Elevated triglyceride levels can be reduced by the following life-style changes: weight loss (if overweight), increased physical activity, restriction of alcohol consumption, and reduced intakes of simple sugars (sweets) and saturated fats (as recommended by *Eater's Choice*). Some people may have to use drugs if diet does not normalize their triglyceride levels.

Stress

It is a commonly held belief that stress increases the risk of coronary heart disease. Scientists have not been able to confirm or deny this relationship. They are hampered by the difficulty in measuring and quantifying stress. What is stressful to you may not be stressful to others. Furthermore, people react to the same stress in different ways.

Type A Behavior Pattern

People with Type A behavior patterns are characterized as hard-driving, impatient, and time-conscious. Type B people, on the other hand, are easygoing. Numerous studies have shown Type A behavior pattern to be a risk factor for developing coronary heart disease. But in all fairness, it must be said that other studies have not confirmed this observation, and so the jury is still out on the importance of Type A behavior in the development of heart disease.

Remember:

1. The major risk factors of heart disease you cannot control are family history of heart disease, sex, and age.
2. The major risk factors you *can* control (in addition to high blood cholesterol) are high blood pressure and cigarette smoking.
3. Other risk factors include diabetes mellitus, obesity, lack of physical activity, and high blood triglycerides.

THE REAL WORLD 10

YOUR NEW eating pattern is for life — in two ways. It will improve your chances for a long and healthy life, and you must follow it for the rest of your life. Following *Eater's Choice* is easy, and you will find that eating heart-healthy foods can be more satisfying than eating your old heart-risky ones.

HONESTY IS THE HEALTHIEST POLICY

Remember: you *must* be honest with yourself. Don't make exceptions — even for special occasions — or before you know it you will be off the eating plan. Face it: we all have an almost infinite capacity to fool ourselves about how much and how often we eat certain foods. We constantly underestimate the calories, fat, and sugar we consume. We make a small change in our diet and feel so sorry for ourselves that we reward ourselves with treats that negate our progress. We don't want to make a fuss or feel embarrassed, so we eat foods we should avoid when we dine out. We see special occasions deserving of exceptions in everyday occurrences, such as office parties, weekends, birthdays, going out to eat, even when this is a weekly or more frequent event. The favorite expressions of the cheater-eater are "Just this one time" and "This little bit couldn't possibly matter."

These problems do not have to be yours. Be strong. It's your life. Cheater-eaters only cheat themselves. *Eater's Choice* eaters don't need to cheat. They plan ahead. *Eater's Choice* is a flexible plan that allows you to eat your favorite foods as well as enjoy an occasional splurge. (See Chapter 11.)

Heart-Healthy Tips

- Avoid eating on the run, which may necessitate eating fast foods or junk food from vending machines. The time you save in the present may cost you dearly in the future.
- To save yourself from a massive pig-out attack, eat *before* you attend a party where you know high sat-fat foods will be served.
- Try to avoid grocery shopping when you are hungry. In a fit of hunger you might satisfy your craving with a tub of ice cream.
- Make popcorn (with polyunsaturated oil or air-popped with no butter added) for a snack while watching TV or visiting friends. Popcorn is a low-fat, low-calorie, high-fiber food, and it's cheap.
- Turn off the TV or leave the room when food ads appear. (Do not go to the kitchen!) Many of the ads on TV are devoted to glorifying the fattiest, most heart-risky foods available to mankind. Watching food ads will make you hungry for these artery cloggers.

BE PROUD OF THE NEW YOU

You should not be ashamed that you are watching your fat intake. By letting your friends, colleagues, and family know that you are serious about your new eating pattern, you can solicit their support. Do not let them make you feel guilty because you are eating healthfully and they may not be.

Truly good friends *will* help, by cooking or serving foods low in saturated fat for you, encouraging you to stay on your new eating plan, suggesting restaurants that offer low-fat entrees. You should never feel pressured either by words or by the situation to stray from your eating plan. Say no politely, but firmly. You'll be respected for your self-control. And who knows, perhaps your friends and relatives will begin to see how good you look, how great you feel, and how well you are eating. You might just have a positive influence on their lifestyles.

EATING OUT

Here are a few tips that will help you enjoy eating out in restaurants while staying within your saturated fat budget. First, learn which restaurants serve foods low in saturated fat. Most restaurants that serve chicken and fish dishes can prepare them without butter, cream sauces, or other added fats. Do not be afraid to ask what the ingredients are and how the dish is prepared. Perhaps you can eat the cream sauce: just ask what is in it — maybe it will fit into your sat-fat budget.

Special Orders

If you find that every dish on the menu is too fatty, tell the waiter you are on a low-fat diet and wish to have baked or roasted chicken breast without skin or broiled fish with lemon and no butter or cream sauce. Ask if the restaurant has margarine instead of butter and skim milk instead of whole milk. Have your baked potato served without butter or sour cream on it. (Plain baked potatoes taste delicious, too.) If you must have a topping, have it served on the side so you can regulate the amount you use. Most good restaurants will serve fresh fruit for dessert, if you request it.

Many restaurants will gladly honor your wishes. However, if you request low-fat modifications and your chicken comes with skin, your fish is swimming in butter, or your potato is drowning in sour cream, send them back. Don't be shy. After all, they're your arteries, not the waiter's.

If a restaurant is unable or unwilling to satisfy your low-fat needs, you might consider taking your business elsewhere in the future — and letting them know why.

You can clearly see that the secret to eating out is to *ask*. As you and others ask for low-fat options with increasing frequency, restaurants will begin to realize that there is a market for such foods and will respond. It is happening already. Some Big Boy restaurants have devoted a section of their menu to low-fat foods. You will feel no sacrifice in ordering exclusively from this part of the menu. In fact, you will feel sorry for the uninformed diners eating all those artery-choking high-fat foods.

Flying? Call Ahead

Frequent airline travelers know how rarely heart-healthy food graces the airline menu. High-fat meats, sauces, cheeses, butter, and desserts abound, and once up in the air, there are no choices to be had. However, a little forethought may provide you with food you can eat without qualms. At least twenty-four hours before your flight, call the airline reservations clerk and order a special meal. Be as specific as you can in making your request. I usually ask for fish or chicken breast and fruit for dessert. I also tell them I am on a low-fat, low-cholesterol diet.

Some airlines, notably United Airlines, provide tasty meals upon request that conform to your needs. Sad to say, other airlines either feed you boiled carrots as a punishment for trying to be healthy or steak because they think it is a low-fat option. Other things being equal, I often choose an airline on their ability and willingness to meet my dietary needs. Perhaps pressure from passengers who care about their heart health will change airline menus in the future.

THE ART OF READING FOOD LABELS

Now that you are concerned with what is in the food you eat, how do you know the contents of canned or packaged goods that you buy at the store? The answer is *labels*. Learning to read food labels will be invaluable in helping you to balance your saturated fat budget.

Nutrition Information

The majority of packaged foods today have nutrition information labels printed somewhere on their packaging. (To understand this section better, I suggest you get a can or package from the pantry or refrigerator so you can look at the label.) The ingredients are always listed in descending order by weight. For example, the raspberry sherbet I have before me has these ingredients listed: "Skim milk, sugar, water, corn syrup, red raspberries, cream, raspberry juice concentrate, carob bean gum, mono- and diglycerides, natural raspberry flavor, guar gum, dextrose, whey, citric acid, polysorbate 80, pectin."

This label tells you there is more skim milk than any other ingredient in the carton. Unfortunately, since the actual weights of ingredients are not provided, you have no way of knowing if the skim milk is 49 percent or 20 percent of the weight of the sherbet. You know there is less sugar than skim milk, but you do not know the actual amount of sugar or any other ingredient.

Ingredient lists can be very beneficial even when they are not quantitative because they may list ingredients you want to avoid. If the first ingredient listed on your package of cereal is sugar, you might want to avoid eating that cereal. If coconut oil is listed second on the label of your bag of potato chips, you might decide to leave that package of potato chips in the store.

The most helpful kind of label provides nutrient content per serving as well as the ingredients. Find a food package that contains this type of information. First find the serving size or the number of servings per container. Keep this in mind: some labels can be misleading. I am reading a label on a can of tuna. It says that one can contains 3.3 servings and that a serving is 2 ounces (approximately ¼ cup). One serving contains 2 grams of fat. If you only eat ¼ cup tuna fish, then 2 grams of fat is what you are eating. However, since I eat the whole can at one serving, I must multiply the 2 grams by 3.3. I am eating 6.6 grams of fat. Remember: their serving size may not be the same as yours.

The ultimate in usefulness for those of us monitoring our saturated fat intake is for the nutrient content information to include the amount of saturated fat, polyunsaturated fat, total fat, and cholesterol as well as the amounts of protein, carbohydrates, and sodium. The fat, protein, and carbohydrate contents are given in grams. To convert them into calories, multiply the fat grams by 9 and multiply the protein and carbohydrate grams by 4 each.

Unfortunately, very few labels provide saturated and polyunsaturated fat contents. At most, they provide total fat content. For example, the tuna fish label provides only total fat (6.6 grams per can or $6.6 \times 9 = 59.4$ calories of total fat). You can find the amount of calories of saturated fat by checking the food tables at the end of the book.

To determine the sat-fat content of commercial foods not listed in the Food Tables, we have developed an inexpensive "pocket companion" called a Sat-fat Estimator. The Sat-fat Estimator helps you estimate sat-fat calories from the grams of fat listed on a label. See the last page of the book for ordering information.

Comparing Labels May Be Tricky

You can and should use the nutrient content information to make comparisons among products. But *be careful.* Be sure you are comparing equal portion sizes. The manufacturers of some high-fat or high-calorie foods make their portion sizes small so the calorie, fat, sodium, or sugar content does not seem so high. If this is the case, adjust all nutrient content information to the same serving size so you can make meaningful comparisons.

For example, the serving size for one product is 3 ounces and the fat content is 60 calories per serving. The serving size of a similar product is 2 ounces and the fat content is 60 calories per serving. At first glance, both products appear to have equal fat contents. However, the serving size of one product is one and a half times larger than that of the other. You can compare the fat contents of the two by determining the fat content for one ounce of each product. The first product contains 60 calories per 3 ounces, or 20 calories of fat per ounce. The second product contains 60 calories per 2 ounces, or 30 calories of fat per ounce. The second product thus contains 50 percent more fat than the first product.

Oil Labels

Many food products specify the use of some polyunsaturated oil (such as corn oil) that has been hydrogenated or partially hydrogenated. This means that the oil has been treated by a chemical process that converts some or all of the polyunsaturated oil into saturated oil. Polyunsaturated oils that have been hydrogenated, either completely or partially, act just like saturated fats in raising blood LDL cholesterol levels and thus increasing your risk of heart disease.

Products are often labeled as containing one or more oils; for example, corn, soybean, palm, or coconut oil. As you know from the food tables, there are large and important differences among these oils. Soybean is a predominantly polyunsaturated oil, while palm and especially coconut and palm kernel oils are predominantly saturated oils. In cases where a choice of oils is listed, the manufacturer uses whichever is cheapest at the moment. As you do not know which oil was used, the best course of action is to avoid the food altogether.

Unfortunately, coconut, palm kernel, palm, and hydrogenated oils are widely used in commercial baked products, frozen dinners, and candies. Coconut oil is often used to make commercial popcorn, including the popcorn sold in movie theaters. (Bring your own next time. It is healthier and cheaper.) Coconut, palm kernel, palm, and hydrogenated oils are so widely used because they are solid at room temperature. They have longer shelf lives because they do not become rancid as readily as the more polyunsaturated oils. Also, they have a higher burning point and thus do not require as much care and attention during use.

Consumer Beware

Know how to read labels and avoid being misled by the following kinds of advertising claims.

1. CLAIM: Cholesterol-free.
   TRUTH: The average consumer translates "cholesterol-free" to "heart-healthy." Hah! Of course, coconut, palm, and hydrogenated plant oils are cholesterol-free. Cholesterol is found only in animal products. Coconut and palm are plants. What the advertisers fail to say is the saturated fat in coconut, palm, and hydrogenated plant oils is much more heart-risky than cholesterol and should be avoided more assiduously.

2. CLAIM: Light, lower-fat, or lean.
   TRUTH: A food that is described as light, lower-fat, or lean may be lower in fat than other foods of the same type while still being a high-fat food. For example, some brands of cream cheese are advertised as light, containing 50 percent less fat. While it is true that 5 grams of fat is half as much as 10 grams of fat, 5×9 calories per gram of fat or 45 calories of fat is still a lot of fat in one tablespoon of cream cheese.

3. CLAIM: 2% milk is low-fat.
   TRUTH: 2% milk is lower in fat than whole milk but is hardly a low-fat food item. The percentages refer to the percent of the weight of the milk that is fat. Since most of the weight of the milk is water, the weight contributed by fat is small. However, 2% milk derives 34.6 percent of its calories from fat (45 calories of fat per cup). This is not what you would call a low-fat item. Expressing the fat content as a percentage of the weight trivializes the high-fat content.

4. CLAIM: Frankfurters contain no more than 30 percent fat.
   TRUTH: The Food and Drug Administration allows franks to contain up to 30 percent fat. This means at most 30 percent of the weight of the franks comes from fat. But about 80 percent of the calories of a frank come from

fat. This amounts to 151 calories of fat in each beef frank. Expressing fat content in terms of weight grossly underestimates its contribution. You get a much better appreciation for the fat content when you express it in terms of calories.

5. CLAIM: 93% fat-free corned beef.

TRUTH: This corned beef claims it is 93% fat-free. Only 7% fat — that sounds like a low-fat item. Food producers know that consumers are interested in buying low-fat foods. However, the 7% fat refers to the fat content as a percentage of the weight. Actually, each slice of corned beef contains 2 grams of fat or 18 (2 × 9) calories of fat. The food label indicates that 1 ounce contains 40 calories. Thus, 18 calories of fat is 45% (18/40) of the total calories. The claim really should be 55% fat-free. This is not such a low-fat food after all.

MODIFYING RECIPES

You will find many low-fat recipes in this book. We have chosen only low-fat recipes so that you may easily fit them into your daily sat-fat budget. To help you keep track of your saturated fat intake, the sat-fat calories are listed at the end of each recipe along with total calories.

And you can easily make a whole range of old and new favorites perfect for your new low-fat eating plan with a few simple adaptations.

Substituting Ingredients

Sour Cream Herb Bread can be modified easily without sacrificing taste or texture. Substitute 3 tablespoons of margarine for 3 tablespoons of butter, for a saving of 141 calories of saturated fat. Substitute ½ cup of buttermilk for ½ cup of sour cream for a saving of 135 calories of saturated fat. Buttermilk Herb Bread is just as delicious as Sour Cream Herb Bread and, with 276 fewer calories of saturated fat per loaf, it is much healthier.

Sour Cream Herb Bread	**Buttermilk Herb Bread**
1 tablespoon dry yeast	same
¼ cup very warm water	same

pinch of sugar	same
3 tablespoons **butter**	3 tablespoons **margarine**
3 cups flour	same
3 tablespoons sugar	2 tablespoons sugar
1 teaspoon salt	same
¼ teaspoon marjoram	same
¼ teaspoon oregano	same
¼ teaspoon thyme	same
½ cup **sour cream**	½ cup **buttermilk**
1 egg	same

	TOTAL CALORIES		SAT-FAT CALORIES	
	LOAF	SLICE	LOAF	SLICE
Sour Cream Herb Bread:	2145	126	351	21
Buttermilk Herb Bread:	1874	110	75	4

Silent Substitutions

These substitutions are termed silent because there is often little or no reduction in the quality (taste and texture) of the final product when ingredients rich in saturated fat are replaced by their low-fat counterparts.

When the recipe calls for:	Use instead:
Butter	Margarine*
Lard or solid shortening	Liquid vegetable oil or margarine with a high P/S ratio
Sour cream	Low-fat yogurt or buttermilk
Whole milk	Skim milk
1 tablespoon chocolate	1 tablespoon cocoa + 3 tablespoons margarine
3 egg yolks	1 egg yolk
2 whole eggs	1 egg + 1 egg white
Pork	Chicken, white meat
Chicken livers	Chicken, white meat
Veal cutlets	Turkey cutlets

---

*Margarine and butter have the same fat content and total calories, but margarine is made from vegetable oil and so has no cholesterol, less saturated fat, and more polyunsaturated fat. Use margarine with a high P/S ratio (see Chapter 7).

COOKING TIPS

Here are some tips for cooking that will help you stay within your sat-fat budget:

- Steam vegetables. Purchase an inexpensive metal steamer that can be placed in any size saucepan. Buy fresh vegetables. Place about an inch of water in the saucepan. Spread out your steamer and place your vegetables on top. Cover the saucepan. Steam the vegetables until they are tender. Overcooking destroys taste, texture, and vitamins.
- Always remove skin *before* cooking chicken. The skin increases the saturated fat content by 2½ times. Bake, broil, or roast chicken. Sauté in a small amount of oil, preferably in a wok.
- Bake, broil, or poach fish. Fried vegetables or meats absorb fat that you do not need. Use a wok for sautéing.
- When cooking beef, trim off all visible fat. Broil or bake on a rack to drain the fat. Remove more fat from the cooked meat with paper towels. Avoid pan-frying.
- *Never* deep-fry foods.

Is Cooking the Low-Fat Way Expensive?

NO. NO. NO. Replacing foods high in saturated fat with vegetables, fruits, and whole grains will save you money as well as improve your health. Convenience foods that are highly processed and full of saturated fat are expensive. Beef is more expensive than chicken, turkey, and many fish. A rice dish with small amounts of chicken or even beef is much less expensive than a steak. Sour cream and sweet cream are costly, both in price and health. Get the picture? Popcorn (made with polyunsaturated oil or air-popped) is one of the healthiest and least expensive snack foods available. In contrast, commercial snack foods such as cookies, chips, and candies are highly saturated, heart-risky, and extremely expensive.

A NEW BEGINNING

You are making a dramatic change in your life. You have learned why it is so important for you to eat heart-healthy foods. In time you will find that a menu low in saturated fat and high in complex carbohydrates will be the most satisfying for you.

Making these changes may not be easy at first, but soon you will find that cooking and eating right is a normal part of your life. I can see you now, sitting in front of the fireplace with your great-great-great-grandchildren, sharing a bowl of popcorn (made with polyunsaturated oil or air-popped).

Remember:

1. Take time to eat. Eating junk food from vending machines or at fast-food restaurants saves you time in the present but may cost you dearly in the future.

2. When eating out, *ask* what ingredients are in dishes. Choose broiled, baked, or roasted turkey or chicken without skin or fish. Choose dishes without butter or high-fat sauces. Ask for margarine instead of butter. Ask for dressings and toppings to be served on the side so you can regulate the amount you eat. Don't hesitate to send food back if it is not prepared the way you requested.

3. Learn to read labels carefully. Ingredients are listed in descending order according to weight. Pay particular attention to serving sizes when comparing foods or determining their contribution of saturated fat.

4. Consumer beware: All plant products are cholesterol-free. What they may not be is low in saturated fat. Foods advertised as light, lean, or lower-fat may be high in saturated fat. Some food labels list a choice of vegetable oils. If coconut, palm, palm kernel, or hydrogenated vegetable oils are among the choices, avoid the product.

11 TWO WEEKS OF MEALS

THE FOLLOWING sample meal plans were designed to help you plan your own daily menus. Here are two whole weeks of menus with a different breakfast, soup, main course, and dessert for each day to show you the variety of foods you can eat and still stay within your sat-fat budget. All the sample meal plans are based on a total consumption of 2000 calories per day. You can find the recipes for dishes printed in italics in the Cook's Choice section.

The first weekly meal plan provides menus that add up to approximately 200 sat-fat calories a day and thus conform to the *Eater's Choice* 10 Percent Plan. In addition, a 6 Percent Plan (120 sat-fat calories per day) is provided, which illustrates how you can modify your eating in the event the 10 Percent Plan does not lower your blood cholesterol sufficiently. Bold print highlights differences in foods or portion sizes between the 10 Percent and the 6 Percent eating plans.

The second weekly meal plan is based on the 6 Percent Plan. This meal plan illustrates how you can save up sat-fat calories to spend on a splurge later in the week. The saturated fat intake in the meals from Sunday through Friday is lower than allowed on the 6 Percent budget. Despite the fact that you will actually be eating more like a 5 Percent *Eater's Choice* Plan, you will have a most satisfying week. You will even have scrumptious desserts each day.

By eating below your sat-fat budget all week, you will be able to save up calories (in this plan, you will save 156 sat-fat calories) to spend at the end of the week. You can spend these calories any way you wish. Of course, since you ate so well all week, you might choose not to spend these calories at all. Eating less saturated fat than is in your sat-fat budget is always an option — a healthy option.

MEAL PLANS — WEEK I

FOOD	PORTION	10% PLAN TOTAL CALORIES	SAT-FAT CALORIES	PORTION	6% PLAN TOTAL CALORIES	SAT-FAT CALORIES
SUNDAY — WEEK 1						
Breakfast						
French Toast	2	212	16	2	212	16
Syrup	1 tbsp	61	0	1 tbsp	61	0
Orange juice	**6 fl oz**	83	0	**8 fl oz**	110	0
Coffee	1 cup	0	0	1 cup	0	0
2% milk	1 tbsp	8	2	1 tbsp	8	2
Breakfast subtotal		364	18		391	18
Lunch						
Lentil and Everything Soup	1 cup	82	2	1 cup	82	2
Oriental Chicken Salad	1 serving	325	20	1 serving	325	20
French Bread	**1 piece**	85	2	**2 pieces**	170	4
Coffee	1 cup	0	0	1 cup	0	0
2% milk	1 tbsp	8	2	1 tbsp	8	2
Apple				1 large	125	1
Lunch subtotal		500	26		710	29
Dinner						
Vegetable Soup Provençal	1 cup	90	5	1 cup	90	5
Calzone	1 serving	322	12	1 serving	322	12
2% milk	1 cup	121	27	1 cup	121	27
Mixed salad	1 serving	23	0	1 serving	23	0
Italian dressing	1 tbsp	69	9			
Low-cal Italian				1 tbsp	16	2
Ice cream	1 cup	269	80			
Ice milk				½ cup	92	16
Chocolate Cake with Chocolate Icing	1 slice	300	15	1 slice	300	15
Dinner subtotal		1194	148		964	77
Daily total		2058	192		2065	124

MEAL PLANS — WEEK 1

FOOD	10% PLAN			6% PLAN		
	PORTION	TOTAL CALORIES	SAT-FAT CALORIES	PORTION	TOTAL CALORIES	SAT-FAT CALORIES
MONDAY — WEEK 1						
Breakfast						
Water bagel	1	200	3	1	200	3
Margarine	2 tsp	60	12			
Edam cheese	1 oz	101	45			
Peanut butter				1 tbsp	95	12
Jam				1 tbsp	55	0
Orange juice	6 oz	83	0	6 oz	83	0
Coffee	1 cup	0	0	1 cup	0	0
2% milk	1 tbsp	8	2	1 tbsp	8	2
Breakfast subtotal		452	62		441	17
Lunch						
Turkey sandwich						
White meat turkey w/o skin	3 oz	114	3	3 oz	114	3
Mayonnaise	1 tbsp	99	11			
Low-cal mayonnaise				1 tbsp	35	5
Whole-wheat bread	2 slices	140	8	2 slices	140	8
Tomato	¼ tomato	6	0	¼ tomato	6	0
Potato chips	1 oz	210	32			
Coffee	1 cup	0	0	1 cup	0	0
2% milk	1 tbsp	8	2	1 tbsp	8	2
Pear	1	100	0	1	100	0
Lunch subtotal		677	56		403	18
Dinner						
Carrot Soup	1½ cups	128	6	1½ cups	128	6
Chicken Kiev	1 serving	256	27	1 serving	256	27
Rice	½ cup	113	1	½ cup	113	1
Sesame Broccoli	1 serving	50	3	1 serving	50	3
Mixed salad	1 serving	23	0	1 serving	23	0
Thousand Island dressing	1 tbsp	59	8			
Low-cal Thousand Island				2 tbsp	48	4

MEAL PLANS — WEEK 1

| | | 10% PLAN | | | 6% PLAN | |
FOOD	PORTION	TOTAL CALORIES	SAT-FAT CALORIES	PORTION	TOTAL CALORIES	SAT-FAT CALORIES
Coffee	1 cup	0	0	1 cup	0	0
2% milk	1 tbsp	8	2	1 tbsp	8	2
Ice milk	1 cup	184	32			
Applesauce Cake				1 slice	250	14
Dinner subtotal		821	79		876	57
Snack						
Mixed nuts				1½ oz	254	27
Daily total		1950	197		1974	119

TUESDAY — WEEK 1

Breakfast

Cheerios	1 oz	110	3	1 oz	110	3
2% milk	1 cup	121	27			
Skim milk				1 cup	86	3
Whole-wheat bread	**2 slices**	140	8	**1 slice**	70	4
Margarine	**2 tsp**	60	12	**1 tsp**	30	6
Jelly	1 tbsp	50	0	1 tbsp	50	0
Coffee	1 cup	0	0	1 cup	0	0
2% milk	1 tbsp	8	2	1 tbsp	8	2
Orange juice	**6 fl oz**	83	0	**8 fl oz**	110	0
Breakfast subtotal		572	52		464	18

Lunch

Roy Rogers' roast beef sandwich	1	356	29	1	356	29
French fries	1 serving	220	33			
Apple juice				1 cup	115	0
Coffee	1 cup	0	0	1 cup	0	0
2% milk	1 tbsp	8	2	1 tbsp	8	2
Apple	**1 small**	80	1	**1 large**	125	1
Lunch subtotal		664	65		604	32

Dinner

Zucchini Soup	1 cup	80	1	1 cup	80	1
Scallop Creole	1 serving	199	10	1 serving	199	10

MEAL PLANS — WEEK 1

FOOD	PORTION	10% PLAN		PORTION	6% PLAN	
		TOTAL CALORIES	SAT-FAT CALORIES		TOTAL CALORIES	SAT-FAT CALORIES
White rice	½ cup	113	1	½ cup	113	1
Caraway Carrots	1 serving	45	3	1 serving	45	3
Mixed salad	1 serving	23	0	1 serving	23	0
Russian dressing	1 tbsp	76	10			
Low-cal French dressing				2 tbsp	44	2
Coffee	1 cup	0	0	1 cup	0	0
2% milk	1 tbsp	8	2	1 tbsp	8	2
Tante Nancy's Apple Crumb Cake	1 serving	225	15	1 serving	225	15
Dinner subtotal		769	42		737	34
Snack						
Swiss cheese	1 oz	107	45			
Wheat Thins	4	35	5			
Skim milk	1 cup	86	3			
Ice milk				1 cup	184	32
Daily total		2233	212		1989	116

WEDNESDAY — WEEK 1

Breakfast

Whole-wheat toast	2 slices	140	8	2 slices	140	8
Peanut butter	1 tbsp	95	12	1 tbsp	95	12
Orange juice	**6 fl oz**	83	0	**8 fl oz**	110	0
Coffee	1 cup	0	0	1 cup	0	0
2% milk	1 tbsp	8	2	1 tbsp	8	2
Breakfast subtotal		326	22		353	22

Lunch

Tuna sandwich						
White tuna (water packed)	3.25 oz	146	3	3.25 oz	146	3
Whole-wheat bread	2 slices	140	8	2 slices	140	8

MEAL PLANS — WEEK 1

FOOD	10% PLAN			6% PLAN		
	PORTION	TOTAL CALORIES	SAT-FAT CALORIES	PORTION	TOTAL CALORIES	SAT-FAT CALORIES
Mayonnaise	1 tbsp	99	14			
Low-cal mayonnaise				1 tbsp	35	5
Apple	**1 small**	80	1	**1 large**	125	1
Coffee	1 cup	0	0	1 cup	0	0
2% milk	1 tbsp	8	2	1 tbsp	8	2
Lunch subtotal		473	28		454	19
Dinner						
Sirloin steak	**6 oz**	372	72	**4 oz**	248	48
Spinach, cooked	½ cup	20	0	½ cup	20	0
Baked potato w/skin, large	1	220	1	1	220	1
Margarine	**2 tsp**	60	12	**1 tbsp**	90	18
Mixed salad	1 serving	23	0	1 serving	23	0
French dressing, **regular**	2 tbsp	134	28			
low calorie				2 tbsp	44	2
Coffee	1 cup	0	0	1 cup	0	0
2% milk	1 tbsp	8	2	1 tbsp	8	2
Ice milk	½ cup	92	16			
Fruit cocktail				1 cup	185	0
Dinner subtotal		929	131		838	71
Snack						
Grapes				2 cups	194	2
Popcorn	**4 cups**	220	20	**2 cups**	110	10
Daily total		1948	201		1949	124

THURSDAY — WEEK 1

FOOD	PORTION	TOTAL CALORIES	SAT-FAT CALORIES	PORTION	TOTAL CALORIES	SAT-FAT CALORIES
Breakfast						
Oat bran cereal	½ cup dry	165	2	½ cup dry	165	2
Raisins	1 tbsp	27	0	1 tbsp	27	0
Margarine	1 tsp	30	6	1 tsp	30	6
Orange juice	**6 fl oz**	83	0	**8 fl oz**	110	0
Coffee	1 cup	0	0	1 cup	0	0
2% milk	1 tbsp	8	2	1 tbsp	8	2
Breakfast subtotal		313	10		340	10

MEAL PLANS — WEEK 1

		10% PLAN			6% PLAN	
FOOD	PORTION	TOTAL CALORIES	SAT-FAT CALORIES	PORTION	TOTAL CALORIES	SAT-FAT CALORIES
Lunch						
Hamburger, lean broiled	**4 oz**	324	100	**3 oz**	243	75
Hamburger roll	1	115	5	1	115	5
Coleslaw	½ cup	42	2	½ cup	42	2
Coffee	1 cup	0	0	1 cup	0	0
2% milk	1 tbsp	8	2	1 tbsp	8	2
Grapes	1 cup	97	0			
Apple				1 large	125	1
Popcorn				2 cups	110	10
Lunch subtotal		586	109		643	95
Dinner						
Mushroom Soup	1 cup	95	5			
Minestrone				1½ cups	180	3
Turkey Scaloppine Limone	1 serving	280	19			
Turkey Mexique				1 serving	180	9
Steamed Zucchini Matchsticks	1 serving	17	0	1 serving	17	0
Whole-wheat bread	2 slices	140	8			
Rice	½ cup	113	1	½ cup	113	1
Cucumber Salad	1 serving	20	0	1 serving	20	0
Carrot Cake sans Oeufs	1 serving	122	5			
Apricots, canned				1 cup	215	0
2% milk	1 cup	121	27			
Dinner subtotal		908	65		715	13
Snack						
Nonfat fruit yogurt	8 oz	200	0			
Anjou pear				1 pear	120	0
Skim milk				1 cup	86	3
Daily total		2007	184		1914	121

MEAL PLANS — WEEK 1

FOOD	10% PLAN			6% PLAN		
	PORTION	TOTAL CALORIES	SAT-FAT CALORIES	PORTION	TOTAL CALORIES	SAT-FAT CALORIES
FRIDAY — WEEK 1						
Breakfast						
Whole-wheat toast	**1 slice**	70	4	**2 slices**	140	8
Banana slices	**½ banana**	53	1	1 banana	105	2
1% cottage cheese	**¼ cup**	41	4	**½ cup**	82	7
Cantaloupe	½ melon	95	1	½ melon	95	1
Coffee	1 cup	0	0	1 cup	0	0
2% milk	1 tbsp	8	2	1 tbsp	8	2
Breakfast subtotal		267	12		430	20
Lunch						
Dijon Chicken Rice Salad	1 serving	305	15	1 serving	305	15
Apple Oat Bran Muffin	1 muffin	125	4	1 muffin	125	4
Orange	1 fruit	60	0	1 fruit	60	0
Coffee	1 cup	0	0	1 cup	0	0
2% milk	1 tbsp	8	2	1 tbsp	8	2
Pear				1 large	125	1
Lunch subtotal		498	21		623	22
Dinner						
Cucumber Soup	1 cup	78	0	1 cup	85	3
Rib chops	**2**	480	120	**1**	240	60
Potato Skins	1 serving	79	3	1 serving	79	3
Italian Mixed Vegetables	1 serving	65	6	1 serving	65	6
White wine	3½ fl oz	80	0	3½ fl oz	80	0
Coffee	1 cup	0	0	1 cup	0	0
2% milk	1 tbsp	8	2	1 tbsp	8	2
Cinnamon Sweet Cakes	1 piece	148	8			
Apple				1 large	125	1
Dinner subtotal		938	139		682	75

MEAL PLANS — WEEK I

	10% PLAN			6% PLAN		
FOOD	PORTION	TOTAL CALORIES	SAT-FAT CALORIES	PORTION	TOTAL CALORIES	SAT-FAT CALORIES
Snack						
Nonfat yogurt w/fruit	8 oz	200	0			
Grapes				1 cup	97	1
Skim milk	_____	_____		1 cup	86	3
Daily total		1903	172		1918	121
SATURDAY — WEEK 1						
Breakfast						
Buttermilk Waffles	1 square	188	9	1 square	188	9
Syrup	1 tbsp	61	0	1 tbsp	61	0
Grapefruit	1 fruit	95	0	1 fruit	95	0
Coffee	1 cup	0	0	1 cup	0	0
2% milk	1 tbsp	8	2	1 tbsp	8	2
Breakfast subtotal		352	11		352	11
Lunch						
Pawtucket Chili	1½ cups	173	6	1½ cups	173	6
Anjou pear	1 fruit	120	0	1 fruit	120	0
Popcorn	4 cups	220	20	4 cups	220	20
Coffee	1 cup	0	0	1 cup	0	0
2% milk	1 tbsp	8	2	1 tbsp	8	2
Lunch subtotal		521	28		521	28
Dinner						
Pesto on Spaghetti	1 serving	315	21	1 serving	315	21
Pink salmon steak	6 oz	246	12	6 oz	246	12
Cauliflower Sauté	1 serving	67	5	1 serving	67	5
Baked sweet potato	1	115	0	1	115	0
Mixed salad	1 serving	23	0	1 serving	23	0
Blue cheese dressing	1 tbsp	77	14			
Low-cal Italian dressing				1 tbsp	16	2
Ice cream	½ cup	135	40			
Sherbet				½ cup	135	11

MEAL PLANS — WEEK 1

		10% PLAN			6% PLAN	
FOOD	PORTION	TOTAL CALORIES	SAT-FAT CALORIES	PORTION	TOTAL CALORIES	SAT-FAT CALORIES
Coffee	1 cup	0	0	1 cup	0	0
2% milk	1 tbsp	8	2	1 tbsp	8	2
Dinner subtotal		986	94		925	53
Snack						
Blue cheese	1 oz	100	48			
Wheat Thins	8	70	10			
Oat Bran Muffin				1	160	6
Daily total		2029	191		1958	98

MEAL PLANS — WEEK 2

FOOD	PORTION	TOTAL CALORIES	SAT-FAT CALORIES
SUNDAY — WEEK 2			
Breakfast			
Buttermilk Pancakes	3	135	9
Syrup	3 tbsp	183	0
Orange sections	1 cup	85	0
Coffee, black	1 cup	0	0
Breakfast subtotal		403	9
Lunch			
Gazpacho I	1 cup	100	8
Scallop Curry	1 serving	197	10
Rice	¾ cup	170	2
Keema Eggplant	1 serving	100	4
Mixed salad	1 serving	23	0
Low-cal Russian dressing	1 tbsp	23	1
Banana Cake	1 slice	263	12
Lunch subtotal		876	37
Dinner			
Corn Chowder	1½ cups	288	12
Tomato Quiche	1 slice	220	21
Spinach with mushroom salad	1 cup	15	0
Dressing (oil, vinegar, Dijon mustard)	2 tbsp	119	16
Coffee, black	1 cup	0	0
Kiwi	1	45	0
Dinner subtotal		687	49
Daily total		1966	95

6% Plan sat-fat daily budget	120
+ Carry-over	0
Total	120
− Day's expenditure	− 95
New carry-over	25

MEAL PLANS — WEEK 2

FOOD	PORTION	TOTAL CALORIES	SAT-FAT CALORIES
MONDAY — WEEK 2			
Breakfast			
Strawberries	1 cup	45	0
w/nonfat yogurt	½ cup	55	0
Oat Bran Muffins	2	320	12
Orange juice	6 fl oz	83	0
Coffee, black	1 cup	0	0
Breakfast subtotal		503	12
Lunch			
Tuna salad sandwich			
water-packed tuna	3¼ oz	146	3
whole-wheat toast	2 slices	140	8
low-cal salad dressing	1 tbsp	45	9
Orange	1	60	0
Marvelous Cookies	2	160	10
Skim milk	8 fl oz	86	3
Lunch subtotal		637	33
Dinner			
Watercress Soup	1 serving	97	11
Indonesian Chicken with Green Beans	1 serving	200	15
Rice	1 cup	226	1
Indian Vegetables	1 serving	100	6
Cucumber Salad	1 serving	20	0
Apple Cake	1 slice	220	13
Dinner subtotal		863	46
Daily total		2003	91
	6% Plan sat-fat daily budget	120	
	+ Carry-over	25	
	Total	145	
	− Day's expenditure	− 91	
	New carry-over	54	

MEAL PLANS — WEEK 2

FOOD	PORTION	TOTAL CALORIES	SAT-FAT CALORIES
TUESDAY — WEEK 2			
Breakfast			
Cocoa	1 cup		
Cocoa	1 tsp	20	7
Sugar	2 tsp	30	0
Skim milk	8 fl oz	86	3
Low-fat cottage cheese	¼ cup	41	4
Honey Whole-Wheat Bread	1 slice	130	2
Orange juice	6 fl oz	83	0
Banana	1	105	2
Breakfast subtotal		495	18
Lunch			
Cold Ginger Carrot Soup	1 cup	70	4
Peppery Chicken	1 half breast	180	12
Whole-Wheat Bagels	2	230	2
Carrot sticks	1 carrot	30	0
Grapes	1 cup	97	1
Lunch subtotal		607	19
Dinner			
Lentil and Everything Soup	1 cup	82	2
Broiled Ginger Fish	1 serving	209	6
Rice Pilau with Apricots	½ cup	106	4
Cauliflower Sauté	1 serving	67	5
Mixed salad	1 serving	23	0
Dressing made with olive oil, vinegar, herbs	2 tbsp	179	24
Ice milk	¾ cup	138	24
Skim milk	8 fl oz	86	3
Dinner subtotal		890	68
Daily total		1992	105
6% Plan sat-fat daily budget		120	
+ Carry-over		54	
Total		174	
− Day's expenditure		− 105	
New carry-over		69	

MEAL PLANS — WEEK 2

FOOD	PORTION	TOTAL CALORIES	SAT-FAT CALORIES
WEDNESDAY — WEEK 2			
Breakfast			
Oat bran cereal	½ cup dry	165	2
Raisins	1 tbsp	14	0
Margarine	1 tsp	30	6
Orange	1	60	0
Breakfast subtotal		269	8
Lunch			
Fruit Salad with Cottage Cheese	1 serving	280	7
Honey Whole-Wheat Bread	1 slice	130	2
Margarine	1 tsp	30	6
Popcorn (sunflower oil)	4 cups	220	20
Lunch subtotal		660	35
Dinner			
Avgolemono Soup	1 cup	99	2
Chicken with Rice, Tomatoes, and Artichokes	1 serving	320	10
Sweet potato, baked	1	115	trace
Sliced tomato	1	23	0
Skim milk	8 fl oz	86	3
Cocoa Brownie	1 square	115	9
Dinner subtotal		758	24
Snack			
Focaccia	2½ pieces	300	8
Daily total		1987	75
6% Plan sat-fat daily budget		120	
+ Carry-over		69	
Total		189	
− Day's expenditure		− 75	
New carry-over		114	

MEAL PLANS — WEEK 2

FOOD	PORTION	TOTAL CALORIES	SAT-FAT CALORIES
THURSDAY — WEEK 2			
Breakfast			
Nonfat yogurt w/fruit	8 fl oz	200	0
Whole-wheat toast	2 pieces	140	8
Jelly	1 tsp	15	0
Coffee, black	1 cup	0	0
Breakfast subtotal		355	8
Lunch			
Curried Tuna Salad w/Pears	1 serving	220	11
Apricot Oat Muffin	2	270	8
Fresh blueberries, cherries or grapefruit sections	1 cup	80	0
Skim milk	8 fl oz	86	3
Lunch subtotal		656	22
Dinner			
Apple Squash Soup	1 cup	155	9
Turkey Cutlets with Artichokes and Cream Sauce	1 serving	260	21
Rice	¾ cup	170	2
Acorn Squash	1 serving	125	8
Eastern Spinach Salad	1 serving	70	5
Mocha Cake with Mocha Frosting	1 square	180	14
Dinner subtotal		960	59
Daily total		1971	89

6% Plan sat-fat daily budget	120
+ Carry-over	114
Total	234
− Day's expenditure	− 89
New carry-over	145

MEAL PLANS — WEEK 2

FOOD	PORTION	TOTAL CALORIES	SAT-FAT CALORIES
FRIDAY — WEEK 2			
Breakfast			
Cheerios	1 oz	110	3
Skim milk	½ cup	43	1
Banana, sliced	½	53	1
Orange juice	6 fl oz	83	0
Whole-wheat toast	1 piece	70	4
Margarine	1 tsp	30	6
Coffee, black	1 cup	0	0
Breakfast subtotal		389	15
Lunch			
Turkey submarine sandwich			
White meat turkey	3 oz	114	3
Low-cal mayonnaise	1 tbsp	45	9
Submarine roll	1	215	8
Bosc pear	1	100	0
Skim milk	8 fl oz	86	3
Lunch subtotal		560	23
Dinner			
Broccoli Soup	1 cup	125	7
Pizza	2 pieces	310	10
Mixed salad	1 serving	23	0
Low-cal Italian dressing	2 tbsp	32	4
Green Beans Basilico	1 serving	44	4
Deep-Dish Pear Pie	1 slice	236	11
Coffee, black	1 cup	0	0
Dinner subtotal		770	36
Snack			
Popcorn (sunflower oil)	4 cups	220	20
Daily total		1939	94
6% Plan sat-fat daily budget		120	
+ Carry-over		145	
Total		265	
− Day's expenditure		− 94	
New carry-over		171	

MEAL PLANS — WEEK 2

FOOD	PORTION	TOTAL CALORIES	SAT-FAT CALORIES
SATURDAY — WEEK 2 — Day to Splurge			
Breakfast			
Poached egg	1	79	15
Canadian bacon	2 slices	86	12
Buttermilk Waffles	2 squares	376	18
Orange juice	6 fl oz	83	0
Coffee, black	1 cup	0	0
Breakfast subtotal		624	45
Lunch			
Chili non Carne	1½ cups	235	11
with salad vegetables	¼ cup	15	0
Bran Muffin	1	116	4
Tangerine	1	35	0
Skim milk	8 fl oz	86	3
Lunch subtotal		487	18
Dinner			
Rib roast (lean, trimmed)	6 oz	420	102
Large baked potato	1	220	0
with sour cream	1 tbsp	26	14
Mixed salad	1 serving	23	0
Low-cal Italian dressing	1 tbsp	16	2
Cheese cake	1 slice	280	89
Coffee, black	1 cup	0	0
Dinner subtotal		985	207
Daily total		2096	270
6% Plan sat-fat daily budget		120	
+ Carry-over		171	
Total		291	
− Day's expenditure		− 270	
New carry-over		21	

CHOICES

12

THIS CHAPTER groups foods together according to their sat-fat calorie content. You can use it in meal planning to find foods that have the exact number of sat-fat calories you need to fill out your sat-fat budget. (Of course, you need not feel compelled to spend your entire sat-fat budget each day. The less sat-fat you eat, the better.)

This is how it works: turn to Chapter 11 and look at the meal plans for Monday — Week 1. At the end of the day, the person following the 6 Percent Plan has 28 surplus sat-fat calories to spend on a snack. He has chosen to have mixed nuts for a total of 27 sat-fat calories. Maybe that wouldn't be your choice. Instead, you could look at the 0–10, 11–20, and 21–30 columns of the Choices chart and choose a snack that would appeal to you. Perhaps you would like 3 slices of the pizza (15 sat-fat calories) you made and froze last week or 3 oatmeal cookies (12 sat-fat calories) and a cup of low-fat fruit-flavored yogurt (15 sat-fat calories).

The Choices chart dramatically illustrates the abundance and variety of low-fat dishes (including desserts) available on a low sat-fat eating plan. Just look at the many choices you have in the 0–10, 11–20, and 21–30 columns. (Recipes for the dishes in italicized print can be found in Part II of this book.)

The Choices chart may not include all your favorite foods. Feel free to add the sat-fat values of your favorite foods and recipes to the appropriate columns in "Your Own Choices." Check the food tables at the back of the book and the recipes in Part II to estimate these values.

CHOICES: 0–20 SAT-FAT CALORIES

0–10   **11–20**

Meats and Fish

4 oz broiled cod (1)

1 serving *Scallops Caribbean* (3)

4 oz turkey breast w/o skin (4)

4 oz solid tuna in water (4)

4 oz baked flounder or sole (4)

1 serving *Dill Fish* (4)

1 serving *Shanghai Fish* (4)

1 serving *Tortillas con Pollo* (5)

1 serving *Broiled Ginger Fish* (6)

1 serving *Chinese Chicken* (7)

1 serving *Fish Baked in Olive, Chili Pepper, and Tomato Sauce* (8)

1 serving *Chicken Marrakesh* (8)

1 serving *Tandoori Chicken* (8)

1 serving *Chicken with Rice, Tomatoes, and Artichokes* (9)

1 serving *Turkey with Snow Peas* (9)

1 serving *Turkey Mexique* (9)

1 serving *Salmon Soufflé* (9)

1 serving *Turkey Roll-ups Firenze* (10)

1 serving *Flounder Fillets Stuffed with Fennel Rice* (10)

1 serving *Grilled Apricot-Ginger Chicken* (11)

4 oz pink salmon, canned (11)

1 serving *Peppery Chicken* (12)

4 oz chicken breast w/o skin (12)

4 oz roasted turkey leg w/o skin (12)

4 oz fried chicken breast w/o skin (12)

1 serving *Scallops Provençal* (13)

1 serving *Broiled Monkfish with Orange Sauce* (13)

1 serving *Chicken Couscous* (13)

1 serving *Singapore Chicken* (13)

1 serving *Ma-Po Bean Curd* (13)

1 serving *Chicken with Apples and Onions* (14)

1 serving *Coq au Vin* (14)

1 serving *Baghdad Chicken* (14)

1 serving *Kung Pao Chicken with Broccoli* (14)

1 serving *Fish with Mushroom Sauce* (14)

1 serving *Turkey Véronique* (15)

1 serving *Turkey Cutlet* (15)

1 serving *Chicken Paprikash* (15)

1 serving *Lemon Chicken* (15)

1 serving *Indonesian Chicken with Green Beans* (15)

1 serving *Marinated Fish Steaks* (16)

1 serving *Chicken Smothered in Vegetables* (16)

4 oz lean roasted pork tenderloin (16)

1 serving *Chicken with Apricots, Sweet Potatoes, and Prunes* (16)

1 serving *Turkey Sautéed with Onions and Almonds* (17)

1 serving *Pineapple Chicken* (17)

1 serving *Chicken Curry* (17)

1 serving *Cuban Chicken* (18)

1 serving *Apricot Chicken Divine* (18)

1 serving *Curry Fish* (18)

1 serving *Turkey Scaloppine Marsala* (19)

1 serving *Turkey Scaloppine Limone* (19)

1 serving *Broccoli Baked Turkey* (19)

1 serving *Keema Matar* (19)

1 serving *Lime-Peanut-Ginger Chicken* (19)

1 serving *Sate Ajam* (19)

1 serving *Lemon-Mustard Chicken* (20)

CHOICES: 21–50 SAT-FAT CALORIES

21–30	31–40	41–50

Meats and Fish

1 serving *Phyllo Chicken with Rice, Artichokes, and "Cream" Sauce* (21)

1 serving *Turkey Cutlets with Artichoke-Cream Sauce* (21)

1 serving *Phyllo-Wrapped Fish and Mushroom Sauce* (22)

1 serving *Creamy Turkey Casserole* (22)

1 serving *Sesame Chicken Brochettes* (22)

4 oz roasted chicken breast w/skin (24)

4 oz roasted chicken leg w/o skin (24)

1 serving *Breaded Turkey Cutlet* (26)

1 serving *Chicken Kiev* (27)

4 oz grilled Canadian bacon (28)

4 oz lean broiled trimmed round steak (28)

1 serving *Creamy Chicken Pie* (29)

4 oz roasted regular cured ham (32)

1 serving *Mongolian Hot Pot* (35)

4 oz roasted trimmed lean lamb leg (40)

4 oz broiled lean trimmed lamb loin chop (40)

4 oz lean trimmed rump roast (44)

4 oz broiled lean trimmed sirloin steak (48)

4 oz braised lean flank steak (48)

4 oz veal cutlet (48)

4 oz lamb lean trimmed arm or blade chop (48)

CHOICES: 0–20 SAT-FAT CALORIES

0–10   **11–20**

Meats and Fish

1 serving *Oriental Fish
  Kebabs* (10)
1 serving *Scallop Creole*
  (10)
1 serving *Scallop Curry*
  (10)

Luncheon Meats

1 serving *Indonesian
  Peanut Chicken* (20)
4 oz chunk light tuna in
  oil (20)
4 oz baked red salmon
  (20)

4 slices (4 oz) extra
  lean ham (16)
4 slices (4 oz) light
  turkey roll (20)

Dairy

8 oz plain skim milk
  yogurt (2)
1 cup skim milk (3)
4 oz 1% cottage cheese
  (7)
1 tbsp grated Parmesan
  cheese (9)
1 tbsp half-and-half
  (10)

4 oz 2% cottage cheese
  (12)
1 cup 1% milk (14)
1 tbsp sour cream (14)
1 whole egg (15)
8 oz fruit-flavored low-
  fat yogurt (15)
1 tbsp light cream (16)
½ cup ice milk (16)

Fats and Oils

1 tbsp low-cal French
  dressing (1)
1 tbsp low-cal Russian
  dressing (1)
1 tbsp low-cal Italian
  dressing (2)
1 tbsp low-cal
  Thousand Island
  dressing (2)
1 tbsp soy coffee
  whitener (3)
1 tbsp Thousand Island
  dressing (8)
1 tbsp diet or whipped
  soft margarine (9)
1 tbsp Italian dressing (9)
1 tbsp Russian dressing
  (10)

1 tbsp safflower oil (11)
1 tbsp coconut oil
  coffee whitener (13)
1 tbsp sunflower oil
  (13)
1 tbsp mayonnaise (14)
1 tbsp blue cheese salad
  dressing (14)
1 tbsp French dressing
  (14)
1 tbsp corn oil (15)
1 tbsp olive oil (16)
1 tbsp soybean oil (18)

CHOICES: 21–50 SAT-FAT CALORIES

21–30	31–40	41–50

Luncheon Meats

21–30	31–40	41–50
1 chicken frank (22)	4 slices (4 oz) regular ham (36)	1.6 oz beef frank (48)
	5 slices (1 oz) pepperoni (40)	

Dairy

21–30	31–40	41–50
1 oz part skim mozzarella (26)	1 tbsp whipping cream (31)	8 oz whole milk yogurt (43)
1 tbsp cream cheese (26)	½ cup regular ice cream (40)	1 cup whole milk (45)
1 cup 2% milk (27)		4 oz whole milk ricotta (46)
4 oz creamed cottage cheese (29)		1 oz blue cheese (48)
		1 oz American cheese (50)

Fats and Oils

21–30	31–40	41–50
1 tbsp peanut oil (21)	1 tbsp cottonseed oil (32)	1 tbsp pork lard (45)
1 pat butter (23)	1 tbsp chicken fat (34)	
1 tbsp Crisco (30)		

CHOICES: 0–20 SAT-FAT CALORIES

0–10	11–20	

Desserts and Snacks

1 serving *Cocoa Angel Food Cake* (0)

1 serving *Strawberry Mousse* (0)

1 vanilla wafer (2)

1 fig bar (2)

10 pretzels (0–4)

1 slice *Foccaccia* (3)

1 *Apple-Nut Cookie* (4)

1 serving *Carrot Cake sans Oeufs* (5)

1 *Marvelous Cookie* (5)

1 serving *Pears Hélène* (5)

1 slice *Pizza* (5)

1 cup popcorn popped in oil (5)

4 saltines (5)

1 *Oatmeal Cookie* (6)

¼ oz Goldfish (6)

1 chocolate chip cookie (7)

5 Triscuits (7)

1 serving *Cinnamon Sweet Cakes* (8)

10 cheese crackers (8)

1 *Cocoa Brownie* (9)

1 serving *Pineapple Pound Cake* (9)

1 serving *Raspberry Cake* (9)

1 square gingerbread (10)

1 serving *Strawberry Tart* (10)

1 serving *Apple Pandowdy* (11)

½ cup sherbet (11)

1 serving *Deep-Dish Pear Pie* (11)

1 serving *Banana Cake* (12)

1 serving *Calzone* (12)

10 cheese tidbits (12)

1 oz snack sticks (12–15)

1 tbsp peanut butter (12)

1 serving *Key Lime Pie* (12)

1 serving *Apple Cake* (13)

1 oz almonds (13)

1 small slice dark fruit cake (14)

1 oz pecans or walnuts (14)

1 serving *Ginger Cake with Pear Sauce* (14)

1 serving *Applesauce Cake* (14)

1 serving *Mocha Cake* (14)

1 serving *Chocolatey-Chocolate Cocoa Cake* (15)

1 serving *Marble Cake* (15)

1 serving *Orange Cake* (15)

1 serving *Tante Nancy's Apple Crumb Cake* (15)

1 serving *Peach Pound Cake* (16)

1 oz pistachios (16)

10 potato chips (16)

1 oz peanuts (18)

½ cup vanilla instant pudding (20)

CHOICES: 21–50 SAT-FAT CALORIES

21–30	31–40	41–50

Desserts and Snacks

1 serving *Lemon Loaf* (21)

½ cup chocolate pudding (22)

1 oz cashews (23)

1 small slice pound cake (27)

1 oz macadamia nuts (29)

½ cup custard, baked (31)

1 small slice devil's food cake with chocolate frosting (32)

1 slice peach pie (37)

1 slice carrot cake with cream cheese frosting (37)

1 slice blueberry pie (39)

1 oz Brazil nuts (41)

1 slice apple pie (41)

1 slice cherry pie (42)

1 slice pecan pie (42)

1 slice custard pie (50)

CHOICES: 0–20 SAT-FAT CALORIES

0–10	11–20

Fast Foods

Arthur Treacher's coleslaw (10)

1 Kentucky Fried Chicken drumstick (15)

CHOICES: 51–200 SAT-FAT CALORIES

51–60	61–70	71–200

Meats

4 oz broiled lean trimmed porterhouse steak (52)	4 oz roasted lean veal chuck (63)	4 oz braised trimmed blade pot roast (72)
4 oz broiled extra lean ground beef (56)	4 oz broiled lean trimmed club steak (64)	4 oz veal rib roast (84)
4 oz broiled lean veal round (56)	4 oz trimmed lean rib roast (68)	1 pan-fried center loin pork chop (88)
4 oz roasted lean trimmed lamb shoulder (56)	4 oz braised lean trimmed chuck (68)	1 pan-fried center rib pork chop (94)
4 oz broiled lean trimmed lamb rib chop (60)	4 oz broiled lean veal loin (68)	4 oz broiled lean ground beef (100)
		4 oz braised lean veal breast (104)
		4 oz cooked bacon (176)

Luncheon Meats

4 links cooked pork sausage (52)	1.6 oz beef frank (61)	4 oz kielbasa (100)
4 oz ham salad spread (52)	4 slices (3.2 oz) beef salami (68)	4 slices (4 oz) beef luncheon meat loaf (116)
2 oz beef and pork frank (55)	2.4 oz link smoked pork sausage (69)	4 oz beef bologna (120)
		1 Polish pork sausage (211)

CHOICES: 21–50 SAT-FAT CALORIES

21–30	31–40	41–50

Fast Foods

Kentucky Fried Chicken wing, original recipe (21)	Burger King cheeseburger (33)	McDonald's hotcake and butter (43)
McDonald's English muffin with butter (26)	McDonald's regular French fries (33)	Kentucky Fried Chicken extra crispy breast (44)
McDonald's cookies (28)	McDonald's apple pie (33)	Burger King chopped beef steak (45)
Kentucky Fried Chicken breast, original recipe (29)	McDonald's hamburger (33)	McDonald's shake or sundae (47)
Roy Rogers' roast beef (29)	Wendy's chili (38)	McDonald's chocolate chip cookies (49)
		McDonald's Quarter Pounder (50)
		Burger King Whaler (50)

CHOICES: 51–200 SAT-FAT CALORIES

51–60	61–70	71–200

Dairy

1 oz cheddar cheese (54)		
1 oz cream cheese (56)		

Fats and Oils

1 tbsp beef tallow (58)		1 tbsp palm kernel oil (100)
1 tbsp palm oil (60)		1 tbsp coconut oil (106)

Desserts and Snacks

1 slice yellow cake with chocolate frosting (51)		⅛ cheesecake (85)
1 fried apple pie (52)		1 oz dried, toasted coconut (107)
1 fried cherry pie (52)		1 slice cream pie (135)
1 slice pumpkin pie (58)		

CHOICES: 51–200 SAT-FAT CALORIES

51–60	61–70	71–200

Fast Foods

Kentucky Fried Chicken original snack box (55)

McDonald's cheeseburger (58)

Egg McMuffin (59)

Burger King hot dog (60)

Pizza Hut supreme ¼ medium pizza (65)

Arby's Ham n' Cheese sandwich (70)

Long John Silver's fish (70)

McDonald's Filet-o-Fish (71)

Hardee's cheeseburger (76)

Dairy Queen chocolate-dipped cone (83)

Wendy's Old Fashioned (85)

Dairy Queen banana split (91)

Burger King Whopper (95)

Kentucky Fried Chicken dinner, wing and breast (95)

Hardee's double cheeseburger (127)

Dairy Queen Big Brazier with cheese (128)

Dairy Queen chocolate malt (128)

Hardee's Deluxe (137)

McDonald's Quarter Pounder with cheese (150)

McDonald's Big Mac (155)

YOUR OWN CHOICES: 0–40 SAT-FAT CALORIES

0–10	**11–20**

21–30	**31–40**

13 FOOD NUTRIENTS AND WHAT THEY DO FOR YOU

IN YOUR FERVOR to lower your sat-fat intake, don't forget to balance your diet with foods that will give you adequate amounts of vitamins, minerals, protein, and fiber. Eating a well-balanced diet should be no problem if you replace your excess sat-fat calories with fruits, vegetables, and whole grains.

More specifically, to maintain your health it is essential that you eat foods from each of the following food groups every day.

VEGETABLES

Vegetables contribute vital fiber, vitamins, and minerals to your diet. They should be varied and eaten daily.

Dark green vegetables should be included several times a week. They are an excellent source of vitamins A and C, riboflavin, folic acid, iron, and magnesium. Choose from:

beet greens	endive	spinach
broccoli*	escarole	turnip greens
chard	kale	watercress
chicory	romaine lettuce	

Deep yellow vegetables are an excellent source of vitamin A. Choose from:

carrots	sweet potatoes
pumpkin	winter squash

---

*These cruciferous vegetables may reduce your risk of colon cancer.

142

Other vegetables also contribute varying amounts of vitamins and minerals. Choose from:

artichokes	chinese cabbage	okra
asparagus	cucumbers	onions
beets	eggplant	radishes
brussels sprouts*	green beans	summer squash
cabbage*	green peppers	tomatoes
cauliflower*	lettuce	turnips*
celery	mushrooms	zucchini

Starchy vegetables are rich in starch, fiber, vitamin B_6, folic acid, iron, magnesium, potassium, and phosphorus. Choose from:

corn	potatoes (white)
green peas	rutabaga*
lima beans	sweet potatoes (rich in vitamin A)

Dried beans and peas are excellent sources of protein, soluble fiber (known to reduce blood cholesterol levels), calcium, magnesium, phosphorus, potassium, iron, and zinc.

Choose from these dried beans and peas, which should be included as a starchy vegetable several times a week:

black beans	lentils	split peas
black-eyed peas	lima beans	other types of dried
chickpeas	navy beans	beans and peas
kidney beans	pinto beans	

FRUITS

Fruits contain fiber, vitamins, and minerals. They should be varied and eaten daily.

Citrus, melon, and berries are rich sources of vitamin C, other vitamins, folic acid, and minerals. Choose from:

blueberries	lemon	tangerine
cantaloupe	orange	watermelon
grapefruit	orange juice	other citrus fruits,
grapefruit juice	raspberries	melons, and
honeydew melon	strawberries	berries

Other fruits have smaller amounts of the same nutrients. Choose from:

apples	nectarines	prunes
apricots	peaches	raisins
bananas	pears	other fruit
cherries	pineapples	fruit juices
grapes	plums	

NOTE: Avoid dates and figs. They are high in saturated fat.

WHOLE GRAINS, BREADS, AND CEREALS

Whole grains, breads, and cereals are rich in protein, starch, fiber, vitamins, and minerals and should be consumed daily.

The following whole-grain products are rich in starch, fiber, protein, thiamine, riboflavin, niacin, folic acid, vitamin E, iron, phosphorus, magnesium, zinc, and other trace minerals. Choose from:

brown rice	oatmeal	whole-wheat bread
buckwheat groats	pumpernickel	and rolls
bulgur	bread	whole-wheat pasta

The following enriched-grain products contain starch and protein, but thiamine, riboflavin, niacin, and iron have been added. Be careful that saturated fat has not also been added. *Read the labels carefully!*

Eat these foods in moderation; they are often a source of little nutrition and empty calories. Whole-grain products are far more nutritious.

bagels	corn bread	noodles
biscuits	corn muffins	pasta
cereal (ready-to-eat)	French bread	rice

MILK PRODUCTS

Milk products are rich in protein, calcium, riboflavin, vitamin B_{12}, magnesium, vitamin A, thiamine, and, if fortified, vitamin D. Milk products need not be high in saturated fat to contain high amounts of calcium. In fact, low-fat milk products contain more calcium than their high-fat counterparts. Choose from these milk products daily:

buttermilk	low-fat yogurt
low-fat cottage cheese (1%)	skim milk

Calcium is also found in peanuts and dark green vegetables.

Women need more calcium than men in order to avoid developing the bone-thinning disease osteoporosis.

MEATS, POULTRY, FISH, AND EGGS

Meats, poultry, fish, and eggs are good sources of protein, phosphorus, niacin, iron, zinc, and vitamins B_6 and B_{12}.

Choose often from the following:

white meat chicken with no skin
white meat turkey with no skin
fish
shellfish

Choose less often from the following:

beef	lamb	veal
ham	pork	eggs

Do not eat organ meats such as liver. They are loaded with cholesterol.

Cooked dried beans or peas, as well as nuts and seeds, may be substituted for meat, poultry, fish, and eggs. However, as these plant foods lack vitamin B_{12}, this vitamin must be supplied by other foods. Nuts and seeds are high in fat and should be eaten in moderation.

TWO

COOK'S CHOICE

INTRODUCTION

COOK'S CHOICE is different and special. In the following pages, you will find only recipes that are *very low* in saturated fat. Not only are these recipes healthy, they make for delicious eating.

We wrote Cook's Choice to show you that low-fat, heart-healthy foods can be just as tasty and satisfying as heart-risky foods. This is especially important for people who need to lower their blood cholesterol. It is also a must for those who want to lower their blood pressure or lose weight, and for diabetics.

But beyond any health considerations, this cookbook is for people who want to eat well. Dishes need not be filled with cream, sour cream, or cheese to taste good. Try Spinach Quiche (page 266), try Key Lime Pie (page 332), try Watercress Soup (page 164) — in fact, try any of the following recipes for a real taste treat.

A note to sodium watchers: If you are monitoring your sodium intake, you may want to cut down on the amount of salt in some of these recipes.

Here are some tips for superior taste or nutritional benefits without excess effort or expense:

- In the recipes that call for pepper, use freshly ground black pepper. There really is a difference between the stale, tasteless pepper that comes in a can and the bright taste of pepper that has just been ground. It is definitely worth buying a peppermill (not necessarily expensive) and whole peppercorns (available in the spice section of your local grocery store).
- Grate a whole nutmeg (available in the spice section of your local grocery store) with a hand grater for a fresher, nuttier taste.
- Fresh garlic is available at grocery stores and is far superior to

garlic powder or garlic salt. It will stay fresh for weeks in the refrigerator.
- Fresh ginger root is available at many grocery stores and is easily kept for months in the refrigerator in a jar filled with sherry. Slice off the outer covering and use ginger root with superior results in recipes that call for ginger.
- In any recipes that call for canned chicken broth, either strain the broth (we often skim the fat off the surface, then pour the broth through a fine tea strainer) or if the fat is hardened, lift it off the soup with a spoon.
- Use *unbleached* white flour. When flour is bleached, it loses many of its important nutritional qualities.

NOTE: $\boxed{Q}$ indicates recipes that are quick and easy to prepare. But beware: some $\boxed{Q}$ recipes require marinating for several hours or overnight. Read recipes through before beginning!

STOCKING UP

For some of you, reducing your saturated fat will mean a big change in the foods you cook. You may wonder what foods will replace the cream in your refrigerator or the Twinkies in your cupboard. What foods should you have on hand to make cooking the following recipes a snap? Here is a list of foods and spices to keep in your cupboard, your freezer, and your refrigerator.

Foods to keep on your shelves:

almonds, slivered	onions
anchovies	pastas (spaghetti, noodles, etc.)
apricots, dried	pineapple chunks, canned
apricot jelly	peaches, canned
artichoke hearts in water	peanuts, unsalted
baking powder	potatoes
baking soda	prunes
barley	raisins
beans, dried (black, pinto, etc.)	salt
beans, kidney, canned	sesame paste (tahini)
chicken broth	sherry, dry
chickpeas	sugar, brown
cocoa, unsweetened	sugar, white

cornstarch
flour, unbleached white
flour, whole-wheat
honey
lentils
molasses
oat bran
oatmeal (not quick)
oil, olive
oil, sunflower or safflower
olives, black and green

sugar, confectioners'
tomatoes, canned
tomato juice
tomato paste (6 oz)
tomato sauce (8 oz)
vanilla
vermouth
vinegar
walnuts, shelled
yeast (if you plan to make
    bread)

Spices:

basil leaves
caraway seeds
cardamom, ground
cayenne pepper
chili powder, hot (if you like)
chili powder, mild
cinnamon, ground
cinnamon sticks
cloves, ground
cloves, whole
coriander
cream of tartar
cumin, ground and seeds
curry powder

dillweed
garam masala*
ginger, ground
mustard seed, black
nutmeg, whole
oregano
paprika
peppercorns, black
rosemary leaves
sesame seeds
tarragon
thyme leaves
turmeric

Foods from the Oriental food store:

bamboo shoots, canned
bean sauce
black beans (fermented)
chili paste with garlic
hoisin sauce

mushrooms, dried black
sesame chili oil
sesame oil
soy sauce and double black
    soy sauce
water chestnuts, canned

---

*Available in Indian groceries and specialty stores.

Foods* to keep in your refrigerator:

buttermilk (for baking)
carrots
celery
garlic cloves
ginger root (store in jar with
   sherry)
lemons

limes
margarine
mayonnaise or salad dressing
mustard, Dijon
yogurt, nonfat plain

Foods to keep in your freezer:

boned and skinned chicken
   breasts
corn, frozen
margarine

peas, frozen
turkey cutlets
whole-wheat bread
whole-wheat pita bread

These all-season foods will enhance your meals — keep some on hand:

broccoli
carrots**
celery**
eggplant
mushrooms (always good in
   salads)
peppers, red or green

potatoes, white or sweet**
snow peas (Chinese peapods)
spinach
squash** (acorn, butternut,
   etc.)
tomatoes
zucchini

Buy fruits in season. Apples, oranges, and pears can usually be purchased year-round. Use for baking, cooking, and snacks.

---

*These foods will stay fresh at least several weeks.
**These vegetables will keep fresh at least several weeks.

SOUPS

14

SOUP! What a wonderful invention! Hot, cold, spicy, sweet, thick, thin, bland, tart — an unlimited source of goodness. Soup is the perfect way to start a meal. It is a delight to the senses and it is filling. In fact, a bowl of soup makes you feel so satisfied that by the time you get to the main course, your ravenous hunger is abated and you may eat less for the rest of the meal.

These are the major advantages of making your own soup:

- It will taste much better than anything you can buy.
- You have an enormous choice of great soups to make.
- You need not worry about whether the soup is too salty or fatty because you control the amount of salt and fat in your soup.
- You make the kind of soup you want when you want it: hot soup to warm you in the winter; cold soup to refresh you in the summer.
- You can make a large amount at one time and freeze it in small containers for use at a later time. Frozen soup is like money in the bank.

CHICKEN STOCK

Instead of using canned chicken broth, you can make your own chicken stock and freeze it in small amounts. It will be tastier, and it will have no fat or salt. There are many ways to make chicken stock; here is one example.

4 pounds chicken backs, or a
    4–5 pound stewing chicken,
    or 6–8 boneless chicken
    breasts
1 onion, sliced
2 carrots, cut into thirds

1 stalk celery, cut into thirds
1 bay leaf
2 sprigs parsley
¼ teaspoon thyme
1 can (10¾ oz) chicken broth,
    strained

In your largest kettle, combine all ingredients, cover with water, and bring to a boil. Reduce heat, cover, and simmer for 1½ hours.

Remove chicken and vegetables. (You may save both the chicken and the vegetables for another use.)

Refrigerate stock in kettle overnight.

Skim off fat.

Freeze in storage containers.

Q

AVGOLEMONO SOUP
(Greek Lemon Soup)

½ cup long-grain rice
2 quarts chicken stock, or 3 cans
    (10¾ oz each) chicken broth,
    strained, + 3 cans water
1 teaspoon salt

¾ cup spaghetti broken into
    ½-inch pieces
1 egg
1 egg white
Juice of 1½ lemons

In a soup pot, bring stock to a boil, reduce heat, and simmer with rice until tender (about 20 minutes).

Add salt and spaghetti pieces and simmer for 6 minutes more.

Just before serving, beat together egg and egg white.

Slowly add lemon juice to the eggs, beating constantly.

Take 1 cup of the broth from the soup pot and add it to the lemon-egg mixture, beating constantly.

Pour lemon-egg broth back into the soup pot, beating constantly. Bring to a boil and serve immediately.

Makes 9 one-cup servings
Per serving: 99 Total calories; 2 Sat-fat calories

Q   MATZO BALL SOUP

The traditional matzo ball soup is made with chicken fat and several eggs. This low sat-fat version is as light as a feather and is equally tasty.

¼ cup water
2 tablespoons margarine
1 egg
1 egg white
½ cup matzo meal

¼ teaspoon salt
6 cups chicken stock, or 2 cans (10¾ oz each) chicken broth, strained, + 2½ cans water

Combine water, margarine, egg, and egg white.
Blend in matzo meal and salt and refrigerate for 20 minutes.
Form chilled dough into balls.
Bring chicken stock to a full boil.
Add matzo balls and simmer, covered, for 20 minutes.

Serves 4 (2 matzo balls each)
Per serving: 167 Total calories; 6 Sat-fat calories

Q   MUSHROOM SOUP

A must! In no more than ten minutes you can make this sophisticated and soothing soup and set it before your family or guests.

½ pound fresh mushrooms, sliced
1 tablespoon margarine
2 cans (10¾ oz each) chicken broth, strained

Juice of 1 lemon (about ¼ cup)
2 tablespoons dry vermouth
1 tablespoon dry sherry
Dash of Tabasco sauce

In a medium saucepan, sauté mushrooms in margarine until just tender.
Gently mix in strained chicken broth.

Add lemon juice, vermouth, sherry, and Tabasco sauce, and heat until warm.

Makes 5 one-cup servings
Per serving: 95 Total calories; 5 Sat-fat calories

POTATO SOUP WITH LEEKS AND BROCCOLI

2 tablespoons margarine
1 ½ cups sliced leeks* (white part)
2 tablespoons unbleached white flour
4 cups hot water
4 cups peeled and sliced potatoes

1 teaspoon salt
¼ teaspoon freshly ground pepper
2 cups broccoli flowerets
2 cups skim milk

In a soup pot, melt margarine.
Mix in leeks, cover pot, and cook slowly until leeks are soft.
Blend in flour and cook for a few seconds. Remove pot from heat.
Add ½ cup of the hot water and blend thoroughly.
Add the remaining hot water, potatoes, salt, and pepper.
Bring to a boil, reduce heat, and simmer, partially covered, for about 40 minutes or until potatoes are tender.
While the potatoes are cooking, steam the broccoli until it is just tender. Set aside.
Pour the cooked potatoes and their liquid into a blender and purée until they are almost smooth (they should still have some texture).
Return soup to pot, add 1 cup of the skim milk, and blend well.
Slowly add the second cup of skim milk, ¼ cup at a time. Do not add so much skim milk that the soup becomes too thin. Soup should be *thick*.
Mix in broccoli, correct seasoning, and finish with several twists of your peppermill.

Makes 8 one-cup servings
Per serving: 113 Total calories; 5 Sat-fat calories

-----

*If you have no leeks, you may use onions, but the special flavor of leeks enhances the soup.

Q

CARROT SOUP

Carrot soup is a great spur-of-the-moment soup because it is simple to make and you probably have the ingredients on hand. It is thick and tasty — wonderful to warm the soul and body on a nippy winter day.

1 medium onion, chopped	1 bay leaf
3 small cloves garlic, minced	Freshly ground pepper to taste
2 tablespoons margarine	2 cans (10¾ oz each) chicken
1 teaspoon thyme	broth, strained
12 carrots, sliced (about 6 cups)	
2 potatoes, peeled and sliced (about 2 cups)	

In a soup pot or large casserole, sauté onion and garlic in margarine until soft.

Stir in thyme.

Mix in carrots, potatoes, bay leaf, and pepper.

Add chicken broth and enough water to cover vegetables.

Bring soup to a boil. Reduce heat, cover, and simmer for 30 minutes.

Remove bay leaf and purée soup in blender.

Makes 11 one-cup servings
Per serving: 85 Total calories; 4 Sat-fat calories

Q

PEANUT BUTTER SOUP

A tasty soup that can be easily made in about 15 minutes.

1 cup chopped celery	1 cup tomato juice
½ cup chopped onion	½ teaspoon coriander
2 tablespoons olive oil	Freshly ground pepper to taste
¼ cup natural all-peanut peanut butter	
1 can (10¾ oz) chicken broth, strained, + 1 can water	

In a soup pot or large casserole, sauté celery and onion in olive oil until tender.

Stir in peanut butter.

Add chicken broth, water, tomato juice, coriander, and pepper. Bring to a boil, reduce heat, and simmer for 10 minutes.

Makes 5 one-cup servings
Per serving: 160 Total calories; 16 Sat-fat calories

APPLE-SQUASH SOUP

Acorn squash makes the richest soup, even though it is a pain to peel; butternut or even yellow zucchini may be substituted.

3 tablespoons margarine
2 cups chopped onion
5 teaspoons curry powder
About 3 pounds acorn squash, peeled, seeded, and cubed (about 6 cups)
2 Granny Smith or other tart apples, peeled, cored, and cubed

3 cups chicken stock, or 1 can (10¾ oz) chicken broth, strained, + water to equal 3 cups
1 teaspoon salt
1 cup apple cider or apple juice
Freshly ground pepper to taste
1–2 Granny Smith or other tart apples, for garnish

In a large soup pot, melt margarine. Add onion and sauté until tender.

Stir in curry powder.

Add squash, apples, chicken stock, and salt. Bring to a boil, reduce heat, and simmer for 25 minutes or until squash and apples are tender.

Remove 2 cups of liquid and set aside.

Purée remaining soup in blender and return to soup pot.

Stir cider into puréed soup.

Add liquid that you set aside, a bit at a time, making sure that soup remains thick, but not *too* thick.

If necessary, reheat soup until hot.

Pepper liberally.

Grate or chop apples into tiny pieces *just* before serving and garnish each bowl of soup.

Makes 9 one-cup servings
Per serving: 155 Total calories; 9 Sat-fat calories

⊡ TARRAGON SQUASH SOUP

A rich, creamy soup that uses no cream. Puréed bread is the secret ingredient.

2 pounds butternut squash, peeled, seeded, and coarsely chopped
2 cloves garlic, peeled
1 teaspoon salt
2 cans (10¾ oz each) chicken broth, strained, + ½ cup water

2 slices stale bread, crusts removed
¼ teaspoon freshly ground pepper
1 teaspoon dried tarragon, or 1 tablespoon fresh tarragon, chopped

In a large pot, combine squash, garlic, salt, chicken broth, and water and bring to a boil. Reduce heat and simmer until squash is tender (about 20–25 minutes).

Tear bread into small pieces and add to squash. Simmer for 3 minutes more.

Purée in blender or food processor.

Just before serving, stir in pepper and tarragon.

Makes 6 one-cup servings
Per serving: 122 Total calories; 2 Sat-fat calories

⊡ GREEN TOMATO SOUP

What does one do with all the green tomatoes left on the vine at the end of the summer growing season? Cook tangy, tasty Green Tomato Soup.

1 cup chopped green tomatoes
4 cups sliced green tomatoes
1 cup sliced onion
2 tablespoons margarine

1 can (10¾ oz) chicken broth, strained, + 1 can water
2 cups shredded fresh spinach

Set aside the 1 cup chopped green tomatoes.

In a medium skillet, briefly sauté sliced green tomatoes and onion in margarine. Cover and cook at low heat until tender.

Purée tomato-onion mixture in blender or food processor. Pour into casserole or soup pot.

Add chicken broth and water and heat through.

Five minutes before serving, add spinach and reserved chopped tomatoes.

Makes 7 one-cup servings
Per serving: 75 Total calories; 5 Sat-fat calories

☒ SWEET CABBAGE SOUP

4 cups chopped cabbage
3 cups grated carrot
1 large can (28 oz) tomatoes
  with juice
1 teaspoon tarragon

1 teaspoon basil
1 teaspoon salt
Water
Juice of 1 lemon
¼ cup raisins

In a large pot, combine cabbage, carrots, tomatoes and their juice, tarragon, basil, and salt. Add water to cover.

Bring to a boil. Reduce heat, cover, and simmer until vegetables are tender.

Purée soup lightly in blender so it still has texture.

Add lemon juice and raisins.

Makes 9 one-cup servings
Per serving: 56 Total calories; 0 Sat-fat calories

☒ BROCCOLI SOUP

1 cup chopped onion
½ cup chopped celery
2 tablespoons margarine
1 cup water
⅓ cup long-grain rice

⅛–¼ teaspoon cayenne pepper
½–1 teaspoon salt
6 cups broccoli flowerets (about
  2 heads)
3 cups skim milk

In a soup pot or large casserole, sauté onion and celery in margarine until tender.

Stir in water, rice, cayenne pepper, and salt, and simmer, covered, for about 10 minutes.

Meanwhile, steam broccoli until just tender. Reserve 1 cup for garnish.

Stir remaining broccoli into soup and continue cooking for 10 minutes more or until rice is cooked and broccoli is soft.

Place in blender. Add skim milk and blend until smooth.
Reheat slowly. Add reserved broccoli and serve.

Makes 7 one-cup servings
Per serving: 125 Total calories; 7 Sat-fat calories

Q CORN CHOWDER

2 tablespoons margarine
2 tablespoons flour
2 cups skim milk

2 cans creamed corn (16 oz
  each)
½ teaspoon salt
½ red pepper or green pepper,
  chopped

In a large pot, melt margarine.
Remove pot from heat and mix in flour until smooth.
Slowly stir in 1 cup of the skim milk.
Return pot to burner and heat slowly until milk thickens.
Stir creamed corn and salt into milk.
Slowly stir in the remaining 1 cup of skim milk. Heat but do not boil.
Stir in peppers and serve.

Makes 6 one-cup servings
Per serving: 192 Total calories; 8 Sat-fat calories

Q CUCUMBER SOUP

Cucumber soup gets a gold star for excellence. It is as refreshing as a dip in a cool lake on a hot summer day. It is simple, quick, and impressive.

2 cucumbers
2 cups nonfat yogurt
1 can (10¾ oz) chicken broth,
  strained

1 clove garlic, crushed
Walnuts, for garnish

Peel cucumbers and cut into bite-size cubes. Salt heavily and set aside.
Spoon yogurt into a medium casserole and stir until smooth.

Stir in chicken broth.

Mix in garlic.

Rinse salt off cucumbers and add them to yogurt mixture. Add salt to taste.

Chill in refrigerator for several hours. Garnish with chopped walnuts.

Makes 5 one-cup servings
Per serving: 78 Total calories; 0 Sat-fat calories

Q ## ZUCCHINI SOUP

One of the greatest recipes known to mankind. Hot or cold, summer or winter, for family or company, zucchini soup is delicious — and easy. You can even prepare it 20 minutes before you eat. If you want to make more and freeze it, just add a few more zucchini and more broth. This recipe is very flexible. Add more or less of any ingredient, and it will still taste superb.

3 large or 4 medium zucchini
  (or more or less), sliced
½ cup chopped onion
¼ cup long-grain rice
Chicken stock to cover zucchini,
  or 2 cans (10¾ oz each)
  chicken broth, strained, +
  water to cover zucchini

1 teaspoon salt
1 teaspoon curry powder
  (approximately)
1 teaspoon Dijon mustard
  (approximately)
½–1 cup nonfat yogurt

In a large soup pot, combine zucchini, onion, rice, chicken stock, water, and salt (add more water, if necessary, to cover zucchini).

Simmer for 15 minutes or until zucchini are tender.

Purée in blender, adding curry powder, mustard, and yogurt to taste.

Eat warm or cool.

This soup freezes well. Reheat frozen soup for best results. Eat immediately or cool for later.

Makes 8 (approximately) one-cup servings
Per serving: 80 Total calories; 1 Sat-fat calorie

COLD GINGER-CARROT SOUP

This soup can be eaten either cold or warm. The lime and ginger give it an interesting flavor.

1 tablespoon minced ginger root	2 cans (10¾ oz each) chicken
2 cloves garlic, minced	broth, strained, + 1 can
½ cup chopped onion	water
2 tablespoons margarine	¼ cup fresh lime juice
5 cups sliced carrots	(approximately)
	Nonfat yogurt, for garnish

In a soup pot or large casserole, sauté ginger, garlic, and onion in margarine until tender.

Stir in carrots.

Add chicken broth and water and simmer until carrots are tender (about 20 minutes).

Add lime juice and purée soup in blender until smooth.

Chill or serve warm. Top each soup bowl with a large dollop of yogurt.

Makes 10 one-cup servings
Per serving: 70 Total calories; 4 Sat-fat calories

SOUR CHERRY SOUP

Sour Cherry Soup is a sweet soup. It is ideal for a luncheon or dinner party and *very* simple to make. It has no fat but does have quite a lot of sugar.

2 cans (1 lb each) undrained sour cherries packed in water	2 tablespoons unbleached white flour
¾ cup sugar	6 tablespoons cold water
1 stick cinnamon	2 cups water

Remove about 12 cherries from one can and put aside for garnish. (Or buy another whole can of cherries.)

In a medium saucepan, cook cherries with their juice, sugar, and cinnamon stick for 10 to 15 minutes.

In a small bowl, mix flour and 3 tablespoons of the cold water until smooth. Blend in remaining 3 tablespoons cold water.

Remove cinnamon stick from cooked cherries and set aside.

Pour cherry mixture into blender. Add flour mixture and blend until soup is smooth.

Return soup to saucepan, add 2 cups water, and heat just to boiling.

Return cinnamon stick to soup and chill.

Garnish each bowl of soup with a few cherries before serving.

Makes 6 one-cup servings
Per serving: 165 Total calories; trace Sat-fat calories

WATERCRESS SOUP

Watercress Soup is thick and creamy in texture but low in fat. It makes a refreshing first course in summer or winter.

3 tablespoons margarine	½ teaspoon freshly ground
1 cup chopped onion	pepper
2 bunches watercress, washed	1 teaspoon tarragon
and stems removed	1 teaspoon dillweed
2 tablespoons unbleached white	1 quart buttermilk
flour	2 tablespoons fresh lemon juice
5 cups chicken stock, or 2 cans	1 teaspoon Worcestershire sauce
(10¾ oz each) chicken broth,	½ teaspoon curry powder
strained, + 2 cans water	10 sprigs watercress, for garnish
1½ teaspoons salt	

In a large soup pot, melt margarine. Add onion and cook until soft.

Stir in watercress.

Cover and cook slowly for 10 minutes or until watercress wilts.

Sprinkle on flour and mix well.

Add chicken stock, salt, and pepper. Cover and simmer for 30 minutes. Add tarragon and dillweed at the last minute.

Cool slightly. Purée in blender or food processor.

Return soup to pot. Add buttermilk, lemon juice, and Worcestershire sauce and stir until smooth.

Add curry powder and heat through.

Cool and refrigerate.

Makes 10 one-cup servings
Per serving: 97 Total calories; 11 Sat-fat calories

Q

GAZPACHO I

4 large tomatoes, quartered	3 tablespoons olive oil
1 medium onion, quartered	¼ cup white vinegar
2 cloves garlic	1 cup tomato juice
1 green pepper, coarsely chopped	Salt to taste
1 cucumber, peeled and coarsely chopped	Stale bread (1 or 2 slices, or bagel)

In a blender, roughly purée tomatoes, onion, garlic, green pepper, cucumber, olive oil, vinegar, tomato juice, and salt. Chill.

Before serving, make croutons by cutting bread (bagel, wholewheat bread — whatever you have around) into cubes and toasting until crispy in toaster oven.

(You may also sauté the croutons in oil and garlic.)

Garnish soup with croutons.

Makes 6 one-cup servings

Per serving:	Total calories	Sat-fat calories
Without croutons	100	8
With croutons	124	9

Q

GAZPACHO II

If you hate wasting the juice from canned tomatoes, the following two recipes (Gazpacho II and Tomato-Rice Soup) will appeal to you. Each time you use canned tomatoes, accumulate their juice in a storage container in the freezer for future soups.

8 cups juice from canned
  tomatoes
2 green peppers, coarsely
  chopped
1 medium onion, coarsely
  chopped

2 cloves garlic, minced
1 cucumber, peeled and coarsely
  chopped
½ cup white vinegar
¼ cup olive oil
Salt and pepper to taste

Purée all ingredients in blender. Chill.
Add croutons as in Gazpacho I (page 165).

Makes 8 one-cup servings

Per serving:	Total calories	Sat-fat calories
Without croutons	113	8
With croutons	130	9

Q

TOMATO-RICE SOUP

6 cups juice from canned
  tomatoes
1 tablespoon grated onion
1 pinch ground cloves

½ cup long-grain rice
1 cup frozen peas
1 cup frozen corn

Combine tomato juice, onion, cloves, and rice and bring to a boil. Reduce heat and simmer for about 25 minutes.
Add peas and corn and cook about 5 minutes more.

Makes 8 one-cup servings
Per serving: 93 Total calories; 0 Sat-fat calories

HOT AND SOUR SOUP

The ingredients in Hot and Sour Soup seem exotic, but they are all available at Oriental food stores. This wonderful soup is worth an extra shopping trip. The ingredients may be used in many recipes.

NOTE: This soup is spicy hot. Reduce chili oil and white pepper for a milder soup.

10 large dried black mushrooms*

½ cup tree ear fungi*

⅓ cup tiger lily stems (golden needles)*

2 tablespoons cornstarch

3 tablespoons water

¾ cup diced uncooked chicken breast

1 tablespoon olive oil

1 tablespoon soy sauce

1 can (8 oz) bamboo shoots,* sliced

6 cups chicken stock, or 3 cans (10¾ oz each) chicken broth, strained, + 2 cans water

3 tablespoons white vinegar

1 tablespoon double black soy sauce**

2 cakes tofu (fresh bean curd),* cubed

2 teaspoons chili oil*

½–1 teaspoon ground white pepper

2 egg whites, beaten

4 green onions, sliced

Place mushrooms, tree ears, and tiger lily stems in a small bowl and cover with boiling water. In about 15 minutes or when they are soft, drain off the water and chop off stems or any hard parts.

Slice mushrooms and tree ears and pull tiger lily stems into shreds. Set aside.

Combine cornstarch and water into a smooth paste. Set aside.

In a heated wok or skillet, sauté chicken in oil until chicken is cooked through.

Stir in regular soy sauce.

Stir in mushrooms, tree ears, tiger lily stems, and bamboo shoots.

Add chicken stock, vinegar, and double black soy sauce.

Stir cornstarch mixture into soup. Let thicken.

Add tofu and bring soup to a boil.

Stir in the chili oil and white pepper.

Turn off the heat for 1 minute and then slowly pour the egg whites into the soup, stirring constantly.

Garnish each bowl of soup with chopped green onions.

Makes 10 one-cup servings
Per serving: 105 Total calories; 5 Sat-fat calories

---

*Available at Oriental food stores and some supermarkets
**If double black soy sauce is not available, make your own by mixing 2 teaspoons regular soy sauce with 1 teaspoon molasses.

Q

MULLIGATAWNY SOUP

Customarily, Mulligatawny Soup is made with cream. Our Mulligatawny Soup dispenses with the cream (at 335 sat-fat calories a cup) or cream substitute. The spicy flavors and interesting textures make this one of our favorite soups.

½ cup chopped onion
½ cup chopped carrot
½ cup chopped celery
2 tablespoons olive oil
1 tablespoon margarine
1½ tablespoons flour
2 teaspoons curry powder
5 cups chicken stock, or 2 cans
    (10 oz each) chicken broth,
    strained, + 2 cans water

½ cup diced uncooked chicken
1 apple, peeled and diced
½ cup cooked long-grain rice
¼ teaspoon thyme
1 teaspoon salt
¼ teaspoon freshly ground
    pepper

In a soup pot or large casserole, sauté onion, carrot, and celery in oil and margarine until vegetables are tender.

Stir in flour and curry powder and cook for about 1 minute.

Pour in chicken stock and bring to a boil.

Add chicken. Reduce heat, cover, and simmer for 15 minutes.

Add apple, rice, thyme, salt, and pepper and simmer for 15 minutes more.

Makes 6 one-cup servings
Per serving: 156 Total calories; 10 Sat-fat calories

Q   # MONHEGAN ISLAND FISH CHOWDER

Eating Monhegan Island Fish Chowder will show you that fish chowders need not be made with cream to be delicious. This chowder uses one large can of evaporated skim milk, which has 3 calories of saturated fat. A comparable amount of cream has 335 calories of saturated fat.

3 large potatoes (about 4 cups)
1 cup chopped onion
2 tablespoons margarine
2 cups water
1 teaspoon salt
1 teaspoon basil

¼ teaspoon freshly ground
   pepper
1 pound cod fillets
2 cups frozen corn kernels
1 large can (12 oz) evaporated
   skim milk

Scrub potatoes well and cut into bite-size pieces. *Do not peel.* Steam until just tender. Set aside.

In a large pot, sauté onion in margarine until tender.

Add potatoes, water, salt, basil, and pepper and bring to a boil. Reduce heat, cover, and simmer for 15 minutes.

Gently place cod fillets on top of potatoes, cover, and simmer until fish flakes easily (about 10 minutes).

Carefully stir in corn and evaporated milk. Heat until corn and milk are hot and serve. Do not allow soup to boil.

Makes 9 one-cup servings
Per serving: 172 Total calories; 5 Sat-fat calories

MILD FISH CHOWDER

2 cans (10¾ oz each) chicken
   broth, strained, + 2 cans
   water
3 cups cubed potatoes
2 tablespoons long-grain rice
½ cup sliced carrot
1 teaspoon dillweed
1 tablespoon margarine
1 cup sliced leeks

2 green onions, sliced
1 tablespoon unbleached white
   flour
1 cup frozen corn
⅓ pound mild white fish (such
   as turbot)
½ can (6½ oz) solid white
   albacore tuna packed in water

In a large pot, combine chicken broth, water, potatoes, rice, carrots, and dillweed.

In a skillet, melt margarine. Sauté leeks and green onions until soft. Mix in flour until smooth and remove from heat.

Add leek-flour mixture to soup.

Simmer soup until potatoes are fully cooked (about 20 minutes).

Stir in corn, fish, tuna, and tuna liquid. Cook 5 minutes more or until fish is fully cooked.

Makes 7 one-cup servings
Per serving: 181 Total calories; 4 Sat-fat calories

Ⓠ MINESTRONE

Almost every Italian restaurant in Italy offers its own minestrone, or vegetable soup. Each one is slightly different and all are wonderful. You can take whatever vegetables you have in the refrigerator, add some water or broth, pasta, rice and/or beans, and you have created your own minestrone.

½ onion, sliced	¼ cup long-grain rice
1 tablespoon olive oil	1 teaspoon basil
2 potatoes, diced	1 teaspoon oregano
4 carrots, sliced	½–1 teaspoon salt
2 celery stalks, sliced	1 can (15½ oz) kidney beans

In a soup pot or large casserole, sauté onion in olive oil until tender.

Mix in potatoes, carrots, and celery. Add water to cover.

Add rice, basil, oregano, salt, and kidney beans.

Bring to a boil. Reduce heat, cover, and simmer until rice is cooked and vegetables are tender (about 25 minutes).

Makes 8 one-cup servings
Per serving: 120 Total calories; 2 Sat-fat calories

VEGETABLE SOUP PROVENÇAL

A hearty Mediterranean soup with a distinctive taste. Use whatever vegetables you have on hand. The more the better! The secret ingredient is the pistou. Italy has its pesto and France has its pistou. Both sauces are combinations of basil, garlic, cheese (omitted here because it is so high in sat-fat), and olive oil, added to soups and pasta to enhance and enrich the flavor.

Make a lot of Vegetable Soup Provençal. It freezes well.

CAUTION: Reheat slowly.

1 large onion, chopped
3 cups chopped carrot
2–3 potatoes, diced
2½ quarts water
1–2 teaspoons salt
Any vegetables, such as:
   1 zucchini, sliced
   2 cups broccoli flowerets
   1 cup cauliflower flowerets
   2 cups green beans

2 slices stale bread, shredded
½ cup broken pieces of
   spaghetti

Pistou

8 cloves garlic, minced
⅓ cup chopped parsley
1 can (6 oz) tomato paste

3 tablespoons dried basil, or ½
   cup fresh basil
¼ cup olive oil

In a large soup pot, combine onion, carrot, and potato.

Add water and salt and heat to boiling. Reduce heat, cover, and simmer for 20 minutes.

Add zucchini, broccoli, cauliflower, green beans, any other vegetables of your choice, bread, and spaghetti and simmer, covered, for 15 minutes more.

Make pistou in food processor, blender, or with a fork by blending garlic, parsley, tomato paste, basil, and olive oil until smooth.

Stir the pistou into the soup, a little at a time.

Makes 15 one-cup servings
Per serving: 90 Total calories; 5 Sat-fat calories

GREEN PESTO SOUP

3 cups shredded spinach,
washed, stems removed
6 green onions, sliced
3 tablespoons margarine
1 cup shredded leaf lettuce
2 potatoes, peeled and diced
(about 2 cups)

8 cups water
1 teaspoon salt
¼ teaspoon freshly ground
pepper
1 cup broken pieces of thin
spaghetti

Pesto

2 cloves garlic
3 tablespoons olive oil
2 tablespoons basil
2 tablespoons chopped parsley

2 cups spinach, washed and
stems removed
½ cup water

In a soup pot, sauté spinach and green onions in margarine until tender.

Stir in lettuce, potatoes, water, salt, and pepper.

Cover pot and simmer until potatoes are tender (about 25 minutes).

Add spaghetti and bring soup to a boil. Reduce heat and simmer for 6 minutes.

Meanwhile, make pesto in a blender or food processor by blending garlic, olive oil, basil, parsley, spinach, and water until smooth.

Mix pesto into soup and serve.

Makes 11 one-cup servings
Per serving: 100 Total calories; 9 Sat-fat calories

BARLEY-VEGETABLE SOUP

½ cup pearl barley, washed
2 quarts homemade chicken
stock, or 3 cans (10¾ oz
each) chicken broth, strained,
+ 3 cans water
1 small onion, cut into fourths
1 carrot, cut into thirds
1 stalk celery, cut into 1 inch
slices

1 teaspoon thyme
1 bay leaf
Freshly ground pepper to taste
3–5 carrots, sliced
2 stalks celery, sliced
½ zucchini, sliced
½ cup onion, chopped
2 cups fresh spinach, chopped

Place barley, chicken stock, onion quarters, carrot thirds, celery slices, thyme, and bay leaf in a large soup pot and bring to a boil. Reduce heat, cover, and simmer for about 1 hour or until barley is tender.

Add sliced carrots, celery, zucchini, and chopped onion and cook until tender.

Add spinach a few minutes before serving.

Makes 9 one-cup servings
Per serving: 100 Total calories; Trace Sat-fat calories

Q ## LENTIL AND EVERYTHING BUT THE KITCHEN SINK SOUP

Lentils are legumes, which, besides tasting very good, are quite nutritious. They are rich in vitamin C, folic acid, and many minerals. They are a good source of soluble fiber, which has been found to lower blood cholesterol.

1 cup lentils	6 cups water
1 clove garlic, minced	1 cup tomato juice
2 stalks celery, sliced	1 teaspoon salt
½ cup chopped onion	1 teaspoon thyme
1 tablespoon margarine	1 tablespoon soy sauce
1 cup grated carrot	⅓ cup brown rice
1½–2 cups coarsely chopped potato	1½ cups frozen corn

Place lentils in a bowl and cover with water.

In a large pot, sauté garlic, celery, and onion in margarine until tender.

Stir in carrot and potatoes.

Drain water from lentils and add lentils to vegetables.

Add water, tomato juice, salt, thyme, soy sauce, and brown rice. Bring to a boil. Reduce heat, cover, and simmer until lentils and potatoes are tender (about 30 minutes).

Add corn and cook 10 to 20 minutes more.

Makes 10 one-cup servings
Per serving: 82 Total calories; 2 Sat-fat calories

Q TORTILLA SOUP

This is an instantaneous soup that always gets rave reviews.

6 corn tortillas*
1 medium onion, diced
3 cloves garlic, minced
1 tablespoon olive oil
2 tablespoons chili powder
1 teaspoon oregano

1 large can (28 oz) heavy
  concentrated crushed
  tomatoes
1 can (10¾ oz) chicken broth,
  strained, + 1 can water
1 green pepper, diced
1 cup frozen corn
Salt and pepper to taste

About 15 minutes before you serve soup, heat tortillas in a slow oven (325°F), until crisp.

In a soup pot, sauté onion and garlic in oil until soft.

Stir in chili powder and oregano.

Stir in tomatoes, chicken broth, and water.

Bring to a boil and simmer for a few minutes.

Add green pepper and corn.

Add salt and pepper to taste.

For each serving, break a tortilla into small pieces and place at the bottom of a soup bowl. Ladle soup over the tortilla and serve.

Makes 7 one-cup servings
Per serving: 155 Total calories; 4 Sat-fat calories

Q CANTALOUPE SOUP

Cantaloupes are excellent sources of vitamins A and C and fiber as well as being just plain delicious. Combined with ginger, orange juice, and buttermilk, cantaloupe makes a refreshing and unusual summer soup.

2 cantaloupes, chilled if possible
¼ cup orange juice
1 teaspoon chopped ginger root

3 tablespoons sweet vermouth
½ cup buttermilk

---

*Corn tortillas can be found in the refrigerator section of most supermarkets. Be sure they contain no lard or other saturated fat.

Halve melons, discard seeds, scoop out meat, and place it in blender.

Add orange juice, ginger, vermouth, and buttermilk, and blend.

If cold, serve immediately. Otherwise, chill.

Makes 6 one-cup servings
Per serving: 80 Total calories; 1 Sat-fat calorie

Q   CHILLED STRAWBERRY SOUP

Ron says this soup should be in the dessert section. It is sweet and refreshing and easy to make.

2 oranges, peeled and thinly sliced	2 cups sliced strawberries*
1 cinnamon stick	Dash of salt
2 cups water	1 ½ tablespoons cornstarch
¼ cup sugar	1 tablespoon water

Simmer orange pieces and cinnamon stick in 2 cups of water for 5 minutes.

Remove the cinnamon stick and set aside.

Add sugar, strawberries, and a dash of salt and bring to a boil. Turn heat to low.

Blend cornstarch with 1 tablespoon water and stir into soup until clear.

Chill with cinnamon stick.

Makes 5 one-cup servings
Per serving: 90 Total calories; 0 Sat-fat calories

---

*Try peaches, cherries, apricots, or a combination of fruits.

Q

VEGETABLE SOUP WITH SPINACH, POTATOES, RICE, AND CORN

2 cloves garlic, minced
1 tablespoon olive oil
5 ounces fresh spinach, torn
  into bite-size pieces
1 can chicken broth (10¾ oz),
  strained, + 2 cans water

½ teaspoon salt, optional
2 small potatoes, peeled and
  cubed
¼ cup long-grain rice
1 cup frozen corn

In soup pot, sauté garlic in oil until soft.

Stir in spinach and cook for about 1 minute.

Add broth, water, salt, potatoes, and rice, and bring to a boil.

Reduce to a simmer and cook for about 15 minutes or until potatoes are tender and rice is cooked.

Add corn and cook for about 1 minute.

Makes 5 one-cup servings
Per serving: 145 Total calories; 4 Sat-fat calories

Q

ORIENTAL NOODLE SOUP

Also a great last-minute soup. The dried Chinese noodles can be stored forever. The tofu and snow peas should be fresh.

2 cans chicken broth (10¾ oz
  each), strained, + 2 cans
  water
2 ounces cellophane noodles*
1 tablespoon soy sauce

¼ teaspoon white pepper
1 cake tofu,* cubed
1 green onion, sliced
10–15 snow peas

Bring broth and water to a boil in a soup pot. Add cellophane noodles.

Simmer about 10 minutes, until noodles are soft.

Add soy sauce and white pepper. Simmer a minute or two.

Add tofu, green onion, and snow peas and serve.

Makes 6 one-cup servings
Per serving: 64 Total calories; 1 Sat-fat calorie

---

*Available at Oriental food stores and some supermarkets.

CUBAN BLACK BEAN SOUP

Beans are an excellent source of protein, soluble fiber, calcium, magnesium, phosphorus, potassium, iron, and zinc. Experiment with different types of beans to make this hearty, tasty soup. Spoon it over rice and top it with chopped onions.

½ pound dried black beans
2 cloves garlic, minced
1 large onion, chopped
1 green pepper, chopped
1 tablespoon olive oil
1 teaspoon cumin

1 teaspoon oregano
1 teaspoon salt, optional
1¼ cups cooked rice
½ cup chopped onions, for garnish
2½ teaspoons vinegar

Cover black beans with cold water and soak overnight, or cover beans with boiling water and let soak for 4 hours.

Drain the beans and place in soup pot. Add water to cover. Simmer until tender (about 1–1½ hours).

In a medium skillet, sauté garlic, onions, and green pepper in olive oil until tender.

Stir in cumin, oregano, and salt. Add 1 tablespoon of water and simmer for one more minute to blend flavors.

Add vegetable mixture to beans.

Place ¼ cup of rice in each soup bowl. Spoon soup over rice. Top with chopped onions and sprinkle ½ teaspoon of vinegar over each bowl.

Makes 5 one-cup servings
Per serving: 215 Total calories; 4 Sat-fat calories

15 CHICKEN

CHICKEN IS ONE of the most versatile meats. You can sauté it, bake it, broil it, boil it, roast it, or make it into chicken salad, chicken pot pie, or chicken brochettes. You can cook it with fruit, vegetables, grains, wine, herbs, or spices and it will be different and delicious each time.

Almost all of the following recipes use chicken breasts without skin. Chicken breast without skin is the preferred chicken choice for anyone concerned about saturated fat intake. Both thighs and drumsticks without skin are low in saturated fat (8 calories of sat-fat per ounce for a thigh, which amounts to about 14 sat-fat calories per thigh or 28 sat-fat calories for two thighs. There are 4 calories of sat-fat per ounce for a drumstick, which amounts to 6 sat-fat calories per drumstick or 12 sat-fat calories for 2). However, chicken breasts are even lower (3 calories of sat-fat per ounce, which amounts to about 8 sat-fat calories per breast) and more versatile. If you do substitute chicken thighs or drumsticks in any of the recipes, make sure you adjust the total sat-fat values to reflect that change.

Chicken breasts may be purchased with bones or already boned. You may have avoided buying *boneless* chicken breasts without skin because of their expense. However, the skin and bones of a chicken breast account for half their weight. You are paying much more for chicken breasts with skin and bones than you think. Look for boned chicken breasts without skin on sale for a real bargain.

NOTE: It is easier to slice chicken when it is slightly frozen. If you do not mind unusual-looking chicken pieces, the following advice will save you time. Slice frozen (but not rock-hard frozen) boneless chicken breasts without skin lengthwise into 1½-inch-wide chunks. Feed into food processor using the thickest slicer you have. Sauté the chicken in oil and freeze for later use.

If you use canned chicken broth in any of these recipes, either strain the broth (pour it through a fine tea strainer) or, if the fat is hardened, lift it off the surface of the broth with a spoon.

▣ INDONESIAN CHICKEN WITH GREEN BEANS

A beautiful dish — green beans set against ochre-colored sauce — and very tasty. This is one of our all-time favorites.

6 boned and skinned chicken breast halves, cut into bite-size pieces

4 tablespoons olive oil

10 cloves garlic, minced

1 tablespoon minced ginger root

1 small onion, chopped

1 pound green beans, washed and cut into bite-size pieces

Juice of 1 lime (preferred) or lemon

1 tablespoon double black soy sauce*

2 teaspoons brown sugar

2 teaspoons turmeric

1 teaspoon salt

½ cup water

Sauté chicken in 2 tablespoons of the olive oil until chicken turns white and is cooked through. Set aside.

Heat the remaining 2 tablespoons olive oil and sauté garlic, ginger, and onion until soft.

Add green beans. Stir until green beans turn bright green.

Add lime juice, soy sauce, brown sugar, turmeric, salt, and ¼ cup of the water.

Slowly add remaining water, if necessary, but sauce should not be watery.

Add chicken pieces and stir until completely covered with sauce. Serve over rice.

Serves 8
Per serving: 200 Total calories; 15 Sat-fat calories

---

*Double black soy sauce is available at Oriental food stores and some supermarkets. You can make your own by mixing 2 teaspoons soy sauce with 1 teaspoon dark molasses.

⟨Q⟩   # LEMON CHICKEN

A delicate blending of tart and sweet, Lemon Chicken can't help but become one of your most popular family or company dishes.

8 boned and skinned chicken
   breast halves
Juice of 2½ lemons
2 tablespoons margarine
1 tablespoon olive oil
1 cup unbleached white flour
1 teaspoon salt
½ teaspoon paprika

¼ teaspoon freshly ground
   pepper
2 tablespoons grated lemon peel
¼ cup brown sugar
2 tablespoons fresh lemon juice
   + 2 tablespoons water
1–2 lemons, sliced thin

Place chicken in a bowl or casserole. Cover with lemon juice and marinate in refrigerator for several hours or overnight, turning chicken periodically.

Preheat oven to 425°F.

Put margarine and olive oil in a shallow baking pan and place in oven until margarine melts (about 5 minutes).

Meanwhile, combine flour, salt, paprika, and pepper in plastic bag.

Remove chicken breasts from marinade and coat each with flour by shaking it in the plastic bag.

Remove baking pan from oven and lower heat to 350°F.

Place chicken in the baking pan in a single layer.

Either peel the yellow (zest) from two lemons and chop it fine with the brown sugar in your food processor, or grate the zest and mix it with the brown sugar.

Sprinkle the lemon zest–sugar mixture evenly over the chicken breasts. Combine lemon juice and water and sprinkle evenly over chicken.

Put 1 lemon slice on each chicken breast and bake chicken for 35–40 minutes or until it is cooked through.

Serves 8
Per serving: 223 Total calories; 15 Sat-fat calories

LIME-PEANUT-GINGER CHICKEN

8 boned and skinned chicken
  breast halves
½ cup fresh lime juice
1 clove garlic
1 tablespoon sliced ginger root
1 teaspoon whole peppercorns
1 teaspoon dried basil
1 tablespoon soy sauce
1 tablespoon white vinegar
1 teaspoon honey
1 tablespoon water

1 tablespoon grated lemon peel
5 tablespoons olive oil
1 tablespoon sesame oil
2 tablespoons natural all-peanut
  peanut butter
2–3 cups sliced mushrooms
1 tablespoon cornstarch diluted
  in 2 tablespoons water
¼–½ cup sliced green onions

Cut chicken into bite-size pieces and marinate in lime juice for at least 2 hours in refrigerator.

Make a dressing by chopping garlic, ginger, and peppercorns in food processor or blender until pepper is no longer whole. (It will probably be impossible to break up all peppercorns.)

Blend in basil, soy sauce, vinegar, honey, water, and grated lemon peel.

Pour 2 tablespoons of the olive oil into the processor or blender and process until smooth. Set dressing aside.

Remove chicken from marinade and sauté it in sesame oil and the remaining 3 tablespoons of olive oil until it turns white.

Add dressing and stir until chicken is well coated and sauce is warm.

Mix in peanut butter. Stir in mushrooms. Add cornstarch mixture to thicken sauce.

Sprinkle green onions on top and serve over rice.

Serves 10
Per serving: 221 Total calories; 19 Sat-fat calories

Q

CHICKEN KIEV

This recipe is a gem: it uses ingredients you probably have on hand; it takes no time to make; and the resulting dish is so special you can proudly serve it to the most discriminating of guests.

2 cloves garlic, finely chopped
1 teaspoon basil
1 teaspoon oregano
½ teaspoon salt
2 cups fine bread crumbs made from 3–4 slices of white bread or challah*

½ cup margarine
8 boned and skinned chicken breast halves
¼ cup dry white wine or vermouth
¼ cup sliced green onions

Preheat oven to 375°F.

Mix garlic, basil, oregano, and salt with bread crumbs and place on a large plate. (You can mince the garlic in a food processor, add bread slices and process until they become crumbs, then add spices and process again.)

Melt ¼ cup of the margarine. Dip each chicken breast in the melted margarine, roll it in bread crumbs, and place it in a shallow baking pan.

Bake near center of oven for 50–60 minutes or until fully cooked.

Melt the remaining ¼ cup margarine. Mix in wine and green onions.

Pour sauce over chicken.

Return chicken to oven for 3–5 minutes or until sauce is hot. Serve over rice.

Serves 8
Per serving: 256 Total calories; 27 Sat-fat calories

---

*Avoid commercial bread crumbs. They are high in total calories (390 per cup) and high in saturated fat calories (14 per cup). Use your food processor or blender to make your own bread crumbs from a few slices of bread (about 65 total calories and 2 sat-fat calories per slice).

⃞Q⃞ INDONESIAN PEANUT CHICKEN

Peanuts are a major ingredient in Indonesian cooking. The spicy peanut sauce that covers this chicken dish is called a satay. The satay may also be used as a dip for vegetables or slices of cold chicken.

6 boned and skinned chicken breast halves	3 tablespoons olive oil

Satay sauce

1 clove garlic	1 teaspoon turmeric
1 small onion	Juice of 1 lime or lemon
1-inch piece ginger root	1–3 hot chili peppers
1 cup shelled roasted peanuts, unsalted	1 cup water
	1 large onion, sliced
1 tablespoon soy sauce	1 tablespoon olive oil

Cut chicken into bite-size pieces. (Cutting the chicken into small pieces takes a few minutes, but everything else is quick and easy. You may also keep the chicken pieces whole and bake them covered with the satay sauce.)

Sauté chicken in olive oil until white and cooked through. Set aside.

Blend garlic, onion, ginger, peanuts, soy sauce, turmeric, lime or lemon juice, chili peppers, and water in blender or food processor until smooth.

Place sauce in top of double boiler and heat water to boiling. Cover pot and cook sauce for 20 minutes or until thick.

Sauté onion rings in olive oil until soft.

Pour satay sauce over chicken and stir until chicken is well coated. Stir in onion rings and serve over rice.

Serves 10
Per serving: 230 Total calories; 20 Sat-fat calories

Ⓠ
TANDOORI CHICKEN

2 cloves garlic, minced
1 tablespoon sliced ginger root
¼ cup chopped onion
1 teaspoon Dijon mustard
¼ teaspoon cardamom
¼ teaspoon coriander

½ teaspoon salt
¼ teaspoon pepper
3 tablespoons fresh lemon juice
1½ cups nonfat yogurt
8 skinned chicken breast halves

Combine all ingredients except chicken (may be done in food processor, mincing garlic and ginger first) and pour over chicken breasts.

Marinate in refrigerator for at least 24 hours.

Place chicken with marinade in a shallow baking pan.

Bake at 375°F for 40 minutes or until chicken is fully cooked.

Serves 8
Per serving: 165 Total calories; 8 Sat-fat calories

Ⓠ
CHICKEN WITH APPLES AND ONIONS

6 skinned chicken breast halves
1 cup sliced onion
1 tablespoon olive oil
2 cups sliced tart apples

1 tablespoon margarine
1½ cups apple juice
2 tablespoons honey
½–1 teaspoon salt

Preheat oven to 350°F.

Place chicken breasts in a shallow baking pan.

In a skillet, sauté onions in olive oil until tender. Add apples and sauté for 1 more minute.

Pour onions and apples over chicken.

Melt margarine in a small saucepan. Combine apple juice, honey, salt, and margarine and pour over chicken and vegetables.

Bake for 45 minutes or until chicken is cooked through.

Serves 6
Per serving: 258 Total calories; 14 Sat-fat calories

▢ CHICKEN SMOTHERED IN VEGETABLES

8 boned and skinned chicken
   breast halves
½ cup unbleached white flour
1 teaspoon salt
¼ teaspoon freshly ground
   pepper
¼ cup olive oil

2 cloves garlic, minced
1½ cups sliced onion
1 green pepper, sliced
2 cups sliced mushrooms
2 teaspoons oregano
10 cherry tomatoes or 3 whole
   tomatoes, sliced

Preheat oven to 375°F. Grease a shallow baking pan with margarine.

Cut each chicken breast into four pieces.

Coat chicken by shaking in a plastic bag with flour, salt, and pepper.

Place chicken in baking pan and grind additional pepper over it.

In a large skillet, sauté garlic and onion in oil until soft.

Stir in green pepper, mushrooms, and oregano and cook for 1 minute.

Add tomatoes.

Pour vegetables over chicken and bake for 45 minutes or until chicken is fully cooked.

Serves 8
Per serving: 242 Total calories; 16 Sat-fat calories

▢ PEPPERY CHICKEN

A very peppery chicken that tastes good grilled or roasted in the oven.

8 skinned chicken breast halves
2 tablespoons olive oil
2 tablespoons soy sauce
2 tablespoons honey
½ teaspoon thyme
½ teaspoon paprika

¼ teaspoon cayenne pepper
1 tablespoon white vinegar
½ teaspoon allspice
1 teaspoon freshly ground
   pepper
2 cups sliced mushrooms

Preheat oven to 375°F.
Place chicken in a shallow casserole.

Combine olive oil, soy sauce, honey, thyme, paprika, cayenne pepper, vinegar, allspice, and pepper and pour over chicken. Marinate in refrigerator for about 1 hour.

Bake chicken for 30–45 minutes or until cooked through.

Surround chicken with sliced mushrooms, spoon the sauce over them, and bake 5 minutes more.

For grilling: remove breasts from marinade and grill until cooked through, basting periodically with marinade.

Add mushrooms to the marinade and simmer for 5 minutes. Spoon over grilled chicken breasts.

Serves 8
Per serving: 180 Total calories; 12 Sat-fat calories

Q MA-PO BEAN CURD

This dish may be used as a main dish although it barely has any meat (chicken) in it. It is extremely tasty.

2 tablespoons olive oil
1 tablespoon minced ginger root
2 boned and skinned chicken breast halves, ground (can be ground in food processor)
3 cakes tofu (fresh bean curd),* cubed
½ cup water
1½ tablespoons soy sauce

½ teaspoon sugar
1–3 teaspoons chili paste with garlic*
1 tablespoon fermented black beans*
1 tablespoon cornstarch mixed with 2 tablespoons water
½ tablespoon sesame oil*
2 tablespoons sliced green onion

*Available at Oriental food stores and some supermarkets

Heat a wok or large skillet to hot. Add olive oil and sauté ginger until fragrant (about 10 seconds).

Add chicken and stir until it turns white.

Stir in tofu, water, soy sauce, and sugar.

Reduce heat, cover, and simmer for 5–10 minutes.

Uncover and stir in chili paste with garlic and fermented black beans.

Raise heat and stir in cornstarch mixture and sesame oil until sauce thickens.

Stir in green onion and serve over rice.

Serves 6
Per serving: 150 Total calories; 13 Sat-fat calories

CHICKEN COUSCOUS

Couscous is the national dish of the Maghreb region of Morocco, Algeria, and Tunisia. The grain, made from semolina, is eaten as a cereal, as a main dish with meat and vegetables, and as a dessert with fruit and nuts. Our Chicken Couscous combines interesting textures and exotic tastes to create a complete meal in one dish.

6 boned and skinned chicken breast halves, cut into bite-size pieces	½ teaspoon paprika
	3 tablespoons slivered almonds
1 cup sliced carrot	2 cups sliced onion
½ cup sliced celery	2 tablespoons olive oil
2 small turnips, quartered	1 teaspoon coriander
1 cup dry white wine or vermouth	¼ cup raisins
	1½ cups chopped tomatoes
1 teaspoon thyme	1 teaspoon cinnamon
½ teaspoon rosemary	2 cups quick-cooking couscous
½ teaspoon salt	1 tablespoon margarine

In a large casserole, combine chicken, carrots, celery, turnips, wine, thyme, rosemary, salt, paprika, and water to cover.

Bring to a boil, reduce heat, and simmer, covered, until chicken is cooked (about 20 minutes).

Meanwhile, in a medium skillet, toast almonds over low heat until golden. Remove and set aside.

In same skillet, cook onion in olive oil over low heat, covered, until soft, stirring often.

Mix in coriander and raisins and cook slowly for 5 minutes more. Set aside.

When chicken is finished cooking, pour out all but about ½ cup of the liquid.

Add tomatoes and cinnamon to the chicken mixture and mix well. Cook, covered, for 5 minutes more.

Make couscous according to package directions. It takes about 5 minutes. (Add 1 tablespoon margarine instead of any amount of butter they suggest.)

Reheat onion-raisin mixture and sprinkle almonds over it.

Place couscous on a large platter. Cover with onions. Top with chicken and vegetables. Spoon on remaining sauce from casserole.

Serves 10
Per serving: 304 Total calories; 13 Sat-fat calories

Q APRICOT CHICKEN DIVINE

One-half cup of nonfat yogurt (0 sat-fat calories, 55 total calories) replaces ½ cup of sour cream (135 sat-fat calories, 247 total calories) to create this divine chicken.

2 tablespoons margarine	⅓–½ cup apricot preserves
2 tablespoons olive oil	1 tablespoon Dijon mustard
8 skinned chicken breast halves	½ cup nonfat yogurt
½ cup unbleached white flour	2 tablespoons slivered almonds
1 teaspoon salt	

Preheat oven to 375°F.

Melt margarine with oil in a shallow baking pan.

Meanwhile, shake chicken in a plastic bag filled with flour and salt until chicken is coated.

Place chicken in a single layer in the baking pan and bake for 25 minutes.

Combine apricot preserves, mustard, and yogurt.

Spread apricot mixture on chicken and bake for 30 minutes more or until done.

Just before serving, brown almonds lightly in toaster oven. Sprinkle almonds over chicken and serve over rice.

Serves 8
Per serving: 280 Total calories; 18 Sat-fat calories

Q   GRILLED APRICOT-GINGER CHICKEN

1½ cups dried apricots	¼–½ teaspoon cayenne pepper
Juice of 1 lemon (about ¼ cup)	½–1 teaspoon salt
2 cloves garlic, minced	2 tablespoons olive oil
1 teaspoon minced ginger root	10 skinned chicken breast
½–1 teaspoon cardamom	halves

In a small saucepan, place apricots and add water to cover. Add lemon juice, bring to a boil, reduce heat, and simmer until tender.

In a blender or food processor, purée apricots and liquid with garlic, ginger, cardamom, cayenne pepper, salt, and olive oil. Add more water if too thick. Score the chicken breasts several times on each side. Cover with the apricot mixture and marinate in refrigerator for several hours or overnight.

Remove chicken from marinade and reserve marinade.

Preheat oven to broil or prepare grill.

Broil or grill chicken until cooked through.

Heat marinade and spoon over chicken.

Serve over rice.

Serves 10
Per serving: 214 Total calories; 11 Sat-fat calories

Q ## SESAME CHICKEN BROCHETTES

6 boned and skinned chicken
  breast halves
¼ cup soy sauce
¼ cup olive oil
½ cup dry white wine or
  vermouth

1 clove garlic, minced
3 tablespoons sesame seeds,
  lightly toasted

Cut chicken breasts into 1-inch cubes and place in a bowl or casserole.

Combine soy sauce, olive oil, wine, and garlic and pour over chicken. Marinate in refrigerator for at least 30 minutes.

Preheat oven to broil or prepare grill.

Remove chicken from marinade and reserve marinade.

Skewer chicken and broil or grill until cooked through, basting occasionally with marinade.

Roll chicken in sesame seeds and serve over rice.

Heat marinade and spoon over chicken and rice.

Serves 6
Per serving: 268 Total calories; 22 Sat-fat calories

Q ## CHICKEN WITH RICE,
TOMATOES, AND ARTICHOKES

4 boned and skinned chicken
  breast halves
2 cloves garlic, minced
½ cup chopped onion
2 tablespoons olive oil
1 large can (28 oz) tomatoes,
  chopped
2 cups water

½ teaspoon thyme
½ teaspoon oregano
1 teaspoon salt
¼ teaspoon freshly ground
  pepper
1 bay leaf
2 cups uncooked long-grain rice
1 jar (11½ oz) artichoke hearts,
  packed in water

Cut chicken into bite-size pieces and set aside.

In a large casserole, sauté garlic and onion in olive oil until soft.

Stir in tomatoes and their liquid, water, thyme, oregano, salt, pepper, and bay leaf and bring to a boil.

Add chicken and rice, cover casserole, and reduce heat to low.

Cook for 25 minutes or until rice is tender, most liquid is absorbed, and chicken is cooked through.

Stir in artichokes and serve.

Serves 8
Per serving: 320 Total calories; 10 Sat-fat calories

BAGHDAD CHICKEN

¾ cup chopped onion
2 teaspoons garam masala*
2 tablespoons olive oil
⅓ cup uncooked long-grain rice
⅔ cup water
3 tablespoons raisins
3 tablespoons chopped peanuts

¼ cup nonfat yogurt
8 boned and skinned chicken
  breast halves
Salt and freshly ground pepper
  to taste
4 cups cooked long-grain rice
  (optional)

Preheat oven to 375°F.

Sauté onion in garam masala and olive oil until soft. Stir in rice.

Add water, cover saucepan, and cook over low heat until liquid is absorbed (about 20 minutes).

Remove from heat. Stir in raisins, peanuts, and yogurt. Let cool.

Flatten chicken breasts between two sheets of wax paper. Salt and pepper chicken.

Put a portion of the rice mixture in the center of each breast.

Bring together the sides of the breast to enclose the rice.

Place the breast seam-side down in a shallow casserole.

Bake until chicken is cooked through (about 45 minutes).

Combine any rice mixture you have remaining with plain rice and serve on the side.

Serves 8
Per serving: 238 Total calories; 14 Sat-fat calories

---

*Available at specialty food stores. Or make your own by combining ½ teaspoon ground cloves, ¾ teaspoon ground cardamom, and ¾ teaspoon cinnamon.

☑ CHINESE CHICKEN

6 tablespoons soy sauce
  (approximately)
¼ cup dry sherry
1 clove garlic
3 or 4 shakes ground ginger or 1
  thin slice ginger root
½ cup + 1 tablespoon sugar
  (approximately)

5–6 star anise*
2 cups water (approximately)
10 boned and skinned chicken
  breast halves**
2 tablespoons soy sauce
1 tablespoon sugar

Place ¼ cup soy sauce, sherry, garlic, ginger, ½ cup sugar, star anise, and 1 cup of the water in an electric frying pan (or large frying pan). Add chicken in one layer and cook over medium heat for 20 minutes. Sauce will be thick.

Turn chicken. Add remaining 1 cup water, 2 tablespoons soy sauce, and 1 tablespoon sugar.

Taste. If too salty, add more sugar. If too sweet, add more soy sauce.

Cook for 30 minutes more or until chicken is cooked through. Keep adding water when sauce gets too thick. Periodically turn chicken. Keep tasting sauce and add soy sauce or sugar if necessary.

Chicken should be a deep brown.

Serves 10

	Total calories	Sat-fat calories
1 breast	196	7
1 thigh	161	13
1 drumstick	132	6

*Available at Oriental food stores and some supermarkets

**You may substitute chicken thighs or drumsticks without skin for some of the chicken breasts.

PHYLLO CHICKEN WITH RICE, ARTICHOKES, AND CREAM SAUCE

What a wonderful combination of tastes and textures! This very elegant chicken can be made a day ahead and refrigerated. (We recommend that you do make this chicken dish ahead because it involves many steps. To cook it along with all the other dishes that comprise a dinner will make you a nervous wreck and frazzled host.)

Phyllo dough that has been stored in the freezer has to be thawed in the refrigerator 8 hours or overnight and then set out at room temperature for 2–4 hours before using. Take this into account when planning to cook this dish.

Chicken

10 boned and skinned chicken
   breast halves
1 cup dry white wine or
   vermouth

1 teaspoon salt
1½ teaspoons thyme
½ teaspoon rosemary
1 bay leaf

Rice

3 tablespoons margarine
2 cloves garlic, minced
½ cup chopped onion

½ pound sliced mushrooms
¾ cup long-grain rice

Cream Sauce

3 tablespoons margarine
¼ cup unbleached white flour

½ cup skim milk

Assembly

1 package (9 oz) frozen
   artichoke hearts, thawed, or 1
   jar (11½ oz) artichoke hearts,
   packed in water and drained

3 tablespoons margarine
16 sheets phyllo dough,*
   thawed (usually comes in
   16-oz package)

---

*Available at Greek or Mideast food stores or in the freezer section of many supermarkets

The Chicken and Broth

In a large pot, combine chicken, wine, salt, thyme, rosemary, bay leaf, and water to cover. Bring to a boil. Reduce heat, cover, and simmer for 25 minutes or until chicken is cooked through.

Remove chicken and cut into bite-size pieces. Set aside.

Boil chicken broth gently, uncovered, until it is reduced to about 3½ cups.

Set aside and make the rice.

The Rice

In a large saucepan, melt margarine.

Add garlic, onion, and mushrooms and cook until tender.

Stir in rice.

Add 1½ cups of the reduced chicken broth. Simmer, covered, until liquid is absorbed (about 20 minutes).

While rice is cooking, make the cream sauce.

The Cream Sauce

Melt margarine over low heat.

Stir in the flour and cook until bubbly.

Remove from heat and slowly stir in remaining 2 cups of broth.

Gradually add skim milk. Return to low heat and stir until thick.

Back to the Rice and Chicken

When the rice is cooked, stir in the artichoke hearts and 1 cup of the cream sauce. Set aside.

Stir remaining cream sauce into chicken pieces. Set aside.

Putting It All Together

Preheat oven to 350°F.

Grease a 9 × 13-inch baking pan with margarine.

Melt the 3 tablespoons margarine.

Unfold phyllo leaves. Cover with plastic or damp towel.

Place 1 phyllo sheet into bottom of pan. Brush lightly with melted margarine.

Repeat procedure with 6 more sheets of phyllo.

Spread half of the rice mixture over phyllo dough.

Spread chicken over rice mixture.

Spread remaining rice mixture over chicken.

Cover with 6 sheets of phyllo, brushing with margarine between each sheet.

Tuck in edges of last sheet and brush the top with margarine.

Cut lightly through 3 or 4 layers of phyllo dough to indicate pieces to be cut later.

Bake chicken for 45 minutes or until golden brown and bubbly. Or refrigerate it for up to 24 hours and bake later for 60 minutes.

Serves 12
Per serving: 303 Total calories; 21 Sat-fat calories

CUBAN CHICKEN

2 potatoes, peeled and cubed
1 tablespoon margarine
1 tablespoon olive oil
6 boned and skinned chicken
   breast halves, cut into thirds
½ cup unbleached white flour
⅓ cup water
1 large can (28 oz) tomatoes
   with juice

1 large green pepper, chopped
¾ cup chopped onion
2 cloves garlic, minced
¾ teaspoon oregano
¾ teaspoon cumin
½ teaspoon salt
¼ cup raisins
½ cup stuffed green olives

Preheat oven to 425°F.

Place potatoes in a saucepan, cover with water, and boil for 10 minutes.

Put margarine and olive oil in shallow baking pan and place in oven until margarine melts.

Shake chicken breasts, one at a time, in a plastic bag filled with flour until breast is completely coated.

Arrange floured chicken in baking pan in one layer. Add water. Place potatoes evenly over chicken.

Reduce heat to 375°F and bake chicken for 20 minutes.

Meanwhile, chop tomatoes either in food processor or by hand and place them with juice in a large bowl.

Add green pepper, onion, garlic, oregano, cumin, salt, raisins, and olives.

Spread tomato mixture over chicken and bake for 20 minutes more or until chicken is fully cooked.

Serve over rice.

Serves 6
Per serving: 300 Total calories; 18 Sat-fat calories

Ｑ LEMON-MUSTARD CHICKEN

6 skinned chicken breast halves
¼ cup margarine
3 tablespoons Dijon mustard

3 tablespoons fresh lemon juice
1 teaspoon tarragon
½ teaspoon salt

Preheat oven to 375°F.
Place chicken in a shallow baking pan.
In a small saucepan, melt margarine. Stir in mustard, lemon juice, tarragon, and salt. Pour over chicken.
Bake chicken for 45 minutes or until cooked through.
Spoon sauce from pan over chicken.

Serves 6
Per serving: 204 Total calories; 20 Sat-fat calories

COQ AU VIN

2 whole frying chickens
¼ cup olive oil
¼ cup cognac or brandy
2 cups full-bodied red wine (*not* Hearty Burgundy)
1 can (10¾ oz) chicken broth, strained
2 cloves garlic, minced

1 teaspoon salt
1 bay leaf
½ teaspoon thyme
12 small white onions, peeled
½–1 pound mushrooms
4 tablespoons margarine
3 tablespoons unbleached white flour

Cut chickens into parts and remove skin. If you cannot remove the skin from a part (such as the wings) do not use that part.
In a large casserole, brown chicken on all sides in olive oil.
Pour cognac over chicken and ignite it. Shake pan while cognac is burning.
When flame subsides, add wine, chicken broth, garlic, salt, bay leaf, thyme, and onions and simmer, covered, until chicken is tender (about 25 minutes).
Remove chicken from casserole and cover to keep warm.
Boil liquid in casserole until it is reduced to about 3 cups (about 10 minutes). Remove from heat.
Sauté mushrooms in 2 tablespoons of the margarine for about 1 minute and set aside.

Make a paste of the remaining 2 tablespoons margarine and the flour.

Mix the paste into the reduced liquid in the casserole. Reheat slowly until liquid is thickened.

Return chicken and mushrooms to casserole and heat through.

Serve over noodles (shells, rotini, etc.).

Serves 10

	Total calories	Sat-fat calories
1 chicken breast half	230	14
1 drumstick	164	13
1 thigh	193	20

Q PINEAPPLE CHICKEN

2 tablespoons margarine
2 tablespoons olive oil
1 cup unbleached white flour
1 teaspoon salt
1 teaspoon paprika
¼ teaspoon freshly ground
  pepper

8 skinned chicken breast halves
1 can (20 oz) pineapple chunks
  in heavy syrup
½ cup sliced green pepper
2 green onions, sliced
1 tablespoon brown sugar
¼ cup dry sherry

Preheat oven to 425°F.

In a large shallow baking pan, melt margarine with oil in the oven. Remove pan.

Combine flour, salt, paprika, and pepper in a plastic bag.

Piece by piece, coat chicken by shaking it in the bag with the seasoned flour.

Arrange floured chicken in baking pan in one layer. Bake at 425°F for 20 minutes. Turn chicken.

Combine pineapple, green pepper, green onions, brown sugar, and sherry and pour over chicken.

Lower heat to 375°F and bake until chicken is golden brown and sauce is thick (about 45 minutes).

Serves 8
Per serving: 275 Total calories; 17 Sat-fat calories

CREAMY CHICKEN PIE

Creamy Chicken Pie is so rich and creamy you will think you are eating something that is clogging your arteries. Not so! Low-fat cottage cheese is the secret ingredient. This recipe is great for using up leftover turkey or chicken.

Partially baked nonsweet pie
   crust (page 330)
3 tablespoons margarine
½ cup chopped onion
3 cups sliced mushrooms
3 tablespoons unbleached white
   flour
1 cup low-fat (1%) cottage
   cheese

2 cups diced cooked chicken or
   turkey breast
⅓ cup chopped parsley
¼ teaspoon freshly ground
   pepper
¼ teaspoon rosemary

Prepare partially cooked nonsweet pastry for pie bottom crust but use 1¾ cups flour, and ⅓ cup margarine. Refrigerate remaining dough.

Preheat oven to 375°F.

In a large skillet, melt margarine over medium heat.

Cook onion and mushrooms until most liquid has evaporated.

Stir in flour and cook until bubbly. Remove skillet from heat.

Stir in cottage cheese, chicken, parsley, pepper, and rosemary.

Spoon chicken mixture into partially baked pie shell.

Roll out extra dough and cut it into strips. Place over chicken, making a lattice top.

Bake for 45 minutes or until crust is golden brown.

Serves 7
Per serving: 175 Total calories; 29 Sat-fat calories

KUNG PAO CHICKEN
WITH BROCCOLI

Most Chinese cooking is low-fat. Vegetables or rice are mixed with small amounts of poultry or other meats to create tantalizing combinations of textures and tastes. This recipe calls for some exotic ingredients, which are available at Oriental food stores and may be stored forever (almost) in the refrigerator or pantry.

1 egg white
1 tablespoon cornstarch
6 boned and skinned chicken breast halves, cut into bite-size pieces
4 tablespoons bean sauce*
2 tablespoons hoisin sauce*
1 tablespoon chili paste with garlic*
1½ teaspoons sugar

2 tablespoons dry sherry
2 tablespoons white vinegar
4 cloves garlic, peeled and flattened
1 large head broccoli, stem trimmed, cut into flowerets
3 tablespoons olive oil
½ cup unsalted roasted peanuts, shelled
4–6 dried hot red peppers

Combine egg white and cornstarch.

Mix with chicken pieces and refrigerate for 30 minutes.

Combine bean sauce, hoisin sauce, chili paste with garlic, sugar, sherry, vinegar, and garlic and set aside.

Steam broccoli in wok or saucepan until tender but still crisp. Set aside.

Sauté chicken in olive oil in wok or large frying pan until cooked through.

Add sauce and stir until chicken is well coated.

Stir in peanuts and red peppers. Add broccoli and mix until well coated with sauce.

Serve over rice.

Serves 10
Per serving: 195 Total calories; 14 Sat-fat calories

*Available at Oriental food stores and some supermarkets

Q

CHICKEN MARRAKESH

8 boned and skinned chicken
    breast halves
1/3 cup fresh lemon juice
2 tablespoons grated lemon peel
1 clove garlic, minced
2 tablespoons thyme

1 teaspoon salt
1 teaspoon freshly ground
    pepper
2 lemons, thinly sliced
    (optional)

Place chicken in a bowl or casserole.

Mix together lemon juice, lemon peel, garlic, thyme, salt, and pepper and pour over chicken. Marinate chicken in refrigerator for at least 3 hours.

Preheat oven to 350°F.

Remove chicken from marinade and place in shallow baking dish.

Pour marinade over chicken and bake chicken for 30–45 minutes or until cooked through.

Garnish with lemon slices.

Serves 8
Per serving: 145 Total calories; 8 Sat-fat calories

CHICKEN PAPRIKASH

Paprikash dishes typically use sour cream. Nonfat yogurt has been substituted here without affecting the taste. Half a cup of nonfat yogurt contains 0 sat-fat calories. Half a cup of sour cream contains about 135 sat-fat calories.

6 boned and skinned chicken
    breast halves, cut into bite-
    size pieces
1/4 cup olive oil
1/2 cup chopped onion
1 1/2 cups sliced mushrooms
1/2 tablespoon paprika
1/2 teaspoon dillweed

1/4 teaspoon freshly ground
    pepper
1/2–1 teaspoon salt
1/2 cup chicken broth, strained
1 1/2 tablespoons cornstarch
    mixed with 3 tablespoons
    water
1/2 cup nonfat yogurt

In a large skillet or wok, sauté chicken in 3 tablespoons of the olive oil until cooked through. Remove chicken from skillet. Set aside.

Add 1 tablespoon olive oil to the skillet and cook onions and mushrooms briefly until just tender.

Stir in chicken, paprika, dillweed, pepper, salt, and chicken broth. Cover and cook over low heat for 10 minutes.

Add cornstarch mixture and bring to a boil, stirring constantly.

Remove from heat and stir in yogurt.

Serve over rice or noodles.

Serves 8
Per serving: 197 Total calories; 15 Sat-fat calories

Q CHICKEN WITH APRICOTS, SWEET POTATOES, AND PRUNES

This dish is colorful to look at and a pleasure to eat. What's more, it is quick and easy and can be prepared ahead of time.

8 boned and skinned chicken breast halves	¼ cup olive oil
	¼ cup white vinegar
¾ cup dried prunes	1 cup dry vermouth
¾ cup dried apricots	2 tablespoons brown sugar
2 cups cubed sweet potatoes	4 teaspoons oregano

Place chicken breasts, prunes, apricots, and sweet potatoes in medium-large bowl or casserole.

Combine olive oil, vinegar, vermouth, brown sugar, and oregano and pour over chicken, fruit, and sweet potatoes. Cover and marinate in refrigerator for several hours or overnight.

Preheat oven to 375°F.

Remove chicken from casserole. Arrange in shallow baking pan.

Pour marinade over chicken and bake, covered (you can use aluminum foil), for 45 minutes to 1 hour or until chicken is cooked through and sweet potatoes are soft.

Serves 8
Per serving: 341 Total calories; 16 Sat-fat calories

SINGAPORE CHICKEN

Singapore Chicken includes salad greens, but it is more like a main dish than a salad. You can eat it warm or chilled. It tastes even better the second day.

8 boned and skinned chicken breast halves
1 teaspoon minced garlic
1 teaspoon minced ginger root
2 tablespoons soy sauce
2 tablespoons hoisin sauce*
1 tablespoon white vinegar
1 teaspoon five-spice powder**
1 teaspoon Dijon mustard
2 teaspoons sugar
½ cup white vinegar

2 teaspoons soy sauce
3 tablespoons olive oil
1 Chinese celery cabbage, or 1 head lettuce, chopped (about 6 cups)
4 green onions, thinly sliced
3 tablespoons slivered almonds, toasted
1 tablespoon sesame seeds, toasted

Place chicken breasts in a bowl or small casserole.

Combine garlic, ginger, soy sauce, hoisin sauce, vinegar, and five-spice powder and pour over chicken. Cover bowl and marinate chicken in refrigerator overnight.

Preheat oven to 350°F.

Bake chicken in marinade for 45–60 minutes or until cooked through.

Meanwhile, prepare dressing by combining mustard, sugar, vinegar, soy sauce, and olive oil in a jar and shaking well.

Slice chicken into narrow strips and combine with celery cabbage and green onions.

Pour dressing over all and mix until well coated.

Top with almonds and sesame seeds.

Serve or refrigerate overnight.

Serves 10
Per serving: 192 Total calories; 13 Sat-fat calories

---

*Available at Oriental food stores and some supermarkets
**Five-spice powder is available at Oriental food stores, or you can make your own by pulverizing the following in a blender: 30 peppercorns, 2 whole star anise (optional), 1 teaspoon fennel seeds, 2 one-inch pieces cinnamon stick, ¼ teaspoon cloves. Store excess in covered jar.

TORTILLAS CON POLLO

Chicken, yogurt, and rice make this tortilla unusual, low-fat, and, of course, delicious.

Tomato Sauce

1 clove garlic, minced
⅓ cup chopped onion
1 teaspoon olive oil
1 large can (28 oz) tomatoes,
    drained and chopped

¼ cup chopped green pepper
½ teaspoon cumin seed
½ teaspoon oregano

Filling

3 cups cooked long-grain rice
1½ cups diced cooked chicken
½–1 teaspoon chili powder

½ teaspoon ground cumin
½ cup nonfat yogurt

8 tortillas*

At least 30 minutes before serving, prepare the tomato sauce: Cook garlic and onion in olive oil until soft. Add tomatoes, green pepper, cumin seed, and oregano and cook until thick (about 30 minutes).

Preheat oven to 350°F. Grease a shallow baking dish with margarine.

Combine rice, chicken, chili powder, cumin, and yogurt.

Place ½ cup rice mixture in center of each tortilla and roll.

Place seam-side down in baking dish.

When all eight tortillas have been placed in baking dish, cover with tomato sauce and bake for 25 minutes.

Serves 8
Per serving: 222 Total calories; 5 Sat-fat calories

---

*Read the label. Packaged tortillas should contain only corn (perhaps some lime) and should *not* contain any of the following: shortening, fat, salt, or preservatives.

Q   # CHICKEN CURRY

6 boned and skinned chicken
    breast halves, cut into bite-
    size pieces
2 tablespoons olive oil
1 tablespoon margarine
2 cloves garlic, minced
¾ cup chopped onion

½ cup chopped green pepper
2 teaspoons curry powder
½ teaspoon thyme
½ teaspoon salt
2 cups cherry tomato halves (or
    whole tomatoes or drained
    canned tomatoes, chopped)

In a large skillet or wok, sauté chicken in olive oil until chicken is
cooked through.

Remove chicken and set aside.

Melt margarine in same skillet. Sauté garlic, onion, and green pepper until soft.

Blend in curry powder, thyme, and salt.

Add chicken and stir until well coated with sauce. Stir in tomatoes.

Serves 6
Per serving: 218 Total calories; 17 Sat-fat calories

MONGOLIAN HOT POT

Making this dish is a group activity that allows each person to be
his own cook. It works like a fondue. Everyone skewers a piece of
meat or vegetable and dips it into simmering broth in a large Oriental
"hot pot" or in an electric frying pan or wok. When the meat is
finished cooking, the enriched broth becomes an after-dinner soup.

You will notice that Mongolian Hot Pot is more caloric than most
dishes in this cookbook, but 591 total calories and 35 sat-fat calories
makes a whole meal of soup, vegetables, and meat.

6 boned and skinned chicken
    breast halves

Marinade

2 cloves garlic, minced
¼ cup olive oil
1 tablespoon white vinegar

2 tablespoons honey
¼ cup soy sauce

Sauce

3 cloves garlic, minced
½ teaspoon minced ginger root
1 green onion, sliced
½ cup olive oil
6 tablespoons natural all-peanut
   peanut butter

¼ cup dry sherry
1 tablespoon soy sauce
1 tablespoon white vinegar

The Rest

4 ounces cellophane noodles*
4 cakes fresh tofu (bean curd),*
   cubed
½ pound snow peas
1 zucchini, cut into ¼-inch
   slices

½ head celery cabbage, coarsely
   chopped
1 pound bay scallops

Broth

10 cups chicken stock, or 2 cans
   (10¾ oz each) chicken broth,
   strained, + 6 cans water

3 green onions, sliced
1½ teaspoons sliced ginger root
2 cloves garlic, minced

4 cups hot cooked rice

Slice chicken breasts into slender, bite-size pieces. Marinate in garlic, olive oil, vinegar, honey, and soy sauce in refrigerator for several hours or overnight.

Prepare sauce by puréeing all sauce ingredients in a blender until smooth.

Pour boiling water over cellophane noodles and let stand for 5–10 minutes or until soft. Drain and set aside.

Remove chicken from marinade and arrange artistically on a plate.

Arrange another plate with tofu, snow peas, zucchini slices, and celery cabbage. Set aside.

Arrange bay scallops on another plate.

Pour chicken broth and water in a hot pot, chafing dish, or electric

---

*Available at Oriental food stores and some supermarkets

wok or frying pan set in the center of the table. Heat to a slow boil.

Mix in green onions, ginger, and garlic.

Give each person a bowl of rice and a plate. Pass around the trays of chicken, scallops, and vegetables so people may take what they wish. Each person should also have a fondue fork, skewer, or sharp implement to dip chicken, scallops, and vegetables in broth until cooked.

When food is all devoured or everyone is almost full, add noodles and celery cabbage to the broth and cook for 2–3 minutes.

Serve resulting soup in bowls.

Serves 8
Per serving:

	Total calories	Sat-fat calories
2 tablespoons peanut sauce	144	19
Meat and vegetables	263	15
Broth	184	1
Total	591	35

Q

SATE AJAM
(BROILED CHICKEN ON SKEWERS)

6 boned and skinned chicken breast halves	⅛ teaspoon freshly ground pepper
18 small mushrooms	½ teaspoon cumin
¼ cup olive oil	1 teaspoon minced garlic
2 tablespoons fresh lime juice	

Cut chicken into 1-inch pieces and cut stems off mushrooms.

Alternate pieces of chicken with mushrooms on 6 skewers. (Push skewers through the *tops* of the mushrooms so the mushrooms will not split.)

Place skewered chicken in a shallow casserole.

Combine olive oil, lime juice, pepper, cumin, and garlic and pour over chicken.

Turn skewers to coat chicken and mushrooms with oil mixture.

Refrigerate for at least 30 minutes.

Preheat broiler.

Place skewers on broiler pan and broil 6 inches from heat for about 10 minutes or until cooked through. Turn and baste several times.

Serve over rice and spoon warm marinade over chicken pieces.

Serves 6
Per serving: 225 Total calories; 19 Sat-fat calories

KEEMA MATAR

Traditionally, Keema Matar is made with ground lamb or beef. It tastes equally good with ground chicken, and instead of spending 111 sat-fat calories using ground lean beef, you spend a mere 19.

5 boned and skinned chicken breast halves	2–3 tablespoons curry powder
¼ cup olive oil	1 cinnamon stick
1 tablespoon minced garlic (about 4–5 cloves)	½ teaspoon salt
	1 cup frozen peas

Grind chicken breasts in a food processor or a meat grinder. If you are using a food processor, first cut the cold (but not frozen) chicken breasts into 1-inch cubes. Place the cubes in the work bowl. Press the Pulse/Off button until chicken is ground (not puréed!). In a large skillet, sauté ground chicken in olive oil, stirring constantly, until it is cooked through.

Mix in garlic, curry powder, cinnamon stick, and salt.

Add peas and stir until heated through.

Serve over Indian Rice (p. 276).

Serves 6
Per serving: 241 Total calories; 19 Sat-fat calories

Q

CAJUN CHICKEN

1 tablespoon margarine
1 tablespoon olive oil
8 boned and skinned chicken
    breast halves

½ cup unbleached white flour
½ teaspoon salt, optional

Seasoning Mix (Use more or less of the peppers for a hotter or milder taste.)

¾ teaspoon oregano
½ teaspoon thyme
½ teaspoon basil
½ teaspoon salt

½ teaspoon paprika
¼ teaspoon freshly ground
    black pepper
½ teaspoon cayenne pepper
¼ teaspoon white pepper

3 cloves garlic, minced
¾ cup chopped onion
2 stalks celery, diced
½ cup chopped green pepper
1 tomato, coarsely chopped

2 tablespoons olive oil
1 can (10¾ oz) chicken broth,
    strained
1 small can (8 oz) tomato sauce
1 potato, peeled and diced
2 bay leaves

Preheat oven to 425°F.

Melt margarine with oil in a shallow baking pan in the oven (about 5 minutes).

Meanwhile, shake chicken in a plastic bag filled with flour and salt until chicken is coated.

Place chicken in a single layer in baking pan and bake for 25–30 minutes at 350°F, until almost cooked through.

While chicken is baking, combine oregano, thyme, basil, salt, paprika, and peppers, and set aside.

In a large frying pan, sauté garlic, onion, celery, green pepper, and tomato in oil until soft.

Mix in seasoning mixture and let simmer for about a minute.

Mix in broth and tomato sauce. Bring to a boil, then simmer for 5 minutes.

Lower heat and add chicken breasts and potato. Cook until potatoes are soft and chicken is done.

NOTE: If you find the finished dish too "hot" for your taste, dilute with an additional can of tomato sauce.

Serves 8
Per serving: 255 Total calories; 17 Sat-fat calories

Q ## BAR-B-QUE CHICKEN

1 tablespoon Dijon mustard
2 tablespoons vinegar
2 tablespoons molasses
¼ cup ketchup

½ teaspoon Worcestershire sauce
1 clove garlic, minced
Dash of Tabasco sauce
8 skinned chicken breast halves or thighs*

In a large bowl, mix together Dijon mustard, vinegar, molasses, ketchup, Worcestershire sauce, garlic, and Tabasco for marinade.

Marinate chicken for an hour (or less, if you haven't planned ahead).

Remove chicken and reserve remaining marinade.

Barbecue or broil chicken for 10 minutes.

Turn and coat chicken with marinade and continue cooking until done.

Heat reserved marinade to boiling, simmer for 2 minutes, and spoon over chicken before serving.

Serves 8

	Total calories	Sat-fat calories
1 breast	165	8
1 thigh	150	14

---

*For a barbecue, you may want greater quantities of chicken. Just double, triple, quadruple, etc., the recipe.

☑ GINGER CHICKEN WITH GREEN ONIONS

5 boned and skinned chicken
  breast halves
1 teaspoon ground ginger
2 tablespoons cornstarch
½ cup water
3 tablespoons soy sauce

2 tablespoons olive oil
2 cloves garlic, minced
2 teaspoons minced ginger root
2 dried red peppers, crushed, or
  1 teaspoon dried red pepper
  flakes
1½ cups green onions cut into
  1-inch pieces

Cut chicken into bite-size pieces, sprinkle with ground ginger, and set aside for 15 minutes.

Make a smooth paste of the cornstarch and 2 tablespoons of the water.

Stir in 2 more tablespoons of water and soy sauce. Set aside.

Sauté chicken in oil until cooked through.

Stir in garlic, ginger root, and red pepper flakes.

Mix in soy sauce mixture and heat until the sauce thickens.

If sauce is too thick, mix in up to ¼ cup of water, a little at a time.

Stir in green onion strips and serve over rice.

Serves 6
Per serving: 183 Total calories; 12 Sat-fat calories

☑ ORANGE-SOY CHICKEN

4 boned and skinned chicken
  breast halves
2 tablespoons soy sauce
1½ tablespoons cornstarch
½ tablespoon hoisin sauce
3 tablespoons dry sherry
⅓ cup water
1 clove garlic, minced

1 teaspoon minced ginger root
2 tablespoons orange peel slivers
1 tablespoon olive oil
1 teaspoon marmalade
½–1 teaspoon red pepper flakes
1 orange, peeled and cut into
  bite-size pieces
10–20 snow peas

Place chicken between two pieces of wax paper and pound with a meat mallet to flatten. Then steam in a vegetable steamer or on a steamer tray in a wok until cooked through. Pull or slice them into thin strips about 2–3 inches long.

Mix soy sauce into cornstarch, a tablespoon at a time, creating a smooth paste.

Mix in hoisin sauce, sherry, and water, and set aside.

Sauté garlic, ginger, and orange peel slivers in oil until soft.

Stir in cooked chicken pieces.

Stir in cornstarch mixture and cook until it thickens. Add more water if too dry.

Mix in marmalade, red pepper, orange pieces, and snow peas, and serve over rice.

Serves 6
Per serving: 145 Total calories; 8 Sat-fat calories

CHICKEN VERDE

16 spears asparagus
4 boned and skinned chicken
   breast halves
1 clove garlic, minced
1 teaspoon basil

6 anchovies
2 tablespoons olive oil
2 tablespoons fresh lemon juice
1 teaspoon water

Preheat oven to 375°F.

Snap off bottoms of asparagus.

Pound breasts between two sheets of wax paper with a meat mallet, until flat. This is important, as they must be thin to cook quickly.

Combine garlic, basil, anchovies, olive oil, and lemon juice into a sauce in blender or food processor, or mash and mix by hand.

In a small rectangular glass casserole, place four asparagus spears closely together and wrap a chicken breast around them. Repeat this process for the rest of the breasts.

Spread sauce over chicken.

Sprinkle teaspoon of water over exposed asparagus.

Cover casserole tightly with aluminum foil.

Bake for 20–30 minutes, or until chicken is cooked through.

DO NOT OVERCOOK. If you cook asparagus too long, it becomes soggy and the sauce becomes watery.

Serves 4
Per serving: 230 Total calories; 18 Sat-fat calories

VEGETABLES, CHICKEN, AND CELLOPHANE NOODLES

2 ounces cellophane noodles*
2 boned and skinned chicken
  breast halves
8 mushrooms (approximately)
2 carrots
1 zucchini
4 green onions
4 leaves chinese cabbage*

3 cloves garlic, minced
1 tablespoon olive oil
1 tablespoon sesame oil*
3 tablespoons soy sauce
½ teaspoon sugar
½ teaspoon salt, optional

Cover cellophane noodles with warm water and set aside.

Steam chicken breasts in a vegetable steamer. When cooked through (about 10 minutes), cut them into bite-size pieces and set aside.

Cut mushrooms into thin slices. Cut carrot and zucchini into julienne strips. Cut green onions into 1-inch pieces. Set aside.

Remove the green leaf from the cabbage. Cut into bite-size pieces. Julienne the white part of the leaf. Set aside.

Drain water from cellophane noodles.

Sauté garlic in both oils.

Add vegetables and stir-fry until tender but crisp.

Stir in chicken.

Stir in soy sauce, sugar, salt, and cellophane noodles. Mix to distribute sauce evenly. Serve over rice.

Serves 6
Per serving: 115 Total calories; 8 Sat-fat calories

---

*Available at Oriental food stores and some supermarkets

▣ CHICKEN NUGGETS CHEZ GOOR

The chicken nuggets that you get at fast-food chains are deep-fried in highly saturated oils. Instead of devouring 46 calories of saturated fat per serving, try Chicken Nuggets Chez Goor, marinated in olive oil and garlic and baked in the oven. A mere 13 sat-fat calories per serving.

4 boned and skinned chicken breast halves	1 cup finely ground bread crumbs, made from 2–3 slices French or other bread
2 tablespoons olive oil	¼ teaspoon cayenne pepper
2 cloves garlic, minced	2½ teaspoons honey
¼ teaspoon freshly ground pepper	2 tablespoons Dijon mustard

Preheat oven to 475°F.

Cut each chicken breast half into 8 pieces.

Mix oil, garlic, and pepper with chicken pieces and marinate about 30 minutes.

Combine bread crumbs and cayenne and place on plate.

Roll chicken pieces in bread crumbs and place on large cookie sheet in a single layer.

Bake for about 15 minutes until browned and cooked through. For extra browning, broil for a few more minutes.

Combine honey and mustard. Dip nuggets into honey-mustard sauce.

Serves 4

	Total calories	Sat-fat calories
Per serving	234	13
with honey-mustard sauce	254	13

SHEPHERD'S CHICKEN CHILI PIE

1½–2 pounds potatoes, peeled and cut into chunks
4 boned and skinned chicken breast halves, cubed
1 can (16 oz) whole tomatoes, with juice
1 large onion, sliced
3 cloves garlic, minced
2 tablespoons olive oil
1½ tablespoons chili powder
½ teaspoon oregano
1 teaspoon cumin
2 tablespoons water
1 tablespoon tomato paste
1 teaspoon margarine
Salt and pepper to taste
1 tablespoon skim milk

Place potatoes in a saucepan with water to cover, bring to a boil, and simmer for about 10–15 minutes, until tender.

Steam chicken pieces in a vegetable steamer or on a steamer tray in a wok until cooked through, about 10 minutes.

Drain tomatoes. Reserve liquid.

Preheat oven to 350°F.

In a large skillet, sauté onion and garlic in olive oil until soft.

Mix in chili powder, oregano, and cumin.

Add water, tomato paste, and tomatoes. Cook until sauce is thick. If sauce becomes *too* thick, add a few tablespoons of the reserved tomato juice.

Mix chicken cubes into sauce.

Drain potatoes and whip them. Add margarine, salt, and pepper. Add skim milk and mix until potatoes are smooth. Add more milk if necessary.

Place chicken mixture in a shallow casserole. Spread potatoes on top. Bake for about 30 minutes.

Serves 6
Per serving: 247 Total calories; 12 Sat-fat calories

TURKEY

Turkey is the heart of any Thanksgiving dinner, but it makes delicious eating throughout the rest of the year. Turkey can be stuffed and roasted and the leftovers made into numerous interesting dishes. Turkey cutlets can replace veal cutlets with no one being the wiser (but everyone being the healthier).

White meat turkey breast is a must for everyone who wants to consume less saturated fat and who also enjoys eating. One ounce of turkey breast has only 1 calorie of saturated fat!

NOTE: Turkey contains so much protein and so little fat, it tends to cook quickly. Be careful. Overcooking makes turkey tough.

BASIC TURKEY CUTLET

Turkey cutlets provide a quick and extremely elegant meal. In addition, they are low in fat (even lower than chicken), they are inexpensive, and they can be substituted for exorbitantly expensive veal scaloppine. Turkey cutlets can usually be found in the poultry section of your grocery store.

2 pounds turkey cutlets
½ cup unbleached white flour
3 tablespoons olive oil

2 tablespoons margarine
Salt and freshly ground pepper
   to taste

To Prepare Turkey Cutlets for Any Veal Scaloppine Recipe:

Place cutlets between two pieces of wax paper and pound with meat mallet or rolling pin until thin.

Place flour on a plate. Dip each cutlet in flour, coating it on both sides, and place it on a large plate. When the plate is completely covered with one layer of cutlets, cover them with a sheet of wax paper to hold the next layer.

Heat olive oil and margarine in a large frying pan or wok.

When very hot (margarine should bubble) place cutlets in frying pan. Do not crowd cutlets.

When the edges turn white, turn the cutlets and cook them until they become light brown and are no longer pink inside. Cutlets cook very quickly. Turn again. Do not overcook or cutlets will be tough.

Remove cutlets to a plate and salt and pepper them liberally.

Do not clean skillet. Remove all but 1–2 tablespoons of oil. Now you are ready for any number of scaloppine recipes.

Serves 8
Per serving: 245 Total calories; 15 Sat-fat calories

Q TURKEY SCALOPPINE LIMONE

2 pounds turkey cutlets
2 tablespoons margarine
¼ cup fresh lemon juice (about
   1 lemon)
1 tablespoon unbleached white
   flour

⅓ cup chopped parsley
1 pound mushrooms, sliced
2 lemons, thinly sliced

Prepare turkey cutlets as in master recipe (page 215).

Melt margarine in skillet. Add lemon juice.

Sprinkle on flour and blend into mixture. Add cutlets. Stir and turn cutlets until they are covered with sauce but do not overcook them.

Add parsley and mushrooms, stirring until mushrooms are covered with sauce.

Garnish with lemon slices and serve immediately.

Serves 8
Per serving: 280 Total calories; 19 Sat-fat calories

Q TURKEY SCALOPPINE MARSALA

2 pounds turkey cutlets
½ cup Marsala
2 tablespoons margarine

1 tablespoon unbleached white flour
1 pound mushrooms, sliced

Prepare turkey cutlets as in master recipe (page 215).

Add Marsala to pan over high heat. When it begins to boil, add margarine and reduce heat to medium.

Sprinkle on flour and blend.

Add cutlets and stir and turn until covered with sauce.

Add mushrooms and stir until covered with sauce.

Serve immediately.

Serves 8
Per serving: 290 Total calories; 19 Sat-fat calories

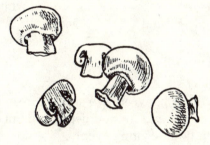

Q TURKEY CUTLETS WITH ARTICHOKE-CREAM SAUCE

This turkey dish is so creamy, you would swear it was a no-no! But it has nothing bad in it. With only 21 sat-fat calories per serving, it is a good choice for keeping your family healthy and impressing your company.

1 pound turkey cutlets
2 tablespoons margarine
3 tablespoons unbleached white flour

1 cup skim milk
1 jar (11½ oz) artichoke hearts, packed in water

Prepare cutlets as in master recipe (page 215), but use only 2 tablespoons of margarine and 1 tablespoon of olive oil to sauté cutlets.

In a medium saucepan, melt margarine. Remove from heat and stir in flour to make a smooth paste.

Slowly stir in skim milk and liquid from artichokes. Heat until thick.

Mix in artichoke hearts.

Pour sauce over cutlets and serve.

Serves 5
Per serving: 260 Total calories; 21 Sat-fat calories

TURKEY VÉRONIQUE

6 turkey cutlets (about 1 pound)
½ cup unbleached white flour
1 teaspoon tarragon
¼ teaspoon salt
¼ teaspoon freshly ground
   pepper
3 tablespoons margarine

1 tablespoon olive oil
½ cup minced onion
1 cup sliced mushrooms
⅔ cup dry white wine or
   vermouth
2 cups seedless grapes

Preheat oven to 375°F.

Flatten turkey cutlets between two sheets of waxed paper.

Combine flour, tarragon, salt, and pepper and place on plate.

Dredge cutlets in flour, coating evenly.

Melt margarine and olive oil in a large skillet.

Brown cutlets (they brown quickly), adding 1 more tablespoon of margarine if necessary.

Remove cutlets with a slotted spoon and place in a shallow baking pan.

Sauté onions and mushrooms in skillet until tender.

Add wine and heat to boiling. Pour over cutlets.

Cover with foil, place in oven, and bake for 10 minutes.

Add grapes and bake for 5 minutes more.

Serves 6
Per serving: 245 Total calories; 15 Sat-fat calories

TURKEY ROLL-UPS FIRENZE

Avoid commercial bread crumbs. They are high in total calories (390 per cup) and high in saturated fat calories (14 per cup). Use your food processor or blender to make your own from a few slices of bread (about 65 total calories and 2 sat-fat calories per slice).

If you forget to thaw the spinach, cook it first until it is no longer frozen.

2 cups bread crumbs made from
   3–4 slices bread
2 cloves garlic, minced
1 teaspoon thyme
1 teaspoon oregano
6 turkey cutlets (about 1 pound)
1 package frozen spinach,
   thawed, or 10 ounces fresh
   spinach

¼ cup low-fat (1%) cottage
   cheese
¼ cup chopped mushrooms
¼ cup chopped onion
2 tablespoons margarine, melted

Preheat oven to 400°F.

Combine bread crumbs, garlic, thyme, and oregano. Or chop garlic in food processor, then add bread slices and spices.

Pound cutlets between two sheets of wax paper until thin.

Squeeze liquid out of spinach.

Combine spinach, cottage cheese, mushrooms, and onions.

Place ⅙ spinach mixture on one side of each cutlet.

Roll up cutlets. Dip in melted margarine. Roll in bread crumbs.

Place rolled cutlets in a shallow casserole greased with margarine.

Bake for 10–20 minutes or until cooked through.

Serves 6
Per serving: 176 Total calories; 10 Sat-fat calories

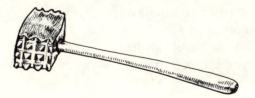

Q BREADED TURKEY CUTLET

¼ cup margarine
2 pounds turkey cutlets
½ teaspoon salt
½ teaspoon basil or oregano

1 cup bread crumbs made from
2 slices of bread
¼ cup olive oil
2 tablespoons margarine

Melt ¼ cup margarine and set aside.

Pound turkey cutlets between two sheets of wax paper until thin.

Combine salt, herbs, and bread crumbs and place on a plate.

Dip cutlet into melted margarine, then coat on both sides with bread crumbs and shake off excess.

Heat olive oil and 2 tablespoons margarine in large skillet until bubbly.

Cook cutlets a few at a time until golden brown on each side.

Place on paper towels to absorb excess fat and serve immediately.

Serves 8
Per serving: 287 Total calories; 26 Sat-fat calories

Q TURKEY MEXIQUE

A great dish with a chili taste.

1 cup chopped onion
2 teaspoons minced garlic
2 tablespoons olive oil
1–2 tablespoons chili powder
1 tablespoon cumin seed
½ teaspoon salt
1 tablespoon unbleached white
   flour

1½ cups chicken broth, strained
3 tablespoons tomato paste
3 cups diced cooked turkey
   breast
1 green pepper, diced
¼ cup stuffed green olives,
   sliced

In a large skillet, sauté onion and garlic in olive oil until soft.

Stir in chili powder, cumin seed, salt, and flour.

Add chicken broth and tomato paste and blend well.

Cook for 5 minutes over low heat.

Stir in turkey, green pepper, and olives and heat through.

Serve over rice.

Serves 6
Per serving: 180 Total calories; 9 Sat-fat calories

TURKEY SAUTÉED WITH ONIONS AND ALMONDS

Q

3 tablespoons slivered almonds
2 cups thinly sliced onion
2 tablespoons margarine
2 tablespoons olive oil
¼ teaspoon cardamom
½ teaspoon coriander

1 teaspoon salt
⅓ cup dry sherry
¼ cup raisins
3 cups diced cooked turkey
    breast
¼ cup chopped parsley

Brown almond slivers in a toaster oven and set aside. Watch them carefully — they burn quickly.

In a large skillet or wok, sauté onion in margarine and olive oil until tender.

Stir in cardamom, coriander, salt, sherry, and raisins. Cook until all excess liquid evaporates.

Stir in turkey, parsley, and almonds and heat through.

Serves 6
Per serving: 250 Total calories; 17 Sat-fat calories

BROCCOLI BAKED TURKEY

Q

1 head broccoli
2 tablespoons margarine
3 tablespoons unbleached white
    flour
1 can (10¾ oz) chicken broth,
    strained

½ teaspoon salt
½ pound mushrooms, sliced
2 cups diced cooked turkey
    breast

Trim stems and leaves off broccoli and separate flowerets.

Steam flowerets until just tender. Set aside.

In a medium saucepan, melt margarine.

Remove from heat and stir flour into margarine to make a smooth paste.

Return to low heat and blend in chicken broth, stirring constantly until sauce is thick and smooth.

Stir salt and mushrooms into sauce.

Preheat oven to 375°F. Grease a shallow baking pan with margarine.

Place broccoli in baking pan, cover with turkey, and pour mushroom sauce over both.

Bake, uncovered, 15–25 minutes.

Serves 6
Per serving: 145 Total calories; 19 Sat-fat calories

CREAMY TURKEY CASSEROLE

2 egg whites
2 tablespoons margarine
3 tablespoons unbleached white flour
1 can (10¾ oz) chicken broth, strained
1 cup diced celery
2 tablespoons minced green onion
½ cup (2 oz) chopped pecans

½ teaspoon salt
¼ teaspoon Worcestershire sauce
1 egg yolk
1 tablespoon fresh lemon juice
¼ cup reduced-calorie mayonnaise
3 cups diced cooked turkey breast

Preheat oven to 400°F. Grease a casserole with margarine.

Whip egg whites until stiff but not dry and set aside.

In a medium saucepan, melt margarine. Remove from heat and stir in flour to make a paste. Gradually blend in chicken broth over low heat. Stir constantly until sauce is thick and smooth.

Stir celery, green onion, pecans, salt, Worcestershire sauce, egg yolk, and lemon juice into sauce.

Fold in egg whites.

Mix mayonnaise with turkey so that turkey is well coated.

Add turkey mixture to sauce and pour into casserole. Bake for 20 minutes.

Serves 6
Per serving: 255 Total calories; 22 Sat-fat calories

TURKEY WITH SNOW PEAS

1 pound turkey tenderloin
2 tablespoons white vinegar
2 tablespoons soy sauce
1 tablespoon brown sugar
2 slices ginger root
2 tablespoons dry sherry

1 tablespoon cornstarch
¼ cup water
3 ounces (about 1 cup) snow peas
10 water chestnuts, thinly sliced

Place turkey in a casserole.

Combine vinegar, soy sauce, brown sugar, ginger, and sherry and pour over turkey.

Simmer for about 20 minutes or until tender. *Do not overcook.*

Remove turkey from casserole and slice into bite-size pieces.

Return sliced turkey to casserole and refrigerate in marinade for several hours or overnight.

Place turkey in a large skillet or wok.

Combine cornstarch and water into a smooth paste. Stir into remaining marinade.

Heat turkey. Pour marinade over turkey and stir until well coated. Stir in snow peas and water chestnuts.

Serves 5
Per serving: 162 Total calories; 9 Sat-fat calories

17 FISH AND SEAFOOD

FISH IS AN excellent choice for heart-healthy eating. It is a fine source of complete protein. The quality of this protein is about the same as that of red meat. Fish also contains important vitamins and minerals. And, in addition to all this good nutrition, fish contains much less fat than red meat. While 6 ounces of trimmed sirloin steak contains 150 calories of saturated fat, 6 ounces of haddock or flounder contain 6 calories of saturated fat. Fish oils are polyunsaturated and have an unusually potent effect in lowering blood triglyceride levels.

Fish cooks quickly — within minutes — and may be prepared in a multitude of tasty ways: broiled, baked, poached, oven-fried. Fish may be used as the base for soups, salads, pastas, and stews. Even when prepared most simply to enhance its delicacy, fish is delicious.

Q BROILED MONKFISH WITH ORANGE SAUCE

Very special and delicious. Skim milk makes a great cream sauce. (And look at the difference in sat-fat calories per cup: 3 for a cup of skim milk versus 335 for a cup of cream.)

2 tablespoons margarine
2 tablespoons unbleached white
  flour
¼ cup orange juice
¾ cup skim milk
Grated rind of 1 orange
1 green onion, sliced
¼ teaspoon salt

¼ cup flour
½ teaspoon salt
¼ teaspoon freshly ground
  pepper
1½ pounds monkfish fillets (or
  any whitefish fillets)
2 teaspoons margarine

Preheat broiler and grease broiler pan with oil.

Melt margarine in a small saucepan. Remove from heat and mix in 2 tablespoons flour to make a smooth paste.

Mix in orange juice and skim milk, stirring until smooth.

Cook over medium heat until sauce thickens, stirring constantly.

Stir in 2 tablespoons grated orange rind, green onion, and salt and set aside.

Combine ¼ cup flour, salt, and pepper and place on large plate.

Dredge fillets in flour so both sides are coated.

Lay fillets on broiler pan and dot them with 2 teaspoons margarine.

Sprinkle remaining orange rind on fillets (grate more if needed).

Broil for 5–15 minutes, depending on the thickness of the fish, or until fish flakes easily.

Reheat orange sauce and spoon 1 tablespoon over each serving.

Serves 6
Per serving: 194 Total calories; 13 Sat-fat calories

Q   ## MARINATED FISH STEAKS

1½ pounds fish steaks   1 teaspoon oregano
   (swordfish, monkfish, halibut,   ½ teaspoon salt
   etc.)   1 tablespoon olive oil
2 tablespoons ketchup   ¼ cup orange juice
1 tablespoon fresh lemon juice   ¼ cup dry vermouth
1 clove garlic, minced   ¼ cup chopped parsley

Place steaks in a shallow casserole.

Combine ketchup, lemon juice, garlic, oregano, salt, olive oil, orange juice, vermouth, and parsley and pour over fish. Marinate several hours or overnight in refrigerator.

Preheat broiler and grease broiler pan with oil.

Broil fish for 5–15 minutes or until it flakes easily.

Heat marinade and spoon over fish.

Serves 4
Per serving: 297 Total calories; 16 Sat-fat calories

Q

FISH BAKED IN OLIVE,
CHILI PEPPER, AND TOMATO SAUCE

¾ cup chopped onion
2 cloves garlic, minced
1 tablespoon olive oil
1 tablespoon cornstarch
1 can (16 oz) tomatoes,
    chopped, juice reserved
⅓ cup sliced stuffed green olives

1 teaspoon chopped red or
    green chili pepper
1½ pounds flounder fillets (or
    other mild fish)
Salt to taste
1 tablespoon fresh lemon juice

Preheat oven to 375°F.

In a medium skillet, sauté onion and garlic in olive oil until soft. Mix in cornstarch.

Add tomatoes and their juice and mix until well blended.

Cook over medium-high heat until sauce thickens.

Stir in olives and chili pepper.

Spoon half the sauce into a baking pan large enough to hold the fillets in one layer. Place fillets over sauce.

Salt fillets and sprinkle them with lemon juice.

Cover fillets with remaining sauce and bake for 10 minutes or until they flake easily.

Serves 6
Per serving: 163 Total calories; 8 Sat-fat calories

Q ## SALMON WITH CUCUMBER-GRAPE SAUCE

½ cup nonfat yogurt
3 tablespoons reduced-calorie
    mayonnaise
1 tablespoon fresh lemon juice
⅓ cup grated cucumber

1 cup seedless grapes
6 salmon steaks* (6 oz each)
3 tablespoons margarine
¼ cup fresh lemon juice

Preheat broiler and grease broiler pan.

Combine yogurt, mayonnaise, lemon juice, cucumber, and grapes. Set aside.

---

*Salmon varies greatly in total calories and sat-fat calories depending on the species. This will affect the total calories per serving.

Place salmon steaks on broiler pan.
Melt margarine and combine it with lemon juice.
Baste salmon with lemon-margarine sauce.
Broil 3–5 minutes, turn salmon, and baste again.
Broil 3–5 minutes more or until fish flakes easily.
Spoon cucumber-grape sauce over salmon steaks and serve.

Serves 6

Per serving:	*Total calories*	*Sat-fat calories*
Atlantic	528	30
Chinook	540	60
Pink	330	24
Sockeye (red)	365	42

BROILED GINGER FISH

1 cup flour
1 teaspoon salt
½ teaspoon freshly ground
  pepper
4 six-ounce fish fillets
  (monkfish, haddock, etc.)

4 teaspoons margarine
4 teaspoons diced ginger root
Lemon slices to cover fillets

Set oven to broil and grease broiler pan with oil.
Combine flour, salt, and pepper on a large plate.
Dredge fillets in flour, covering both sides.
Dot fillets with margarine, sprinkle them with ginger, and cover
with lemon slices.
Broil for 5–15 minutes or until fish flakes easily.

Serves 4
Per serving: 209 Total calories; 6 Sat-fat calories

Q

CURRY FISH

A simple but impressive dish, which tastes as good as it looks. Fun for company.

2 pounds any white fish fillets
2 teaspoons margarine
Salt to taste
¼ cup margarine
1–2 tablespoons curry powder
5 cups cooked long-grain rice
3–4 hard-boiled egg whites,
  chopped

Raisins
Peanuts
Crushed pineapple
Scallions
Chutney

Preheat oven to 425°F. Grease a baking dish with margarine.

Place fillets in baking dish, dot with 2 teaspoons margarine, salt lightly, and bake for 20 minutes.

Flake the fish. (If you wish to serve it later, you can refrigerate the fish now.)

Melt ¼ cup margarine in a large skillet and mix in curry powder.

Add fish and stir until it is covered with curry sauce.

Mix cooked rice and fish together gently.

Place egg whites, raisins, peanuts, crushed pineapple, scallions, and chutney in small dishes and pass with main dish.

Serves 10

Per serving:	*Total calories*	*Sat-fat calories*
Without condiments	251	12
With teaspoon of each	317	18

Q

DILL FISH

1½ pounds fish fillets (flounder,
  sole, turbot, etc.)
¼ cup fresh lime juice
1 teaspoon dillweed

1 clove garlic, minced
Salt and freshly ground pepper
  to taste

Preheat oven to 350°F.

Squeeze lime juice over fillets and marinate for at least 30 minutes in refrigerator.

Grease a shallow baking pan with margarine.

Place fillets in baking pan and sprinkle with dill, garlic, salt, and pepper.

Bake for 5–10 minutes or until fish flakes easily.

Serves 6
Per serving: 115 Total calories; 4 Sat-fat calories

FLOUNDER FILLETS STUFFED WITH FENNEL RICE

Raw fennel, or *finocchio*, as the Italians call it, tastes of licorice or anise. The taste of cooked fennel is more subtle and sweet. Cook sliced fennel bulb with margarine and water to cover for a delicious vegetable dish. You may substitute celery in this recipe but try to find fennel at your grocery store or an Italian market for a more unusual dish. Despite its lack of cream or whole milk, this dish is quite creamy.

⅓ cup sliced fennel stalks
⅓ cup sliced mushrooms
1 teaspoon fennel seeds
1 tablespoon margarine

1½ cups cooked long-grain rice
2 tablespoons margarine
3 tablespoons fresh lemon juice
8 flounder fillets

Preheat oven to 375°F. Grease a shallow baking pan with margarine.

In a medium skillet, sauté fennel and mushrooms in 1 tablespoon margarine until just tender.

Add fennel seeds and cooked rice. Stir for a minute and set aside.

Melt 2 tablespoons margarine in a small saucepan. Add lemon juice and set aside.

Lay out fillets on waxed paper.

Place several tablespoons of rice mixture in the middle of each fillet.

Roll up the fillets and place them seam-side down in the baking dish. (The sides may barely reach each other, but that is okay.)

Pour margarine-lemon mixture over fish and bake for about 20 minutes or until fish flake easily. (Measure thickness of rolled fish and allow 10 minutes per inch.)

If you have any rice mixture left over, reheat and serve with the fish.

Serves 8
Per serving: 140 Total calories; 10 Sat-fat calories

PHYLLO-WRAPPED FISH
AND MUSHROOM SAUCE

Fish wrapped in phyllo dough is an elegant company dish. If you want a simpler (as in less work) dish, just ignore the phyllo part of the recipe. The fish with the mushroom sauce is still luscious.

NOTE: If you are using phyllo dough, the directions on the box usually recommend that you thaw it in the refrigerator overnight and 2–3 hours at room temperature before you use it.

Fish

8 fillets (6 oz each) pollack,
   monkfish, or other white fish
Salt and freshly ground pepper

1 pound phyllo leaves
¼ cup melted margarine

Mushroom Sauce

2 tablespoons margarine
¼ cup unbleached white flour
3 cups sliced mushrooms
3 tablespoons margarine
¼ cup dry sherry

1½ cups skim milk
¼ teaspoon salt
⅛ teaspoon freshly ground
   pepper
Grated nutmeg to taste

The Fish

Preheat oven to 350°F. Grease a baking sheet with margarine.
Check fillets for small bones and remove them.

Lightly salt and pepper fish.

Unroll phyllo dough and cover it with plastic wrap or a towel to keep it from drying out and becoming brittle.

Place one sheet of phyllo dough on the counter with a narrow end toward you. Brush phyllo with melted margarine. Cover with a second sheet of phyllo and brush it with melted margarine. Repeat process for third sheet.

Place fillet on the phyllo edge nearest you. (If fillet is long and narrow, you may have to fold the fillet in half.) Fold left side, then right side of phyllo over fillet and roll it up.

Place seam-side down on baking sheet.

Wrap each fillet in phyllo dough and place on baking sheet.

Bake for 20 minutes. Make a small slit in phyllo to see if fish is done. Bake until fish flakes easily and is opaque.

While fish is baking, make mushroom sauce.

The Mushroom Sauce

In a medium saucepan, melt margarine.

Lower heat and mix in flour.

In a medium skillet, sauté mushrooms in 3 tablespoons of margarine until tender.

Add sherry to mushrooms and boil until alcohol is evaporated.

Add skim milk to mushrooms and heat until steaming but *not boiling*.

Slowly pour milk mixture into flour mixture, blending until sauce is smooth.

Return saucepan to burner and slowly heat sauce to boiling.

Add salt, pepper, and nutmeg to thickened sauce.

Serve over phyllo-wrapped fish.

Serves 8

Per serving:	Total calories	Sat-fat calories
With mushroom sauce	431	22
Without mushroom sauce	342	10

Q FISH WITH MUSHROOM SAUCE

8 fillets (6 oz each) pollack,   1 tablespoon margarine
   monkfish, or other white fish

Make mushroom sauce (see pages 230–231).
Preheat oven to 350°F. Grease a shallow baking pan with margarine.
Place fish in baking pan and dot with margarine.
Bake for 5–10 minutes or until fish flakes easily and is opaque.
Spoon mushroom sauce over fish and serve.

Serves 8
Per serving: 302 Total calories; 14 Sat-fat calories

Q ORIENTAL FISH KEBABS

1¼ pounds swordfish steaks
½ cup fresh lime juice
1 tablespoon soy sauce
1 tablespoon brown sugar
2 cloves garlic, minced
2 tablespoons sliced green onion

1 medium onion, cut into
  eighths
1 green pepper, cut into 1½-
  inch pieces
8 cherry tomatoes

Cut fish into 1½-inch cubes.
Combine lime juice, soy sauce, brown sugar, garlic, and green onion and pour over fish. Marinate for at least 2 hours in refrigerator.
Arrange fish, onion chunks, green pepper, and tomatoes on skewers.
Broil for 10 minutes per inch of thickness of fish or until it flakes easily.
Heat remaining marinade and spoon over fish.

Serves 4
Per serving: 243 Total calories; 10 Sat-fat calories

Q SHANGHAI FISH

1½ pounds white fish fillets	1 tablespoon dry sherry
1 tablespoon soy sauce	3 green onions, sliced
1 clove garlic, minced	½ tablespoon hoisin sauce*

Marinate fish in soy sauce, garlic, sherry, green onions, and hoisin sauce for several hours in refrigerator.

Broil for 5–10 minutes or until fish flakes easily and is opaque.

Heat marinade to boiling and serve over fish.

Serves 6
Per serving: 117 Total calories; 4 Sat-fat calories

Q FISH WITH PEPPERCORNS, THYME, AND MUSTARD

¼–½ teaspoon black peppercorns	2 tablespoons vermouth
	½ teaspoon olive oil
4 teaspoons Dijon mustard	1 pound fish fillets (sole,
1 teaspoon thyme	flounder, etc.)

Preheat oven to 450°F. With margarine, grease shallow glass casserole or baking pan large enough to hold fish.

Crush peppercorns coarsely in food processor or mortar and pestle.

Combine and mix with mustard, thyme, vermouth.

Make several diagonal slashes across the fillets.

Place fish in baking pan and spread mustard mixture over it.

Bake for 5–20 minutes, until fish flakes easily.

Serves 3
Per serving: 70 Total calories; 5 Sat-fat calories

*Available at Oriental food stores and some supermarkets

234

Q

SALMON SOUFFLÉ

1 can (8 oz) salmon	3 egg whites
1 cup skim milk	
1 cup fine bread crumbs made from 2 slices whole-wheat bread	

Preheat oven to 350°F. Grease a small casserole with margarine.

Prepare salmon by carefully rinsing it with water and removing any bones. Set aside.

Heat skim milk and bread crumbs slowly in a double boiler until thick.

Meanwhile, whip egg whites until stiff but not dry. Set aside.

Flake salmon with a fork and add it to the thickened milk mixture. Remove from heat.

Fold salmon mixture into egg whites.

Pour into casserole and bake for 30 minutes.

Serves 4
Per serving: 149 Total calories; 9 Sat-fat calories

SCALLOPS AND SHRIMP

Both scallops and shrimp are low sat-fat gems. They take only 3–5 minutes to cook, may be added to innumerable sauces with no fuss or bother, are extremely low in saturated fat (1 ounce of either contains only 1 sat-fat calorie), and are delicious.

You may have been told to avoid shrimp because it is higher in cholesterol than other shellfish. While this is true, shrimp is also high in omega-3 polyunsaturated fats, which largely neutralize the cholesterol.

Ⓠ SCALLOP OR SHRIMP CURRY

Delight your guests or family with this unusual curry. The apples and lime create a unique combination of sweet and sour tastes.

1 cup chopped onion
1 apple, peeled, cored, and chopped
2 cloves garlic, minced
1 tablespoon curry powder
2 tablespoons margarine
¼ cup unbleached white flour
½ teaspoon salt
¼ teaspoon cardamom
¼ teaspoon freshly ground pepper
1 can (10¾ oz) chicken broth, strained
1 tablespoon fresh lime juice
1¼ pounds bay scallops or shrimp, shelled and deveined
1 cup sliced mushrooms

In a large skillet, sauté onion, apple, garlic, and curry powder in margarine until tender.

Remove skillet from heat and blend in flour, salt, cardamom, and pepper.

Stir in chicken broth and lime juice until curry sauce is well blended.

Bring curry sauce to a boil, reduce heat, and simmer, uncovered, for about 5 minutes. Stir occasionally.

Meanwhile, place scallops or shrimp in a pot of boiling water and cook until just tender (5–10 minutes). Drain and set aside.

When curry sauce is finished cooking, add shellfish and mushrooms and serve over rice.

Serves 6
Per serving: 197 Total calories; 10 Sat-fat calories

Q

SCALLOPS PROVENÇAL

It takes only about 15 minutes and very little effort to create this delightful combination of color, texture, and taste.

1 pound bay scallops	2 cups snow peas (about ½
¼ cup unbleached white flour	pound)
3 cloves garlic, minced	2 cups sliced red pepper
3 tablespoons olive oil	1 cup sliced mushrooms

Rinse scallops, dry with a paper towel, and roll scallops in flour.

In a wok or large skillet, sauté scallops and garlic in olive oil until tender (about 5–10 minutes).

Add snow peas, red peppers, and mushrooms and mix until heated through.

Serve over rice.

Serves 5
Per serving: 214 Total calories; 13 Sat-fat calories

Q

SCALLOPS OR SHRIMP CARIBBEAN

¼ cup sugar	2 teaspoons grated orange peel
2 tablespoons cornstarch	½ pound mushrooms, sliced
⅛ teaspoon salt	1 medium orange, peeled and
½ cup orange juice	cut into bite-size pieces
⅓ cup white vinegar	¼ pound snow peas
½ cup water	¼ cup sliced green onions
1 pound bay scallops or shrimp,	3 cups cooked long-grain rice
shelled and deveined	3 tablespoons sliced almonds

In a large skillet, combine sugar, cornstarch, and salt. Slowly stir in orange juice, vinegar, and water.

Stir constantly over medium heat until mixture thickens.

Add scallops or shrimp and orange peel.

When shellfish is cooked through (5–10 minutes), add mushrooms, orange pieces, snow peas, and green onions.

Serve over rice, topped with almonds.

Serves 6
Per serving: 170 Total calories; 3 Sat-fat calories

SCALLOP OR SHRIMP CREOLE

2 green peppers, chopped
1 cup chopped onion
2 cloves garlic, minced
2 tablespoons margarine
1 teaspoon brown sugar
¼ teaspoon freshly ground
   pepper
½ teaspoon thyme
¼ teaspoon cayenne pepper
1 bay leaf

½ teaspoon salt
2 large cans (28 oz each)
   tomatoes, drained, juiced, and
   chopped
½ cup sliced celery
1½ cups sliced mushrooms
3 tablespoons chopped parsley
1 pound bay scallops or shrimp,
   shelled and deveined

Sauté green peppers, onion, and garlic in margarine until soft.

Add brown sugar, pepper, thyme, cayenne pepper, bay leaf, and salt and stir well.

Stir in tomatoes and cook over low heat for 30 minutes or until sauce is thick.

Add celery and mushrooms and cook for a few minutes more.

Mix in parsley and scallops or shrimp and cook for 5–10 minutes or until shellfish is cooked through.

Serve immediately so shellfish will not overcook.

Serve over rice.

Serves 6
Per serving: 199 Total calories; 10 Sat-fat calories

SPICY SHRIMP LOUISIANA

1–1¼ pounds shrimp
¼ teaspoon ground white
  pepper
⅛ teaspoon freshly ground
  black pepper
¼ teaspoon cayenne pepper
½ teaspoon basil
¼ teaspoon thyme
¼ teaspoon salt
¼ cup water

¼ cup unbleached white flour
2 tablespoons olive oil
½ cup chopped onion
1 green pepper, chopped
2 stalks celery, chopped
2 cloves garlic, minced
1 can (10¾ oz) chicken broth,
  strained
1 tablespoon tomato paste
¼ cup chopped green onions

Shell, devein, and clean shrimp. Cook in boiling water for about 3 minutes. Discard water. Set shrimp aside.

Combine the white, black, and cayenne pepper, basil, thyme, and salt. Set aside.

Slowly add water to flour and mix into a paste. Set aside.

Heat oil in wok or large frying pan until hot.

Stir in onion, green pepper, celery, and garlic, and cook until soft. Mix in spice mixture.

Stir in broth and tomato paste.

Stir in flour mixture and cook until sauce thickens.

Add shrimp and green onions and serve over rice.

Serves 6
Per serving: 115 Total calories; 6 Sat-fat calories

VEGETABLES   18

Hooray for vegetables! Vegetables provide meals with texture, color, dietary fiber, vitamins, and minerals. They score high in a cancer prevention eating plan as well as a heart-healthy eating plan. And, in addition, they are delicious! They fill you up without filling you out.

One of the best ways to cook vegetables is also the easiest. Cook vegetables in a steamer until they are just tender (a few minutes at most). Perhaps add some melted margarine or oil and vinegar. Steaming vegetables minimizes loss of vitamins. It also brings out the unique taste of each vegetable.

In addition to steaming, vegetables may be prepared in a variety of enticing ways, as you will find in the recipes below.

[Q]   SWEET VEGETABLE MÉLANGE

2 large onions, sliced (about 2 cups)
2 tablespoons olive oil
2 cups sliced carrot
2 small sweet potatoes, cubed (about 2 cups)

1½ tablespoons brown sugar
1 teaspoon cinnamon
¼ cup raisins
½ cup water

In a medium casserole, sauté onions in olive oil until soft.
Cover with carrots, then sweet potatoes.
Mix brown sugar, cinnamon, and raisins and sprinkle over vegetables.
Pour water over vegetables.

Cover and bake at 400°F for 45 minutes or until vegetables are tender.

Serves 8
Per serving: 105 Total calories; 4 Sat-fat calories

INDIAN VEGETABLES

This recipe makes a large pot of colorful, tasty vegetables, which may be eaten warm or cold. Try it as a main dish served over rice.

¼ cup olive oil
1 teaspoon black mustard seeds*
3 cloves garlic, chopped
1 medium onion, chopped
1 green pepper, chopped
2–3 potatoes, peeled and cubed
1 small eggplant, peeled and cubed
1½ teaspoons turmeric
1 teaspoon salt
¼ cup water
1 teaspoon cumin
1 teaspoon coriander

1 teaspoon garam masala*
Any vegetables, for example:
 1 head broccoli, cut into flowerets (about 3 cups)
 1 cup or more cauliflower flowerets
 6 carrots, sliced
 1 cup or more green beans, cut in half
 1 cup sliced celery
 1 zucchini, sliced
1 cup water

In a large pot, heat olive oil and add black mustard seeds.

When the mustard seeds begin to pop, add garlic, onion, and green pepper and cook until soft.

Stir in potatoes and eggplant.

Add turmeric and salt and mix until vegetables are covered with turmeric sauce.

Add ¼ cup water, reduce heat to low, cover the pot, and cook for 10 minutes.

Stir in cumin, coriander, garam marsala, and vegetables.

Add 1 cup water and increase heat to medium.

After 10 minutes, lower heat and cook until vegetables are tender.

Serves 12
Per serving: 100 Total calories; 6 Sat-fat calories

---

*Available at Indian or Oriental food stores

VEGETABLE SOUFFLÉ
WITH TAHINI SAUCE

This recipe is a lot of work, but it's worth it. You may prepare the vegetable purée one or two days before serving and refrigerate it.

1 turnip, peeled and grated
6 carrots, peeled and grated
3 cups broccoli flowerets (about 1 head)
2 tablespoons margarine
2 tablespoons firmly packed brown sugar

1 tablespoon curry powder
½ teaspoon salt
¼ teaspoon freshly ground pepper
⅛ teaspoon grated nutmeg

Tahini Sauce

1 clove garlic
1 tablespoon parsley
3 tablespoons tahini (sesame seed paste)*

1 cup nonfat yogurt
1 tablespoon fresh lemon juice
½ tablespoon fresh dill, or ½ teaspoon dried dillweed

4 egg whites

The Vegetable Purée

Steam turnip and carrot 2–3 minutes or until tender. Set aside.
Steam broccoli flowerets about 5 minutes or until tender.
Purée turnip, carrot, and broccoli in food processor or blender until smooth. Set aside.
Melt margarine in a large skillet over low heat.
Stir in brown sugar until well blended.
Stir in curry powder, salt, pepper, and nutmeg.
Add puréed vegetables and mix well, stirring frequently until most moisture has evaporated.
Cool. (Cover and refrigerate if you wish to finish dish later.)
While vegetable purée is cooling, make tahini sauce.

The Tahini Sauce

Chop garlic and parsley in food processor or blender.

---

*Available at Mideast food stores and many supermarkets

Add tahini, yogurt, lemon juice, and dill.
Blend until smooth. Chill.

The Soufflé
Preheat oven to 450°F. Grease a 1- or 2-quart casserole with margarine.

Beat egg whites until stiff but not dry.

Fold vegetable purée into egg whites, ⅓ at a time. Place in baking dish and bake at 450°F for 15 minutes.

Reduce heat to 350°F and bake for 30 minutes more or until puffed and golden brown.

Serve with tahini sauce.

Serves 8

	Total calories	Sat-fat calories
Per serving:	75	5
Tahini sauce	19	3
per tablespoon		

Ⓠ MURIEL'S CHINESE VEGETABLES

2 ounces cellophane noodles*
2 cloves garlic, minced
2 tablespoons olive oil
1 tablespoon sesame oil
3 cups broccoli flowerets (about 1 head)

2 cups cauliflower flowerets
1 red pepper, sliced
2 tablespoons dry white wine or vermouth
1 teaspoon five-spice powder*
2 tablespoons soy sauce

Pour boiling water over cellophane noodles and let them soak for 15–30 minutes.

Sauté garlic in olive oil and sesame oil for a few seconds.

Stir in broccoli, cauliflower, and red pepper, and stir-fry until just tender.

Stir in vermouth and five-spice powder.

Drain cellophane noodles and stir into vegetables.

Stir in soy sauce until vegetables are well covered with sauce.

Serves 9
Per serving: 85 Total calories; 6 Sat-fat calories

---

*Available in Oriental food stores and some supermarkets

☒ ITALIAN MIXED VEGETABLES

1 clove garlic, minced
1 onion, sliced
3 tablespoons olive oil
3 cups combined red and/or
yellow and/or green sweet
peppers, sliced

2 zucchini, sliced (about 2 cups)
Salt to taste
1 teaspoon thyme, oregano, or
basil, or combination

In a large skillet, sauté garlic and onion in olive oil until tender.
Stir in peppers, zucchini, salt, and herbs.
Cover. Cook until tender.

Serves 8
Per serving: 65 Total calories; 6 Sat-fat calories

RATATOUILLE

Add eggplant, bay leaf, and tomatoes to Italian mixed vegetables
and you have a French dish — ratatouille.

2 cloves garlic, minced
1 onion, sliced
3 tablespoons olive oil
3 cups combined red and/or
yellow and/or green sweet
peppers, sliced
2 zucchini, sliced (about 2 cups)
4 fresh tomatoes, cubed, or 1
large can (28 oz) Italian plum
tomatoes, drained

Salt to taste
1 bay leaf
1 teaspoon dried basil, or 2
tablespoons fresh basil,
chopped
1 small eggplant, cubed and
steamed (about 2 cups)*

Sauté garlic and onion in olive oil in a medium-large casserole.
Add peppers, zucchini, tomatoes, salt, bay leaf, and basil.
Cover and simmer until vegetables are tender (about 15–20
minutes).
Add steamed eggplant and cook for 5 minutes more.

Serves 10
Per serving: 60 Total calories; 5 Sat-fat calories

*See page 249 for eggplant preparation

◻

ARTICHOKE

Artichokes make a great appetizer. Watch your family gobble them up and then fight for the delectable hearts.

1 artichoke for two people   Margarine

Trim the stem and pull off the small leaves at the base of the artichoke.

With scissors, cut off the tips of the bottom leaves.

Drop artichoke into a large pot of boiling water and boil slowly for 40–45 minutes or until a leaf will pull off easily.

To eat artichoke, pull off a leaf, dip the bottom in a small bowl of melted margarine, and scrape the leaf between your teeth to extract the "meat." Discard the leaf.

When no more edible leaves are left, you have reached the heart. Remove excess leaves and scrape off the hairy fibers above the heart. Dip the heart in margarine.

Per serving:	Total calories	Sat-fat calories
Artichoke	26	0
Margarine per tablespoon	90	18

CURRIED BEANS

2 cups dried beans (½ cup each chickpeas, black-eyed peas, pinto beans, small red chili beans, or any combination)
1 teaspoon minced ginger root
1 cup chopped onion
2 tablespoons olive oil

1 cup chopped tomato
1 teaspoon coriander
2 teaspoons cumin
1 teaspoon turmeric
¼ teaspoon cayenne pepper
1 teaspoon salt
2 tablespoons tomato paste

Place dried beans in a large bowl or casserole. Rinse and remove any foreign matter.

Cover beans with boiling water and let them soak for at least 4 hours.

Drain water. Cover beans with fresh water and simmer for 40–60 minutes or until tender.

In a skillet, sauté ginger and onion in olive oil until soft.

Stir in tomato, coriander, cumin, turmeric, cayenne pepper, salt, and tomato paste.

Stir periodically for about 5 minutes. If beans become too dry, add a few tablespoons of water.

Makes 11 half-cup servings
Per serving: 155 Total calories; 4 Sat-fat calories

BEANS

If you have been avoiding beans because eating them produces more gas than you care to discuss, here is a way to prepare dried beans (except lentil and split peas) that reduces their gas-producing potential.

1. Rinse beans and pick out foreign matter.
2. Pour boiling water over beans and let them soak for four hours.
3. Drain beans and cook them in fresh water.

CHICKPEAS WITH LEMON AND HERBS

2 cups dried chickpeas	1 teaspoon salt
½ cup fresh lemon juice	2 teaspoons oregano
2 tablespoons olive oil	4 green onions, sliced

Place chickpeas in a large bowl or casserole. Rinse and remove any foreign matter.

Cover chickpeas with boiling water and let them soak for at least 4 hours.

Drain water. Cover chickpeas with fresh water and simmer for 40–60 minutes or until tender.

Combine lemon juice, olive oil, salt, oregano, and green onions and pour over chickpeas. Mix thoroughly.

Makes 10 half-cup servings
Per serving: 170 Total calories; 5 Sat-fat calories

Q

GREEN BEANS BASILICO

1 clove garlic, minced
½ cup chopped onion
½ cup chopped green pepper
1 tablespoon margarine
1 teaspoon basil

½ teaspoon oregano
½ teaspoon salt
3 cups green beans, trimmed
    and cut in half

In a large skillet sauté garlic, onion, and green pepper in margarine until soft.

Stir in basil, oregano, and salt.

Toss green beans with the vegetables until beans are bright green.

Cover skillet and let vegetables cook for 1 minute. If green beans are crisp but tender, they are ready to be served. Otherwise cook them longer.

Serves 6
Per serving: 44 Total calories; 4 Sat-fat calories

Q

BROCCOLI AND MUSHROOMS

Because broccoli is a cruciferous vegetable, it is highly recommended in both heart-healthy and cancer-healthy eating. Even if it were not so healthy it would still be a pleasure to eat.

1 tablespoon olive oil
2 cloves garlic, minced
2 heads broccoli, cut into
    flowerets

½ pound mushrooms, sliced

In a large skillet or wok, heat olive oil.

Add garlic, broccoli, and mushrooms and stir for about 1 minute.

Add 2 tablespoons of water, cover, and cook over low heat until broccoli is just tender (about 5–10 minutes).

Serves 6
Per serving: 65 Total calories; 5 Sat-fat calories

[Q]
SESAME BROCCOLI

1 tablespoon soy sauce	2 heads broccoli, cut into
1 tablespoon sesame oil	flowerets
¼ cup dry sake or vermouth	1 tablespoon sesame seeds,
2 teaspoons honey	toasted

Combine soy sauce, sesame oil, wine, and honey in bowl. Set aside.

Steam broccoli until tender.

Toss broccoli and dressing together.

Sprinkle sesame seeds over broccoli and serve.

Serves 8
Per serving: 50 Total calories; 3 Sat-fat calories

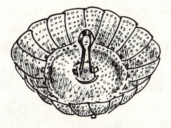

[Q]
CARAWAY CARROTS

Carrots are an excellent source of vitamin A. They keep well in the refrigerator and make great snacks. They are perfect for last-minute chefs because they cook quickly and taste wonderful with very little embellishment.

6 carrots, sliced (about 3 cups)	2 teaspoons caraway seeds
1 tablespoon margarine	

Place sliced carrots in a small saucepan with water to cover.

Gently simmer until carrots are soft. Drain.

Add margarine and mix until carrots are covered.

Stir in caraway seeds.

Serves 6
Per serving: 45 Total calories; 3 Sat-fat calories

Q CARROTS AND LEEKS

1 leek, cleaned thoroughly and
the white bulb sliced
1 tablespoon olive oil

2 cups sliced carrots
¼ teaspoon thyme

In a small saucepan, sauté leeks in olive oil until tender.
Add carrots and thyme.
Cover and cook over low heat until carrots are tender.

Serves 4
Per serving: 71 Total calories; 4 Sat-fat calories

Q CAULIFLOWER SAUTÉ

2 cups cauliflower flowerets
2 cloves garlic, minced
1 small onion, sliced (about ¼
cup)
2 tablespoons olive oil

1 cup snow peas
1 red pepper, sliced
1 cup sliced mushrooms
1 teaspoon oregano

Steam cauliflower until just tender. Set aside.
In large skillet or wok, sauté garlic and onion in olive oil until soft.
Add steamed cauliflower, snow peas, red pepper, mushrooms, and
oregano and stir until heated through.

Serves 6
Per serving: 67 Total calories; 5 Sat-fat calories

Q

CELERY-MUSHROOMS

3 cups sliced celery | 1 cup sliced onions
½ teaspoon salt | 1 cup sliced mushrooms
2 tablespoons margarine

Place celery and salt in a medium saucepan with water to cover.

Bring to a boil, reduce heat, and simmer for 8–10 minutes or until celery is tender.

Meanwhile, melt margarine in a medium skillet over low heat. Sauté onions in margarine until golden.

Add mushrooms and stir for several minutes to blend flavors.

Drain celery and stir it into onion-mushroom mixture.

Serves 6
Per serving: 52 Total calories; 7 Sat-fat calories

Cooking with Eggplant Choose the blackest eggplant you can find. Peel it, cut it into bite-size pieces, and salt them heavily. Place a heavy plate on top of the pieces to help squeeze out the bitter juices. In 30–60 minutes, wash off the salt and gently squeeze eggplant pieces to rid them of bitter juices.

Steam eggplant in a vegetable steamer until tender. There are two advantages to steaming eggplant: steamed eggplant needs no oil (eggplant absorbs an enormous amount of oil) and thus has fewer sat-fat and total calories; and you can test the pre-cooked eggplant for bitterness before using it in a recipe.

Q

KEEMA EGGPLANT

1 medium eggplant, cubed (about 4 cups) | 3 tablespoons fresh lemon juice
1 cup sliced onion | 1 tablespoon brown sugar
1 tablespoon olive oil | 1 tablespoon ketchup
2 teaspoons curry powder | ¼ cup water
 | 1 cup canned chickpeas

Prepare eggplant as explained above.

Meanwhile, sauté onion slices in olive oil until tender.

Stir in curry powder.

Combine lemon juice, brown sugar, ketchup, and water and stir into eggplant mixture. Cook for 5 minutes.

Add chickpeas and cook for 2 minutes more.

Serves 6
Per serving: 100 Total calories; 4 Sat-fat calories

[Q] HOT AND GARLICKY EGGPLANT

1 medium eggplant (about 1 pound)

5 small, dried black Chinese mushrooms*

1 tablespoon chili paste with garlic*

1 tablespoon vinegar

½ tablespoon soy sauce

½ tablespoon double black soy sauce*

2 tablespoons dry sherry

½ teaspoon sugar

1 large green pepper, chopped

1 tablespoon olive oil

½ cup water

Prepare eggplant as explained on page 249.

Place mushrooms in a small bowl and cover with boiling water.

After about 15 minutes remove mushrooms. Squeeze out the excess water and discard stems. Slice mushrooms. Set aside.

Combine chili paste with garlic, vinegar, soy sauces, sherry, and sugar and set aside.

In a large skillet, sauté green pepper and mushrooms in oil until tender.

Stir in eggplant.

Mix in soy sauce mixture until vegetables are covered and then stir in water.

Simmer for about 5 minutes.

Makes 8 half-cup servings
Per serving: 35 Total calories; 2 Sat-fat calories

---

*Available at Oriental food stores

Ⓠ EGGPLANT WITH A GREEK INFLUENCE

1 large or 2 small eggplants
1 tablespoon olive oil
¼ cup fresh lemon juice

12 pitted black olives
1 teaspoon capers
½ teaspoon oregano

Prepare eggplant as explained on page 249. Taste steamed eggplant. If not bitter, proceed.

In a saucepan, combine eggplant, olive oil, lemon juice, olives, capers, and oregano.

Cook over low heat for 10 minutes or until heated through.

Serves 6
Per serving: 51 Total calories; 4 Sat-fat calories

Ⓠ LENTILS AND POTATOES

Lentils, a type of legume, are both delicious and nutritious. They are rich in vitamin C, folic acid, and many minerals, including iron and calcium. They are a good source of soluble fiber, which has been shown to lower blood cholesterol.

Lentils and Potatoes may be served at room temperature on a bed of lettuce or warm as a side dish.

1 cup lentils
1 cup peeled and cubed potato
   (about 1 medium potato)
½ teaspoon salt

2 cloves garlic, minced
⅓ cup chopped onion
1 tablespoon olive oil

Wash lentils and place them in a medium saucepan with potatoes, salt, and water to cover.

Bring to a boil. Reduce heat, cover, and simmer for about 20–25 minutes or until vegetables are tender.

Drain and set aside.

In a large skillet, sauté garlic and onion in olive oil.

Stir in cooked lentils and potatoes and serve or refrigerate.

Serves 6
Per serving: 55 Total calories; 3 Sat-fat calories

Q BRAISED MUSHROOMS ORIENTAL

These mushrooms make a tasty hors d'oeuvre or side dish.

1 pound mushrooms, sliced	4 teaspoons soy sauce
2 tablespoons olive oil	1 cup water
2 teaspoons sugar	2 teaspoons sesame oil

Sauté mushrooms in olive oil until tender.
Stir in sugar, soy sauce, and water.
Cover and simmer for 25 minutes or until water is absorbed.
Add sesame oil.

Serves 6 as a side dish
Per serving: 83 Total calories; 6 Sat-fat calories

Q POTATO SKINS

Leslie Goodman-Malamuth of the Center for Science in the Public Interest devised this recipe as a substitute for the highly saturated potato skins you often find in restaurants. Not only is this recipe quick and easy, the resulting potatoes are scrumptious.

4 large potatoes	Paprika to taste
1 tablespoon olive oil	

Preheat oven to 450°F.
Scrub potatoes well, cut them lengthwise into six wedges the size and shape of dill pickle spears, and dry them on a paper towel.
In a large bowl, toss potato spears with olive oil until they are well covered.
Spread potatoes on a baking sheet, dust them with paprika, and bake for 20–30 minutes or until fork-tender.

Serves 6 (So good, 2 people can easily finish them off!)
Per serving: 79 Total calories; 3 Sat-fat calories

POTATOES

Of all vegetables, potatoes are probably the most maligned. Many people consider them highly caloric and devoid of nutritional value. What injustice! Potatoes are filled with vitamins (particularly vitamin C), minerals, and protein. Eaten plain they are low in calories, have no fat, and are extremely filling.

POTATOES LYONNAISE

2 pounds boiling or all-purpose
  potatoes (about 4 large)
2 tablespoons margarine
½ teaspoon salt
¼ teaspoon freshly ground
  pepper

1½ cups sliced onion (about 2
  onions)
1 tablespoon olive oil
¼ cup chopped parsley

Peel and halve potatoes, then steam or boil them until just tender (about 10 minutes).

Cut potatoes into ¼-inch-thick slices.

Melt margarine in a large skillet. Add potato slices and cook for 15 minutes, shaking pan periodically. After 10 minutes, add salt and pepper and turn potatoes.

In a small skillet, sauté onions in olive oil until browned.

Add onions and parsley to potatoes and cook for 5 minutes more.

Serves 8
Per serving: 90 Total calories; 7 Sat-fat calories

SWEET POTATOES

Sweet potatoes are often considered a fattening treat. They are a healthy treat, but not fattening. One sweet potato has only 115 calories and is chock-full of vitamins A and C and many minerals.

[Q] SWEET POTATOES WITH ORANGES, APPLES, AND SWEET WINE

8 cups sweet potatoes cut into
  ½-inch slices
1 cup diced apple
1 orange, cut into bite-size
  pieces

2 tablespoons fresh lemon juice
1 tablespoon brown sugar
½ cup plum wine or other
  sweet wine
5 whole cloves

Preheat oven to 375°F.

Place sweet potato slices in a saucepan with water to cover. Bring to a boil. Reduce heat, cover, and simmer until just tender when pierced with a fork.

Drain sweet potatoes and place in a casserole.

Mix apple, orange, lemon juice, brown sugar, wine, and cloves. Pour mixture over sweet potatoes.

Bake, covered, for 30 minutes or until apples are tender.

Serves 12
Per serving: 123 Total calories; 0 Sat-fat calories

FLUFFY SWEET POTATOES

3 sweet potatoes (to make 2
  cups mashed)
⅔ cup orange juice
½ teaspoon grated orange peel

2 tablespoons brown sugar
2 tablespoons margarine, melted
1 egg yolk
2 egg whites

Peel sweet potatoes, cut into chunks, place in a medium saucepan, and cover with water.

Bring to a boil, then reduce heat and simmer until tender (about 10–15 minutes).

Preheat oven to 375°F. Grease a casserole with margarine.

Drain potatoes and mash in a large bowl.

Mix in orange juice, orange peel, brown sugar, melted margarine, and egg yolk.

Whip egg whites until stiff but not dry and fold into sweet potato mixture.

Pour sweet potato mixture into casserole and bake for 30 minutes.

Serves 6
Per serving: 133 Total calories; 9 Sat-fat calories

SPINACH AND TOMATOES

Spinach is an excellent source of vitamin A. It is also rich in vitamin C and iron. It may be eaten raw in a salad or cooked in many interesting ways.

10 ounces fresh spinach, washed and shredded	1 1/2 tablespoons olive oil
2 cloves garlic, minced	1 tomato, diced
	1 tablespoon raisins

In a medium saucepan, cook spinach in boiling water to cover until tender (about 2 minutes). Drain well and chop coarsely.
Sauté garlic in olive oil.
Mix in spinach.
Add tomatoes and raisins and heat through.

Serves 4
Per serving: 75 Total calories; 6 Sat-fat calories

SPINACH ORIENTAL

10 ounces fresh spinach, washed and shredded	1 teaspoon chopped ginger root
1 tablespoon olive oil	1 teaspoon double black soy sauce*

In a large skillet, lightly sauté spinach in oil until soft.
Stir in ginger and soy sauce.

Serves 4
Per serving: 50 Total calories; 4 Sat-fat calories

---

*Available at Oriental food stores and some supermarkets

SQUASH

Squash, both winter and summer varieties, is rich in vitamin A, vitamin C, niacin, and iron. Squash is delicious when simply baked, boiled, or steamed and enhanced with a little margarine and freshly ground pepper. Or it may be prepared in a variety of other interesting ways.

Q

ACORN SQUASH

3 medium acorn squash	2 tablespoons margarine
1 cup boiling water	Freshly ground pepper to taste

Preheat oven to 400°F.

Cut each squash in half and scoop out seeds and fibers.

Slice a small piece off the bottom of each half so that they will not roll over.

Place squash halves, cut-side down, in a shallow casserole.

Pour boiling water into the casserole and cover it tightly with aluminum foil.

Bake for 45 minutes or until squash is soft when pierced with a fork.

Turn squash cut-side up and fill each half with 1 teaspoon margarine.

Bake for 5 minutes more.

Grind pepper over squash and serve.

Serves 6
Per serving: 125 Total calories; 8 Sat-fat calories

Q
GLAZED ACORN SQUASH

2 acorn squash   ¾ cup orange juice
2 tablespoons brown sugar

Cut squash crosswise (not through the stem) into ½-inch slices. Clean out fibers and seeds and peel.

Place squash in a large skillet.

Combine brown sugar and orange juice and pour over squash.

Cover and cook over medium heat for 15 minutes. Turn squash.

Raise heat and cook, uncovered, for 10 minutes more or until squash is tender and sauce is reduced.

Serves 6
Per serving: 58 Total calories; 1 Sat-fat calorie

Q
AFGHAN SQUASH

½ cup sliced onion   ¼ teaspoon cardamom
2 tablespoons olive oil   ¼ teaspoon ground cloves
½ teaspoon salt   1 butternut squash, peeled and
½ teaspoon cumin   cubed (about 3 cups)
½ teaspoon coriander

Sauté onion in olive oil in a small casserole.

Stir in salt, cumin, coriander, cardamom, and cloves.

Add squash and 1 cup water.

Cook until tender (about 25 minutes).

Serves 8
Per serving: 50 Total calories; 5 Sat-fat calories

Q
STEAMED ZUCCHINI MATCHSTICKS

So light, so tasty — you don't even need to add salt, spices, or fat. But you may want to crush garlic into one teaspoon of melted margarine and combine it with the vegetables.

2 small zucchini (or ½ small   1 thick carrot, peeled
   zucchini per person)   1 teaspoon margarine (optional)
                                   1 clove garlic (optional)

Cut zucchini and carrot into 2-inch lengths.

Place a zucchini section on a cutting surface, skin-side down.

Holding the sides of the section, slice lengthwise at ⅛-inch intervals. Hold the slices together.

Roll the section one-quarter turn, making sure the slices stay together.

Again, make parallel slices, ⅛-inch apart lengthwise.

Result: zucchini matchsticks.

Repeat for remaining sections of zucchini and carrot.

Place zucchini sticks on top of carrot sticks in a vegetable steamer and steam until just tender (about 1 or 2 minutes).

Serves 4

	Total calories	Sat-fat calories
Per serving	17	0
with margarine	24	2

Q

CURRIED ZUCCHINI

You can use this basic recipe for any vegetable.

1 clove garlic, minced
½ cup chopped onion
3 tablespoons olive oil
½ teaspoon salt
½–1 teaspoon turmeric

¼–½ teaspoon cumin
½ teaspoon red pepper flakes
  (optional)
3 zucchini, sliced (about 3 cups)
2 tomatoes, chopped

In a large skillet, sauté garlic and onion in olive oil until soft.
Add salt, turmeric, cumin, and red peppers. Blend well.
Stir in zucchini and cook until tender.
Stir in tomatoes and serve.

Serves 8
Per serving: 65 Total calories; 6 Sat-fat calories

PIZZA, CHILI, QUICHE, AND TORTILLAS

19

"**O**H, WOE IS ME," says the sat-fat counter. "How can I go on without pizza and chili? Life will be bare." STOP! The following recipes for pizza, chili, quiche, and tortillas are delectable. The only thing they lack is saturated fat. So don't feel sorry for yourself. You *can* have your cake — or pizza — and eat it too!

PIZZA

You might think that a low-fat diet would eliminate pizza, but the following recipes will prove to you how fabulous low-sat-fat pizzas can be. They make good snacks as well as main courses for lunch or dinner. Freeze leftovers (if there are any!). Then, in the future when you want a treat, heat the frozen slices in your toaster oven.

To make pizza with a crisper crust, buy four inexpensive unglazed quarry tiles (each about a 5-inch square) at a tile store or purchase a pizza tile at a store that sells kitchen supplies. Pizza baked directly on hot tiles has a crunchier crust.

To slide the pizza onto the tiles it helps to have a pizza peel. It looks like this:

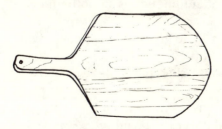

You may devise other gizmos to slide the pizza onto the tiles if you wish, but a pizza peel really works well. Of course, you may forgo both the tiles and the pizza peel and use a metal pizza pan or cookie sheet instead.

PIZZA

Dough

1 tablespoon active dry yeast
¼ cup warm water
Pinch of sugar
4 cups unbleached white flour

1 teaspoon salt
1 cup warm water
3 tablespoons olive oil

Topping

2 cloves garlic
3 tablespoons olive oil
Salt to taste
1½ cups tomato sauce (page 263)
2 cups sliced mushrooms
1½ sliced green peppers (about 1½ cups)

1 cup sliced onion
1⅓ cups low-fat (1%) cottage cheese
3 teaspoons oregano
4 teaspoons olive oil

The Dough

Place yeast, the ¼ cup warm (but not hot) water, and sugar in a large bowl or the work bowl of your food processor. Let proof (become bubbly).

Mix in flour and salt.

Mix in the 1 cup warm (but not hot) water and olive oil.

Knead or process until dough is smooth and elastic, adding more flour if needed.

Place dough in a large greased bowl, cover with a towel, and let rise for about 45 minutes.

While the dough is rising, place tiles (see above) in oven and heat oven to 450°F.

After the dough has risen, divide it into four parts, form each into a smooth ball, and cover for 10 minutes.

Roll the dough into four small circles, 10 to 12 inches each. Wait 10 minutes more. Roll the dough thinner.

To Make Each Pizza

Cover pizza peel with a thin layer of cornmeal or grease pizza pan with oil.

Place one rolled circle of dough on the pizza peel or in the pizza pan.

Crush garlic into olive oil. Paint the surface of the dough with garlic oil and sprinkle with salt.

Spoon about ¼ cup tomato sauce over the dough.

Arrange mushrooms, green peppers, and onions over tomato sauce.

Put cottage cheese on top (as if it were mozzarella).

Sprinkle with ¾ teaspoon oregano and drizzle with olive oil.

Bake for 10–20 minutes or until crust is golden brown.

4 pizzas, 4 slices per pizza
Per slice: 155 Total calories; 5 Sat-fat calories

CALZONE

A recipe that you can enjoy with no pangs of remorse. This seems like a lot of work, but once you do it, it goes quickly and is quite delicious.

Dough

1 tablespoon active dry yeast
pinch of sugar
½ cup warm water
3–4½ cups unbleached white
    flour

1–1½ teaspoons salt
1 cup skim milk
2 tablespoons olive oil

Tomato Sauce*

3 tablespoons olive oil
1 cup chopped onion
4 large cans (28 oz each)
   tomatoes

1 can (6 oz) tomato paste
2 teaspoons basil
1 teaspoon salt

Filling

1 clove garlic
¼ cup olive oil
Salt to taste
1 cup low-fat (1%) cottage
   cheese

1 green pepper, sliced
1 cup sliced mushrooms
1 cup sliced onion

The Dough

Place yeast, sugar, and warm water in food processor or large bowl and let proof.

Add 3 cups flour and salt and mix.

Add skim milk and olive oil and process until dough masses into a ball or knead until smooth and elastic. Add more flour if dough is too sticky.

Place dough in a bowl greased with oil and cover with a towel. Let rise in a warm place for about 1 hour.

If you are using pizza tiles (see page 259), place them in preheated 450°F oven 30 minutes before baking pizza.

While dough is rising, make the tomato sauce.

The Tomato Sauce

Place olive oil in large saucepan.

Add onion and cook over low heat until tender.

Strain juice from canned tomatoes. (Freeze juice for soups.) Chop tomatoes (easily done in food processor).

Mix tomato paste into tomatoes. Add tomato mixture to saucepan.

Add basil and salt and cook until thick (about 45 minutes).

To Make the Calzone

When dough has risen, divide it into 8 parts and form each part into a smooth ball. Cover with a towel or plastic wrap for about 10

---

*This recipe makes 8 cups of tomato sauce. You will need only about one cup for calzone. Freeze the rest for future use in other recipes or as spaghetti sauce.

minutes. It is important that you let the dough "rest" or it will be difficult to roll flat.

Roll each ball into a flat circle. Wait 10 minutes more.

Make each circle thinner. Place dough on floured surface or pizza peel sprinkled with cornmeal (see page 259).

Crush garlic into olive oil. Brush dough with the garlic oil, then sprinkle it with salt.

Spread about 2 tablespoons of tomato sauce over half the dough, leaving a border of ½ inch.

Spread 2 tablespoons cottage cheese evenly over tomato sauce.

Top with a few slices of green pepper, mushroom, and onion.

Fold the top half of the dough over and pinch the top and bottom edges together. Paint the top with garlic oil and salt lightly.

Slide calzone onto hot tiles or onto cookie sheet.

Bake for about 10–20 minutes or until browned.

Makes 8 calzone
Per calzone: 322 Total calories; 12 Sat-fat calories

FOCACCIA

The whole-wheat flour in this pizza not only makes it healthier but also gives it a toasty taste and crunchy texture. Try it! It is easy and makes great snacks. Freeze it in snack-size slices.

Dough

1½ teaspoons dry active yeast
½ teaspoon honey
1 cup warm water

2½ cups whole-wheat flour
¾ teaspoon salt
1 tablespoon olive oil

Tomato Sauce

1 large can (28 oz) tomatoes, or
   3 large tomatoes
2 cloves garlic, minced
1 small onion, chopped
1 tablespoon olive oil

½ teaspoon oregano
¼ teaspoon basil
Ground hot cherry peppers
   (optional)

The Dough

Place yeast, honey, and warm water in food processor or large bowl. Let proof.

Add flour, salt, and olive oil and process or knead until smooth and elastic, adding flour if needed.

Place dough in an oiled bowl, cover with a towel, and let rise in a warm place for about 1 hour.

Punch down dough and let it rest on floured counter for 10 minutes.

Preheat oven to 400°F and grease a 10 × 15-inch cookie sheet with oil.

Roll dough out (or press with your hands) onto the cookie sheet.

Pinch a rim around the edge. Cover with a towel and let rise for 30 minutes.

Meanwhile, make the tomato sauce.

The Tomato Sauce

If using canned tomatoes, drain liquid and chop tomatoes. If using whole tomatoes, chop fine.

In a medium skillet, sauté garlic and onion in olive oil until tender.

Stir in tomatoes, oregano, and basil and let simmer until thick (about 10–15 minutes).

Let cool.

Spread the sauce over the dough.
Add hot cherry peppers, if desired.
Bake for 20–25 minutes.

Makes 12 pieces
Per piece: 120 Total calories; 3 Sat-fat calories

PISSALADIÈRE

An onion pizza of Provence. Pissaladière makes a perfect luncheon dish, snack, or light dinner. Although it looks as if it took a lot of work, it is quite simple to make. Cook the onions ahead to save time later.

Filling

3 cups chopped onion
2 cloves garlic, minced

3 tablespoons olive oil

Dough

1 teaspoon dry yeast
pinch of sugar
¼ cup water
2–3 cups unbleached white
  flour

¼ teaspoon salt
¾ cup warm water
2 tablespoons olive oil

12 pitted black olives, halved

6 anchovies

The Filling

Slowly cook onion and garlic in olive oil until soft (about 30 minutes). Set aside. (You can refrigerate cooked onions for a few days.)

The Dough

About 1 hour before serving, place yeast, sugar, and ¼ cup warm water in bowl or food processor. Let proof.

Mix in 2 cups of flour and salt.

Add ¾ cup warm water and olive oil and knead or process for 15 seconds.

Add more flour until dough is smooth and elastic.

Place dough in oiled bowl, cover with towel, and let rise for about 45 minutes.

After 35 minutes, preheat oven to 450°F.

On a greased round pizza pan or cookie sheet, roll out or push the dough into a 10-inch circle.

Spoon onions evenly over dough.

Starting from the center of the circle, place olives in lines like the spokes of a wheel.

Place anchovies between the lines of olives.
Bake for 20 minutes or until dough is slightly golden brown.

Makes 8 slices
Per slice: 256 Total calories; 12 Sat-fat calories

QUICHE

The word "quiche" conjures up images of dozens of eggs and tons of cream, ham, and cheese. The following wonderful quiches will expand your definition. They are made with only low-sat-fat ingredients and make perfect appetizers or light meals.

SPINACH QUICHE

Partially baked nonsweet pie
  crust (page 330)
1 tablespoon chopped parsley
1 teaspoon basil
1 package (10 oz) fresh spinach
  (or frozen spinach, thawed)
1 cup low-fat (1%) cottage
  cheese

1 cup buttermilk
1 egg
1 egg white
½ teaspoon salt
¼ teaspoon freshly ground
  pepper
¼ teaspoon grated nutmeg
2 tablespoons sliced green onion

Preheat oven to 375°F.

Combine parsley with basil (easily done in food processor) and set aside.

If using fresh spinach, wash leaves and tear off stems.

In a medium saucepan, cook fresh or thawed spinach for about 3 minutes in ½ cup boiling water. Drain.

Combine cottage cheese, buttermilk, egg, egg white, salt, pepper, and nutmeg in food processor or bowl.

If using processor, add spinach and process. If mixing in bowl, chop spinach finely and add to cottage cheese mixture.

Stir in green onion and parsley-basil mixture and pour into partially baked pie crust.

Bake for about 30 minutes.

Makes 9 slices
Per slice: 200 Total calories; 17 Sat-fat calories

TOMATO QUICHE

Another quiche you can eat with no qualms is this one, which has a Mediterranean flavor. It is absolutely delicious. If you are an anchovy-hater, do not avoid this recipe. The anchovies enhance the flavor but are not discernible in the taste.

Partially baked nonsweet pie
  crust (page 330)
⅓ cup chopped onion
1 tablespoon olive oil
1 large can (28 oz) + 1 small
  can (16 oz) tomatoes
1 clove garlic, minced
¼ teaspoon basil
½ teaspoon oregano

½ teaspoon salt
6 sprigs parsley, stems removed
1 tin (2 oz) anchovies
1 egg
1 egg white
3 tablespoons tomato paste
25 large pitted black olives, cut
  in half
½ tablespoon olive oil

In a medium skillet, sauté onion in olive oil until tender.

Meanwhile, drain the juice from the tomatoes. (Freeze the liquid for future use.) Chop tomatoes and add to onion.

Mix in garlic, basil, oregano, and salt.

Increase heat to high. When tomato mixture begins to bubble, reduce heat to medium.

Cook tomatoes for about 50 minutes or until thick, stirring occasionally. You may have to reduce heat if mixture begins to boil. Make sure there is no excess liquid.

When sauce is very thick, remove skillet from heat. Cool sauce slightly.

Preheat oven to 375°F.

In a food processor or blender, mix parsley, anchovies, egg, egg white, and tomato paste.

Fold anchovy mixture into tomato sauce and pour into partially baked pie crust.

Artistically arrange olive halves on top of tomato mixture.

Dribble oil over quiche and bake for 25–30 minutes or until puffy and browned on top.

Makes 9 slices
Per slice: 220 Total calories; 21 Sat-fat calories

CHILI

Chili is traditionally made with beef. You will not miss the beef in the following vegetarian recipes. They are delicious and filling — wonderful for a fall or winter day.

CHILI NON CARNE

This is one of the best chili recipes we have ever tasted. It is filled with nutritious vegetables that provide texture but do not interfere with the delicious chili taste. Eat it hot in a bowl mixed with chopped onions, tomatoes, and lettuce, or spoon it into pita bread with chopped onion, lettuce, and tomatoes. Dried beans such as kidney beans and navy beans have been shown to be effective in lowering blood cholesterol.

¾ cup chopped onion
2 cloves garlic, minced
3 tablespoons olive oil
2 tablespoons chili powder
¼ teaspoon basil
¼ teaspoon oregano
¼ teaspoon cumin
2 cups finely chopped zucchini
1 cup finely chopped carrot
1 large can (28 oz) tomatoes +
 1 small can (14½ oz) tomatoes, drained and chopped

1 can (15 oz) kidney beans,
 undrained
2 cans (15 oz each) kidney
 beans, *drained* and thoroughly
 rinsed
Chopped onions, tomatoes,
 lettuce, or green peppers, for
 garnish

In a large pot, sauté onion and garlic in olive oil until soft.

Mix in chili powder, basil, oregano, and cumin.

Stir in zucchini and carrots until well blended. Cook for about 1 minute over low heat, stirring occasionally.

Stir in chopped tomatoes, undrained kidney beans, and drained kidney beans.

Bring to a boil. Reduce heat and simmer for 30–45 minutes or until thick.

Top with chopped onions, tomatoes, and lettuce or green peppers.

Makes 8 one-cup servings
Per serving: 157 Total calories; 7 Sat-fat calories

CRAIG LEFEBVRE'S PAWTUCKET CHILI

Craig Lefebvre, community director of the Pawtucket Heart Health Program, created this scrumptious heart-healthy chili recipe for a contest, the Hot Healthy Chili Challenge. Eat it and you'll see why it's a winner!

1 large can (40 oz) kidney beans, or 2 small cans (16 oz each)
1 can (15 oz) chickpeas
2 cloves garlic, minced
1 medium onion, chopped
1 tablespoon olive oil

1 can (8 oz) tomato sauce
1 can (14½ oz) whole tomatoes
1 tablespoon oregano
½ teaspoon thyme
1 teaspoon cumin
½ teaspoon basil
3 tablespoons chili powder

Rinse kidney beans and chickpeas to remove salt. Set aside.
Sauté garlic and onion in olive oil.
Add beans, chickpeas, and remaining ingredients and bring to a boil.
Simmer for 20 minutes (or longer) until thick.

Makes 8 one-cup servings
Per serving: 115 Total calories; 4 Sat-fat calories

TORTILLAS

Who says you can't have tortillas on a low-sat-fat diet? Admittedly, these tortillas contain no meat or cheese, but they are spicy and great tasting, just like their Mexican counterparts. As a bonus, your arteries will be happier with these than with beef or cheese.

Corn Tortillas* Filling

1 cup dried lentils
2 cups water
2½ tablespoons raisins
3 cloves garlic, minced
¼ teaspoon red pepper flakes

2 teaspoons chili powder
½ teaspoon cumin
¼ teaspoon basil
7 tablespoons tomato paste
2 cups water

---

*Corn tortillas can be found in the refrigerator section of most supermarkets. Be sure they contain only corn, water, and lime — no lard or other saturated fat.

Toppings

Shredded zucchini   Nonfat yogurt

The Filling

In a large pot, combine lentils and 2 cups water and simmer for 10 minutes.

Add raisins, garlic, red pepper flakes, chili powder, cumin, basil, tomato paste, and 1 cup of the remaining 2 cups water and mix well.

Cook slowly for 15 minutes, adding additional 1 cup water when lentil mixture becomes too thick. Stir periodically.

Continue cooking, stirring occasionally (15–30 minutes more) until lentil mixture is thick.

Makes filling for 16 tortillas. Freeze half for future use.

Meanwhile, wrap tortillas completely in aluminum foil and bake at 350°F for 10–15 minutes.

Assembling the Tortillas

Place about 3 tablespoons lentil mixture in center of each tortilla.
Cover with about 1 tablespoon shredded zucchini.
Top with about 1 tablespoon yogurt. Serve.

Makes 8 tortillas
Per tortilla: 90 Total calories; trace Sat-fat calories

PASTA, RICE, AND OTHER GRAINS

20

PASTA, BARLEY, rice, and bulgur are filling and low in saturated fat. As side dishes or complete meals, they add texture and variety to your eating.

Q ## ASPARAGUS PASTA

Asparagus pasta makes a delightful luncheon dish, first course for an elegant meal, or light dinner. No one consuming this dish will believe how incredibly simple it is to make.

2 pounds asparagus, sliced on the diagonal into 1-inch pieces
¼ cup Dijon mustard
¼ cup olive oil
½ cup thinly sliced shallots
2 cloves garlic, minced

4 anchovy fillets
½ teaspoon thyme
¼ cup chopped parsley
1 pound very thin spaghetti or pasta of your choice
Salt and pepper to taste

In a large pot of boiling water, cook asparagus until tender and still bright green (about 3 minutes).

Combine mustard, olive oil, shallots, garlic, anchovies, thyme, and parsley. Set aside.

Cook pasta. Drain, but reserve 1 cup of the cooking water.

Combine pasta with dressing and asparagus and mix well. Add some of the cooking water if too dry. Add salt and pepper to taste.

Serves 8
Per serving: 295 Total calories; 9 Sat-fat calories

Variation: Follow the above recipe but halve all ingredients and add two boned and skinned chicken breast halves that have been steamed and cut into bite-size pieces.

Serves 4
Per serving: 366 Total calories; 13 Sat-fat calories

CREAMY FETTUCCINE WITH VEGETABLES

1 cup sliced carrots
1 cup sliced zucchini
1 cup broccoli flowerets
1 cup green beans, cut in half
8 ounces fettuccine

1½ cups low-fat (1%) cottage
  cheese
⅔ cup skim milk
2 teaspoons basil
¼ cup chopped parsley

Steam carrots, zucchini, broccoli, and green beans until tender. Put in serving bowl to cool.

Cook pasta according to package directions, drain, and set aside to cool.

Using blender or food processor, purée cottage cheese until smooth. Blend in skim milk, basil, and parsley.

Combine vegetables and pasta.

Pour sauce over cool vegetables and pasta and mix until they are thoroughly coated. Serve at room temperature.

Serves 6
Per serving: 74 Total calories; 4 Sat-fat calories

PEASANT PASTA

Any combination of vegetables will do. Try these:

2 cups broccoli flowerets
1 cup cauliflower flowerets
1 zucchini, sliced
5 spears asparagus
20 green beans
½ pound very thin sphaghetti
¼ cup chopped fresh parsley
2 cloves garlic

8 anchovy fillets
3 tablespoons olive oil
1 large tomato, coarsely
  chopped
1 sweet red pepper, coarsely
  chopped
10–15 snow peas
2 dried chili peppers or ½
  teaspoon red pepper flakes

Steam broccoli, cauliflower, and zucchini until tender, and set aside.

Snap off the bottoms of the asparagus and boil for 1–2 minutes, until just tender. Set aside.

Submerge green beans in boiling water for 1–3 minutes, until just tender. Set aside.

While spaghetti is boiling (6 minutes), blend together parsley, garlic, anchovy fillets, and olive oil in a blender or food processor.

Drain spaghetti. Reserve 1 cup of water.

Stir anchovy sauce into spaghetti. If spaghetti is too dry, add a little water.

Stir in cooked vegetables, tomato, red pepper, and snow peas, until well covered with sauce.

Stir in red pepper flakes.

Serves 6
Per serving: 260 Total calories; 11 Sat-fat calories

Q   PASTA MEXICALI

½ pound fancy pasta (fusilli, rigatoni, shells, etc.)
1 zucchini
1 tablespoon margarine
½ cup chopped onion

1 teaspoon cumin
1 teaspoon chili powder
¼ teaspoon salt
1 red pepper, sliced
¼ cup tomato juice

Cook pasta according to package directions. Set aside.
Cut zucchini in quarters lengthwise. Slice into bite-size chunks.
Steam zucchini until just tender. Set aside.
In a small skillet, melt margarine.
Add onion and cook until soft.
Stir in cumin, chili powder, and salt.
Add onion mixture to pasta and mix well.
Add zucchini and red pepper. Add tomato juice and mix well.
Serve warm or at room temperature.

Serves 6
Per serving: 170 Total calories; 4 Sat-fat calories

Q

PASTA WITH PESTO

Pesto hails from Genova, Italy, where the salty soil makes the basil particularly wonderful. Even in the United States, pesto can be superb. It is easy to make and freezes well. This is the only recipe in this book that uses cheese. The recipe uses a food processor or blender; you can also use a mortar and pestle.

2 cups fresh basil	2 tablespoons Parmesan cheese
3 cloves garlic	1 tablespoon Romano cheese
1 teaspoon salt	1 package (16 oz) very thin
¼ cup olive oil	spaghetti
3 tablespoons margarine	

Prepare basil by rinsing it and tearing off the leaves. Discard the stems.

Chop garlic in a food processor or blender.

Add basil and salt. Process.

Add olive oil. Process until smooth. At this point you can put pesto aside for later use or freeze.

When ready to serve, mix margarine into pesto with a fork and blend well.

Blend in cheeses. Set aside.

Make spaghetti according to package directions.

Drain, but reserve 1 cup of the cooking water.

Mix pesto into pasta. If pesto is too dry, carefully stir in a small amount of spaghetti water.

Serves 8
Per serving: 315 Total calories; 21 Sat-fat calories

Q   # EASY SPAGHETTI SAUCE À LA SICILIA

Make a basic tomato sauce and add steamed eggplant and mushrooms for an appetizing spaghetti sauce that needs no ground meat.

1 small eggplant, peeled and cubed	2 cups sliced mushrooms
	12 ounces spaghetti
6 cups Basic Tomato Sauce (see page 275)	

Prepare eggplant (see page 249) and steam until tender. Set aside.

In a medium saucepan, heat 6 cups of tomato sauce.

Stir in eggplant and mushrooms, cook 5 minutes more.

While spaghetti sauce is cooking, prepare spaghetti according to package directions.

Pour tomato sauce over spaghetti and serve.

Serves 6
Per serving: 325 Total calories; 6 Sat-fat calories

BASIC TOMATO SAUCE

1 cup chopped onion

3 tablespoons olive oil

4 large cans (28 oz each) tomatoes, drained

1 can (6 oz) tomato paste

2 teaspoons basil

1 teaspoon salt

In a large saucepan, cook onion in olive oil until soft.

Chop tomatoes and add to onion.

Stir in tomato paste. (Tomatoes can easily be chopped and tomato paste blended in food processor.)

Stir in basil and salt.

Simmer until thick (at least 1 hour).

This tomato sauce freezes well.

Makes 8 cups
Per cup: 104 Total calories; 5 Sat-fat calories

SPAGHETTI TOURAINE

1¼ pounds fresh tomatoes

4 cloves garlic, peeled

¼ cup olive oil

Salt to taste

1 tablespoon margarine

1 tablespoon minced carrot

1 tablespoon minced celery

1 tablespoon minced leek

1 tablespoon minced shallot

1 cup dry white wine or vermouth

Bouquet garni (2 parsley sprigs, ⅓ bay leaf, and ⅛ teaspoon thyme wrapped in cheesecloth)

½ cup + 2 tablespoons evaporated skim milk

¼ teaspoon salt

1 tablespoon dried tarragon (or fresh, if available)

10 ounces spaghetti

Place tomatoes in a large saucepan of boiling water. Immediately pour out hot water and pour in cold water.

Peel tomatoes, cut them in half crosswise (not across the stem), squeeze out the seeds and juice, and coarsely chop.

In a medium skillet, cook tomatoes and garlic in olive oil until reduced to a thick sauce (about 20 minutes). Stir occasionally. Add salt.

Meanwhile, melt margarine in a small saucepan. Stir in carrot, celery, leek, and shallot.

Add wine and bouquet garni.

Reduce until thick and stir in evaporated skim milk.

Remove bouquet garni and pour mixture through a sieve to strain out the vegetables. Add tarragon.

Mix with tomato sauce and pour over pasta.

Serves 4
Per serving: 268 Total calories; 21 Sat-fat calories

Q INDIAN RICE

1 tablespoon olive oil	1 teaspoon coriander
2 cloves garlic, minced	1/4 teaspoon cinnamon
1 tablespoon minced ginger root	1/4 teaspoon ground cloves
3/4 cup chopped onion	1/4 teaspoon salt
1/4 teaspoon cardamom	1 1/2 cups long-grain rice
1/4 teaspoon caraway seeds	3 3/4 cups water

In a medium saucepan, heat olive oil.

Add garlic, ginger, and onion and cook until soft.

Mix in cardamom, caraway seeds, coriander, cinnamon, cloves, salt, and rice and blend well.

Add water, cover, and bring to a boil. Reduce heat and cook until all water is absorbed (about 25 minutes).

Makes 12 half-cup servings
Per serving: 97 Total calories; 2 Sat-fat calories

Q

OLIVE-ARTICHOKE RICE

3¾ cups water
1½ cups long-grain rice
½ teaspoon salt
3 tablespoons olive oil
1 tin (2 oz) anchovies (omit if
   you hate anchovies)

1 red pepper, sliced
½ cup artichoke hearts, diced
12 pitted black olives, sliced

In a medium saucepan, bring water to a boil.

Add rice and salt, cover, reduce heat to low, and cook for 25 minutes or until all water is absorbed.

Mix in remaining ingredients and cool to lukewarm.

Makes 14 half-cup servings
Per serving: 105 Total calories; 5 Sat-fat calories

Q   ## RICE PILAU WITH APRICOTS AND RAISINS

3 tablespoons slivered almonds
2 tablespoons margarine
1 teaspoon minced ginger root
1 clove garlic, minced
¼ cup chopped onion
1 teaspoon salt
2 whole cloves

½ cinnamon stick
1 teaspoon turmeric
1½ cups long-grain rice
3¾ cups water
¼ cup apricots, sliced
2 tablespoons raisins

In a medium casserole, sauté slivered almonds in margarine over medium heat until golden.

Add ginger, garlic, and onion and sauté until soft.

Mix in salt, cloves, cinnamon stick, and turmeric.

Add rice and stir until well coated.

Add water and bring to a boil. Cover, reduce heat to low (or off), and cook until water is absorbed (about 25 minutes).

Mix in apricots and raisins.

Makes 14 half-cup servings
Per serving: 106 Total calories; 4 Sat-fat calories

Q
LEMON RICE WITH SPINACH AND RED PEPPER

⅓ cup chopped onion
1 tablespoon olive oil
1 cup long-grain rice
½ teaspoon salt
2½ cups water

1 cup chopped spinach
2 tablespoons fresh lemon juice
1 red pepper, chopped (about ½ cup)

In a medium saucepan, sauté onion in olive oil until soft.

Mix in the rice and salt. Add water and bring to a boil. Reduce heat to low or off and cover saucepan.

After 15 minutes, stir spinach and lemon juice into rice.

Cook for 10 minutes more or until liquid is completely absorbed.

Mix in red pepper and serve.

Makes 8 half-cup servings
Per serving: 100 Total calories; 2 Sat-fat calories

⌨ FRIED RICE

2 egg whites
½ egg yolk
2 tablespoons olive oil
3 green onions, cut into ¼-inch pieces

3 cups boiled rice (cold)
1 tablespoon soy sauce
¼ teaspoon sugar
¼ cup cooked diced chicken, shrimp, turkey, or combination

Beat egg whites and yolk together.
In a small skillet, scramble eggs in 1 tablespoon oil. Set aside.
In a large skillet, sauté green onions in 1 tablespoon oil.
Add rice and mix thoroughly.
Stir in soy sauce and sugar.
Stir in eggs and meat.

Makes 6 one-half cup servings
Per serving: 180 Total calories; 8 Sat-fat calories

⌨ BULGUR WITH TOMATOES AND OLIVES

1 cup bulgur (cracked wheat)
2 tablespoons margarine
1 cup tomato juice
1 cup water

1 tomato, chopped
¼ cup sliced green olives
2 stalks celery, chopped
3 green onions, sliced

In a large skillet, sauté bulgur in margarine until bulgur begins to color and crackle.

Add tomato juice, water, and tomato and simmer until most liquid is absorbed (about 35 minutes).

Add olives, celery, and green onions and mix until heated through.

Makes 9 half-cup servings
Per serving: 79 Total calories; 2 Sat-fat calories

Q

BARLEY PLUS

An interesting alternative to rice.

¾ cup chopped onion
½ cup chopped mushrooms
2 tablespoons margarine
1 cup pearl barley, rinsed

1 can (10¾ oz) chicken broth, strained
½ teaspoon salt

Sauté onion and mushrooms in margarine until tender. Stir in barley.

Add 1 cup of the chicken broth plus salt and bring to a boil. Cover and simmer for 25 minutes.

Add remaining broth plus water to equal 1 cup. Cook 25 more minutes until liquid is absorbed.

Fluff barley with a fork before serving.

Serves 6
Per serving: 167 Total calories; 7 Sat-fat calories

SALADS

21

SALADS ARE refreshing. They can be quite nutritious and add texture and bulk to a meal. Salads by themselves generally contain very little fat. But beware of high-fat salad dressings! These culprits turn many a healthy salad into a no-no dish for people watching their fat intake and calories.

Gourmet food shops specialize in a variety of salads — pasta salad, rice salad, chicken, turkey, and fish salads. Here are a few you can make yourself and eat without hesitation.

▣ TARRAGON-RAISIN CHICKEN SALAD

4 boned and skinned chicken
  breast halves
½ teaspoon salt
1 small onion
1 small carrot
4 whole peppercorns

2 tablespoons reduced-calorie
  mayonnaise
2 tablespoons nonfat yogurt
2 teaspoons tarragon
2 tablespoons golden raisins

In a medium saucepan, combine chicken, salt, onion, carrot, and peppercorns. Add water to cover and bring to a boil.

Reduce heat and simmer until chicken is cooked through.

Strain broth. (Freeze for future use.)

Cut chicken into large chunks and set aside.

Combine mayonnaise, yogurt, tarragon, and raisins.

Add to chicken and mix until chicken is well coated.

Serves 4
Per serving: 180 Total calories; 12 Sat-fat calories

Q
CORIANDER CHICKEN SALAD

6 boned and skinned chicken
  breast halves
1 carrot
2 cloves garlic
1 bay leaf
½ teaspoon salt

¼ teaspoon coriander
2 cups broccoli flowerets
2 tablespoons reduced-calorie
  mayonnaise
2 tablespoons nonfat yogurt
2 teaspoons Dijon mustard

In a medium saucepan, combine chicken, carrot, garlic, bay leaf, and salt. Add water to cover and cook at slow boil until chicken breasts are completely cooked.

Strain broth and freeze for future use.

Cut chicken into large chunks, mix with coriander, and set aside to cool.

Steam broccoli until just tender.

Combine salad dressing, yogurt, and mustard.

Mix mustard-yogurt dressing with chicken.

Stir in broccoli until coated with dressing.

Serves 8
Per serving: 90 Total calories; 12 Sat-fat calories

Q
CHICKEN SALAD WITH SHALLOTS
AND MUSHROOMS

4 boned and skinned chicken
  breast halves
2 tablespoons olive oil
2 tablespoons white vinegar

2 teaspoons minced shallot
1 cup sliced mushrooms
1 teaspoon thyme
¼ teaspoon salt

Cook chicken as in Tarragon-Raisin Chicken Salad (page 281). Combine remaining ingredients and pour over chicken. Mix until chicken is well coated.

Serves 6
Per serving: 140 Total calories; 11 Sat-fat calories

⧄ DIJON CHICKEN-RICE SALAD

3¾ cups water
1½ cups long-grain rice
½ teaspoon salt
2 tablespoons Dijon mustard
2 tablespoons white vinegar
¼ cup olive oil

½–1 cup diced green and/or red
  pepper
¼ cup pitted black olives, sliced
¼ cup sliced green onion
2 cooked chicken breast halves,
  diced

In a medium saucepan, bring water to a boil.

Add rice and salt, reduce heat, cover, and simmer for 20–25 minutes or until water is absorbed.

Place rice in a bowl.

Combine mustard, vinegar, and olive oil and mix into rice.

Add green pepper, olives, green onion, and chicken and mix well.
Tastes best when tepid.

Serves 6
Per serving: 305 Total calories; 15 Sat-fat calories

⧄ ORIENTAL CHICKEN SALAD

4 boned and skinned chicken
  breast halves
1 carrot
¼ small onion
1 head broccoli, cut into
  flowerets (about 3 cups)
3 tablespoons walnut oil

3 tablespoons soy sauce
1 tablespoon dry vermouth
2 teaspoons minced ginger root
¼ cup chopped walnuts
½ pound mushrooms, sliced
1 head red-leaf or Boston
  lettuce

In a large pot, combine chicken, carrot, and onion. Cover with water and boil until chicken is cooked through.

Cut chicken into bite-size pieces. Set aside.

Steam broccoli flowerets until *just* tender.

Combine walnut oil, soy sauce, and ginger in a large bowl.

Add walnuts, mushrooms, and chicken and mix until all are coated with sauce. Stir in broccoli.

Place some lettuce on each salad plate. Top with chicken salad.

Serves 4
Per serving: 325 Total calories; 20 Sat-fat calories

◻ CURRIED TUNA SALAD WITH PEARS

3 tablespoons reduced-calorie
  mayonnaise
1½ tablespoons nonfat yogurt
¾–1 teaspoon curry powder

2 cans (6½ oz each) water-
  packed tuna, drained
3 tablespoons diced pear
Lettuce

Combine mayonnaise, yogurt, and curry powder.
Mix into tuna fish.
Stir in pear.
Serve over lettuce.

Serves 3
Per serving: 220 Total calories; 11 Sat-fat calories

SALADE NIÇOISE

A salad that is a meal in itself. Our Salade Niçoise is just like those served on the Riviera, but the egg yolks have been removed.

Dressing

1 clove garlic, minced
Juice of ½ lemon (about 2
  tablespoons)
2 tablespoons white vinegar

1 tablespoon Dijon mustard
1 teaspoon basil
½ teaspoon salt
½ cup olive oil

Salad

4 potatoes
3 cups green beans, tips
  removed and cut in half
1 medium head red-leaf or
  Boston lettuce, shredded
4 tomatoes, cut into eighths

Whites from 3 hard-boiled eggs
¼ cup pitted black olives
2 tablespoons capers
1 tin (2 oz) anchovy fillets
1 can (6½ oz) water-packed
  solid white tuna, drained

Combine all dressing ingredients in a jar and shake vigorously. Set aside.

Steam potatoes until tender, peel, and cut into bite-size pieces.

Mix potatoes with ¼ cup dressing and set aside.

Cook green beans in boiling water for 5 minutes or until just tender and bright green.

Mix green beans with 2 tablespoons dressing and set aside.

Put lettuce and tomatoes in a large salad bowl and toss them with the remaining dressing.

Add potatoes, green beans, egg whites, olives, capers, anchovies, and drained tuna and mix until well coated with dressing. Traditionally each vegetable is segregated on a plate. We prefer them mixed into the salad.

Serves 10
Per serving: 195 Total calories; 15 Sat-fat calories

INDONESIAN VEGETABLE SALAD

2 cups shredded lettuce or
    Chinese celery cabbage
1 cup sliced carrot
1 cup green beans, cooked in
    boiling water until just tender

2 tomatoes, sliced
1 cucumber, peeled and sliced

Sauce

1 tablespoon sliced green onion
½ tablespoon olive oil
4 tablespoons natural all-peanut
    peanut butter
1 clove garlic, minced
½ teaspoon red pepper flakes

1 bay leaf
1 slice lemon
1 teaspoon sugar
½ teaspoon salt
¾ cup skim milk
2 tablespoons water

Place lettuce on a platter.

Artistically arrange carrots, green beans, tomatoes, and cucumber over lettuce. Cover with plastic wrap and chill in refrigerator.

In a small saucepan, sauté green onion in olive oil.

Mix in peanut butter, garlic, red pepper flakes, bay leaf, lemon, sugar, and salt until peanut butter starts to melt.

Gradually blend in skim milk. Cook over low heat, stirring constantly, until thick. Chill dressing.

Before serving, dilute dressing with water.

Pass platter and dressing separately so everyone can take what they want.

Serves 6
Per serving: 108 Total calories; 10 Sat-fat calories

TABBOULI

1 cup bulgur (cracked wheat)	2 cloves garlic, minced
3 cups boiling water	1 small onion, chopped
1 can (15 oz) chickpeas, drained	½ cup chopped green pepper
¼ cup fresh mint, minced, or ½ teaspoon dried mint	2 medium tomatoes, chopped
	2 tablespoons olive oil
1 teaspoon oregano	2 tablespoons fresh lemon juice
½ teaspoon salt	¼ cup chopped parsley
¼ teaspoon freshly ground pepper	

Place bulgur in a large bowl and cover with boiling water.

Let stand for about 1 hour or until fluffy. Squeeze out excess water.

Combine bulgur with remaining ingredients.

Chill for at least 1 hour.

Makes 10 half-cup servings
Per serving: 135 Total calories; 5 Sat-fat calories

Q

CUCUMBER SALAD

2 cucumbers, peeled and sliced
thin
1 medium onion, sliced thin
1 teaspoon salt

1 teaspoon sugar
1 teaspoon dill weed
1 cup white vinegar

Mix cucumbers and onion together in a ceramic or glass bowl.

Add salt, sugar, and dill weed to vinegar and pour over cucumbers and onion.

Chill 1 hour.

Serves 6
Per serving: 20 Total calories; 0 Sat-fat calories

Q

EASTERN SPINACH SALAD

1 package (10 oz) fresh spinach,
washed and shredded
10 water chestnuts, sliced
3 green onions, sliced
1 cup sliced mushrooms
1 cucumber, peeled and sliced
thin

2 tablespoons olive oil
2 tablespoons soy sauce
3 tablespoons fresh lemon juice
1½ tablespoons honey
1 tablespoon sesame seeds,
toasted

In a salad bowl, combine spinach, water chestnuts, green onions, mushrooms, and cucumber slices.

Mix together olive oil, soy sauce, lemon juice, and honey and pour over salad.

Sprinkle with sesame seeds.

Serves 8
Per serving: 70 Total calories; 5 Sat-fat calories

Q

POTATO SALAD

4–5 Russet (red) potatoes
½ cup nonfat yogurt
3 tablespoons reduced-calorie
mayonnaise

1 teaspoon tarragon
1 tablespoon white vinegar
1 teaspoon Dijon mustard
½ teaspoon salt

Scrub potatoes thoroughly. Steam until tender.
Meanwhile, combine remaining ingredients. Set aside.
Cut potatoes into chunks (do not remove skin).
Pour sauce over potatoes so they are thoroughly coated.
Serve warm or cold.

Serves 6
Per serving: 105 Total calories; 5 Sat-fat calories

Q   FRUIT SALAD WITH COTTAGE CHEESE OR YOGURT

This high-protein, low-fat dish makes a filling lunch. Round it off with a piece of Honey Whole-Wheat Bread (page 303) and, for dessert, home-popped popcorn.

Spring or Summer Fruits

¼ cantaloupe   1 peach
½ cup blueberries   ⅙ honeydew melon

Fall or Winter Fruits

½ Golden Delicious apple   ½ Bosc pear
1 kiwi   ½ orange

½ cup low-fat (1%) cottage
   cheese or nonfat yogurt

Cut fruit into bite-size pieces and place in bowl.
Mix in cottage cheese or yogurt.

Serves 1

	Total calories	Sat-fat calories
Spring or summer salad:		
with cottage cheese	280	7
with nonfat yogurt	250	0
Fall or winter salad:		
with cottage cheese	270	7
with nonfat yogurt	245	0

SANDWICHES AND DIPS 22

SOUR CREAM need not be the basis for your dips and sandwich spreads. Sour cream has 270 sat-fat calories per cup. In its place, use nonfat or low-fat yogurt, tofu, eggplant, chickpeas, or cottage cheese for delicious, low-fat dips and spreads.

⧉ TOFU (MOCK EGG SALAD) SANDWICH

Fresh tofu is available at Oriental food stores, health food stores, and even some supermarkets. Tofu is actually soybean curd. It is an excellent source of protein and has a negligible amount of saturated fat. Store tofu in water in a covered container in the refrigerator. Change water daily to keep tofu fresh for up to a week.

1 cake fresh tofu	1 green onion, sliced
1 tablespoon reduced-calorie mayonnaise	½ tomato, chopped
½–1 teaspoon curry powder	2 six-inch whole-wheat pita bread pockets

In a small bowl, break up tofu with a fork.
Mix in mayonnaise, curry powder, green onions, and tomatoes.
Spoon tofu spread into pita bread pockets.

Makes 2 sandwiches

Double the amount of ingredients and use tofu spread as a dip with fresh raw vegetables.

Makes about 2 cups

	Total calories	Sat-fat calories
Per sandwich	150	9
Per tablespoon	9	1

Q

BABA GHANOUSH

1 medium eggplant
¼ cup or more fresh lemon
   juice
3 tablespoons tahini (sesame
   seed paste)

1–2 cloves garlic
¼ cup chopped parsley
Salt to taste

Peel eggplant, cut into bite-size pieces, and salt heavily. Set aside for 15 minutes. Rinse and squeeze eggplant and steam in vegetable steamer until soft.
Purée eggplant in food processor or blender.
Blend in lemon juice and tahini.
Just before you serve, crush garlic into purée and mix in parsley and salt.
Taste. Add more lemon juice if you wish.
Serve with whole-wheat or plain pita bread cut into pieces.

Makes about 2 cups
Per tablespoon: 12 Total calories; 1 Sat-fat calorie

Q

CHICKPEA SANDWICH OR DIP

1 can chickpeas
2 cloves garlic
⅓ cup parsley
1 tablespoon tahini (sesame
   seed paste)*
Juice of 1 lemon (about ¼ cup)

4 six-inch whole-wheat pita
   bread pockets
Chopped tomatoes, green
   onions, and lettuce, for
   garnish

Drain chickpeas. Reserve liquid. In blender or food processor, chop garlic and parsley.
Add chickpeas, tahini, and lemon juice.
Blend until smooth, adding more chickpea liquid if spread is too stiff.
Make sandwiches by spooning chickpea spread into pita bread pockets.
Garnish with chopped tomatoes, green onions, and lettuce.

Makes 4 sandwiches

---

*Available at Mideast food shops and many supermarkets

Use as a dip for vegetables, crackers, squares of pita, etc.

Makes about 1½ cups

	Total calories	*Sat-fat calories*
Per sandwich	195	4
Per tablespoon	20	1

EGGPLANT APPETIZER

A tasty appetizer. Eat with quartered pita bread or crackers or heat and serve as a vegetable.

4 cups peeled, cubed eggplant	½ cup Spanish olives
½ cup chopped onion	½ cup black olives
4 cloves garlic, minced	2 teaspoons capers
2 stalks celery, sliced	2 teaspoons brown sugar
3 tablespoons olive oil	2 tablespoons white vinegar

Salt eggplant heavily and set aside for 15 minutes.

Rinse salt off eggplant under running water while squeezing out bitter juices.

Steam eggplant until tender.

Taste. If not bitter, set aside. If bitter, find a recipe without eggplant!

Sauté onion, garlic, and celery in olive oil until soft.

Mix in eggplant, olives, capers, brown sugar, and vinegar and heat until warm.

Eat hot, at room temperature, or chilled.

Serves 10
Per serving: 70 Total calories; 9 Sat-fat calories

VEGEBURGERS

For those who crave hamburgers but do not want the saturated fat they contain, Vegeburgers are a meatless substitute. Worthington Foods sells a soy product called GranBurger. It may be used to make Vegeburgers, spaghetti sauce, soup — any food that calls for hamburger meat.

1⅓ cups hot water	½ teaspoon salt
1⅔ cups GranBurger	¼ teaspoon poultry seasoning
¼ cup chopped onion	1 egg
2 tablespoons unbleached white flour	2 egg whites
1 cup bread crumbs made from 2 slices bread	2 tablespoons skim milk
	2 tablespoons olive oil

Add hot water to GranBurger and let sit for 3–5 minutes.

Stir in onion, flour, bread crumbs, salt, and poultry seasoning.

Beat together egg, egg whites, and skim milk and mix into GranBurger mixture.

Form patties. They will probably fall apart, so handle with care.

Heat olive oil in large frying pan.

Fry as with hamburgers.

Makes about 10 burgers
Per burger: 73 Total calories; 3 Sat-fat calories

BREADS 23

STARCHES HAVE received bad press over the years. Bread, rice, pasta, and potatoes have been associated with weight gain. Weight problems begin not with starch but with the fat that is put on the starch: bread slathered with margarine, potatoes stuffed with sour cream. An ounce of carbohydrate has less than *half* as many calories as an ounce of fat. An average piece of bread has a mere 80 calories. Cover it with margarine and the caloric value goes up to 180. And, of course, the saturated fat content also rises.

You can cut down on saturated fats and cholesterol by replacing fatty meats and high-fat dairy products with grains, potatoes, breads, and pasta. Many starchy foods (such as whole grains and potatoes with skin) provide fiber, bulk, vitamins, and minerals.

Many of the following recipes are for 1 loaf so that you can make them in your food processor. Double ingredients for 2 loaves.

You can make any loaf into baguettes by following the portion of the recipe for French Bread, page 296, beginning with "Divide dough in half."

We have chosen to use olive oil in baking bread because olive oil lowers LDL-cholesterol without lowering HDL-cholesterol. Choose a mild-tasting olive oil, and your taste buds won't notice the difference.

SHAKER DAILY LOAF

1 tablespoon active dry yeast
Pinch of sugar
¼ cup warm water
6 cups unbleached white flour
  (approximately)

2¼ cups skim milk
2 tablespoons margarine
2 tablespoons maple syrup or
  honey
2 teaspoons salt

Dissolve yeast and sugar in the warm water in a large bowl or a food processor. Let proof (become bubbly).

Mix in 3 cups of the flour.

In a small saucepan, scald skim milk. Remove from heat.

Add margarine, maple syrup, and salt to milk and mix until margarine melts.

When liquid has cooled to lukewarm, add to flour in bowl.

Stir in more flour, ½ cup at a time, until dough is fairly stiff.

Knead dough 10 minutes or process 15 seconds or until dough is smooth and elastic.

Place dough in a large oiled bowl, cover with a towel, and let rise in a warm place for 1 hour or until doubled in bulk.

Remove dough from bowl and divide it in half.

Let dough rest, covered, for 10 minutes.

Roll into two loaves and place in loaf pans greased with margarine.

Cover and let rise until doubled (1–2 hours).

Preheat oven to 350°F.

Bake loaves for 35–40 minutes or until they are golden brown and sound hollow when tapped.

Makes 2 loaves

	Total calories	Sat-fat calories
Per ½-inch slice	90	2
Per loaf	1512	28

CARDAMOM BREAD

1 tablespoon active dry yeast
2 tablespoons brown sugar
¼ cup warm water
2–4 cups unbleached white
   flour

1 teaspoon salt
¼–½ teaspoon cardamom*
2 tablespoons margarine
1 cup skim milk

Combine yeast, brown sugar, and water in a large bowl or a food processor. Let proof.

Add 2 cups flour, salt, and cardamom and mix.

In a small saucepan, melt margarine. Remove from heat and stir in milk.

If liquid is still cool, return saucepan to burner and heat until warm, but not *too* warm. Add to flour.

Knead dough 10 minutes or process 15 seconds or until dough is smooth and elastic, adding more flour if necessary.

Place dough in a large oiled bowl, cover with a towel, and let rise in warm place for 1 hour or until doubled in bulk.

Roll into loaf and place in loaf pan greased with margarine.

Cover with a towel and let rise for 1 hour or until doubled in bulk.

Preheat oven to 425°F.

Bake loaves for 10 minutes.

Reduce heat to 350°F and bake for 30 minutes more or until loaves are golden brown and sound hollow when tapped.

Makes 1 loaf

	Total calories	Sat-fat calories
Per ½-inch slice	95	3
Per loaf	1605	45

---

*For a totally different taste, substitute 1 teaspoon cinnamon.

FRENCH BREAD

A French bread of peasant stock. Give yourself a treat and eat it warm, straight from the oven. It also freezes well. Make smaller loaves for submarine sandwiches. Any bread is an impressive gift to bring to friends. And this bread is so easy you'll be embarrassed to answer yes when asked if you made it yourself.

1½ tablespoons active dry yeast
½ teaspoon sugar
¼ cup warm water
2–3 cups unbleached white
    flour

1 teaspoon salt
2 tablespoons margarine
1 cup water

Place yeast, sugar, and very warm, but *not hot*, water in a large bowl or a food processor. Let proof.

Mix in 2 cups flour and the salt.

Melt margarine in a small saucepan. Add water. If liquid is cool, heat until warm but *not hot*.

Add liquid to flour and knead dough 10 minutes or process 15 seconds or until dough is smooth and elastic, adding more flour if necessary.

Place dough in large oiled bowl, cover with a towel, and let rise in a warm place for 1 hour or until doubled in bulk.

Divide dough in half.

Roll each half into a rectangle. Fold over in thirds like this:

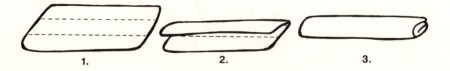

1.   2.   3.

Press the edge into the dough after each fold.

Put into greased (with margarine) French bread pan that looks like this:

Cover and let rise for about 1 hour, or until doubled in bulk.
After 50 minutes, preheat oven to 450°F.
Uncover bread and slash with parallel or diagonal lines like this:

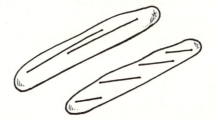

Place bread pan in oven on a diagonal to the right. Put 4 ice cubes in the bottom of the oven to create steam for crustier loaves.
In 5 minutes, add 4 more ice cubes.
In 10 minutes, shift pan so it is on a diagonal to the left, like this:

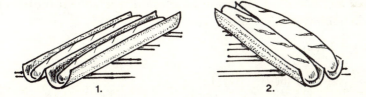

Reduce heat to 400°F and bake for 10 minutes more or until golden brown. Take loaves out of pan and cool or eat immediately.
Freezes nicely. If thawed, slice *before* reheating. Thawed French bread flakes like crazy when cut after reheating.

Makes 2 loaves

	Total calories	Sat-fat calories
Per ½-inch slice	85	2
Per loaf	845	21

BUTTERMILK HERB BREAD

1 tablespoon active dry yeast
2 tablespoons sugar
¼ cup warm water
2–3 cups unbleached white
  flour
1 teaspoon salt

¼ teaspoon marjoram
¼ teaspoon oregano
¼ teaspoon thyme
3 tablespoons margarine
½ cup buttermilk
1 egg

Place yeast, sugar, and water in a large bowl or in your food processor. Let proof.

Mix in 2 cups flour, salt, marjoram, oregano, and thyme.

In a small saucepan, melt margarine. Add buttermilk. If liquid is cool, heat until warm but *not too hot.*

Add liquid to the flour. (If using a food processor, process at least 15 seconds.)

Mix in enough flour to make a stiff but soft dough.

Add egg. Knead dough 10 minutes or process 15 seconds or until dough is smooth and elastic.

Put dough in a large oiled bowl, cover with a towel, and let rise in a warm place for 1 hour or until doubled in bulk.

Form loaf and place in loaf pan greased with margarine. Cover and let rise 1 hour or until doubled in bulk.

Preheat oven to 375°F.

Bake loaf for about 35 minutes or until it is golden brown and sounds hollow when tapped.

Makes 1 loaf

	Total calories	Sat-fat calories
Per ½-inch slice	110	4
Per loaf	1874	75

GINGER-ORANGE BREAD

A very subtle taste of ginger pervades this whole-wheat bread.

1 tablespoon active dry yeast
2 tablespoons brown sugar
¼ cup warm water
1½ cups whole-wheat flour
1½ cups unbleached white flour
  (approximately)

1 teaspoon salt
2 teaspoons ground ginger
2 tablespoons margarine
½ cup buttermilk
½ cup orange juice

Combine yeast, brown sugar, and warm water in a large bowl or a food processor. Let proof.

Mix in whole-wheat flour, white flour, salt, and ginger.

In a small saucepan, melt margarine.

Stir in buttermilk and orange juice and, if necessary, heat to warm.

Add liquid to flour and knead 10 minutes or process 15 seconds or until dough is smooth and elastic, adding more white flour if necessary.

Place dough in a large oiled bowl, cover with a towel, and let rise in a warm place for 1 hour or until doubled in bulk.

Shape into a loaf and place in a loaf pan greased with margarine.

Cover with a towel and let rise in warm place for about 1 hour or until doubled in bulk.

Preheat oven to 400°F.

Bake loaf for 10 minutes.

Reduce heat to 350°F and bake for 30 minutes more or until golden brown.

Makes 1 loaf

	Total calories	Sat-fat calories
Per ½-inch slice	95	3
Per loaf	1620	50

CHALLAH

A delicious bread for the Jewish Sabbath or just for enjoyable eating.

1 tablespoon active dry yeast	½ teaspoon salt
2 tablespoons sugar	¾ cup warm water
¼ cup warm water	2 tablespoons olive or sunflower
2–4 cups unbleached white	oil
flour	1 egg

Place yeast, sugar, and ¼ cup warm water in a large bowl or a food processor. Let proof.

Mix in 2 cups flour and salt.

Add ¾ cup warm water, oil, and egg and mix or process for 15 seconds.

Knead dough 10 minutes or process 15 seconds or until dough is smooth and elastic, adding more flour if necessary.

Place dough in a large oiled bowl, cover with a towel, and let rise in warm place for 1 hour or until doubled in bulk.

Divide dough into two unequal portions, one-third and two-thirds.

Divide the smaller portion of the dough into three pieces. Roll each into a rope.

Divide the larger portion into three pieces. Roll each into a rope.

Braid the three larger ropes and place them on a greased cookie sheet.

Braid the three smaller ropes and place them on top of the larger braided pieces. Pinch the two together.

Cover with a towel and let rise for 1 hour or until doubled in bulk.

Preheat oven to 400°F.

Bake bread for 10 minutes.

Reduce heat to 375°F and bake for 30 minutes more or until golden brown.

Makes 1 large loaf or 2 small loaves

	Total calories	Sat-fat calories
Per ½-inch slice	70	2
Per loaf	1670	47

ANADAMA BREAD

This version of the New England bread has whole-wheat flour added to it to make it healthier while retaining its wonderful taste and texture.

1 tablespoon active dry yeast
Pinch of sugar
¼ cup warm water
¾ cup corn meal
1½ cups whole-wheat flour
1½ cups unbleached white flour
    (approximately)

1–1½ teaspoons salt
2 tablespoons margarine
1 cup water
3 tablespoons molasses

Dissolve yeast with pinch of sugar in ¼ cup warm water in a large bowl or a food processor. Let proof.

Mix in corn meal, whole-wheat flour, 1 cup of the white flour, and salt.

In a small saucepan, melt margarine. Stir in 1 cup warm water and molasses.

Heat to warm but not *too* warm and add liquid to flour mixture.

Knead dough 10 minutes or process 15 seconds or until dough is smooth and elastic, adding more white flour if necessary.

Place dough in a large oiled bowl, cover with a towel, and let rise in a warm place for 1 hour or until doubled in bulk.

Form into a loaf and place in a loaf pan greased with margarine. Cover and let rise for 1 hour or until doubled in bulk.

Preheat oven to 400°F.

Bake loaf for 15 minutes.

Reduce heat to 350°F and bake about 30 minutes more or until loaf is golden brown and sounds hollow when tapped.

Makes 1 loaf

	Total calories	Sat-fat calories
Per ½-inch slice	110	3
Per loaf	1861	46

PEANUT BUTTER BREAD

A bread with a subtle peanut buttery taste and aroma.

1 tablespoon active dry yeast
2 tablespoons sugar
¼ cup warm water
2 cups whole-wheat flour
2½ cups unbleached white flour
  (approximately)

2 teaspoons salt
2 tablespoons margarine
¼ cup natural all-peanut peanut
  butter
1 cup buttermilk

Place yeast, sugar, and warm water in a large bowl or a food processor. Let proof.

Mix in whole-wheat flour, white flour, and salt.

In a small saucepan, melt margarine. Stir in peanut butter. Add buttermilk. If liquid becomes too cool, heat until warm.

Add liquid to flour mixture and knead 10 minutes or process 15 seconds or until dough is smooth and elastic, adding more white flour if necessary.

Place dough in a large oiled bowl, cover with a towel, and let rise in a warm place for about 1 hour or until doubled in bulk.

Divide dough in half and form loaves.

Place in loaf pans greased with margarine, cover, and let rise for about 1 hour or until doubled in bulk.

Preheat oven to 350°F.

Bake for 45–60 minutes or until loaves are golden brown and sound hollow when tapped.

Makes 2 small loaves

	Total calories	Sat-fat calories
Per ½-inch slice	75	5
Per loaf	1300	54

PUMPERNICKEL BREAD

1 tablespoon yeast
¼ cup warm water
Pinch of sugar
1 cup rye flour
2 cups whole-wheat flour
   (approximately)
2 cups unbleached white flour

1 teaspoon salt
2 tablespoons margarine
2 tablespoons molasses
1¼ cups warm water
1 tablespoon caraway seeds
Corn flour

Place yeast in a large bowl or a food processor. Add ¼ cup warm water and sugar. Let proof.

Mix in rye flour, whole-wheat flour, 1½ cups white flour, and salt.

In a small saucepan, melt margarine. Add molasses and 1¼ cups warm water.

When liquid is warm, but not *too* warm, add to flour and knead 10 minutes or process 15 seconds or until dough is smooth and elastic, adding more white flour if necessary.

Knead in caraway seeds.

Place dough in a large oiled bowl, cover with a towel, and let rise in a warm place for 1 hour or until doubled in bulk.

Sprinkle corn flour on a baking sheet.

Form dough into a round or loaf, place on baking sheet, cover, and let rise 1 hour or until doubled in bulk.

Preheat oven to 450°F.

Bake loaf for 10 minutes.

Reduce heat to 350°F and bake for 35 minutes more or until loaf sounds hollow when tapped.

Makes 1 large loaf

	Total calories	Sat-fat calories
Per ½-inch slice	90	2
Per loaf	2215	43

HONEY WHOLE-WHEAT BREAD

Whole-grain breads are much more nutritious than breads made with white flour. In whole-grain flours, the entire kernel is ground into flour so that vitamins, minerals, and fiber are not lost.

Honey Whole-Wheat Bread makes wonderful toast. Top it with

bananas and cottage cheese and you have a filling, nutritious, and scrumptious breakfast. Honey Whole-Wheat Bread freezes well.

This recipe makes 4 loaves of bread. Freeze the ones you are not using.

2 tablespoons active dry yeast
2 tablespoons salt
1 quart-size package nonfat dry milk
1 five-pound bag whole-wheat flour (about 16 cups)
6½ cups water

½ cup honey
½ cup olive or sunflower oil
2 teaspoons cinnamon
½ teaspoon grated nutmeg
1½ cups rolled oats
½ cup raisins

In a mixing bowl, combine yeast, salt, nonfat dry milk, and 2 cups flour.

In a large saucepan, combine water, honey, and oil and heat until quite warm (about 115°F) but *not too hot* or you will kill the yeast.

Add liquid to dry ingredients in mixing bowl and beat for 4 minutes.

Mix in 4 cups flour.

Mix in the cinnamon, nutmeg, oats, and raisins.

Keep adding flour until you produce a stiff dough. Your mixer probably will not be large enough to handle all the dough. When the mixer reaches its limit, remove the dough to a pastry board or counter and add flour until the dough is stiff enough to knead.

Knead dough for 8–10 minutes or until smooth and elastic.

Place dough in large oiled bowl, cover with a towel, and let rise in warm place for about 1 hour or until doubled in bulk.

Form 4 loaves, place in loaf pans greased with margarine, cover with a towel, and let rise 1 hour or until doubled in bulk.

Preheat oven to 350°F.

Bake loaves for 45 minutes to 1 hour or until they are golden brown and sound hollow when tapped.

Makes 4 loaves

	Total calories	Sat-fat calories
Per ½-inch slice	130	2
Per loaf	2222	39

OATMEAL BREAD

1 cup water
1 cup rolled oats
2 tablespoons honey
1 tablespoon margarine
1 teaspoon salt

1 tablespoon active dry yeast
Pinch of sugar
⅓ cup warm water
2½ cups unbleached white flour
    (approximately)

In a small saucepan, boil 1 cup water and add oats, honey, margarine, and salt. Let cool.

Combine yeast, sugar, and ⅓ cup warm water in a large bowl or a food processor. Let proof.

Add 2 cups flour to the yeast mixture.

When oat mixture is warm, but *not hot,* add it to the flour mixture and knead dough 10 minutes or process 15 seconds or until dough is smooth and elastic, adding more flour if necessary.

Place dough in a large oiled bowl, cover with a towel, and let rise in a warm place for 1 hour or until doubled in bulk.

Form dough into a loaf and place in a loaf pan greased with margarine. Cover and let rise about 1 hour or until doubled in bulk.

Preheat oven to 350°F.

Bake for 45 minutes or until golden brown.

Makes 1 loaf

	Total calories	Sat-fat calories
Per ½-inch slice	94	2
Per loaf	1601	33

ONION FLAT BREAD

1 tablespoon active dry yeast
1 teaspoon sugar
1 cup warm water
2½–3 cups unbleached white
    flour*

1 teaspoon + a few shakes salt
2 teaspoons margarine
1 cup chopped onions
1 teaspoon paprika

Place yeast, sugar, and water in large bowl or a food processor. Let proof.

---

*For a slightly different taste, use 1 cup of whole-wheat flour, along with 1½–2 cups unbleached white flour.

Mix in 2 cups flour and salt. Knead for 10 minutes or process for 15 seconds, until smooth and elastic, adding flour if necessary.

Place dough in an oiled bowl, cover with a towel, and let rise in a warm place for an hour or until doubled in bulk.

Punch dough down and split in half. Let rest for 5 minutes.

Meanwhile, grease two 9-inch cake pans with margarine.

Melt 2 teaspoons of margarine.

Press dough into cake pans.

Spread margarine over the tops and press onion into the surface.

Let rise about 45 minutes or until doubled in bulk.

Preheat oven to 450°F.

Sprinkle tops with paprika and a few shakes of salt.

Bake 20–25 minutes, until lightly browned.

Makes 2 loaves, 8 slices per loaf
Per loaf: 700 Total calories; 10 Sat-fat calories
Per slice: 88 Total calories; 1 Sat-fat calorie

WHOLE-WHEAT BAGELS

1 tablespoon active dry yeast	1½ cups unbleached white flour
3 tablespoons sugar	1 teaspoon salt
1 cup warm water	2 tablespoons olive or sunflower
1½ cups whole-wheat flour	oil

Mix yeast, sugar, and warm water in a large bowl or a food processor. Let proof.

Mix in whole-wheat flour, white flour, and salt.

Knead 8–10 minutes or process 15 seconds or until dough is smooth and elastic, adding more flour if necessary.

Place dough in a large oiled bowl, cover with a towel, and let rise in a warm place for 40 minutes. Punch down.

Roll into lengths about 5 inches long and ¾ inch wide. Pinch each into a circle to make a bagel.

Preheat oven to 350°F and grease cookie sheet with oil.

Fill a medium saucepan with water. Add oil and bring to a boil.

Drop a bagel into the boiling water.

When it rises to the top, remove it with a slotted spoon or spatula so the excess water can drip off.

Repeat this process with all the bagels.

Place bagels on cookie sheet and bake for 10 minutes.

Raise heat to 400°F and bake for 10 minutes more.

Makes 12 bagels
Per bagel: 115 Total calories; 1 Sat-fat calorie

SESAME BREADSTICKS

Beware! These breadsticks are habit-forming.

1 teaspoon active dry yeast
¼ cup warm water
⅔ cup whole-wheat flour
2 or more cups unbleached white flour
1 teaspoon salt, optional

⅔ cup nonfat skim milk
2 tablespoons olive oil
1 egg white
2 teaspoons water
7 tablespoons sesame seeds

Place yeast and warm water in large bowl or a food processor. Let proof.

Mix in flours and salt.

Add milk and olive oil, and knead for 10 minutes or process until dough is smooth and elastic, adding more flour if necessary.

Place dough in ungreased bowl, cover with a towel, and let rise 1 hour.

Preheat oven to 400°F.

On a lightly floured surface, roll the dough into a ¼-inch-thick rectangle. One dimension of the rectangle should be the length of your breadsticks.

Cut the dough into ½-inch strips. (If you prefer thicker breadsticks, cut the dough into one-inch strips.)

Roll each strip in your palms to make a breadstick and lay it on an ungreased baking sheet. Place the sticks in a line, about a ½-inch apart.

Beat the egg white and water together and brush onto breadsticks.

Place sesame seeds on a plate and roll each breadstick in the seeds and replace them on the baking sheet.

Count the breadsticks and write down the number so you can calculate their sat-fat calories.

Bake for 10–20 minutes or until golden brown. Cool on a rack.

Makes about 35 six-inch sticks
To determine the total calories and sat-fat calories for each breadstick, divide the number of breadsticks you made into the following numbers:
Total calories: 1824   Total sat-fat calories: 82
For example, 82 sat-fat calories divided by 35 breadsticks = 2.3 sat-fat calories each.

OAT BRAN MUFFINS

Oat bran, a food rich in soluble fiber, has been found to lower blood cholesterol levels. Oat bran is available at supermarkets, packaged as Mother's Oat Bran (Quaker Oats). It may also be purchased in bulk at health food stores.

Q APPLE OAT MUFFINS

1½ cups oat bran
½ cup whole-wheat flour
3 tablespoons brown sugar
2 teaspoons baking powder
½ teaspoon salt
1 teaspoon cinnamon
½ cup apple juice

¼ cup skim milk
1 egg
2 tablespoons olive or sunflower oil
2 tablespoons honey
1 cup apples, peeled, cored, and diced
2 tablespoons raisins

Preheat oven to 400°F. Grease a 12-cup muffin tin with margarine.

Combine oat bran, flour, brown sugar, baking powder, salt, and cinnamon and set aside.

In a large mixing bowl, combine apple juice, skim milk, egg, oil, and honey.

Add flour mixture, apples, and raisins and combine until just moistened.

Fill muffin tin and bake at 400°F for about 20 minutes or until golden brown and a cake tester comes out clean.

Makes 12 muffins
Per muffin: 125 Total calories; 4 Sat-fat calories

 ## MOTHER'S OAT BRAN MUFFINS

These oat bran muffins (an adaptation of the Quaker Oats recipe) are made with no other grain but oat bran. They have twice as much oat bran and thus more soluble fiber than the preceding oat muffins.

2¼ cups oat bran	½ teaspoon salt
¼ cup brown sugar	¾ cup skim milk
¼ cup chopped walnuts	1 egg + 1 egg white, beaten
¼ cup raisins	¼ cup honey
1 tablespoon baking powder	2 tablespoons olive or sunflower oil

Preheat oven to 425°F. Grease a 12-cup muffin tin with margarine.

Combine oat bran, brown sugar, walnuts, raisins, baking powder, and salt.

Add skim milk, eggs, honey, and oil. Mix until ingredients are just moistened.

Fill muffin tin and bake for 15 minutes or until golden brown and a cake tester comes out clean.

Makes 12 muffins
Per muffin: 160 Total calories; 6 Sat-fat calories

Q

ORANGE OAT MUFFINS

Can you believe it? Another oat bran muffin.

1 cup oat bran
½ cup wheat germ
½ cup whole-wheat flour
3 tablespoons brown sugar
2 tablespoons grated orange
   peel

2 teaspoons baking powder
1 egg
2 tablespoons olive or sunflower
   oil
½ cup orange juice
¼ cup skim milk
2 tablespoons raisins

Preheat oven to 400°F. Grease a 12-cup muffin tin with margarine.

Combine oat bran, wheat germ, whole-wheat flour, brown sugar, orange peel, and baking powder. Set aside.

In a mixing bowl, mix egg, oil, orange juice, and skim milk.

Mix in dry ingredients until just moistened.

Carefully mix in raisins.

Fill muffin tin and bake for 15 minutes or until golden brown and a cake tester comes out clean.

Makes 12 muffins
Per muffin: 110 Total calories; 4 Sat-fat calories

Q

APRICOT OAT MUFFINS

Yet another oat muffin. Healthy and delicious — a good snack or breakfast on the run.

½ cup orange juice
1 cup dried apricots, chopped
   (easily done in food
   processor)
¼ cup brown sugar
1 cup oat bran

¼ cup wheat germ
¾ cup whole-wheat flour
2 teaspoons baking powder
2 tablespoons olive or sunflower
   oil
½ cup skim milk
1 egg

Preheat oven to 400°F. Grease a 12-cup muffin tin with margarine.

In a small saucepan, heat orange juice until boiling. Mix in apricots and brown sugar.

Remove saucepan from heat and cool apricot mixture slightly.

In a medium bowl, combine oat bran, wheat germ, whole-wheat flour, and baking powder. Set aside.

In a mixing bowl, beat together oil, skim milk, and egg.

Add dry ingredients and apricot-orange juice mixture to milk mixture and mix until just moistened.

Fill muffin tin and bake for 15 minutes or until golden brown and a cake tester comes out clean.

Makes 12 muffins
Per muffin: 135 Total calories; 4 Sat-fat calories

BRAN MUFFINS

Wheat bran, made from the outer coverings of wheat kernels, is rich in vitamins, minerals, and insoluble dietary fiber. Insoluble dietary fiber promotes regularity and is believed to protect against colon cancer.

1 cup whole-wheat flour	1 cup buttermilk
1 cup wheat bran	1 egg, beaten
3 tablespoons brown sugar	3 tablespoons molasses
¼ teaspoon salt	2 tablespoons olive or sunflower
1 teaspoon baking soda	oil
½ teaspoon baking powder	⅓ cup raisins

Preheat oven to 400°F. Grease a 12-cup muffin tin with margarine.

Combine whole-wheat flour, wheat bran, brown sugar, salt, baking soda, and baking powder. Set aside.

In a mixing bowl, mix buttermilk, egg, molasses, and oil.

Add dry ingredients and mix until just moistened.

Fold in raisins.

Fill muffin tin and bake for about 15 minutes or until golden brown and a cake tester comes out clean.

Makes 12 muffins
Per muffin: 116 Total calories; 4 Sat-fat calories

BANANA-CARROT MUFFINS

Not an oat bran muffin but tasty and healthy anyway. Eat as a snack or for a light breakfast.

3 medium carrots	2 teaspoons double-acting
2 medium bananas	baking powder
¼ cup margarine	¼ teaspoon salt
½ cup brown sugar	¼ teaspoon baking soda
1 large egg	1 teaspoon vanilla
2 cups whole-wheat flour	½ cup chopped walnuts

Preheat oven to 350°F. Grease a 12-cup muffin tin with margarine.

Grate carrots (a food processor does this well) and set aside.

Mash bananas with a fork and set aside.

In a mixing bowl, cream the margarine and brown sugar until fluffy. Add egg and beat well.

Stir in the mashed bananas.

In a small bowl, mix together flour, baking powder, salt, and baking soda.

Add flour mixture to banana mixture. Do not overmix.

Add grated carrots, vanilla, and nuts and combine carefully.

Fill muffin tin and bake for 20–25 minutes or until a cake tester comes out clean.

Makes 12 muffins
Per muffin: 195 Total calories; 11 Sat-fat calories

As an alternative, try substituting 1 cup oat bran + ½ cup wheat germ + ½ cup whole-wheat flour for the 2 cups of whole-wheat flour. Use only 2 tablespoons margarine and ¼ cup brown sugar.

Total calories: 155; Sat-fat calories: 8

GINGERBREAD MUFFINS

These muffins taste like cake. Use self-control! One muffin has only 9 sat-fat calories, but 12 have 108!!

1 cup unbleached white flour
¾ cup whole-wheat flour
¼ cup granulated sugar
¼ cup brown sugar
1 teaspoon baking soda
¼ teaspoon salt
1 teaspoon ginger
1 teaspoon cinnamon
¼ teaspoon cloves
¼ teaspoon allspice
¼ teaspoon grated nutmeg
¾ cup buttermilk
⅓ cup olive or sunflower oil
1 egg + 1 egg white
¼ cup light unsulphured
   molasses

Preheat oven to 400°F and grease a 12-cup muffin tin with margarine.

Combine flours, sugars, baking soda, salt, and spices in a large bowl. Set aside.

In a large mixing bowl, combine buttermilk, oil, egg, egg white, and molasses.

Add flour mixture to buttermilk mixture. Do not overmix.

Pour into cups of muffin pan and bake for 15 minutes, or until cake tester comes out clean.

Makes 12 muffins
Per muffin: 177 Total calories; 9 Sat-fat calories

BUTTERMILK PANCAKES

Breakfast need not be a problem for those watching their sat-fat intake. In addition to the bread and muffin recipes listed above, try these pancakes and the waffles and French toast below.

Instead of using sour cream (270 sat-fat calories per cup) or whole milk (45 sat-fat calories per cup), make your pancakes with buttermilk (12 sat-fat calories per cup). Buttermilk enhances the taste of waffles and pancakes. These delicious buttermilk pancakes will hardly make a dent in your sat-fat budget.

Use maple syrup or powdered sugar to sweeten pancakes and waffles. Butter adds only unneeded sat-fat calories.

2 egg whites	¼ teaspoon salt
1 cup unbleached white flour	1 cup buttermilk
½ cup whole-wheat flour	½ cup skim milk
2 teaspoons baking powder	5 tablespoons olive or sunflower oil

Whip egg whites until stiff but not dry. Set aside.

In a large bowl, combine white flour, whole-wheat flour, baking powder, salt, buttermilk, and skim milk until just moistened.

Fold egg whites into batter. Fold 2 tablespoons of the oil into batter.

Lightly grease skillet with remaining 3 tablespoons of oil.

For each pancake, spoon ¼ cup batter onto hot skillet.

Reduce heat to medium-high and cook pancakes until bottoms are browned.

Turn and continue cooking until golden brown.

Makes 32 pancakes
Per pancake: 45 Total calories; 3 Sat-fat calories

BUTTERMILK WAFFLES

1 egg white at room temperature	½ teaspoon salt
1 cup whole-wheat flour	1 cup buttermilk
1 cup unbleached white flour	1 cup skim milk
2 teaspoons baking powder	¼ cup olive or sunflower oil

Preheat waffle iron.

Beat egg white until stiff but not dry. Set aside.

In a medium bowl, combine whole-wheat flour, white flour, baking powder, and salt.

Add buttermilk and skim milk. *Do not overmix.*

Fold in egg white. Fold in oil.

Place batter on waffle iron in amounts specified by your waffle-iron instructions. Cook accordingly.

Makes 8 Belgian waffles

	Total calories	Sat-fat calories
Total batter	1500	72
Per square*	188	9

CINNAMON FRENCH TOAST

2 egg whites	Pinch of grated nutmeg
3 tablespoons skim milk	3 slices whole-wheat bread or
½ teaspoon vanilla	French bread
½ teaspoon ground cinnamon	2 teaspoons margarine

In a shallow dish, mix egg whites, skim milk, vanilla, cinnamon, and nutmeg.

Soak both sides of bread in mixture.

In a large frying pan, melt margarine over high heat.

Add bread. Reduce heat to medium.

Turn bread after 2 minutes. Cook until golden brown and crispy.

Serves 3
Per serving: 106 Total calories; 8 Sat-fat calories

---

*Because waffle irons come in many sizes, this recipe may make more or less than 8 waffle squares. Divide 1500 by the number of waffle squares you make to figure out the total calories per square (for example, 1500 ÷ 8 = 187.5). Divide 72 by the number of waffle squares to figure out the sat-fat calories per square (for example, 72 ÷ 8 = 9).

24 DESSERTS

Y OU MIGHT think dessert would be the most difficult part of the meal to make low in saturated fat. This is not true. There are many desserts that not only are scrumptious and beautiful but fit perfectly into a low-sat-fat diet. (That is not to say they are necessarily low in calories — so go easy.)

The trick to keeping desserts low in saturated fat is to substitute nonfat yogurt, buttermilk, or skim milk for sour cream, sweet cream, or whole milk and margarine or oil for butter; never to use lard, shortening, palm, or coconut oil; and to reduce eggs to no more than one and substitute egg whites for additional eggs.

You may be surprised that we use olive oil in making these desserts. Olive oil is the oil of choice because it lowers LDL-cholesterol without lowering HDL-cholesterol. Try using a mild-tasting olive oil in your baked goods. Only your arteries will be able to detect a difference.

You will notice that we recommend grated nutmeg in many recipes. Buy whole nutmegs at your grocery store and simply grate one when you need nutmeg in a recipe. The advantage is that each time you grate one it is fresh and thus has the taste it is supposed to have.

We recommend unbleached white flour because when a flour is bleached, it loses many of its important nutritional qualities.

APPLESAUCE CAKE

1 cup raisins
½ cup water
1 cup chunky applesauce
⅓ cup margarine
½ cup sugar
1 egg

1 teaspoon vanilla
1½ cups unbleached white flour
1 teaspoon baking soda
½ teaspoon cinnamon
⅛ teaspoon ground cloves
½ cup chopped walnuts

Preheat oven to 350°F. Grease a loaf pan with margarine.

In a small saucepan, combine raisins and water. Bring to a boil. Reduce heat, cover, and simmer for 1 minute.

Remove from heat. Stir in applesauce. Cool to lukewarm.

Cream margarine and sugar. Beat in egg and vanilla.

Combine flour, baking soda, cinnamon, and cloves and mix into batter.

Add applesauce mixture and nuts.

Pour into greased loaf pan and bake for 1 hour or until a cake tester comes out clean.

Cool for 10 minutes before removing from pan.

Makes 10 slices
Per slice: 250 Total calories; 14 Sat-fat calories

APPLE CAKE

A moist, hearty cake that is easy to make.

¾ cup brown sugar
½ cup olive or sunflower oil
1 teaspoon vanilla
1 egg
1 egg white
¾ cup unbleached white flour
1 cup whole-wheat flour

½ teaspoon salt
1 teaspoon baking soda
1½ teaspoons cinnamon
¼ teaspoon grated nutmeg
4 cups Delicious apples, peeled
    and cut into chunks
½ cup chopped walnuts

Preheat oven to 350°F. Grease an 8-inch springform pan with margarine and dust with flour.

In an electric mixer, beat together brown sugar and oil.

Add vanilla, egg, and egg white and beat until smooth.

Add flours, salt, baking soda, cinnamon, and nutmeg and beat until smooth.

With a large (wooden) spoon or rubber spatula, mix in apples and walnuts. The batter will be *very* sticky and stiff.

Spoon batter into pan and bake for 50–60 minutes or until a cake tester comes out clean.

Makes 12 slices
Per slice: 220 Total calories; 13 Sat-fat calories

BANANA CAKE

This banana cake is out of the ordinary. Rich and full-bodied.

1 cup whole-wheat flour
½ cup unbleached white flour
¼ cup wheat germ
1 teaspoon cinnamon
½ teaspoon grated nutmeg
2 teaspoons baking powder
¼ teaspoon baking soda
¼ teaspoon salt

⅓ cup olive or sunflower oil
½ cup brown sugar
¾ teaspoon vanilla
1 egg
3 bananas, mashed
½ cup chopped walnuts
5 prunes, chopped

Preheat oven to 350°F. Grease a loaf pan with margarine.

Mix flours, wheat germ, cinnamon, nutmeg, baking powder, baking soda, and salt and set aside.

In an electric mixer, mix oil and brown sugar. Add vanilla and egg and mix well.

Add bananas and blend until smooth. Mix in flour mixture.

Fold in nuts and prunes.

Pour batter into loaf pan and bake for 1 hour or until a cake tester comes out clean.

Makes 10 slices
Per slice: 263 Total calories; 12 Sat-fat calories

LEMON LOAF

Crunchy, lemony goodness.

1 cup walnuts*
½ cup sugar
½ cup margarine
Peel of 1 lemon, grated
2 cups unbleached white flour
¼ teaspoon salt

2 teaspoons baking powder
1 teaspoon baking soda
¾ cup buttermilk
¼ cup lemon juice
2 tablespoons fresh lemon juice
3 tablespoons sugar

Preheat oven to 375°F. Grease a loaf pan with margarine.

Chop walnuts with food processor or nut chopper. Set aside.

Cream sugar and margarine with mixer.

Add grated lemon peel and mix until smooth.

Mix together flour, salt, baking powder, and baking soda and set aside.

Mix buttermilk and lemon juice and set aside.

Add flour mixture to creamed mixture alternately with buttermilk mixture. *Do not overmix.*

Stir in walnuts.

Pour into loaf pan and bake for 30–45 minutes or until a cake tester comes out clean.

Let cool in pan 10 minutes.

In a small saucepan, combine lemon juice and sugar and stir over low heat until sugar dissolves.

Pierce top of cake with a fork or skewer. Spoon lemon-sugar mixture into holes.

Let cool for easy slicing. (A whiff of lemon loaf may cause your impatient family to force you to slice the cake warm!)

Makes 10 slices
Per slice: 290 Total calories; 21 Sat-fat calories

---

*Lemon Loaf is delicious even without the walnuts. Eliminate walnuts and reduce total calories to 215, sat-fat calories to 15 per slice.

CARROT CAKE SANS OEUFS

It is difficult to believe that this delicious, rich carrot cake has no eggs, but believe it! Carrot Cake sans Oeufs does not even contain an egg white.

¾ cup sugar
1 cup grated carrot (food processor grates quickly)
1 cup raisins
1 teaspoon cinnamon
1 teaspoon grated nutmeg
1 teaspoon ground cloves

1½ cups water
3 tablespoons margarine
2 cups flour
2 teaspoons baking soda
¼ teaspoon salt
1 cup chopped walnuts

Preheat oven to 325°F. Grease a 13 × 9-inch baking pan with margarine.

In a small saucepan, combine sugar, carrot, raisins, cinnamon, nutmeg, cloves, water, and margarine. Bring to a boil. Reduce heat, and simmer for 5 minutes.

Pour into a mixing bowl and cool to lukewarm.

Add flour, baking soda, and salt. Mix well.

Stir in walnuts.

Pour into pan and bake for 1 hour or until a cake tester comes out clean.

Makes 24 squares
Per square: 122 Total calories; 5 Sat-fat calories

GINGER CAKE WITH PEAR SAUCE

Ginger Cake tastes good with or without pear sauce.

⅓ cup margarine
2 tablespoons maple syrup
⅓ cup sugar
1 egg
1½ cups unbleached white flour
½ teaspoon baking powder
½ teaspoon baking soda

½ teaspoon salt
1 teaspoon cinnamon
1½ teaspoons ginger
½ teaspoon allspice
¼ teaspoon grated nutmeg
1 cup buttermilk

Pear Sauce

| 2 cups water | 3 ripe Anjou or other pears |
| ¼ cup sugar | 1 tablespoon sugar |

The Ginger Cake

Preheat oven to 350°F. Grease an 8 × 8-inch baking pan with margarine.

Cream margarine, maple syrup, and sugar until smooth.

Mix in egg.

Combine flour, baking powder, baking soda, salt, cinnamon, ginger, allspice, and nutmeg. Add to batter, alternating with buttermilk. Mix until smooth. Pour batter into baking pan and bake for 30 minutes or until a cake tester comes out clean.

Meanwhile, make the pear sauce.

The Pear Sauce

In a large saucepan, combine water and ¼ cup sugar and bring to a simmer.

Poach pears in simmering sugar water for about 10 minutes or until soft.

Drain pears and purée them with 1 tablespoon sugar in a blender until smooth.

Serve over cooled cake.

Makes 9 squares

	Total calories	Sat-fat calories
Per square	183	14
with Pear Sauce	194	14

ORANGE CAKE

1½ cups unbleached white flour
2 teaspoons baking powder
¼ teaspoon salt
½ cup margarine
½ cup sugar

½ cup orange juice
3 egg whites
2 tablespoons orange juice

Preheat oven to 350°F. Grease a loaf pan with margarine.

Combine flour, baking powder, and salt. Set aside.

In a large mixing bowl, beat margarine until soft. Gradually add sugar until creamy.

Add flour mixture, alternating with ½ cup orange juice, until batter is smooth.

In another bowl, whip egg whites until stiff but not dry.

Fold egg whites into batter.

Pour batter into loaf pan and bake for 50 minutes or until a cake tester comes out clean.

Cool in pan for 10 minutes.

Poke holes in top of cake. Pour 2 tablespoons orange juice into holes.

Makes 10 slices
Per slice: 180 Total calories; 15 Sat-fat calories

PINEAPPLE POUND CAKE

2½ cups flour
1½ teaspoons baking soda
½ teaspoon salt
½ cup margarine
¾ cup sugar
3 egg whites

1 tablespoon grated orange peel
1 teaspoon vanilla
1 cup nonfat yogurt
1 cup pineapple chunks
¼ cup orange juice
¼ cup sugar

Preheat oven to 375°F. Grease a 10-inch tube pan with margarine.

Mix flour, baking soda, and salt and set aside.

Cream margarine and sugar.

Add egg whites, orange peel, and vanilla and beat well.

Add flour mixture and yogurt alternately to sugar mixture and mix well.

Pour half the batter into pan. Spread pineapple evenly over batter. Cover with remaining batter.

Bake for 40 minutes or until a cake tester comes out clean.

Let the cake cool for 5 minutes.

Meanwhile, in a small saucepan, combine orange juice and sugar. Bring to a boil, reduce heat, and simmer for 3–5 minutes.

Remove cake from pan. Pierce it with a fork and spoon orange juice mixture into holes and over the top of the cake.

Makes 16 slices
Per slice: 177 Total calories; 9 Sat-fat calories

PEACH POUND CAKE

This pound cake and the preceding one will remind you of cakes that are made with a pound of butter and 6 eggs. Nonfat yogurt and margarine make the difference in the saturated fat content of our pound cakes, but not in their taste and appearance.

1 tablespoon unbleached white flour
2 tablespoons brown sugar
2 peaches,* sliced
¾ cup margarine
1 cup sugar
2½ cups unbleached white flour
¼ teaspoon salt
½ teaspoon baking soda
1 teaspoon baking powder
1 teaspoon vanilla
1 carton (8 oz) low-fat lemon yogurt
1 egg
1 egg white

Preheat oven to 325°F. Grease a 12-cup bundt pan with margarine and dust with flour.

In a medium bowl, mix 1 tablespoon flour and the brown sugar.

Add peaches and mix until covered with sugar.

Spread peaches around bottom of bundt pan.

In a large mixing bowl, cream margarine and sugar.

Stir in 2½ cups flour, salt, baking soda, and baking powder.

---

*If it is winter and no fresh peaches are available, use canned peaches or peel, core, and dice two pears instead. Add ¼ teaspoon grated nutmeg to the brown sugar and flour mixture.

Add vanilla, yogurt, egg, and egg white and beat for 3 minutes at medium speed.

Pour batter over peaches and bake for about 1 hour or until a cake tester comes out clean.

Cool for 10 minutes before removing from pan.

Makes 16 slices
Per slice: 210 Total calories; 16 Sat-fat calories

COCOA ANGEL FOOD CAKE

¾ cup cake flour
¼ cup cocoa
1¼ cups sugar
1¼–1½ cups egg whites (about
   10–12)

1 teaspoon cream of tartar
1 teaspoon vanilla
½ teaspoon almond extract

Preheat oven to 350°F.

Sift together three times: cake flour, cocoa, and ¼ cup of the sugar. Set aside.

Sift remaining 1 cup sugar and set aside.

Whip egg whites until foamy. Add cream of tartar. Continue beating until whites are stiff but not dry.

Fold in sugar a little at a time.

Fold in vanilla and almond extract.

Sift flour-cocoa mixture over batter (¼ at a time) and fold into batter.

Pour batter into an ungreased 10-inch tube pan and bake for 45 minutes or until a cake tester comes out clean.

Invert the tube pan and let cake cool.

Makes 12 slices
Per slice: 119 Total calories; trace Sat-fat calories

MARBLE CAKE

To make a special occasion even more special, bake a marble cake and ice it with Cocoa Frosting (see page 328).

3½ cups cake flour
½ teaspoon baking soda
2½ teaspoons baking powder
½ cup buttermilk
½ cup skim milk
1 teaspoon vanilla
½ cup margarine
¾ cup sugar
1 egg yolk

1 tablespoon cocoa
1 tablespoon sugar
1 teaspoon cinnamon
⅛ teaspoon ground cloves
⅛ teaspoon baking soda
1 tablespoon margarine
4 egg whites, at room
  temperature

Preheat oven to 375°F. Grease a 10-inch tube pan with margarine.

Combine cake flour, baking soda, and baking powder and set aside.

Combine buttermilk, skim milk, and vanilla and set aside.

In a large mixing bowl, cream ½ cup margarine and ¾ cup sugar. Mix in egg yolk.

Add half the flour mixture and half the milk mixture and stir until smooth.

Add remaining flour mixture and milk mixture and stir until smooth.

Combine cocoa, cinnamon, cloves, baking soda, and 1 tablespoon sugar.

In a small saucepan, melt 1 tablespoon margarine and blend into cocoa-sugar mixture. Blend 1 cup of batter into cocoa mixture.

Whip egg whites until stiff but not dry.

Fold ⅔ of the egg whites into plain batter and remaining ⅓ egg whites into cocoa batter.

Pour plain batter into tube pan.

Drop spoonfuls of cocoa batter onto plain batter.

With a knife, swirl the cocoa batter through the plain batter.

Bake for 30 minutes or until a cake tester comes out clean.

Makes 12 slices
Per slice: 238 Total calories; 15 Sat-fat calories

DIVINE BUTTERMILK POUND CAKE

You will not believe how light and fine-grained this cake is.

1¾ cup cake flour
½ teaspoon baking soda
1 teaspoon baking powder
¼ teaspoon salt
½ cup margarine

¾ cup sugar
1 egg + 2 egg whites
½ teaspoon vanilla
¼ teaspoon almond extract
¾ cup buttermilk

Preheat oven to 375°F and grease a 9-inch springform pan with margarine.

Combine flour, baking soda, baking powder, and salt, and set aside.

In an electric mixer, cream margarine and sugar.

Add egg and egg whites, vanilla, and almond extract, and mix until smooth.

Add flour mixture and buttermilk, and mix until smooth.

Pour into springform pan and bake for 30–40 minutes, or until cake tester comes out clean.

When cool, frost it with Cocoa or Mocha Frosting (pages 328–329), or the following walnut glaze.

Walnut Glaze

¼ cup brown sugar
½ tablespoon cornstarch
¼ cup cold water

½ teaspoon margarine
1 tablespoon chopped walnuts

In a small saucepan, mix together brown sugar and cornstarch.

Slowly add water, making sure mixture is smooth.

At medium-high temperature, stir for 3–4 minutes, until mixture is thick and begins to boil.

Stir in margarine and walnuts. Spoon over cool cake.

Makes 12 slices

	Total calories	Sat-fat calories
Per slice	175	13
with Mocha Frosting	225	18
with Walnut Glaze	199	14

SPICE CAKE

2⅓ cups cake flour
1½ teaspoons baking powder
½ teaspoon soda
1 teaspoon grated nutmeg
1 teaspoon cinnamon
½ teaspoon cloves

½ teaspoon salt
¾ cup margarine
1 cup sugar
1 egg yolk
1 cup less 2 tablespoons
  buttermilk
3 egg whites

Preheat oven to 350°F and grease 10-inch tube pan with margarine.

Mix together flour, baking powder, baking soda, nutmeg, cinnamon cloves, and salt, and set aside.

In a large mixing bowl, cream margarine and sugar until fluffy.

Mix in 1 egg yolk.

Add dry mixture alternately with buttermilk.

Whip 3 egg whites until stiff but not dry and fold them into batter.

Pour into prepared pan and bake for 45–60 minutes, or until cake tester comes out clean.

Cool and ice with Cocoa Frosting (page 328) or Mocha Frosting (page 329).

Makes 12 slices

	Total calories	*Sat-fat calories*
Per slice	238	19
with frosting	288	24

CHOCOLATEY-CHOCOLATE COCOA CAKE

3 tablespoons cocoa
4 tablespoons margarine
1 cup boiling water
1 cup sugar
1 teaspoon vanilla
1 egg yolk

1 teaspoon baking soda
½ cup buttermilk
2 cups unbleached white flour
1 teaspoon baking powder
2 egg whites

Cocoa Frosting

3 tablespoons margarine
3 tablespoons cocoa
1 teaspoon vanilla

1½ cups confectioners' sugar
1 tablespoon skim milk

Preheat oven to 350°F. Grease a 10-inch tube pan with margarine and dust with flour.

Place cocoa and margarine in a large mixing bowl and add boiling water.

When margarine is melted, stir in sugar and vanilla and beat until smooth.

Stir in egg yolk and beat until smooth.

Stir baking soda into buttermilk. Add to batter and mix well.

Add flour and baking powder and mix well.

Whip egg whites until stiff but not dry and fold into batter.

Pour batter into pan and bake on middle rack of oven for 40–50 minutes or until a cake tester comes out clean.

Cool. Then make cocoa frosting.

The Cocoa Frosting

In a mixing bowl, blend margarine and cocoa.
Add vanilla.
Beat in confectioners' sugar.
Add milk.
If too stiff, add more milk. If too runny, add more sugar.
Frost top and sides of cake.

Makes 10 slices
Per slice: 273 Total calories; 13 Sat-fat calories

MOCHA CAKE

A rich, dark chocolate cake with a taste of mocha.

1¾ cups unbleached white flour ¾ cup sugar
⅓ cup cocoa 1 egg
1 teaspoon baking soda 1 egg white
½ teaspoon baking powder ⅔ cup buttermilk
¼ teaspoon salt ⅔ cup brewed coffee
1 teaspoon cinnamon 1 teaspoon vanilla
½ cup margarine

Mocha Frosting

3 tablespoons margarine Dash of salt
1 cup confectioners' sugar 1 tablespoon brewed coffee
2 tablespoons cocoa ¼ teaspoon vanilla

Preheat oven to 350°F. Grease an 8 × 8-inch baking pan or a 9-inch springform pan with margarine.

Combine flour, cocoa, baking soda, baking powder, salt, and cinnamon. Set aside.

In a large mixing bowl, cream margarine and sugar.

Add egg and egg white and beat well.

Combine buttermilk, coffee, and vanilla.

Alternately add flour mixture and buttermilk mixture to sugar mixture, beating until smooth.

Pour into baking pan and bake for 40 minutes or until a cake tester comes out clean.

Cool. Then make the frosting.

The Mocha Frosting

Cream margarine. Add confectioners' sugar. Beat until smooth.

Add cocoa, salt, coffee, and vanilla. Beat until smooth.

Add more sugar if frosting is too thin.

Add more coffee if frosting is too thick.

Frost top and sides of cake.

Makes 16 squares

	Total calories	Sat-fat calories
Per square	140	10
with icing	180	14

TANTE NANCY'S APPLE CRUMB CAKE

Apple Crumb Cake is our first choice. The crust is thick, crunchy, and sweet. The slightly tart apples melt in your mouth. Luscious.

2–2½ pounds tart apples*
   (about 6–7 large), peeled,
   cored, and sliced
⅓ cup water
¼ cup sugar
2 cups unbleached white flour

¾ cups sugar
1½ teaspoons baking powder
½ cup margarine
1 egg yolk
2 teaspoons margarine

Preheat oven to 350°F. Grease a 9-inch springform pan with margarine.

In a large pot, cook apple slices with water and ¼ cup sugar until apples are tender but not mushy. Drain and reserve.

In a small bowl, mix flour, ¾ cup sugar, and baking powder.

With a pastry blender, cut in ½ cup margarine.

Cut in egg yolk.

Reserve 1 cup of flour mixture for the topping. Press remainder into bottom and sides of pan.

Spoon drained apples into pan.

Cover with reserved topping and dot with 2 teaspoons margarine.

Bake for about 1 hour or until crust is golden brown.

Makes 12 slices
Per slice: 225 Total calories; 15 Sat-fat calories

PIE CRUST

1 ice cube
⅓–½ cup cold water
1½ cups unbleached white flour
2 tablespoons sugar
Pinch of salt

¼ cup tub margarine, frozen
1½ tablespoons olive or
   sunflower oil
(For nonsweet pie dough,
   eliminate sugar and add ¾
   teaspoon salt)

Place ice cube in the cold water. Set aside.

---

*You can use as few as 5 large apples, but more is better. Or substitute 2–2½ pounds peaches or 4 cups blueberries.

Place 1½ cups flour in food processor fitted with steel blade or in a mixing bowl.

Add sugar and salt and mix until well blended.

Cut margarine into ½-inch pieces and add to flour mixture.

Process briefly or use pastry blender until flour mixture resembles coarse meal or oatmeal flakes.

Add oil and ⅓ cup of ice water (without ice cube).

Process 2–3 seconds or blend until dough begins to collect into a ball. *Do not overprocess.*

If dough is too dry, carefully add a few drops more cold water and blend briefly.

Remove ball of dough, lightly flour, and wrap in wax paper. Place in a plastic bag and chill in refrigerator for at least 2 hours. (Dough will keep 2–3 days in refrigerator or for several months in freezer.)

To Bake

Preheat oven to 450°F. Grease an 8- or 9-inch pie or quiche pan with margarine.

On a piece of wax paper, roll dough into an ⅛-inch-thick circle slightly larger than the pie pan.

Turn over the wax paper so the dough is facing downward and lay it over the pan. Peel wax paper off the dough.

Gently push the dough to conform to the shape of the pan.

Trim excess dough, except for about ¼ inch above the rim of the pan. Form a ridge.

Spread margarine on a piece of aluminum foil larger than the pan.

Set foil, greased-side down, onto pie dough.

Fill with dried beans or aluminum pie weights to keep the crust from bubbling up.

Bake for 7–8 minutes.

Remove foil and beans. Prick crust with a fork to release air bubbles.

For partially baked pie crust, bake 3–4 minutes more or until crust is just beginning to brown and shrink from the edges.

For fully baked pie crust, bake 7–10 minutes more or until lightly browned.

	Total calories	*Sat-fat calories*
Sweet pie crust	1260	95
Nonsweet pie crust	1170	95

GRAHAM CRACKER CRUST

Not only do Honey Graham Crackers make a delicious cookie, Honey Graham Cracker crumbs make a delicious pie crust, particularly for lemon meringue or Key lime pie. Commercial graham crackers, graham cracker crumbs, and ready-to-bake graham cracker crusts are often made with lard or hydrogenated vegetable oil. Make your own graham cracker crumbs and graham cracker crust using the Honey Graham Crackers recipe on page 339.

8 homemade graham cracker crumbs (1¼ cups)
1 teaspoon sugar

¼ cup margarine

Preheat oven to 375°F.

In food processor or blender, crush 8 graham crackers into fine crumbs.

Combine crumbs and sugar and pour into pie plate.

Melt margarine and mix into crumbs.

Press crumbs into pie plate to make a crust.

Bake 8 minutes, or until lightly browned.

Makes one pie crust
Per crust: 920 Total calories; 104 Sat-fat calories

KEY LIME PIE

This pie is as pretty to look at as it is delightful to eat. It never fails to wow guests and please the most discriminating palate. Many Key lime pies call for 3 egg yolks and butter. You will use only 1 egg yolk and margarine to create this divine dessert. You can use lemon juice instead of lime juice and call this Lemon Meringue Pie.

Partially baked sweet pie crust (page 330) or
    Graham Cracker Crust (page 332)

Filling

¾ cup sugar
¼ cup unbleached white flour
3 tablespoons cornstarch
¼ teaspoon salt

½–⅔ cup fresh lime juice + water to equal 2¼ cups
1 egg yolk
1 teaspoon margarine

Meringue

5 egg whites, at room temperature	¼ teaspoon cream of tartar
	½ cup + 2 tablespoons sugar

The Filling

In a medium saucepan, thoroughly mix sugar, flour, cornstarch, and salt.

Add ¼ cup lime water and blend into a smooth paste.

Add remaining lime water and mix until smooth.

Stir filling over medium heat until it begins to boil and thicken. Remove saucepan from heat.

In a small bowl, combine egg yolk with a small amount of filling and blend until smooth. Mix back into filling in saucepan. (This step is important. If you were to add the egg yolk directly into the hot filling, the egg yolk would curdle.) Stir margarine into the filling and pour into crust. Cool until filling gels.

The Meringue

Preheat oven to 375°F.

Whip egg whites with cream of tartar until stiff but not dry.

Add sugar and continue beating until whites form stiff peaks.

Gently cover lime filling with egg whites, making sure whites cover pie completely.

Bake for 8–10 minutes or until meringue is golden brown.

Cool at room temperature.

Makes 10 slices

	Total calories	Sat-fat calories
Per slice		
with pastry crust	270	12
with Graham Cracker Crust	235	13

STRAWBERRY TART

Another pièce de résistance to end any meal on a high note. Make this tart with strawberries, kiwis, peaches, or most any other fruit, even lemons. Try a combination of many fruits on one tart. Tarts are typically filled with crème patissière. Instead of the 6 egg yolks normally used in this French custard, this strawberry tart uses packaged vanilla pudding and pie filling.

Fully baked sweet pie crust
  (page 330)
2 quarts strawberries
1 package vanilla pudding and
  pie filling

1¾ cups skim milk
1 scant tablespoon vanilla
½ cup apricot preserves
1 tablespoon sugar

Wash and hull strawberries.

On a plate the size of your tart pan, make a pleasing arrangement of strawberries.

Make vanilla pudding according to package instructions but use 1¾ cups skim milk and 1 scant tablespoon of vanilla instead of the ingredients listed on the box.

Spread pudding evenly over the bottom of the pie crust.

Immediately arrange fruit on crust.

Combine apricot jam and sugar and heat until syrup is thick and forms a ball at the end of your spoon.

Paint fruit with glaze. Refrigerate tart.

Makes 10 slices
Per slice: 215 Total calories; 10 Sat-fat calories

STRAWBERRY-RHUBARB PIE

Rhubarb gives this pie a wonderful blending of sweet and sour.

Partially baked sweet pie crust
  (page 330)
3 stalks rhubarb
2 pints strawberries, washed
  and hulled

2½ teaspoons margarine
¾–1 cup sugar
2⅔ tablespoons quick-cooking
  tapioca

Prepare partially baked sweet pastry for pie bottom crust, but use 1¾ cups flour.

Refrigerate extra pastry.

Preheat oven to 400°F.

Slice rhubarb into ¼-inch pieces. Cut strawberries into quarters.

Gently sauté rhubarb in 2 teaspoons of the margarine until slightly softened (about 5 minutes).

Combine rhubarb, strawberries, sugar, and tapioca, and set aside for 15 minutes.

Fill crust with fruit mixture.

Dot with the remaining ½ teaspoon margarine.

Roll out remaining pastry and cut into strips. Cover pie with lattice top.

Bake for 25–40 minutes or until crust is browned.

Makes 10 slices
Per slice: 240 Total calories; 11 Sat-fat calories

APPLE PANDOWDY

1¼ cups unbleached white flour
1 tablespoon sugar
¼ teaspoon salt
3 tablespoons margarine
1 tablespoon sunflower oil
3 tablespoons + 1 teaspoon
  skim milk

½ cup brown sugar
1 tablespoon flour
1 teaspoon cinnamon
3 tablespoons molasses
7 cups tart apples (about 7),
  peeled and sliced
½ cup chopped walnuts

Preheat oven to 400°F. Grease a 2-quart shallow baking pan with margarine.

In a small bowl, combine flour, sugar, and salt.

Cut in margarine with a pastry blender until margarine is the size of small peas.

Add oil and 3 tablespoons of skim milk. Mix until dough forms a ball. If too dry, add 1 teaspoon of milk.

Wrap dough in wax paper, place in a plastic bag, and refrigerate for 30 minutes.

In a large bowl, combine brown sugar, flour, and cinnamon.

Mix in molasses. Mixture will be sticky.

Mix in apples and walnuts. Molasses mixture will clump. Don't worry.

Pour into pan. Spread molasses mixture over apples as evenly as possible.

Roll out pastry into a rectangle and place over apples.

Bake for 30–40 minutes or until crust is golden brown.

Makes 10 pieces
Per piece: 243 Total calories; 11 Sat-fat calories

DEEP-DISH PEAR PIE

This pie is absolutely scrumptious! Your fortunate guests will never suspect that nonfat yogurt (absolutely no saturated fat) was substituted for the traditional sour cream (270 sat-fat calories per cup).

Partially baked sweet pie crust
   (page 330)

Filling

5 Anjou pears (or tart apples or
   other pears)
2 tablespoons unbleached white
   flour
½ cup sugar

⅛ teaspoon salt
1 cup nonfat yogurt
1 egg
¼ teaspoon grated nutmeg
1 teaspoon vanilla extract

Topping

3 tablespoons sugar
3 tablespoons unbleached white
   flour

½ teaspoon cinnamon
4 teaspoons margarine

Preheat oven to 400°F.

Peel pears and cut into bite-size pieces. Set aside.

In a large bowl, combine remaining filling ingredients and fold in pears.

Pour pear mixture into pie crust and bake at 400°F for 15 minutes.

Lower heat to 350°F and continue baking for 25 minutes more.

Mix together topping ingredients.

Remove pie from oven and sprinkle topping over filling.

Raise heat to 375°F and bake until topping is brown.

Makes 12 slices
Per slice: 236 Total calories; 11 Sat-fat calories

Q ## COCOA BROWNIES

⅓ cup margarine	1 egg white
½ cup sugar	⅓ cup cocoa
¼ cup light corn syrup	½ cup flour
2 teaspoons vanilla	½ teaspoon salt
1 egg	½ cup chopped walnuts

Preheat oven to 350°F. Grease an 8 × 8-inch baking pan with margarine.

In a large bowl, cream margarine and sugar.

Add corn syrup, vanilla, egg, and egg white and mix until well blended.

Combine cocoa, flour, and salt and slowly add to batter.

Fold in nuts and pour batter into baking pan.

Bake for 25–30 minutes or until a cake tester comes out clean.

Makes 16 squares
Per brownie: 115 Total calories; 9 Sat-fat calories

[Q] CINNAMON SWEET CAKES

A family favorite that can be made on the spur of the moment.

¼ cup olive oil
1 egg
½ cup skim milk
½ cup sugar

¾ cup whole-wheat flour
¾ cup unbleached white flour
2 teaspoons baking powder
½ teaspoon salt

Topping

½ cup brown sugar
½ cup chopped walnuts
1 tablespoon unbleached white
   flour

1 tablespoon margarine
1 teaspoon cinnamon

Preheat oven to 375°F. Grease an 8 × 8-inch baking pan with margarine.

In a large mixing bowl, beat together oil, egg, and skim milk.

Add sugar, whole-wheat flour, white flour, baking powder, and salt and beat until smooth.

Spoon batter into baking pan. (Batter will be thick.)

To make the topping, combine brown sugar, walnuts, flour, and cinnamon in a small bowl.

Melt margarine and stir into mixture.

Sprinkle topping over batter.

Bake for about 25 minutes or until a cake tester comes out clean.

Makes 16 squares
Per square: 148 Total calories; 8 Sat-fat calories

[Q] MANDELBROT

These cookies are addictive. Thank you, Esther Krashes!

⅔ cup sugar
¼ cup olive oil
3 egg whites
1 egg

1½ cups unbleached white flour
1 teaspoon baking powder
½ cup coarsely ground almonds
1 teaspoon orange extract

Preheat oven to 350°F.

Lightly grease a cookie sheet with margarine or olive oil.

In a large mixing bowl, cream sugar and olive oil.

Mix in egg whites and egg.

Add flour and baking powder and mix until smooth.

Stir in almonds and orange extract.

Pour onto cookie sheet. Spread into rectangle (8″ × 10″), about ½ inch thick.

Bake for 20 minutes or until lightly browned.

Remove cookie sheet from oven.

Cut dough into strips about 3 inches wide and then score (do not cut through) into bars about ¾ inch wide.

Turn strips over and bake 10 more minutes or until crisp.

Break into bars.

Makes 4 dozen bars
Per bar: 46 Total calories; 2 Sat-fat calories

Q   HONEY GRAHAM CRACKERS

1 cup whole-wheat flour	¼ cup margarine
½ cup unbleached white flour	2 tablespoons light brown sugar
½ teaspoon baking powder	2 tablespoons honey
¼ teaspoon baking soda	½ teaspoon vanilla
Pinch of salt	2 tablespoons skim milk

Preheat oven to 350°F and grease a cookie sheet with margarine.

Combine flours, baking powder, baking soda, and salt, and set aside.

Cream margarine, sugar, and honey in an electric mixer.

Mix in vanilla.

Add flour mixture and milk.

Gather dough together (add a drop of milk if too dry) and knead into a ball.

Roll dough onto cookie sheet into a rectangle, ⅛ inch thick.

If dough is too sticky, sprinkle it with flour.

Without moving dough, cut into 3-inch squares.

Lightly score a line through the center of each square and pierce each side several times with a fork.

Bake 10–15 minutes, until edges brown. Remove crackers and cool on a wire rack.

Crackers will become crisp as they cool.

Makes 18 crackers
Per cracker: 68 Total calories; 4 Sat-fat calories

Q # MARVELOUS COOKIES

A cookie made with healthy ingredients that is absolutely scrumptious. Refrain from eating too many, as each contains about 80 calories.

¼ cup margarine	¾ teaspoon baking powder
¼ cup olive or sunflower oil	1 cup wheat germ
½ cup brown sugar	1½ cups rolled oats
1 egg	½ cup raisins
1½ teaspoons vanilla	½ cup chopped walnuts
½ cup whole-wheat flour	1–2 tablespoons water, if
½ teaspoon salt	necessary

Preheat oven to 375°F. Grease a cookie sheet with margarine.

Cream margarine, oil, and brown sugar.

Add egg and vanilla and beat well.

Add whole-wheat flour, salt, baking powder, wheat germ, rolled oats, raisins, and nuts and mix well. Add water if too dry.

Drop batter by teaspoonfuls onto cookie sheet and bake 10–12 minutes.

Makes 3 dozen cookies
Per cookie: 80 Total calories; 5 Sat-fat calories

APPLE-NUT COOKIES

⅓ cup margarine
½ cup brown sugar
1 egg
1 cup unbleached white flour
½ cup whole-wheat flour
½ teaspoon baking soda
1 teaspoon baking powder
½ teaspoon salt

1 teaspoon cinnamon
¼ teaspoon grated nutmeg
3 tablespoons milk
¼ cup raisins
½ cup chopped walnuts
2½ cups peeled, diced cooking
    apples

Preheat oven to 400°F. Lightly grease a cookie sheet with margarine.

In a large mixing bowl, cream margarine and brown sugar.

Add egg and beat until batter is smooth.

Combine white flour, whole-wheat flour, baking soda, baking powder, salt, cinnamon, and nutmeg.

Mix into batter alternately with milk.

Stir in raisins and nuts. Fold in apples.

Drop batter by teaspoonfuls onto cookie sheet and bake for 10–12 minutes or until golden brown.

Makes 3 dozen cookies
Per cookie: 62 Total calories; 4 Sat-fat calories

OATMEAL COOKIES

½ cup olive or sunflower oil
⅓ cup brown sugar
2 tablespoons sugar
1 egg white
¾ teaspoon vanilla
3 tablespoons water

2 cups rolled oats
⅓ cup unbleached white flour
⅓ cup whole-wheat flour
¼ teaspoon salt
½ teaspoon baking soda
1 teaspoon cinnamon

Preheat oven to 350°F. Grease a cookie sheet with margarine.
Cream oil and sugars.
Mix in egg white, vanilla, and water.

Add oats, white flour, whole-wheat flour, salt, baking soda, and cinnamon and mix until blended. Do not overmix or you will lose the texture of the oats.

Drop batter by teaspoonfuls onto cookie sheet and bake for 10–15 minutes.

Makes 2 dozen cookies
Per cookie: 85 Total calories; 6 Sat-fat calories

[Q]   # PEARS HÉLÈNE

Pears Hélène made with cocoa and margarine are wonderful, just like their counterpart made with chocolate and butter.

The chocolate sauce is a good all-purpose dessert sauce. You can store it in the refrigerator for weeks.

Pears

4 ripe pears	¼ cup sugar
2 cups water	1 tablespoon fresh lemon juice

Chocolate Sauce

3 tablespoons sugar	1 tablespoon light corn syrup
2 tablespoons cocoa	1 tablespoon margarine
1 tablespoon cornstarch	½ teaspoon vanilla
2 tablespoons water	

The Pears

Peel pears, cut them in half, core them, and cut off the stems.

In a pot large enough to hold pears, combine water, sugar, and lemon juice and bring to a boil.

Spoon pears into liquid, reduce heat, and simmer, covered, for 5 minutes. Pears should be tender, not mushy.

Drain poached pears and chill.

The Chocolate Sauce

In a small saucepan, combine sugar, cocoa, and cornstarch.

Mix in water and corn syrup and blend well.

Cook over medium heat until mixture comes to a boil.

Remove from heat and stir for about 1 minute.

Add margarine and vanilla and continue to stir until sauce is well blended.

On each plate, place 2 pear halves, cut-side up, and pour warm sauce over them.

Serves 4
Per serving: 205 Total calories; 5 Sat-fat calories

STRAWBERRY MOUSSE

1 pint strawberries, washed and hulled
1 tablespoon orange marmalade
1 tablespoon unflavored gelatin
¼ cup orange juice
1 tablespoon cherry liqueur
3 egg whites
3 tablespoons sugar

Purée strawberries in a blender or food processor. Add marmalade.

In a small saucepan, combine gelatin and orange juice.

Add strawberry purée and heat slowly, stirring constantly, until gelatin is dissolved.

Stir in cherry liqueur.

Chill in refrigerator or freezer until mixture thickens.

Beat egg whites until foamy. Add sugar and beat until egg whites are stiff but not dry.

Fold egg whites into strawberry mixture.

Gently pour into a 4-cup soufflé mold. Chill until set.

Makes 6 one-cup servings
Per serving: 67 Total calories; 0 Sat-fat calories

THREE

FOOD TABLES

BEVERAGES

FOOD	PORTION SIZE	TOTAL CALORIES	SAT-FAT CALORIES
Alcoholic			
Beer			
regular	12 fl oz	150	0
light	12 fl oz	95	0
Gin, rum, vodka, whiskey			
80 proof	1½ fl oz	95	0
86 proof	1½ fl oz	105	0
90 proof	1½ fl oz	110	0
Other			
brandy Alexander	5 fl oz	185	65
piña colada	5 fl oz	215	85
eggnog	8 fl oz	342	102
Wine			
dessert	3½ fl oz	140	0
table	3½ fl oz	75	0
Carbonated			
Club soda	12 fl oz	0	0
Cola			
regular	12 fl oz	160	0
diet (artificially sweetened)	12 fl oz	trace	0
Ginger ale	12 fl oz	125	0
Grape	12 fl oz	180	0
Lemon-lime	12 fl oz	155	0
Orange	12 fl oz	180	0
Pepper-type	12 fl oz	160	0
Root beer	12 fl oz	165	0
Other			
Coffee			
brewed	6 fl oz	trace	trace
instant	6 fl oz	trace	trace
Fruit drinks, noncarbonated			
Canned			
fruit punch drink	6 fl oz	85	0
grape drink	6 fl oz	100	0
pineapple-grapefruit juice drink	6 fl oz	90	0
Frozen			
lemonade (diluted)	6 fl oz	80	trace
limeade (diluted)	6 fl oz	75	trace

Fruit juices: see **Fruits and Fruit Juices**

Milk beverages: see **Dairy**

DAIRY

FOOD	PORTION SIZE	TOTAL CALORIES	SAT-FAT CALORIES
Butter			
Regular	1 pat	36	23
	1 stick (½ cup)	813	515
Whipped	1 pat	27	17
	1 stick (½ cup)	542	344

(For margarine, see **Fats and Oils**)

FOOD	PORTION SIZE	TOTAL CALORIES	SAT-FAT CALORIES
Cheese			
American	1 oz	106	50
American cheese spread	1 oz	82	34
American Lite-Line (Borden)	1 oz	50	18
Blue	1 oz	100	48
Brick	1 oz	105	48
Camembert	1 oz	85	39
Caraway	1 oz	90	36
Cheddar	1 oz	114	54
Colby	1 oz	112	52
Cottage			
creamed	½ cup	117	29
dry curd	½ cup	96	3
1% fat	½ cup	82	7
2% fat	½ cup	102	12
Cream			
regular	1 oz	99	56
	1 tbsp	52	26
whipped	1 tbsp	37	19
Edam	1 oz	101	45
Feta	1 oz	75	38
Fontina	1 oz	110	49
Gjetöst	1 oz	132	49
Gouda	1 oz	101	45
Gruyère	1 oz	117	48
Limburger	1 oz	93	43
Monterey Jack	1 oz	100	45
Mozzarella			
whole milk	1 oz	80	34
low moisture	1 oz	90	40
part skim	1 oz	72	26
low moisture, part skim	1 oz	79	28
Muenster	1 oz	104	49
Neufchâtel	1 oz	74	38

DAIRY

FOOD	PORTION SIZE	TOTAL CALORIES	SAT-FAT CALORIES
Ole Smokey (Land O' Lakes)	1 oz	90	36
Parmesan			
grated	1 oz	129	49
	1 tbsp	23	9
hard	1 oz	111	42
Pimento	1 oz	106	50
Port du Salut	1 oz	100	43
Provolone	1 oz	100	44
Ricotta			
whole milk	½ cup	216	93
part skim milk	½ cup	171	55
Romano	1 oz	110	43
Roquefort	1 oz	105	49
Swiss			
natural	1 oz	107	45
processed	1 oz	95	41
Tilsit	1 oz	96	43

Cream

Half-and-half	1 tbsp	20	10
Light, coffee or table	1 tbsp	29	16
	1 cup	469	260

(Coffee whiteners: see **Imitation Dairy Products.**)

Medium (25% fat)	1 tbsp	37	21
	1 cup	583	335
Light whipping	1 tbsp	44	26
	1 cup	699	416
Heavy whipping	1 tbsp	52	31
	1 cup	821	493
Whipped cream topping	1 tbsp	8	4
(pressurized)	1 cup	154	75
Sour	1 tbsp	26	14
	1 cup	493	270

Frozen Desserts

Frozen yogurt			
nonfat (Colombo Lite)	4 oz	90	0
low-fat (Colombo)	4 oz	102	12
regular (ICBIY and TCBY)	4 oz	144	23

DAIRY

FOOD	PORTION SIZE	TOTAL CALORIES	SAT-FAT CALORIES
Ice cream, vanilla			
regular	1 cup	269	80
rich	1 cup	349	133
soft-serve	1 cup	377	122
Ice milk, vanilla			
regular	1 cup	184	32
soft-serve	1 cup	223	26
Sherbet	1 cup	270	21
Imitation Dairy Products			
Coffee whitener, liquid (hydrogenated soybean, cottonseed, sunflower oils)	½ oz	20	3
Coffee whitener, liquid (hydrogenated coconut, palm oil)	½ oz	20	13
Coffee whitener, powdered (hydrogenated palm, coconut oil)	1 tsp	11	6
Dessert topping, powdered (1½ oz topping + ½ cup whole milk)	1 tbsp	8	4
	1 cup	151	77
Dessert topping, pressurized (hydrogenated coconut, palm oils)	1 tbsp	11	7
	1 cup	184	119
Imitation milk (soybean, cottonseed, safflower oils)	1 cup	150	17
Imitation milk (hydrogenated coconut, palm oils)	1 cup	150	67
Imitation sour cream (hydrogenated coconut, palm oils)	1 oz	59	45
	1 cup	479	368
Milk			
Buttermilk	1 cup	99	0
Canned			
condensed, sweetened	1 oz	123	19
	1 cup	982	151
evaporated, skim	1 oz	25	0
	½ cup	99	1
evaporated, whole	1 oz	42	13
	½ cup	169	52

DAIRY

FOOD	PORTION SIZE	TOTAL CALORIES	SAT-FAT CALORIES
Chocolate			
2% milk	1 cup	179	28
whole milk	1 cup	208	47
malted (1 cup milk + ¾ oz powder)	1 cup	233	50
cocoa powder with nonfat dry milk	1 oz	100	5
Low-fat 1%	1 cup	104	14
Low-fat, 2%	1 cup	121	27
Nonfat			
dry	¼ cup	109	1
instant	3.2 oz envelope (for 1 qt)	326	4
Skim	1 cup	86	0–3
Whole	1 cup	150	45
Whole, dry	¼ cup	159	48
Miscellaneous			
Eggnog	1 cup	342	102
Shakes, thick			
Chocolate	10.6 oz	356	45
Vanilla	11 oz	350	53
Yogurt			
coffee and vanilla, low-fat	8 oz	194	16
fruit flavors, low-fat	8 oz	225	15
nonfat (Colombo Natural Lite)	8 oz	110	0
plain, whole milk	8 oz	139	43
low-fat	8 oz	144	20
skim milk	8 oz	127	2
Eggs			
Large, fresh	1	79	15
white	1	16	0
yolk	1	63	15
Large, cooked			
fried in butter	1	83	22
hard-cooked	1	79	15
	1 cup, chopped	215	41
omelet prepared with butter and milk	1 egg	95	25
poached	1	79	15

DAIRY

FOOD	PORTION SIZE	TOTAL CALORIES	SAT-FAT CALORIES
Large, cooked (*cont.*)			
scrambled in butter and milk	1 egg	95	25
	1 cup	325	87
Egg Substitutes			
Egg Beaters			
(Fleischmann's)	¼ cup	40	0
Egg substitute, frozen (egg white, corn oil, nonfat dry milk)	¼ cup	96	10
Egg substitute, liquid (egg white, hydrogenated soybean oil, soy protein)	1½ oz	40	3

FAST FOODS

FOOD	PORTION SIZE	TOTAL CALORIES	SAT-FAT CALORIES
Arby's Ham n' Cheese sandwich	1	380	70
Arthur Treacher's chicken	1 serving	369	36
Arthur Treacher's chowder	1 serving	112	18
Arthur Treacher's fish	1 serving	355	25
Arthur Treacher's fish sandwich	1	440	38
Arthur Treacher's shrimp	1 serving	381	30
Arthur Treacher's coleslaw	1 serving	123	10
Arthur Treacher's chips	1 serving	276	21
Arthur Treacher's Krunch Pup	1 serving	203	36
Arthur Treacher's Lemon Luvs	1 serving	276	20
Burger King cheeseburger	1	317	63
Burger King double cheeseburger	1	478	117
Burger King hamburger	1	275	45
Burger King hot dog	1	291	60
Burger King Whaler	1	488	54
Burger King Whopper	1	626	117
Burger King Whopper Jr.	1	322	54
Burger King French fries	1 serving	227	63
Burger King vanilla shake	1	332	66
Burger King onion rings, regular	1 serving	274	27
Dairy Queen Brazier burger, regular	1	360	60
Dairy Queen Big Brazier burger with cheese	1	553	128

FAST FOODS

FOOD	PORTION SIZE	TOTAL CALORIES	SAT-FAT CALORIES
Dairy Queen Brazier cheese dog	1	330	76
Dairy Queen onion rings	1 serving	300	55
Dairy Queen banana split	1	540	91
Dairy Queen chocolate-dipped cone	1 medium	340	83
Dairy Queen chocolate malt	1 medium	760	128
Dairy Queen soft ice cream cone	1 medium	240	30
Hardee's biscuit with egg	1	383	120
Hardee's Deluxe burger	1	503	137
Hardee's cheeseburger	1	309	90
Hardee's hot dog	1	346	60
Kentucky Fried Chicken Original Recipe Chicken			
breast	1 piece	276	45
drumstick	1 piece	147	18
thigh	1 piece	278	45
wing	1 piece	181	27
Kentucky Fried Chicken Extra Crispy Chicken			
breast	1 piece	354	54
drumstick	1 piece	173	27
thigh	1 piece	371	63
wing	1 piece	218	36
Kentucky Fried Chicken dinner (mashed potatoes, gravy, cole-slaw, roll, 2 pieces chicken)			
wing + breast	1 dinner	755	93
drumstick + thigh	1 dinner	765	95
wing + thigh	1 dinner	902	107
Long John Silver's breaded shrimp	1 order	308	80
Long John Silver's fish + fries	1 order	651	180
McDonald's hamburger	1	263	40
McDonald's cheeseburger	1	318	60
McDonald's Big Mac	1	563	155
McDonald's Quarter Pounder	1	427	82
McDonald's Quarter Pounder w/cheese	1	524	120
McDonald's Filet-o-Fish sandwich	1	432	71
McDonald's regular fries	1 serving	220	40
McDonald's apple pie	1	253	50
McDonald's chocolate or vanilla shake	1	383	47
McDonald's Egg McMuffin	1 order	340	59

FAST FOODS

FOOD	PORTION SIZE	TOTAL CALORIES	SAT-FAT CALORIES
McDonald's hot cakes w/butter and syrup	1 serving	500	43
Pizza Hut Supreme medium pizza	¼ pizza	506	65
Roy Rogers' roast beef sandwich	1	319	29
Wendy's chili	1 serving	266	38
Wendy's baked potato with cheese	1	590	180

FATS AND OILS

FOOD	PORTION SIZE	TOTAL CALORIES	SAT-FAT CALORIES	P/S* RATIO
Oils				
Cocoa butter	1 tbsp	120	73	0.05:1
Coconut	1 tbsp	120	106	0.02:1
Corn	1 tbsp	120	15	4.7:1
Cottonseed	1 tbsp	120	32	2.0:1
Olive	1 tbsp	119	16	0.6:1
Palm	1 tbsp	120	60	0.2:1
Palm kernel	1 tbsp	120	100	0.02:1
Peanut	1 tbsp	119	21	1.9:1
Puritan	1 tbsp	120	9	4.0:1
Safflower	1 tbsp	120	11	8.4:1
Sesame	1 tbsp	120	17	3.0:1
Soybean	1 tbsp	120	18	4.0:1
Sunflower	1 tbsp	120	13	6.3:1
Walnut	1 tbsp	120	11	7.2:1
Animal Fats				
Beef tallow	1 tbsp	116	58	0.08:1
Butter				
regular	1 pat	36	23	0.08:1
	1 tbsp	100	65	
	1 stick	813	515	

*The higher the polyunsaturated to saturated fat (P/S) ratio, the less heart-risky is the food; the lower the ratio, the more heart-risky. In general, a P/S ratio greater than or equal to 1:1 is considered good, and a ratio less than 1:1 is bad. The P/S ratio of some oils may vary. Check the labels of the products you use for the actual P/S ratios.

FATS AND OILS

FOOD	PORTION SIZE	TOTAL CALORIES	SAT-FAT CALORIES	P/S RATIO
Butter (*cont.*)				
whipped	1 tsp	23	12	0.06:1
	1 tbsp	67	38	
Butter oil, anhydrous	1 tbsp	112	71	0.06:1
Chicken fat	1 tbsp	115	34	0.71:1
Duck fat	1 tbsp	115	39	0.40:1
Goose fat	1 tbsp	115	32	0.40:1
Lard (pork)	1 tbsp	116	45	0.28:1
Mutton tallow	1 tbsp	116	55	0.16:1
Turkey fat	1 tbsp	115	34	0.79:1
Commercial Salad Dressings and Spreads				
Blue cheese	1 tbsp	77	14	2.9:1
French				
low calorie	1 tbsp	22	1	5.0:1
regular	1 tbsp	67	14	2.3:1
Italian				
low calorie	1 tbsp	16	2	4.5:1
regular	1 tbsp	69	9	4.1:1
Mayonnaise				
safflower and soybean	1 tbsp	99	11	6.3:1
soybean	1 tbsp	99	14	3.6:1
imitation, milk cream	1 tbsp	14	4	0.25:1
imitation, soybean	1 tbsp	35	5	3.2:1
imitation, soybean w/o cholesterol	1 tbsp	68	10	3.5:1
Kraft Light, reduced calorie	1 tbsp	45	9	3.0:1
Miracle Whip Light, reduced calorie	1 tbsp	45	9	2.0:1
Russian				
low calorie	1 tbsp	23	1	4.0:1
regular	1 tbsp	76	10	4.1:1
Sesame seed	1 tbsp	68	8	4.2:1
Thousand Island				
low calorie	1 tbsp	24	2	5.0:1
regular	1 tbsp	59	8	3.4:1
Sandwich spread	1 tbsp	60	7	3.9:1
Shortenings				
Crisco	1 tbsp	113	30	0.8:1
Household				
hydrogenated soybean and hydrogenated cottonseed	1 tbsp	113	29	1.0:1

FATS AND OILS

FOOD	PORTION SIZE	TOTAL CALORIES	SAT-FAT CALORIES	P/S RATIO
Household (*cont.*)				
hydrogenated soybean and palm	1 tbsp	113	35	0.46:1
lard and vegetable oil	1 tbsp	115	47	0.27:1
Margarines				
Butter blends				
Land O' Lakes Country Morning Blend				
stick	1 tbsp	100	27	1.0:1
tub	1 tbsp	90	27	1.0:1
Mrs. Filbert's I Can't Believe It's Not Butter	1 tbsp	90	18	0.5:1
Diet				
Blue Bonnet	1 tbsp	50	9	N.A.
Fleischmann's	1 tbsp	50	9	N.A.
Imperial	1 tbsp	50	9	2.0:1
Mazola	1 tbsp	50	9	2.0:1
Mrs. Filbert's	1 tbsp	50	9	2.0:1
Parkay	1 tbsp	50	9	2.0:1
Weight Watchers	1 tbsp	50	9	3.0:1
Regular, hard, stick or brick				
Blue Bonnet	1 tbsp	100	18	N.A.
Fleischmann's	1 tbsp	100	18	2.0:1
Land O' Lakes	1 tbsp	100	18	1.0:1
Mazola Premium	1 tbsp	100	18	2.0:1
Parkay	1 tbsp	100	18	0.5:1
Promise	1 tbsp	90	18	2.0:1
Soft, tub				
Blue Bonnet	1 tbsp	100	18	N.A.
Fleischmann's	1 tbsp	100	18	2.5:1
Land O' Lakes	1 tbsp	100	18	2.0:1
Mother's	1 tbsp	100	18	2.0:1
Mrs. Filbert's	1 tbsp	100	18	2.5:1
Parkay	1 tbsp	100	18	2.0:1
Chiffon	1 tbsp	100	18	2.0:1
Promise	1 tbsp	90	18	2.5:1
Whipped, stick				
Blue Bonnet	1 tbsp	70	18	N.A.
Whipped, soft				
Blue Bonnet	1 tbsp	70	18	N.A.
Fleischmann's	1 tbsp	70	18	N.A.

FATS AND OILS

FOOD	PORTION SIZE	TOTAL CALORIES	SAT-FAT CALORIES	P/S RATIO
Whipped, soft (*cont.*)				
Chiffon	1 tbsp	70	9	3.0:1
Mrs. Filbert's Family Spread	1 tbsp	70	9	3.0:1
Shedd's Spread	1 tbsp	70	9	3.0:1

FISH AND SEAFOOD

FOOD	PORTION SIZE	TOTAL CALORIES	SAT-FAT CALORIES
Abalone, raw	1 oz	98	3
Anchovy, canned	1 oz	49	12
Bass, freshwater, steamed or baked	1 oz	33	1
Bass, striped, oven-fried	1 oz	56	5
Bluefish, baked w/margarine	1 oz	45	3
Catfish, freshwater, steamed or baked	1 oz	35	3
Caviar	1 tbsp	42	15
Cisco (lake herring), steamed or baked	1 oz	33	1
Clams			
raw, cherrystones or littlenecks	4 or 5	56	trace
	1 oz	23	trace
canned, drained, chopped	1 cup	157	13
canned, solids and liquid	1 oz	15	1
Mrs. Paul's deviled	1 cake	180	26
Mrs. Paul's fried	2.5 oz	270	35
	1 oz	108	14
Mrs. Paul's Cake Thins	2	310	38
Mrs. Paul's sticks	5	240	17
Cod, broiled w/o added fat	1 oz	29	trace
Crab			
steamed, pieces	1 cup	144	9
steamed	1 oz	26	trace
canned, white or king, not packed	1 cup	135	7
Mrs. Paul's Cake Thins	2	320	40
Mrs. Paul's deviled	1 cake	160	21

FISH AND SEAFOOD

FOOD	PORTION SIZE	TOTAL CALORIES	SAT-FAT CALORIES
Croaker, Atlantic, baked	1 oz	38	3
Crayfish, steamed	1 oz	25	1
Dogfish, spiny (grayfish), baked or steamed	1 oz	53	7
Drum, freshwater, steamed or baked	1 oz	41	3
Eel, baked or steamed	1 oz	79	11
Flounder			
baked or steamed w/o added fat	1 oz	28	1
Mrs. Paul's fried fillets	2	220	19
Mrs. Paul's w/lemon butter	4.25 oz	150	26
	1 oz	35	6
Gefilte fish	1 piece (1.5 oz)	35	2
Grouper (red, black, speckled hind), baked or steamed	1 oz	30	trace
Haddock			
baked or steamed	1 oz	27	trace
oven-fried	1 fillet	182	12
Mrs. Paul's fried fillets	2	230	19
Hake, steamed or baked	1 oz	25	1
Halibut			
baked or steamed	1 oz	34	8
broiled w/margarine	1 fillet	214	17
Herring			
canned	1 piece	221	25
pickled	1 piece	33	4
Lobster			
canned	1 oz	26	1
cooked	1 cup	138	7
	1 lb	431	21
Newburg	1 cup	485	160
Lox (smoked salmon)	1 oz	33	2
Mackerel			
baked or steamed	1 oz	65	11
broiled with butter	1 fillet	248	60
canned	1 oz	52	10
fried in vegetable fat	1 oz	53	10
Mullet, striped, baked or steamed	1 oz	50	4
Mussels, cooked	1 oz	49	2
Ocean perch			
baked or steamed	1 oz	32	1
Mrs. Paul's fried fillets	2	250	33

FISH AND SEAFOOD

FOOD	PORTION SIZE	TOTAL CALORIES	SAT-FAT CALORIES
Oysters			
raw	1 cup (13–19)	160	12
fried	4	108	17
oyster stew (2 parts milk, 1 part oyster)	1 cup	233	80
Perch, white, baked or steamed	1 oz	40	2
Perch, yellow, baked or steamed	1 oz	31	1
Pike, northern, baked or steamed	1 oz	30	trace
Pike, walleye, baked or steamed	1 oz	32	1
Pollock, baked or steamed	1 oz	32	trace
Pompano, baked or steamed	1 oz	57	11
Rockfish, baked or steamed	1 oz	33	1
Sablefish, baked or steamed	1 oz	65	10
Salmon, Atlantic, baked or steamed	1 oz	74	3
Salmon, chinook (king), baked or steamed	1 oz	76	8
Salmon			
chum, canned	1 oz	39	5
coho (silver), canned	1 oz	43	3
pink, baked or steamed	1 oz	41	2
pink, canned	1 oz	40	3
sockeye (red), baked or steamed	1 oz	47	5
Sardines, drained	1 can (3¼ oz)	187	31
Scallops			
steamed	1 oz	32	1
Mrs. Paul's fried	4 oz	240	23
	1 oz	60	6
Mrs. Paul's light batter	3.5 oz	200	21
	1 oz	57	6
Mrs. Paul's Crepes	5.5 oz	220	27
	1 oz	40	5
Mrs. Paul's w/butter and cheese	7 oz	260	45
	1 oz	37	6
Shrimp			
raw, large	1	7	trace
raw, medium	1	4	trace
raw, small	1	2	trace
canned	1 oz	36	trace
	1 cup	148	2
French fried	1 oz	63	7
Mrs. Paul's Cake Thins	2	310	38
Mrs. Paul's Crepes	5.5 oz	250	36

FISH AND SEAFOOD

FOOD	PORTION SIZE	TOTAL CALORIES	SAT-FAT CALORIES
Smelt, baked or steamed	1 oz	33	2
Snapper, red, baked or steamed	1 oz	33	1
Sole			
baked or steamed	1 oz	28	1
Mrs. Paul's w/lemon butter	1 oz	36	6
Squid (floured and fried)	107	50	5
Sturgeon, baked or steamed	1 oz	45	4
Swordfish, baked or steamed	1 oz	40	2
Trout, steamed			
brook	1 oz	38	3
lake	1 oz	57	5
Tuna			
solid white, water packed, drained	1 oz	45	1
chunk light, oil packed, drained	1 oz	56	5
Tuna salad	½ cup	190	15
Whitefish, lake, baked or steamed	1 oz	53	3
Whitefish, smoked	1 oz	30	.5

FRUITS AND FRUIT JUICES

FOOD	PORTION SIZE	TOTAL CALORIES	SAT-FAT CALORIES
Apples, raw			
unpeeled, cored (2¾ inch)	1	80	1
unpeeled, cored (3¼ inch)	1	125	1
unpeeled, sliced	1 cup	64	1
peeled, cored	1	72	1
peeled, sliced	1 cup	65	1
Apple juice	1 cup	115	trace
Applesauce, canned			
sweetened	1 cup	195	1
unsweetened	1 cup	105	trace
Apricots			
raw, pitted	3	50	trace
canned in heavy syrup	1 cup	215	trace
	3 halves	70	trace
canned in juice	1 cup	120	trace
	3 halves	40	trace

FRUITS AND FRUIT JUICES

FOOD	PORTION SIZE	TOTAL CALORIES	SAT-FAT CALORIES
Apricots, dried			
uncooked	1 cup	310	trace
cooked, unsweetened	1 cup	210	trace
Avocados			
California	1	305	41
Florida	1	340	48
Bananas			
whole	1	105	2
sliced	1 cup	140	3
Blackberries	1 cup	75	2
Blueberries			
raw	1 cup	80	trace
frozen, sweetened	10 oz	230	trace
	1 cup	185	trace
frozen, unsweetened	1 cup	78	trace
	20 oz	287	trace
Cantaloupe	½ melon	95	1
Cherries			
sour red, pitted, canned in water	1 cup	90	1
sweet, pitted	10	50	1
Cranberry juice cocktail, sweetened	1 cup	145	trace
Cranberry sauce, sweetened, canned, strained	1 cup	420	trace
Dates			
whole, pitted	10	230	1
chopped	1 cup	490	3
Figs, dried	10	475	4
Fruit cocktail			
canned in heavy syrup	1 cup	185	trace
canned in juice	1 cup	115	trace
Grapefruit			
fresh	½	40	trace
canned, sections	1 cup	150	trace
Grapefruit juice			
fresh	1 cup	95	trace
canned, unsweetened	1 cup	95	trace
canned, sweetened	1 cup	115	trace
Grapes			
Thompson seedless	10	35	1
	1 cup	97	1
Tokay and Emperor	10	40	1
Grape juice, canned or bottled	1 cup	155	1

FRUITS AND FRUIT JUICES

FOOD	PORTION SIZE	TOTAL CALORIES	SAT-FAT CALORIES
Honeydew melon	1/10 melon	45	trace
Kiwis	1	45	trace
Lemons	1	15	trace
Lemon juice			
fresh	1 cup	60	trace
	1 tbsp	4	trace
canned or bottled	1 cup	50	1
	1 tbsp	3	trace
Lime juice			
fresh	1 cup	65	trace
	1 tbsp	4	trace
canned, unsweetened	1 cup	50	1
Mangos	1	135	1
Nectarines	1	65	1
Oranges			
whole	1	60	trace
sections	1 cup	85	trace
Orange juice			
fresh	1 cup	110	0
canned, unsweetened	1 cup	105	trace
diluted concentrate	1 cup	110	trace
Orange and grapefruit juice, canned	1 cup	105	trace
Papaya, fresh, cubed	1 cup	65	1
Peaches			
fresh, whole	1 peach	35	trace
fresh, sliced	1 cup	75	trace
canned in heavy syrup	1 cup	190	trace
	1 half	60	trace
canned in juice	1 cup	110	trace
	1 half	35	trace
dried, uncooked	1 cup	380	1
dried, cooked, unsweetened	1 cup	200	1
Pears			
Bartlett, cored	1	100	trace
Bosc, cored	1	85	trace
D'Anjou, cored	1	120	trace
canned in heavy syrup	1 cup	190	trace
	1 half	60	trace
canned in juice	1 cup	125	trace
	1 half	40	trace
Pineapple			
fresh, diced	1 cup	75	trace

FRUITS AND FRUIT JUICES

FOOD	PORTION SIZE	TOTAL CALORIES	SAT-FAT CALORIES
Pineapple (*cont.*)			
canned in heavy syrup			
crushed, chunks, tidbits	1 cup	200	trace
slices	1 slice	45	trace
canned in juice			
chunks or tidbits	1 cup	150	trace
slices	1 slice	35	trace
Pineapple juice, unsweetened, canned	1 cup	140	trace
Plantains			
fresh	1	220	3
cooked, boiled, sliced	1 cup	180	1
Plums			
fresh, pitted	1 (6.5/lb)	35	trace
	1 (15/lb)	15	trace
canned in heavy syrup	1 cup	230	trace
	3 plums	120	trace
canned in juice	1 cup	145	trace
	3 plums	55	trace
Prunes, dried			
uncooked	10	201	trace
	1 cup	385	1
cooked, unsweetened	1 cup	225	trace
Prune juice	1 cup	180	trace
Raisins, seedless	1 cup	435	2
	1 packet (½ oz)	40	trace
Raspberries			
fresh	1 cup	60	trace
frozen, sweetened	10 oz	295	trace
	1 cup	255	trace
Rhubarb, cooked, sweetened	1 cup	280	trace
Strawberries			
fresh, whole	1 cup	45	trace
frozen, sweetened, sliced	10 oz	275	trace
	1 cup	245	trace
Tangerines			
fresh	1	35	trace
canned in light syrup	1 cup	155	trace
Watermelon	1 slice (4 × 8 inches)	155	3
diced	1 cup	50	1

GRAIN PRODUCTS

FOOD	PORTION SIZE	TOTAL CALORIES	SAT-FAT CALORIES
Bread			
Bagels, plain or water, enriched	1	200	3
Biscuits (baking powder)	1	95	7
Boston brown, canned	½-inch slice	95	3
Cracked wheat	1 loaf (1 lb)	1190	28
	1 slice (18/loaf)	65	2
Crumbs, enriched, dry	1 cup	390	14
French or Vienna, enriched	1 loaf (1 lb)	1270	34
	1-inch slice (French)	100	3
	½-inch slice (Vienna)	70	2
Italian, enriched	1 loaf (1 lb)	1255	5
	¾-inch slice	85	trace
Mixed grain, enriched	1 loaf (1 lb)	1165	29
	1 slice (18/loaf)	65	2
Oatmeal, enriched	1 loaf (1 lb)	1145	33
	1 slice (18/loaf)	65	2
Pita	1 (6½ in.)	165	1
Pumpernickel (⅔ rye flour, ⅓ enriched wheat flour)	1 loaf (1 lb)	1160	23
	1 slice (15/loaf)	80	2
Raisin, enriched	1 loaf (1 lb)	1260	37
	1 slice (18/loaf)	65	2
Rye, light (⅔ enriched wheat flour, ⅓ rye flour)	1 loaf (1 lb)	1190	30
	1 slice (18/loaf)	65	2
Stuffing mix			
dry	1 cup	500	55
moist	1 cup	420	48
Wheat, enriched	1 loaf (1 lb)	1160	35
	1 slice (18/loaf)	65	2
White, enriched	1 loaf (1 lb)	1210	50
	1 slice (18/loaf)	65	3
	1 slice (22/loaf)	55	2

GRAIN PRODUCTS

FOOD	PORTION SIZE	TOTAL CALORIES	SAT-FAT CALORIES
Whole-wheat	1 loaf (1 lb)	1110	52
	1 slice (16/ loaf)	70	4

Breakfast Cereals, Hot

FOOD	PORTION SIZE	TOTAL CALORIES	SAT-FAT CALORIES
Corn (hominy) grits, cooked			
regular and quick	1 cup	145	trace
instant, plain	1 packet	80	trace
Cream of Wheat regular, quick, instant, cooked	1 cup	140	1
Mix'n Eat, plain, cooked	1 packet	100	trace
Malt-O-Meal, cooked	1 cup	120	trace
Oat bran			
cooked	1 cup	110	4
uncooked	1 cup	330	12
Oatmeal or rolled oats			
regular, quick, instant, nonfortified			
cooked	1 cup	110	4
uncooked	1 cup	311	9
instant, fortified, plain, cooked	1 packet	105	3
flavored, cooked	1 packet	160	3

Breakfast Cereals, Cold

FOOD	PORTION SIZE	TOTAL CALORIES	SAT-FAT CALORIES
All-Bran	1 oz (⅓ cup)	70	1
Cap'n Crunch	1 oz (¾ cup)	120	15
Cheerios	1 oz (1¼ cup)	110	3
Corn Flakes	1 oz (1¼ cup)	110	trace
40% Bran Flakes			
Kellogg's	1 oz (¾ cup)	90	1
Post	1 oz (⅔ cup)	90	1
Froot Loops	1 oz (1 cup)	110	2
Golden Grahams	1 oz (¾ cup)	110	6
Grape-Nuts	1 oz (¼ cup)	100	trace
Honey Nut Cheerios	1 oz (¾ cup)	105	1
Lucky Charms	1 oz (1 cup)	110	2
Nature Valley Granola	1 oz (⅓ cup)	125	30
100% Natural Cereal	1 oz (¼ cup)	135	37
Product 19	1 oz (¾ cup)	110	trace
Raisin Bran			
Kellogg's	1 oz (¾ cup)	90	1
Post	1 oz (½ cup)	85	1

GRAIN PRODUCTS

FOOD	PORTION SIZE	TOTAL CALORIES	SAT-FAT CALORIES
Rice Krispies	1 oz (1 cup)	110	trace
Shredded Wheat	1 oz (⅔ cup)	100	1
Special K	1 oz (1⅓ cup)	110	trace
Super Sugar Crisp	1 oz (⅞ cup)	105	trace
Sugar Frosted Flakes	1 oz (¾ cup)	110	trace
Total	1 oz (1 cup)	100	1
Trix	1 oz (1 cup)	110	2
Wheaties	1 oz (1 cup)	100	1

Miscellaneous

FOOD	PORTION SIZE	TOTAL CALORIES	SAT-FAT CALORIES
Barley, pearl, light, uncooked	1 cup	700	3
Buckwheat flour, light, sifted	1 cup	340	2
Bulgur, uncooked	1 cup	600	11
Corn chips	1 oz	155	13
Corn flour	1 tbsp	27	trace
Cornmeal			
whole-ground, dry	1 cup	435	5
degermed			
dry	1 cup	500	2
cooked	1 cup	120	trace
Cornstarch	1 tbsp	29	0
	1 cup	463	trace
Crackers			
cheese, plain	10 (1-inch square)	50	8
sandwich type (peanut butter)	1	40	4
graham, plain	2	60	4
melba toast, plain	1	20	1
rye wafers, whole-grain	2	55	3
saltines	4	50	5
snack-type, standard	1 round	15	2
wheat, thin	4	35	5
whole-wheat wafers	2	35	5
Croissants	1	235	32
Danish pastry			
plain			
packaged ring	1 (12 oz)	1305	196
round piece	1	220	32
fruit, round	1	235	35
Doughnuts			
cake-type, plain	1	210	25
yeast-leavened, glazed	1	235	47

GRAIN PRODUCTS

FOOD	PORTION SIZE	TOTAL CALORIES	SAT-FAT CALORIES
English muffins, plain	1	140	3
French toast	1 slice	155	14
Macaroni, cooked			
firm	1 cup	190	1
tender	1 cup	155	1
Muffins			
blueberry or bran	1 small	140	13
corn	1 small	145	15
Noodles			
egg, cooked	1 cup	200	5
chow mein, canned	1 cup	220	19
Pancakes			
buckwheat	1 (4 inch)	55	8
plain, from mix	1 (4 inch)	60	5
Popcorn			
air-popped	1 cup	30	trace
popped in sunflower oil	1 cup	55	5
candied	1 cup	135	1
microwave			
with hydrogenated soybean oil	1 cup	50–70	6–12
with coconut oil	1 cup	70	39
commercially popped	1 cup	40	22
Pretzels			
sticks	10 (2¼ inch)	10	trace
twisted, Dutch	1	65	1
twisted, thin	10	240	4
Rice			
brown			
raw	1 cup	666	5
cooked	1 cup	230	3
white			
raw	1 cup	670	2
cooked	1 cup	225	1
instant	1 cup	180	1
parboiled	1 cup	185	trace
Rolls			
dinner	1	85	5
frankfurter and hamburger	1	115	5
hard	1	155	4
hoagie or submarine	1	400	16

GRAIN PRODUCTS

FOOD	PORTION SIZE	TOTAL CALORIES	SAT-FAT CALORIES
Spaghetti			
dry	8 oz	838	4
cooked			
firm	1 cup	190	1
tender	1 cup	155	1
Toaster pastries	1	210	15
Tortillas, corn	1	65	1
Waffles, from mix	1 (7 inch)	205	24
Wheat flour			
unbleached white			
sifted	1 cup	420	2
	1 tbsp	26	0
unsifted	1 cup	455	2
cake or pastry			
sifted	1 cup	350	1
self-rising, unsifted	1 cup	440	2
whole-wheat	1 cup	400	3
Wheat bran	1 cup	160	0
Wheat germ	1 tbsp	23	trace

MEATS

FOOD	PORTION SIZE	TOTAL CALORIES	SAT-FAT CALORIES
Beef			
Arm pot roast, braised			
lean and fat	1 oz	99	27
lean only	1 oz	68	11
Bottom round steak, braised			
lean and fat	1 oz	74	14
lean only	1 oz	67	9
Brisket flat half, braised			
lean and fat	1 oz	116	37
lean only	1 oz	77	17
Chuck steak, braised			
lean and fat	1 oz	108	32
lean only	1 oz	78	18

MEATS

FOOD	PORTION SIZE	TOTAL CALORIES	SAT-FAT CALORIES
Club steak, broiled			
lean and fat	1 oz	129	50
lean only	1 oz	69	16
Flank steak, broiled			
lean and fat	1 oz	72	18
lean only	1 oz	69	16
Ground beef, broiled			
lean	1 oz	81	25
extra lean	1 oz	62	14
Porterhouse steak, broiled			
lean and fat	1 oz	85	22
lean only	1 oz	64	13
Rib roast			
lean and fat	1 oz	108	34
lean only	1 oz	70	17
Round steak, broiled			
lean and fat	1 oz	78	19
lean only	1 oz	54	7
Rump roast			
lean and fat	1 oz	98	33
lean only	1 oz	59	11
Shortribs, braised			
lean and fat	1 oz	133	45
lean only	1 oz	84	20
Sirloin steak, broiled			
lean and fat	1 oz	79	19
lean only	1 oz	62	12
T-bone steak, broiled			
lean and fat	1 oz	92	26
lean only	1 oz	61	11
Tenderloin steak, broiled			
lean and fat	1 oz	75	18
lean only	1 oz	58	9
Top round steak, broiled			
lean and fat	1 oz	60	8
lean only	1 oz	55	6

Lamb

FOOD	PORTION SIZE	TOTAL CALORIES	SAT-FAT CALORIES
Arm chop, lean, trimmed, braised	1 oz	79	12
Blade chop, lean, trimmed, broiled	1 oz	65	12
Foreshank, lean, trimmed, braised	1 oz	56	5

MEATS

FOOD	PORTION SIZE	TOTAL CALORIES	SAT-FAT CALORIES
Leg sirloin, lean, trimmed, roasted	1 oz	63	9
Leg shank, lean, trimmed, roasted	1 oz	52	5
Loin chop, lean, trimmed, broiled	1 oz	63	10
Loin chop, lean and fat, broiled	1 oz	83	23
Rib chop, lean, trimmed, broiled	1 oz	60	15
Rib roast, lean, trimmed	1 oz	70	16
Shoulder, lean, trimmed, roasted	1 oz	59	14

Fresh Pork Products
Leg

FOOD	PORTION SIZE	TOTAL CALORIES	SAT-FAT CALORIES
ham, lean and fat, roasted	1 oz	83	19
ham, lean only, roasted	1 oz	62	10
ham, rump half, lean and fat, roasted	1 oz	78	16
ham, rump half, lean only, roasted	1 oz	62	9
ham, shank half, lean and fat, roasted	1 oz	86	20
ham, shank half, lean only, roasted	1 oz	61	9

Loin

FOOD	PORTION SIZE	TOTAL CALORIES	SAT-FAT CALORIES
whole, lean and fat, braised	1 oz	104	26
	1 chop	261	64
whole, lean and fat, broiled	1 oz	98	25
	1 chop	284	73
whole, lean and fat, roasted	1 oz	90	22
	1 chop	262	65
whole, lean only, braised	1 oz	77	13
	1 chop	150	25
whole, lean only, broiled	1 oz	73	13
	1 chop	169	31
whole, lean only, roasted	1 oz	68	12
	1 chop	166	30
blade, lean and fat, braised	1 oz	116	31
	1 chop	275	74
blade, lean and fat, broiled	1 oz	111	31
	1 chop	303	84
blade, lean and fat, pan-fried	1 oz	117	34
	1 chop	368	107
blade, lean and fat, roasted	1 oz	103	28
	1 chop	321	87

MEATS

FOOD	PORTION SIZE	TOTAL CALORIES	SAT-FAT CALORIES
Loin (*cont.*)			
blade, lean only, braised	1 oz	89	18
	1 chop	156	32
blade, lean only, broiled	1 oz	85	19
	1 chop	177	39
blade, lean only, pan-fried	1 oz	80	17
	1 chop	175	38
blade, lean only, roasted	1 oz	79	17
	1 chop	198	42
center loin, lean and fat, braised	1 oz	100	23
	1 chop	266	62
center loin, lean and fat, broiled	1 oz	90	20
	1 chop	275	63
center loin, lean and fat, pan-fried	1 oz	106	28
	1 chop	333	88
center loin, lean and fat, roasted	1 oz	86	20
	1 chop	268	62
center loin, lean only, braised	1 oz	77	12
	1 chop	166	26
center loin, lean only, broiled	1 oz	65	9
	1 chop	166	23
center loin, lean only, pan-fried	1 oz	75	14
	1 chop	178	33
center loin, lean only, roasted	1 oz	68	11
	1 chop	180	30
center rib, lean and fat, braised	1 oz	104	25
	1 chop	246	59
center rib, lean and fat, broiled	1 oz	97	24
	1 chop	264	66
center rib, lean and fat, pan-fried	1 oz	110	30
	1 chop	343	94
center rib, lean and fat, roasted	1 oz	90	22
	1 chop	252	61
center rib, lean only, braised	1 oz	79	13
	1 chop	147	24
center rib, lean only, broiled	1 oz	73	13
	1 chop	162	29
center rib, lean only, pan-fried	1 oz	73	13
	1 chop	160	29
center rib, lean only, roasted	1 oz	69	12
	1 chop	162	28

MEATS

FOOD	PORTION SIZE	TOTAL CALORIES	SAT-FAT CALORIES
Loin (*cont.*)			
sirloin, lean and fat, braised	1 oz	100	24
	1 chop	250	60
sirloin, lean and fat, broiled	1 oz	94	23
	1 chop	278	69
sirloin, lean and fat, roasted	1 oz	82	19
	1 chop	244	56
sirloin, lean only, braised	1 oz	74	11
	1 chop	149	23
sirloin, lean only, broiled	1 oz	69	12
	1 chop	165	29
sirloin, lean only, roasted	1 oz	67	12
	1 chop	175	30
tenderloin, lean only, roasted	1 oz	47	4
top loin, lean and fat, braised	1 oz	108	27
	1 chop	267	66
top loin, lean and fat, broiled	1 oz	102	26
	1 chop	295	76
top loin, lean and fat, pan-fried	1 oz	111	31
	1 chop	337	93
top loin, lean and fat, roasted	1 oz	93	23
	1 chop	274	68
top loin, lean only, braised	1 oz	79	13
	1 chop	147	24
top loin, lean only, broiled	1 oz	73	13
	1 chop	165	30
top loin, lean only, pan-fried	1 oz	73	13
	1 chop	157	29
top loin, lean only, roasted	1 oz	69	12
	1 chop	167	29
Shoulder			
whole, lean and fat, roasted	1 oz	92	24
whole, lean only, roasted	1 oz	69	13
arm picnic, lean and fat, braised	1 oz	98	24
arm picnic, lean and fat, roasted	1 oz	94	24
arm picnic, lean only, braised	1 oz	70	11
arm picnic, lean only, roasted	1 oz	65	11
blade, Boston, lean and fat, braised	1 oz	105	26
	1 steak	594	149
blade, Boston, lean and fat, broiled	1 oz	99	26
	1 steak	647	170

MEATS

FOOD	PORTION SIZE	TOTAL CALORIES	SAT-FAT CALORIES
blade, Boston, lean and fat,	1 oz	91	23
roasted	1 steak	594	151
blade, Boston, lean only, braised	1 oz	83	15
	1 steak	382	71
blade, Boston, lean only, broiled	1 oz	78	16
	1 steak	413	86
blade, Boston, lean only, roasted	1 oz	73	15
	1 steak	404	83
spareribs, lean and fat, braised	1 oz	113	30

Variety Meats and By-Products

Chitterlings, simmered	1 oz	86	26
Feet, simmered	1 oz	55	11
Liver	1 oz	47	4

Pork Products, Cured*

Bacon, cooked	1 oz	163	44
	3 medium slices	109	30
Breakfast strips, cooked	1 oz	130	33
	3 slices	156	39
Canadian-style bacon, grilled	1 oz	52	7
	2 slices	86	12
Feet, pickled	1 oz	58	14

Veal

Breast, lean, braised	1 oz	86	26
Chuck, lean, roasted	1 oz	67	16
Cutlet	1 oz	62	12
Loin, lean, broiled	1 oz	67	17
Rib roast	1 oz	77	21
Round, lean, broiled	1 oz	62	14

*For pork sausage, see **Sausages and Luncheon Meats.**

MIXED DISHES

FOOD	PORTION SIZE	TOTAL CALORIES	SAT-FAT CALORIES
Beef and vegetable stew	1 cup	220	40
Beef potpie (9 inch)	1 slice (3/pie)	515	71
Chicken à la king	1 cup	470	116
Chicken and noodles	1 cup	365	46
Chicken chow mein			
canned	1 cup	95	1
homemade	1 cup	255	37
Chicken potpie (9 inch)	1 slice (3/pie)	545	93
Chili con carne w/beans, canned	1 cup	340	52
Chop suey with beef and pork	1 cup	300	39
Macaroni and cheese			
canned	1 cup	230	42
homemade	1 cup	430	88
Quiche Lorraine (8-inch)	1 slice (8/pie)	600	209
Spaghetti with meatballs and tomato sauce			
canned	1 cup	260	22
homemade	1 cup	330	35

NUTS AND SEEDS

FOOD	PORTION SIZE	TOTAL CALORIES	SAT-FAT CALORIES
Nuts			
Almonds, shelled			
slivered	1 cup	795	60
whole	1 oz (24 nuts)	165	13
Almond butter			
plain	1 tbsp	101	8
honey-cinnamon	1 tbsp	96	7
Almond meal, partially defatted	1 oz	116	4
Almond paste	1 oz	127	7
Almond powder			
full-fat	1 oz	168	13
partially defatted	1 oz	112	4
Brazil nuts, shelled	1 oz (8 medium)	186	41

NUTS AND SEEDS

FOOD	PORTION SIZE	TOTAL CALORIES	SAT-FAT CALORIES
Butternuts, dried	1 oz	174	3
Cashew nuts			
dry-roasted	1 oz (18 medium)	163	23
	1 cup	785	113
oil-roasted	1 oz (18 medium)	163	24
	1 cup	750	112
Cashew butter, plain	1 oz	167	25
	1 tbsp	94	14
Chestnuts, Chinese			
raw	1 oz	64	0
dried	1 oz	103	1
boiled or steamed	1 oz	44	0
roasted	1 oz	68	0
Chestnuts, European			
raw, unpeeled	1 oz	60	1
raw, peeled	1 oz	56	1
dried, unpeeled	1 oz	106	2
dried, peeled	1 oz	105	2
boiled or steamed	1 oz	37	1
roasted	1 oz (3 nuts)	70	1
	1 cup	270	4
Chestnuts, Japanese			
raw	1 oz	44	0
dried	1 oz	102	0
boiled or steamed	1 oz	16	0
roasted	1 oz	57	0
Coconut meat			
raw, shredded or grated	1 cup	283	214
dried, creamed	1 oz	194	157
dried, sweetened, flaked, canned	1 oz	126	72
	1 cup	341	195
dried, sweetened, flaked	1 oz	135	72
	1 cup	351	190
dried, sweetened, shredded	1 oz	142	81
	1 cup	466	263
dried, toasted	1 oz	168	107
Coconut cream			
fresh	1 tbsp	49	42
	1 cup	792	664
canned	1 tbsp	36	27
	1 cup	568	419

NUTS AND SEEDS

FOOD	PORTION SIZE	TOTAL CALORIES	SAT-FAT CALORIES
Coconut milk			
fresh	1 tbsp	35	29
	1 cup	552	457
canned	1 tbsp	30	26
	1 cup	445	385
frozen	1 tbsp	30	25
	1 cup	486	398
Filberts or hazelnuts, chopped	1 oz	180	12
	1 cup	725	48
Formulated, wheat-based			
unflavored	1 oz	177	22
flavored	1 oz	184	24
Hickory nuts, dried	1 oz	187	18
Macadamia nuts			
dried	1 oz	199	28
oil-roasted	1 oz (24 halves)	204	29
	1 cup	960	139
Mixed nuts			
dry-roasted, w/peanuts	1 oz	169	18
oil-roasted, w/peanuts	1 oz	175	22
oil-roasted, w/o peanuts	1 oz	175	23
Peanuts, shelled			
dry-roasted	1 oz (35 kernels)	161	17
oil-roasted	1 oz	165	18
	1 cup	840	89
Peanut butter, smooth	1 tbsp	95	12
Peanut flour	1 tbsp	13	0
Pecans			
dried	1 oz	190	14
	1 cup	720	53
dry-roasted	1 oz	187	13
oil-roasted	1 oz	195	15
Pecan flour	1 oz	93	0
Pine nuts, dried	1 oz	146	20
	1 tbsp	51	7
Pistachio nuts			
dried	1 oz	164	16
dry-roasted	1 oz (47 kernels)	172	17

NUTS AND SEEDS

FOOD	PORTION SIZE	TOTAL CALORIES	SAT-FAT CALORIES
Soybean kernels, roasted or toasted	1 oz	129	8
Walnuts, black, dried	1 oz (14 halves)	172	9
	1 cup	760	41
Walnuts, English or Persian, dried	1 oz (14 halves	182	14
	1 cup	770	60
Seeds			
Pumpkin and squash			
whole, roasted	1 tbsp	18	1
kernels, dried	1 tbsp	47	7
kernels, roasted	1 tbsp	74	10
Sesame, kernels, dried	1 cup	882	104
	1 tbsp	47	6
Sunflower			
in shell, roasted, salted	1 oz	86	8
shelled, dry-roasted, salted	1 tbsp	46	4
shelled, oil-roasted, salted	1 tbsp	51	5
Tahini	1 tbsp	90	10

POULTRY

FOOD	PORTION SIZE	TOTAL CALORIES	SAT-FAT CALORIES
Chicken			
chicken salad	½ cup	340	30
back, meat and skin, fried, batter dipped	1 oz	94	15
	½ back	397	63
back, meat and skin, fried, flour-coated	1 oz	94	14
	½ back	238	36
back, meat and skin, roasted	1 oz	85	15
	½ back	159	28
back, meat and skin, stewed	1 oz	73	13
	½ back	158	28
back, meat only, fried, flour-coated	1 oz	82	10
	½ back	167	22

POULTRY

FOOD	PORTION SIZE	TOTAL CALORIES	SAT-FAT CALORIES
back, meat only, roasted	1 oz	68	9
	½ back	96	13
back, meat only, stewed	1 oz	59	8
	½ back	88	12
breast, meat and skin, fried, batter-dipped	1 oz	74	9
	½ breast	364	44
breast, meat and skin, fried, flour-coated	1 oz	63	6
	½ breast	218	22
breast, meat and skin, roasted	1 oz	56	6
	½ breast	193	19
breast, meat and skin, stewed	1 oz	52	5
	½ breast	202	21
breast, meat only, fried, flour-coated	1 oz	53	3
	½ breast	161	10
breast, meat only, roasted	1 oz	47	3
	½ breast	142	8
breast, meat only, stewed	1 oz	43	2
	½ breast	144	7
drumstick, meat and skin, fried, batter-dipped	1 oz	76	11
	1 drumstick	193	27
drumstick, meat and skin, fried, flour-coated	1 oz	70	9
	1 drumstick	120	16
drumstick, meat and skin, roasted	1 oz	61	8
	1 drumstick	112	14
drumstick, meat and skin, stewed	1 oz	58	7
	1 drumstick	116	15
drumstick, meat only, fried, flour-coated	1 oz	55	5
	1 drumstick	82	8
drumstick, meat only, roasted	1 oz	49	4
	1 drumstick	76	6
drumstick, meat only, stewed	1 oz	48	4
	1 drumstick	78	6
leg, meat and skin, fried, batter-dipped	1 oz	77	11
	1 leg	431	61
leg, meat and skin, fried, flour-coated	1 oz	72	10
	1 leg	285	39
leg, meat and skin, roasted	1 oz	66	9
	1 leg	265	38
leg, meat and skin, stewed	1 oz	62	9
	1 leg	275	40

POULTRY

FOOD	PORTION SIZE	TOTAL CALORIES	SAT-FAT CALORIES
leg, meat only, fried, flour-coated	1 oz	59	6
	1 leg	195	21
leg, meat only, roasted	1 oz	54	6
	1 leg	182	20
leg, meat only, stewed	1 oz	52	6
	1 leg	187	20
liver, simmered	1 oz	53	5
	1 cup	62	7
neck, meat and skin, fried, batter-dipped	1 oz	94	16
	1 neck	172	29
neck, meat and skin, fried, flour-coated	1 oz	94	16
	1 neck	119	21
neck, meat and skin, simmered	1 oz	70	13
	1 neck	94	17
neck, meat only, fried, flour-coated	1 oz	65	8
	1 neck	50	6
neck, meat only, simmered	1 oz	51	5
	1 neck	32	3
thigh, meat and skin, fried, batter-dipped	1 oz	79	11
	1 thigh	238	34
thigh, meat and skin, fried, flour-coated	1 oz	74	10
	1 thigh	162	23
thigh, meat and skin, roasted	1 oz	70	11
	1 thigh	153	24
thigh, meat and skin, stewed	1 oz	66	10
	1 thigh	158	25
thigh, meat only, fried, flour-coated	1 oz	62	7
	1 thigh	113	13
thigh, meat only, roasted	1 oz	59	8
thigh, meat only, roasted (cont.)	1 thigh	109	14
thigh, meat only, stewed	1 oz	55	7
	1 thigh	107	13
wing, meat and skin, fried, batter-dipped	1 oz	92	15
	1 wing	159	26
wing, meat and skin, fried, flour-coated	1 oz	91	15
	1 wing	103	17
wing, meat and skin, roasted	1 oz	82	14
	1 wing	99	17
wing, meat and skin, stewed	1 oz	71	12
	1 wing	100	17

POULTRY

FOOD	PORTION SIZE	TOTAL CALORIES	SAT-FAT CALORIES
wing, meat only, fried, flour-coated	1 oz	60	6
	1 wing	42	4
wing, meat only, roasted	1 oz	58	6
	1 wing	43	4
wing, meat only, stewed	1 oz	51	5
	1 wing	43	4
Duck			
flesh and skin, roasted	1 oz	96	25
	½ duck	1287	332
flesh only, roasted	1 oz	57	11
	½ duck	445	83
Turkey			
back, meat and skin, roasted	1 oz	58	8
	½ back	265	35
back, meat only, roasted	1 oz	48	5
	½ back	164	16
breast, meat and skin, roasted	1 oz	43	2
	½ breast	526	27
breast, meat only, roasted	1 oz	38	1
	½ breast	413	6
leg, meat and skin, roasted	1 oz	48	4
	1 leg	418	37
leg, meat only, roasted	1 oz	45	3
	1 leg	355	26
wing, meat and skin, roasted	1 oz	59	7
	1 wing	186	22
wing, meat only, roasted	1 oz	46	3
	1 wing	98	6

(For chicken and turkey frankfurters and chicken and turkey cold cuts, see **Sausages and Luncheon Meats**)

SAUCES AND GRAVIES

FOOD	PORTION SIZE	TOTAL CALORIES	SAT-FAT CALORIES
Sauces			
Barbecue, ready-to-serve	1 cup	188	6
Béarnaise	1 tbsp	53	29
	½ cup	423	232
Cheese	1 tbsp	28	14
	½ cup	225	110
Curry, dehydrated, prepared w/milk	1 cup	270	54
Curry cream	1 tbsp	40	20
	½ cup	317	160
Hollandaise	1 T	82	47
	½ cup	670	377
Mushroom, dehydrated, prepared w/milk	1 cup	228	49
Sour cream, dehydrated, prepared w/milk	1 cup	509	145
Soy	1 tbsp	11	0
Spaghetti, dehydrated	1 pkt (1.5 oz)	118	2
	1 serving (¼ pkt)	28	1
Spaghetti w/mushrooms, dehydrated	1 pkt (1.4 oz)	118	20
Stroganoff, dehydrated, prepared w/milk and water	1 cup	271	61
Sweet and sour, dehydrated, prepared w/water and vinegar	1 cup	294	0
Teriyaki, dehydrated, prepared w/water	1 cup	131	1
Teriyaki, ready-to-serve	1 tbsp	15	0
White	1 tbsp	24	11
	½ cup	195	88
Gravies			
Au jus, canned	1 cup	38	2
Au jus, dehydrated, prepared w/water	1 cup	19	4
Beef, canned	1 cup	124	25
Brown, dehydrated, prepared w/water	1 cup	9	1
Chicken, canned	1 cup	189	30

SAUCES AND GRAVIES

FOOD	PORTION SIZE	TOTAL CALORIES	SAT-FAT CALORIES
Chicken, dehydrated, prepared w/water	1 cup	83	5
Mushroom			
canned	1 cup	120	9
dehydrated, prepared w/water	1 cup	70	5
Onion, dehydrated, prepared w/water	1 cup	80	4
Pork, dehydrated, prepared w/water	1 cup	76	7
Turkey, canned	1 cup	122	13

SAUSAGES AND LUNCHEON MEATS

FOOD	PORTION SIZE	TOTAL CALORIES	SAT-FAT CALORIES
Barbecue loaf, pork, beef	1 oz	49	8
	1 slice (.8 oz)	40	7
Beerwurst, beer salami			
beef	1 oz	92	31
	1 slice (.8 oz)	75	25
	1 slice (.25 oz)	19	6
pork	1 oz	68	16
	1 slice (.8 oz)	55	13
	1 slice (.25 oz)	14	3
Berliner, pork, beef	1 oz	65	15
	1 slice (.8 oz)	53	13
Blood sausage	1 oz	107	34
	1 slice (.8 oz)	95	30

SAUSAGES AND LUNCHEON MEATS

FOOD	PORTION SIZE	TOTAL CALORIES	SAT-FAT CALORIES
Bockwurst, raw	1 oz	87	26
	1 link (2.3 oz)	200	59
Bologna			
beef	1 oz = 1 slice	89	30
	1 slice (.8 oz)	72	24
beef and pork	1 oz = 1 slice	89	27
	1 slice (.8 oz)	73	22
pork	1 oz = 1 slice	70	18
	1 slice (.8 oz)	57	14
Bratwurst, pork, beef	1 oz	92	25
	1 link (2.5 oz)	226	63
Bratwurst, pork, cooked	1 oz	85	24
	1 link (3 oz)	256	71
Braunschweiger, pork	1 oz	102	28
	1 slice (.6 oz)	65	18
Cheesefurter, cheese smokie, pork, beef	1 oz	93	27
	1 frank	141	40
Chicken roll, light meat	1 oz = 1 slice	45	5
Corned beef loaf, jellied	1 oz = 1 slice	46	7
Dutch brand loaf, pork, beef	1 oz = 1 slice	68	16
Frankfurter			
beef	1 oz	91	31
	1 frank (2 oz)	184	61
	1 frank (1.6 oz)	145	48
beef and pork	1 oz	91	27
	1 frank (2 oz)	183	55
	1 frank (1.6 oz)	144	44
chicken	1 oz	73	14
	1 frank (1.6 oz)	116	22
Ham			
chopped	1 oz	68	16
	1 slice (.74 oz)	50	12
minced	1 oz	75	18
	1 slice (.74 oz)	55	14
sliced, extra lean	1 oz = 1 slice	37	4
sliced, regular	1 oz = 1 slice	52	9
Ham and cheese loaf	1 oz = 1 slice	73	19
Ham and cheese spread	1 oz	69	22
	1 tbsp	37	12

SAUSAGES AND LUNCHEON MEATS

FOOD	PORTION SIZE	TOTAL CALORIES	SAT-FAT CALORIES
Ham salad spread	1 oz	61	13
	1 tbsp	32	7
Headcheese, pork	1 oz = 1 slice	60	13
Honey loaf, pork, beef	1 oz = 1 slice	36	4
Honey roll sausage, beef	1 oz	52	10
	1 slice (.8 oz)	42	8
Italian sausage, cooked, pork	1 oz	92	23
	1 link (5/lb)	216	55
	1 link (4/lb)	268	68
Kielbasa, kolbassy, pork, beef	1 oz	88	25
	1 slice (.9 oz)	81	23
Knackwurst, knockwurst, pork, beef	1 oz	87	26
	1 link (2.4 oz)	209	62
Lebanon bologna, beef	1 oz	64	16
	1 slice (.8 oz)	52	13
Liver cheese, pork	1.3 oz	86	23
	1 slice	115	31
Liver sausage, liverwurst, pork	1 oz	93	27
	1 slice (.6 oz)	59	17
Luncheon meat			
beef, loaved	1 oz = 1 slice	87	29
beef, thin sliced	1 oz	35	3
	5 slices (.74 oz)	26	2
pork, beef	1 oz	100	30
pork, canned	1 oz	95	28
	1 slice (.74 oz)	70	20
Luncheon sausage, pork and beef	1 oz	74	19
	1 slice (.8 oz)	60	16
Luxury loaf, pork	1 oz = 1 slice	40	4
Mortadella, beef, pork	1 oz	88	24
	1 slice (.5 oz)	47	13
Mother's loaf, pork	1 oz	80	20
	1 slice (.74 oz)	59	15
New England brand sausage, pork, beef	1 oz	46	6
	1 slice (.8 oz)	37	5
Olive loaf, pork	1 oz = 1 slice	67	15
Pastrami, turkey	1 oz = 1 slice	40	9
Peppered loaf, pork, beef	1 oz = 1 slice	42	6

SAUSAGES AND LUNCHEON MEATS

FOOD	PORTION SIZE	TOTAL CALORIES	SAT-FAT CALORIES
Pepperoni, pork, beef	1 oz	141	41
	1 slice (.2 oz)	27	8
	1 sausage (9 oz)	1248	364
Pickle and pimento loaf, pork	1 oz = 1 slice	74	20
Picnic loaf, pork, beef	1 oz = 1 slice	66	15
Polish sausage, pork	1 oz	92	26
	1 sausage (8 oz)	739	211
Pork and beef sausage, cooked	1 oz = 1 patty	112	33
	1 link (.46 oz)	52	15
Pork sausage, cooked	1 oz = 1 patty	105	38
	1 link (.46 oz)	48	13
Poultry salad sandwich spread	1 oz	57	9
	1 tbsp	26	4
Salami			
beef, cooked	1 oz	72	22
	1 slice (.8 oz)	58	17
beef and pork, cooked	1 oz	71	21
	1 slice (.8 oz)	57	17
pork, dry or hard	1 oz	115	30
	1 slice (.35 oz)	41	11
pork, beef, dry or hard	1 oz	118	31
	1 slice (.35 oz)	42	11
Sandwich spread, pork, beef	1 oz	67	15
	1 tbsp	35	8
Smoked link sausage			
pork	1 oz	110	29
	1 link (2.4 oz)	265	69
	1 link (.56 oz)	62	16
pork and beef	1 oz	95	27
	1 link (2.4 oz)	229	65
	1 link (.56 oz)	54	15
Thuringer, cervelat, summer	1 oz	98	31
sausage, beef, pork	1 slice (.8 oz)	80	25
Turkey breast meat	1 oz	31	1
	1 slice (.74 oz)	23	1
Turkey ham, cured turkey thigh meat	1 oz = 1 slice	36	4
Turkey roll			
light and dark meat	1 oz = 1 slice	42	5
light meat	1 oz = 1 slice	42	5

SAUSAGES AND LUNCHEON MEATS

FOOD	PORTION SIZE	TOTAL CALORIES	SAT-FAT CALORIES
Vienna sausage, beef and pork, canned	1 oz	79	24
	1 sausage (.56 oz)	45	13

SOUPS

FOOD	PORTION SIZE	TOTAL CALORIES	SAT-FAT CALORIES
Canned			
Asparagus, cream of, condensed			
prepared w/milk	1 cup	161	30
prepared w/water	1 cup	87	9
Bean, black, condensed, prepared w/water	1 cup	116	4
Bean with bacon, condensed, prepared w/water	1 cup	173	14
Bean with frankfurters, condensed, prepared w/water	1 cup	187	19
Bean with ham, chunky, ready-to-serve	1 cup	231	30
Beef broth or bouillon, ready-to-serve	1 cup	6	2
Beef, chunky, ready-to-serve	1 cup	171	23
Beef noodle, condensed, prepared w/water	1 cup	84	10
Celery, cream of, condensed			
prepared w/milk	1 cup	165	36
prepared w/water	1 cup	90	13
Cheese, condensed			
prepared w/milk	1 cup	230	82
prepared w/water	1 cup	155	60
Chicken and dumplings, condensed, prepared w/water	1 cup	97	12
Chicken broth			
condensed	1 cup	78	7
prepared w/water	1 cup	39	4
Chicken, chunky, ready-to-serve	1 cup	178	18

SOUPS

FOOD	PORTION SIZE	TOTAL CALORIES	SAT-FAT CALORIES
Chicken, cream of, condensed			
prepared w/milk	1 cup	191	42
prepared w/water	1 cup	116	19
Chicken gumbo, condensed, prepared w/water	1 cup	56	3
Chicken noodle, condensed, prepared w/water	1 cup	75	6
Chicken noodle with meatballs, ready-to-serve	1 cup	99	10
Chicken rice, chunky, ready-to-serve	1 cup	127	9
Chicken rice, condensed, prepared w/water	1 cup	60	4
Chicken vegetable, chunky, ready-to-serve	1 cup	167	13
Chicken vegetable, condensed, prepared w/water	1 cup	74	8
Chili beef, condensed, prepared w/water	1 cup	169	30
Clam chowder, Manhattan, chunky, ready-to-serve	1 cup	133	19
Clam chowder, Manhattan, condensed, prepared w/water	1 cup	78	4
Clam chowder, New England, condensed			
prepared w/milk	1 cup	163	27
Consommé with gelatin, condensed, prepared w/water	1 cup	29	0
Crab, ready-to-serve	1 cup	76	3
Gazpacho, ready-to-serve	1 cup	57	3
Lentil with ham, ready-to-serve	1 cup	140	10
Minestrone, chunky, ready-to-serve	1 cup	127	13
Minestrone, condensed, prepared w/water	1 cup	83	5
Mushroom, cream of, condensed			
prepared w/milk	1 cup	203	46
prepared w/water	1 cup	129	22
Mushroom with beef stock, condensed, prepared w/water	1 cup	85	14
Onion, condensed, prepared w/water	1 cup	57	2
Onion, French	1 cup	275	70

SOUPS

FOOD	PORTION SIZE	TOTAL CALORIES	SAT-FAT CALORIES
Oyster stew, condensed			
prepared w/milk	1 cup	134	45
prepared w/water	1 cup	59	23
Pea, green, condensed			
prepared w/milk	1 cup	239	36
prepared w/water	1 cup	164	13
Pea, split, with ham, chunky, ready-to-serve	1 cup	184	14
Pea, split, with ham, condensed, prepared w/water	1 cup	189	16
Pepperpot, condensed, prepared w/water	1 cup	103	19
Potato, cream of, condensed			
prepared w/milk	1 cup	148	34
prepared w/water	1 cup	73	11
Scotch broth, condensed, prepared w/water	1 cup	80	10
Shrimp, cream of, condensed			
prepared w/milk	1 cup	165	52
prepared w/water	1 cup	90	29
Stockpot, condensed, prepared w/water	1 cup	100	8
Tomato beef with noodle, condensed, prepared w/water	1 cup	140	14
Tomato bisque, condensed			
prepared w/milk	1 cup	198	28
prepared w/water	1 cup	123	5
Tomato, condensed			
prepared w/milk	1 cup	160	26
prepared w/water	1 cup	86	3
Tomato rice, condensed, prepared w/water	1 cup	120	5
Turkey, chunky, ready-to-serve	1 cup	136	11
Turkey noodle, condensed, prepared w/water	1 cup	69	5
Turkey vegetable, condensed, prepared w/water	1 cup	74	8
Vegetable chunky, ready-to-serve	1 cup	122	5
Vegetable, vegetarian, condensed, prepared w/water	1 cup	72	3
Vegetable with beef, condensed, prepared w/water	1 cup	79	8

SOUPS

FOOD	PORTION SIZE	TOTAL CALORIES	SAT-FAT CALORIES
Vegetable with beef broth, condensed, prepared w/water	1 cup	81	4
Dehydrated			
Asparagus, cream of, prepared w/water	1 cup	59	2
Bean with bacon, prepared w/water	1 cup	106	9
Beef broth or bouillon, prepared w/water	1 cup	19	3
Beef broth, cubed, prepared w/water	1 cup	8	1
Beef noodle, prepared w/water	1 cup	41	2
Cauliflower, prepared w/water	1 cup	68	2
Celery, cream of, prepared w/water	1 cup	63	2
Chicken broth or bouillon, prepared w/water	1 cup	21	2
Chicken broth, cubed, prepared w/water	1 cup	13	1
Chicken, cream of, prepared w/water	1 cup	107	31
Chicken noodle, prepared w/water	1 cup	53	2
Chicken rice, prepared w/water	1 cup	60	3
Chicken vegetable, prepared w/water	1 cup	49	2
Clam chowder, Manhattan	1 cup	65	2
Clam chowder, New England	1 cup	95	6
Consommé, with gelatin added, prepared w/water	1 cup	17	trace
Leek, prepared w/water	1 cup	71	9
Minestrone, prepared w/water	1 cup	79	7
Mushroom, prepared w/water	1 cup	96	7
Onion, prepared w/water	1 cup	28	1
Oxtail, prepared w/water	1 cup	71	11
Pea, green or split, prepared w/water	1 cup	133	4
Tomato, prepared w/water	1 cup	102	10
Tomato vegetable, prepared w/water	1 cup	55	4
Vegetable beef, prepared w/water	1 cup	53	5
Vegetable, cream of, prepared w/water	1 cup	105	13

SUGARS AND SWEETS

FOOD	PORTION SIZE	TOTAL CALORIES	SAT-FAT CALORIES
Candy			
Caramels, plain or chocolate	1 oz	115	20
Carob chips	1 oz or 2⅔ tbsp	140	52
Chocolate			
chips	1 oz or 2⅔ tbsp	140	45
milk, plain	1 oz	145	49
milk, w/almonds	1 oz	150	43
semisweet	1 cup (6 oz)	860	326
sweet, dark	1 oz	150	53
Fondant, uncoated (mints, candy corn, other)	1 oz	105	0
Fudge, chocolate, plain	1 oz	115	19
Hard candies	1 oz	110	0
Jellybeans	1 oz	105	trace
Marshmallows	1 oz	90	0
Other Sweets			
Chocolate mousse	½ cup	300	115
Custard, baked	1 cup	305	61
Gelatin	½ cup	70	0
Honey	1 cup	1030	0
	1 tbsp	65	0
Jams and preserves	1 tbsp	55	0
Popsicle	1	70	0
Puddings			
canned			
chocolate	5-oz can	205	86
tapioca	5-oz can	160	43
vanilla	5-oz can	220	86
dry mix, as purchased, 4 servings/pkg	1 serving	100	0
Dry mix, prepared w/whole milk			
chocolate, instant	½ cup	155	21
chocolate, regular	½ cup	150	22
rice	½ cup	155	21
tapioca	½ cup	145	21
vanilla, instant	½ cup	150	20
vanilla, regular	½ cup	145	21
Sugars			
brown, pressed down	1 cup	820	0
	1 tbsp	51	0

SUGARS AND SWEETS

FOOD	PORTION SIZE	TOTAL CALORIES	SAT-FAT CALORIES
Sugars (*cont.*)			
white			
granulated	1 cup	770	0
	1 tbsp	45	0
	1 pkt	25	0
powdered, sifted	1 cup	385	0
Syrups			
chocolate syrup or topping			
thin-type	1 tbsp	43	1
fudge-type	1 tbsp	63	14
molasses, cane, blackstrap	1 tbsp	43	0
table syrup (corn or maple)	1 tbsp	61	0

Cakes from Mixes (with Enriched Flour)*

FOOD	PORTION SIZE	TOTAL CALORIES	SAT-FAT CALORIES
Angelfood (9¾-inch round)	1 piece (12/cake)	125	trace
Coffeecake, crumb (7¾ × 5⅝ × 1¼ inches)	1 piece (6/cake)	230	18
Devil's food, with chocolate frosting (9-inch round)	1 piece (16/cake)	235	32
Cupcakes	1	120	16
Gingerbread (8-inch square)	1 piece (9/cake)	175	10
Yellow, with chocolate frosting (9-inch round)	1 piece (16/cake)	235	27

Cakes from Scratch (with Enriched Flour)**

FOOD	PORTION SIZE	TOTAL CALORIES	SAT-FAT CALORIES
Carrot, with cream cheese frosting (10-inch tube cake)	1 piece (16/cake)	385	37
Fruitcake, dark (7½-inch round)	1 piece (32/cake)	165	14
Plain sheet cake (9-inch square)			
without frosting	1 piece (9/cake)	315	30
with uncooked white frosting	1 piece (9/cake)	445	41
Pound (8½ × 3½ × 3¼ inches)	1 slice (17/cake)	120	11

---

*Cake mix made with vegetable shortening; frosting made with margarine
**Made with vegetable oil

SUGARS AND SWEETS

FOOD	PORTION SIZE	TOTAL CALORIES	SAT-FAT CALORIES
Cakes, Commercial (with Enriched Flour)			
Cheesecake (9-inch round)	1 piece (12/cake)	280	89
Decadent chocolate cake	1 piece (12/cake)	450	110
Cookies			
brownies with nuts	1	100	14
chocolate chip	4	180	26
fig bars, square	4	210	9
oatmeal, w/raisins	4	245	23
peanut butter	4	245	36
sandwich-type (chocolate or vanilla)	4	195	18
shortbread	4 small	155	26
sugar	4	235	21
vanilla wafers	10	185	16
Devil's food, w/cream filling	1 small cake	105	15
Pound (8½ × 3½ × 3 inches)	1 slice (17/cake)	110	27
Sponge, with cream filling	1 small cake	155	21
White, with white frosting (9-inch round)	1 piece (16/cake)	260	19
Yellow, with chocolate frosting (9-inch round)	1 piece (16/cake)	245	51
Pies (9-inch round)			
Pie crust, from mix (9-inch round)	for 2-crust pie	1485	204
Apple	1 piece (6/pie)	405	41
fried	1 pie	255	52
Blueberry	1 piece (6/pie)	380	39
Cherry	1 piece (6/pie)	410	42
fried	1 pie	250	52
Cream	1 piece (6/pie)	455	135
Custard	1 piece (6/pie)	330	50
Lemon meringue	1 piece (6/pie)	355	39
Peach	1 piece (6/pie)	405	37
Pecan	1 piece (6/pie)	575	42
Pumpkin	1 piece (6/pie)	320	58
Strawberry tart	1 piece (8/tart)	325	60

VEGETABLES AND VEGETABLE PRODUCTS

FOOD	PORTION SIZE	TOTAL CALORIES	SAT-FAT CALORIES
Alfalfa seeds, sprouted, raw	1 cup	10	trace
Artichokes			
raw	1 medium	65	trace
	1 large	83	trace
cooked	1 medium	53	trace
	½ cup hearts	37	trace
Asparagus, raw	4 spears	15	trace
Bamboo shoots, canned	1 cup	25	1
Beans			
black, cooked	1 cup	225	1
great northern, cooked	1 cup	210	1
kidney, raw	1 cup	53	1
lima			
raw	1 cup	176	3
cooked	1 cup	208	1
mung	1 cup	26	trace
pea (navy)			
raw	1 cup	70	1
cooked	1 cup	225	1
pinto			
raw	10 oz	484	2
cooked	1 cup	265	1
snap, raw	1 cup	45	1
Beans, canned			
white, with franks	1 cup	365	67
w/pork in tomato sauce	1 cup	310	22
w/pork in sweet sauce	1 cup	385	39
red kidney	1 cup	230	1
Beets			
raw	2 whole	71	trace
	½ cup sliced	30	trace
cooked, diced or sliced	1 cup	55	trace
cooked, whole	2	30	trace
canned	1 cup	55	trace
Black-eyed peas, cooked	1 cup	190	2
Broccoli			
raw	1 spear	42	1
	1 cup chopped	24	trace
cooked	1 spear	50	1
	1 cup chopped	46	1
Brussels sprouts, cooked	1 cup	60	2

VEGETABLES AND VEGETABLE PRODUCTS

FOOD	PORTION SIZE	TOTAL CALORIES	SAT-FAT CALORIES
Cabbage			
raw	1 cup shredded	20	trace
cooked	1 cup shredded	32	trace
Cabbage, Chinese			
raw	1 cup shredded	9	trace
cooked	1 cup shredded	20	trace
Cabbage, red			
raw	1 cup shredded	19	trace
cooked	1 cup shredded	32	trace
Cabbage, Savoy			
raw	1 cup shredded	19	trace
cooked	1 cup shredded	35	trace
Carrots			
raw	1	30	trace
	1 cup grated	45	trace
cooked	1 cup sliced	70	trace
Cauliflower, raw or cooked	3 flowerets	13	trace
	1 cup flowerets	25	trace
Celery, raw	1 stalk	5	trace
	1 cup diced	18	trace
Chard, Swiss			
raw	1 cup chopped	6	trace
cooked	1 cup chopped	36	trace
Chickpeas, cooked	1 cup	270	4
Coleslaw (made w/light cream)	½ cup	42	2
Collard greens	1 cup chopped	35	1
Corn			
cooked	1 ear	85	2
	1 cup kernels	135	trace
frozen	1 cup	144	2
canned, cream style	1 cup	185	2
Cucumber, raw	1 cucumber	39	trace
	½ cup sliced	7	trace
Eggplant			
raw	1 cup	22	trace
cooked	1 cup cubed	27	trace
Endive, raw	1 cup chopped	8	trace
Garlic, raw	1 clove	4	trace
Kale			
raw	1 cup chopped	33	1
cooked	1 cup chopped	41	1

VEGETABLES AND VEGETABLE PRODUCTS

FOOD	PORTION SIZE	TOTAL CALORIES	SAT-FAT CALORIES
Leeks			
raw	1	76	0
	¼ cup chopped	16	0
cooked	1	38	0
	¼ cup chopped	8	0
Lentils, raw	1 cup	81	0
Lettuce, raw			
butterhead, Boston	1 head (5 inch)	20	trace
	1 outer or 2 inner leaves	trace	trace
crisphead, iceberg	1 head (6 inch)	70	1
	1 wedge (¼ head)	20	trace
	1 cup chopped or shredded	5	trace
looseleaf, romaine	1 cup chopped or shredded	10	trace
Mushrooms			
raw, sliced, chopped	1 cup	20	trace
	1 lb	114	2
cooked	1 cup	40	1
canned	1 cup	35	1
Okra			
raw	8 pods	36	trace
	½ cup sliced	19	trace
cooked	8 pods	27	trace
	½ cup sliced	25	trace
Onion rings, frozen, prepared (breaded and pan-fried in vegetable oil), heated	7 rings	285	54
Onions			
raw	1 cup chopped	55	1
cooked	1 cup chopped	58	trace
Onions, green, raw	½ cup chopped	13	trace
Parsley	10 sprigs	5	trace
Parsnips			
raw	1 cup sliced	100	1
cooked	1 cup sliced	125	1

VEGETABLES AND VEGETABLE PRODUCTS

FOOD	PORTION SIZE	TOTAL CALORIES	SAT-FAT CALORIES
Peas, green			
raw	1 cup	115	1
cooked	1 cup	134	1
Peas and carrots, canned	1 cup	95	1
Peas, split, cooked	1 cup	230	1
Peppers			
hot chili, raw	1	20	trace
	½ cup chopped	30	trace
jalapeño	½ cup chopped	17	trace
sweet, raw	1	20	trace
	½ cup chopped	12	trace
Potatoes			
raw			
flesh	1	88	trace
	½ cup diced	59	trace
skin	from 1 potato	22	trace
baked			
w/skin	1 large	220	1
flesh only	1 large	145	trace
boiled, flesh only	1	120	trace
	½ cup	68	trace
French fries			
frozen, oven heated	10	110	19
fried in vegetable oil (prepared in restaurant)	10	160	23
fried in animal and vegetable oil (prepared in restaurant)	10	158	31
au gratin, dry mix, prepared	1 cup	230	57
hashed brown, frozen, prepared	1 cup	340	63
mashed			
w/whole milk	1 cup	160	6
w/whole milk and margarine	1 cup	225	20
w/whole milk and butter	1 cup	235	65
potato chips	10	105	16
potato salad made w/mayonnaise	1 cup	360	32
scalloped, dry mix	1 cup	230	59
Pumpkin			
raw	1 cup cubed	30	1
cooked	1 cup	50	1
Radishes	4	5	trace
Refried beans, canned	1 cup	295	4
Sauerkraut, canned	1 cup	45	1

VEGETABLES AND VEGETABLE PRODUCTS

FOOD	PORTION SIZE	TOTAL CALORIES	SAT-FAT CALORIES
Shallots, raw	1 tbsp chopped	7	trace
Snow peas, raw or cooked	1 cup	61	1
	1 oz	12	trace
Soy products			
miso	1 cup	470	16
tofu	1 piece (2½ × 2¾ × 1 inches)	85	6
Spinach			
raw	1 cup chopped	10	trace
cooked	1 cup	40	1
Spinach soufflé	1 cup	220	64
Squash			
summer (crookneck, zucchini)			
raw	1 cup sliced	26	1
cooked	1 cup sliced	35	1
winter (acorn, butternut)			
raw	1 cup cubed	43	1
cooked	1 cup cubed	80	3
Succotash, cooked	1 cup	222	3
Sweet potatoes			
baked in skin	1	115	trace
	½ cup mashed	103	trace
boiled w/o skin	1	160	1
	½ cup mashed	172	1
cooked, candied	1 piece (2½ × 2 inches)	145	13
Tomatoes			
raw	1	25	trace
	1 cup chopped	35	trace
cooked	1 cup	60	1
canned	1 cup	50	1
Tomato juice, canned	1 cup	40	trace
Tomato products, canned			
paste	1 cup	220	3
purée	1 cup	105	trace
sauce	1 cup	75	1
Turnips, cooked	1 cup cubed	30	1
Vegetable juice cocktail, canned	1 cup	45	trace
Water chestnuts, canned	1 cup	70	trace
Yam, raw	1 cup cubed	177	1

MISCELLANEOUS

FOOD	PORTION SIZE	TOTAL CALORIES	SAT-FAT CALORIES
Baking powder	1 tsp	5	0
Chili powder	1 tsp	10	1
Chocolate, baking	1 oz	145	81
Cinnamon	1 tsp	5	trace
Cocoa powder	¾ oz	75	3
	1 tbsp	14	trace
w/nonfat dry milk	1 oz	100	5
Curry powder	1 tsp	5	trace
Garlic powder	1 tsp	10	trace
Gelatin, dry	1 envelope	25	trace
Ketchup	1 cup	290	2
	1 tbsp	15	0
Mustard	1 tsp	5	trace
Olives, canned			
green	4 medium or 3 extra large	15	2
ripe, pitted	3 small or 2 large	15	3
Oregano	1 tsp	5	trace
Paprika	1 tsp	5	trace
Pepper, black	1 tsp	5	trace
Pickles			
dill, medium	1	5	trace
fresh-pack, slices	2	10	trace
sweet, gherkin	1	20	trace
Relish, sweet	1 tbsp	20	trace
Salt	1 tsp	0	0
Vinegar, cider	1 tbsp	trace	0
Yeast			
baker's, dry, active	1 packet	20	trace

FROM THE NATIONAL INSTITUTES OF HEALTH
ADULT TREATMENT GUIDELINES
NATIONAL CHOLESTEROL EDUCATION PROGRAM

CRITERIA	ACTION
If total blood cholesterol <200	Repeat total blood cholesterol in 5 years or at physical exam; Recommend general diet
If total blood cholesterol 200–239 and	
• No CHD and <2 risk factors†	Repeat total blood cholesterol annually; Step 1 diet
• CHD or ≥2 risk factors	Determine LDL
If total blood cholesterol ≥240	

If LDL <130	Repeat total blood cholesterol in 5 years; Recommend general diet
If LDL 130–159 and	
• No CHD and <2 risk factors	Repeat total blood cholesterol annually; Step 1 diet
• CHD or ≥2 risk factors	Clinical evaluation; Step 1 or 2 diet
If LDL ≥160	Diet goals: LDL <160 or 　　　　　LDL <130 if CHD present or 　　　　　　　≥2 risk factors

CONTINUE DIETARY TREATMENT FOR 6 MONTHS.
IF GOALS NOT MET, CONSIDER DRUGS.

†RISK FACTORS FOR CORONARY HEART DISEASES (CHD)

• Male sex • Family history • Cigarette smoking • Hypertension • HDL <35 mg/dL
• Cerebrovascular disease or occlusive PVD • Severe obesity • Diabetes mellitus

DIETARY TREATMENT

	STEP 1 DIET	STEP 2 DIET
Saturated fat	<10% of calories	<7% of calories
Dietary cholesterol	<300 mg/day	<200 mg/day

DRUGS

FIRST LINE DRUGS*	DAILY DOSAGE RANGE	MAJOR SIDE EFFECTS	PRECAUTIONS
Cholestyramine	2–6 packets 8–24 grams	GI upset, constipation	Can decrease absorption of other drugs; sudden cessation may cause toxicity from other drugs.
Colestipol	2–6 packets 10–30 grams	GI upset, constipation	
Nicotinic acid	1.5–6.0 grams	Flushing	

*Probucol, gemfibrozil, clofibrate, and lovastatin may be considered for use when bile acid sequestrants or nicotinic acid produces an insufficient reduction in cholesterol. They also may be used in combination with sequestrants.

Verbal Explanation of the Guidelines

• If your total blood cholesterol is **less than 200 mg/dL**:
Have a total blood cholesterol test in 5 years.

• If your total blood cholesterol is between **200 and 239 mg/dL** and you have *no* coronary heart disease and fewer than two risk factors:*

Repeat your total blood cholesterol test annually, and reduce your saturated fat to less than 10% of your daily caloric intake, and your dietary cholesterol to less than 300 mg per day.

• If your total blood cholesterol is between **200 and 239 mg/dL**, and you have coronary heart disease or 2 or more risk factors* for heart disease

OR

If your total blood cholesterol is **240 mg/dL or greater**:

THEN **HAVE YOUR LDL DETERMINED.**

• If your LDL is **less than 130 mg/dL**
Have a total blood cholesterol test in 5 years.

• If your LDL is between **130 and 159 mg/dL**
and you have *no* coronary heart disease and fewer than 2 risk factors* for heart disease:

Repeat your total blood cholesterol test annually, and reduce your saturated fat to less than 10% of your daily caloric intake, and your dietary cholesterol to less than 300 mg per day.

• If your LDL is between **130 and 159 mg/dL** and you *have* coronary heart disease,
or you have two or more than two risk factors* for heart disease, or if your LDL is **160** or greater,

have a clinical evaluation. Reduce your intake of saturated fat to less than 10% (or 7%) of your daily caloric intake and your cholesterol intake to less than 300 (or 200) mg/day.

Your **LDL goals** should be:
If you have *no* coronary heart disease — 160 mg/dL or less
If you have 2 or more risk factors* for heart disease — 130 mg/dL or less.

**Risk Factors
for Coronary Heart Disease (CHD)**
• Male sex • Family history • Cigarette smoking
• High blood pressure • HDL less than 35 mg/dL
• Diabetes mellitus • Severe obesity
• Cerebrovascular disease or occlusive
peripheral vascular disease

DIETARY TREATMENT SHOULD BE CONTINUED FOR AT LEAST 6 MONTHS.

IF GOALS NOT MET, CONSIDER DRUGS.

GLOSSARY

Angina pectoris. An episode of chest pain, often caused by a temporary restriction of oxygenated blood due to narrowing of the coronary arteries supplying the heart muscle. An angina attack is not to be confused with a heart attack, which results from a severe and prolonged lack of oxygenated blood to a part of the heart.

Angiography or angiocardiography. A diagnostic method involving injection of an x-ray dye into the bloodstream. Chest x-rays taken after the injection show the inside dimensions of the heart and blood vessels outlined by the dye.

Aorta. The main trunk artery that carries oxygenated blood from the heart. Lesser arteries branching off from the aorta conduct blood to all parts of the body except the lungs.

Arteriosclerosis. A group of diseases characterized by thickening and loss of elasticity of artery walls. This may be due to an accumulation of fibrous tissue, fatty substances (lipids), and/or minerals.

Artery. A blood vessel that carries blood away from the heart to the various parts of the body. Arteries usually carry oxygenated blood, except for the pulmonary artery, which carries unoxygenated blood from the heart to the lungs for oxygenation.

Atherosclerosis. A type of arteriosclerosis in which the inner layer of the artery wall is made thick and irregular by deposits of a fatty substance. These deposits (called plaques) project above the surface of the inner layer of the artery and thus decrease the diameter of the internal channel of the vessel.

Bile acids. Breakdown products of cholesterol formed in the liver and excreted into the intestine, where they play an important role in the absorption of fats from the foods we eat.

Cholesterol. A fatlike substance found in the cell walls of all animals, including humans. Cholesterol is transported in the bloodstream. Some of it is manufactured by the body and some comes from the foods of animal origin that we eat.

A healthy level of cholesterol is below 200 mg/dL. A higher level is often associated with increased risk of coronary atherosclerosis.

Cholestyramine. A drug used to lower blood levels of cholesterol.

Coronary arteries. Arteries, arising from the base of the aorta, which conduct blood to the heart muscle. These arteries, and the network of vessels branching off from them, come down over the top of the heart like a crown (corona).

Coronary atherosclerosis. Commonly called coronary heart disease. An irregular thickening of the inner layer of the walls of the coronary arteries that conduct blood to the heart muscle. The internal channels of these arteries become narrowed and the blood supply to the heart muscle is reduced.

Coronary bypass surgery. Surgery to improve the blood supply to the heart muscle when narrowed coronary arteries reduce flow of the oxygen-containing blood that is vital to the pumping heart. This reduction in blood flow causes chest pain and leads to increased risk of heart attack. Thus coronary bypass surgery involves constructing detours through which blood can bypass narrowed portions of coronary arteries to keep the heart muscle supplied. Veins or arteries taken from other parts of the body where they are not essential are grafted onto the heart to construct these detours.

Coronary heart disease. Also called coronary artery disease and ischemic heart disease. Heart ailments caused by narrowing of the coronary arteries and therefore a decreased blood supply to the heart.

Electrocardiogram (often referred to as ECG or EKG). A graphic record of the electric currents generated by the heart.

Enzyme. A protein that speeds up specific biochemical processes in the body. Enzymes are universally present in living organisms.

Fats. Also known as lipids. Fats are one of the five major classes of nutrients; the other four are proteins, carbohydrates, minerals, and vitamins. Fats in foods and in the body generally occur as triglycerides.

Heart attack. The death of a portion of heart muscle, which may result in disability or death of the individual, depending on how much of the heart is damaged. A heart attack occurs when a blockage in one of the coronary arteries prevents an adequate oxygen supply to the heart. Symptoms may be none, mild, or severe and may include chest pain (sometimes radiating to the shoulder, arm, neck, or jaw), nausea, cold sweat, and shortness of breath.

Heart disease. A general term applied to ailments of the heart or blood vessels. Some of these are present at birth (congenital) and are either inherited or are the result of environmental influences on the embryo as it develops in the womb. The majority of cases of heart disease, however, are acquired later in life, for example, through the development of atherosclerosis.

High blood cholesterol (hypercholesterolemia). An excess of a fatty substance called cholesterol in the blood, which is often associated with the premature development of atherosclerosis and therefore with increased risk of heart attack and stroke.

High blood pressure (hypertension). An unstable or persistent elevation of blood pressure above the normal range. Uncontrolled, chronic high blood pressure strains the heart, damages arteries, and creates a greater risk of heart attack, stroke, and kidney problems.

High density lipoprotein (HDL). The smallest and most dense lipoprotein, HDL removes cholesterol from LDL and cells and transports it back to the liver, where the cholesterol is broken down into bile acids and excreted into the intestine. HDL is protective against the development of heart disease; high levels of HDL are associated with low risk of heart disease.

Lifestyle. An individual's typical way of life, including diet, kinds of recreation, job, home environment, location, temperament, and smoking, drinking, and sleeping habits.

Lipid. A fatty substance.

Lipoprotein. A complex particle consisting of lipid (fat), protein, and cholesterol molecules bound together to transport lipids through the blood. Lipoproteins are classified according to their density. Three important lipoproteins are Very Low Density Lipoprotein (VLDL), Low Density Lipoprotein (LDL), and High Density Lipoprotein (HDL).

Liver. A large organ in the upper right side of the abdominal cavity, which is involved in the metabolism of fats, produces bile, and performs various other metabolic functions.

Low Density Lipoprotein (LDL). LDL particles are formed by removal of triglycerides from VLDL. LDL is rich in cholesterol. High levels of LDL in the blood are associated with the premature development of atherosclerosis and an increased risk of heart attack.

Metabolism. A general term designating all chemical changes that occur to substances within the body.

Monounsaturated fat. A fat chemically constituted so that it is capable of absorbing additional hydrogen but not as much hydrogen as polyunsaturated fat. These fats in the diet have recently been shown to lower blood cholesterol levels. One example of a monounsaturated fat is olive oil.

Obesity. An increase in body weight beyond physical and skeletal requirements due to an accumulation of excess fat. This puts a strain on the heart and increases the chance of developing two major heart attack risk factors: high blood pressure and diabetes.

Plaque. Also called atheroma. A deposit of fatty (and other) substances in the inner lining of the artery wall, characteristic of atherosclerosis.

Polyunsaturated fat. A fat chemically constituted so that it is capable of absorbing additional hydrogen. These fats are usually liquid oils of vegetable origin, such as corn oil or safflower oil. A diet with a high polyunsaturated fat content tends to lower the amount of cholesterol in the blood. These fats are sometimes substituted for saturated fat in a diet in an effort to lessen the hazard of fatty deposits in the blood vessels.

Saturated fat. A fat chemically constituted so that it is not capable of absorbing any more hydrogen. These are usually the solid fats of animal origin, such as the fats in milk, butter, meat, etc. A diet high in saturated fat content tends to increase the amount of cholesterol in the blood. These fats are restricted in the diet in an effort to lessen the hazard of fatty deposits in the blood vessels.

Sodium. A mineral essential to life, found in nearly all plant and animal tissue. Table salt (sodium chloride) is nearly half sodium. In some types of heart disease, the body retains an excess of sodium and water, and therefore sodium intake is restricted.

Stroke. A blocked blood supply to some part of the brain.

Triglyceride. The main type of lipid (fatty substance) found in the fat tissue of the body and also the main type of fat found in foods. Triglycerides are composed of three fat molecules attached to an alcohol molecule called glycerol. High levels of triglycerides in the blood may be associated with a greater risk of coronary atherosclerosis.

Unsaturated fat. A fat whose molecules have one or more double bonds, so that it is capable of absorbing more hydrogen. Monounsaturated fats, such as olive oil, have only one double bond (the rest are single), and recent evidence indicates that they may lower blood cholesterol levels. Polyunsaturated fats, such as corn oil and safflower oil, have two or more double bonds per molecule and tend to lower blood cholesterol.

Very low density lipoprotein (VLDL). The lightest and largest of the lipoproteins manufactured by the liver, VLDL particles carry triglycerides from the liver to muscle and fat cells throughout the body. VLDL particles are produced and released in large amounts after meals.

TABLE OF EQUIVALENT MEASURES

Volume Measures

1 gallon	4 quarts
1 quart	4 cups 2 pints
1 pint	2 cups
1 cup	8 fluid ounces 16 tablespoons
½ cup	4 fluid ounces 8 tablespoons
⅓ cup	5 tablespoons + 1 teaspoon
¼ cup	2 fluid ounces 4 tablespoons
1 tablespoon	3 teaspoons ½ fluid ounce

Weight Measures

1 pound	16 ounces 454 grams
3.5 ounces	100 grams
1 ounce	28.35 grams

REFERENCES AND RESOURCES

Chapter 1

American Heart Association. *Heart Facts 1985.*

Assembly of Life Sciences, National Research Council. *Diet, Nutrition, and Cancer Committee Report on Diet, Nutrition, and Cancer.* Washington, D.C.: National Academy Press, 1982.

National Cancer Institute, U.S. Department of Health and Human Services. *Diet, Nutrition & Cancer Prevention: A Guide to Food Choices.* NIH Publication No. 85-2711. Washington, D.C.: Government Printing Office, 1984.

National Institutes of Health. *Heart Attacks.* Medicine for the Layman, NIH Publication No. 80-1803. Washington, D.C.: Government Printing Office, 1980.

Pooling Project Research Group. "Relationship of Blood Pressure, Serum Cholesterol, Smoking Habit, Relative Weight, and ECG Abnormalities to Incidence of Major Coronary Events." *Journal of Chronic Diseases* 31 (1978):201–306.

Chapter 2

Brown, M. S., and J. L. Goldstein. "How LDL Receptors Influence Cholesterol and Atherosclerosis." *Scientific American* 251 (November 1984):58–66.

Department of Health, Education, and Welfare. *A Handbook of Heart Terms.* DHEW Publication No. (NIH) 78-131. Washington, D.C.: Government Printing Office.

Department of Health, Education, and Welfare. *The Human Heart: A Living Pump.* DHEW Publication No. (NIH) 78-1058. Washington, D.C.: Government Printing Office.

Heiss, G., et al. "Lipoprotein-Cholesterol Distributions in Selected North American Populations: The Lipid Research Clinics Prevalence Study." *Circulation* 61 (1980):302.

Lipid Research Clinics Program. *The Lipid Research Clinics Population Studies Data Book, Volume 1. The Prevalence Study.* NIH Publication No. 80-1527. Washington, D.C.: Government Printing Office, 1980.

Inter-Society Commission for Heart Disease Resources. "Optimal Resources for Primary Prevention of Atherosclerotic Diseases." *Circulation* 42 (1970, revised 1972):A55–A95.

Chapter 3

Blackburn, H. "Diet and Mass Hyperlipidemia: A Public Health View." In *Nutrition, Lipids, and Coronary Heart Disease — A Global View,* edited by R. I. Levy, et al., 309–48. New York: Raven Press, 1979.

Blankenhorn, D. H., Nessim, S. A., et al. "Beneficial Effects of Combined Colestipol-Niacin Therapy on Coronary Atherosclerosis and Coronary Venous Bypass Grafts." *Journal of the American Medical Association* 257 (1987):3233.

Gordon, T., et al. "High Density Lipoprotein As a Protective Factor Against Coronary Heart Disease: The Framingham Study." *American Journal of Medicine* 62 (1977):707.

Kannel, W. B., et al. "Serum Cholesterol, Lipoproteins, and the Risk of Coronary Heart Disease: The Framingham Study." *Annals of Internal Medicine* 74 (1971):1–12.

Kato, H., et al. "Epidemiologic Studies of Coronary Heart Disease and Stroke in Japanese Men Living in Japan, Hawaii, and California. Serum Lipids and Diet." *American Journal of Epidemiology* 97 (1973):372–85.

Keys, A., ed. "Coronary Heart Disease in Seven Countries." *Circulation* 41 (1970):Supplement 1.

Lipid Research Clinics Program. "The Lipid Research Clinics Coronary Primary Prevention Trial Results. I: Reduction in Incidence of Coronary Heart Disease." *Journal of the American Medical Association* 251 (1984):351.

Lipid Research Clinics Program. "The Lipid Research Clinics Coronary Primary Prevention Trial Results. II: The Relationship of Reduction in Incidence of Coronary Heart Disease to Cholesterol Lowering." *Journal of the American Medical Association* 251 (1984):365.

McGill, H. C., ed. *The Geographic Pathology of Atherosclerosis.* Baltimore: Williams and Wilkins Co., 1968.

Stamler, J. George Lyman Duff Memorial Lecture. "Lifestyles, Major Risk Factors, Proof, and Public Policy." *Circulation* 58 (1978):3.

Stamler, J. "Population Studies." In *Nutrition, Lipids, and Coronary Heart Disease — A Global View,* edited by R. I. Levy, et al., 25–88. New York: Raven Press, 1979.

Chapter 4

American Heart Association. *Eating for a Healthy Heart. Dietary Treatment of Hyperlipidemia.* AHA Publication No. 50-063-A.

American Heart Association. *Recommendations for Treatment of Hyperlipidemia in Adults.* Joint Statement of the Nutrition Committee and the Council on Arteriosclerosis. AHA Special Report No. 72-204-A, 1985.

Goor, R., et al. "Nutrient Intakes Among Selected North American Populations in the Lipid Research Clinics Prevalence Study: Composition of Fat Intake. *American Journal of Clinical Nutrition* 41 (1985):299.

"Highlights of the Report of the National Cholesterol Education Program Expert Panel on Detection, Evaluation, and Treatment of High Blood Cholesterol in Adults." *Archives of Internal Medicine* 148 (1988):36–69.

Chapter 5

Anderson, J. T., F. Grande, and A. Keys. "Cholesterol-Lowering Diets: Experimental Trials and Literature Review. *Journal of the American Dietary Association* 62 (1973):133.

Dennison, D. *The DINE System: The Nutritional Plan for Better Health.* St. Louis: C. V. Mosby, 1982.

Hegsted, D. M., et al. "Quantitative Effects of Dietary Fat on Serum Cholesterol in Man. *American Journal of Clinical Nutrition* 17 (1965):281.

Keys, A., J. T. Anderson, and F. Grande. "Serum Cholesterol Response to Changes in the Diet. II: The Effect of Cholesterol in the Diet." *Metabolism* 14 (1965):759.

U.S. Department of Agriculture. *Composition of Foods.* Agriculture Handbook No. 8. Washington, D.C.: Government Printing Office, rev. December 1963.

Chapter 6

The fat tables are based on data from the following sources:

Dennison, D. *The DINE System: The Nutritional Plan for Better Health.* St. Louis: C. V. Mosby, 1982.

U.S. Department of Agriculture. *Composition of Foods.* Agriculture Handbook No. 8. Washington, D.C.: Government Printing Office, 1963.

U.S. Department of Agriculture. *Composition of Foods.* Agriculture Handbook No. 8. Washington, D.C.: Government Printing Office, sec. 1–12 rev. 1976–84.

U.S. Department of Agriculture. *Nutritive Value of Foods.* Home and Garden Bulletin No. 72. Washington, D.C.: Government Printing Office, rev. 1981.

U.S. Department of Agriculture. *Nutritive Value of American Foods in Common Units.* Agriculture Handbook No. 456. Washington, D.C.: Government Printing Office, November 1975.

Chapter 7

Block, G., et al. "Nutrient Sources in the American Diet: Quantitative Data from the NHANES II Survey. II: Macronutrients and Fats." *American Journal of Epidemiology* 122 (1985):27–40.

Chapter 8

American Heart Association. *Diet in the Healthy Child.* AHA Publication No. 72-203-A; also in *Circulation* 67 (1983):1411A.

Anderson, J. W., et al. "Hypocholesterolemic Effects of Oat Bran or Bean Intake for Hypercholesterolemic Men." *American Journal of Clinical Nutrition* 40 (1984):1146–55.

Kirby, R. W., et al. "Oat Bran Intake Selectively Lowers Serum Low-Density Lipoprotein Cholesterol Concentrations of Hypercholesterolemic Men." *American Journal of Clinical Nutrition* 34 (1981):824–29.

Liebman, B. "What Is This Thing Called Oat Bran?" and "Hot Cereals." *Nutrition Action Health Letter* 12, No. 9 (December 1985):7–11. Center for Science in the Public Interest, 1501 16th Street N.W., Washington, D.C. 20036.

Chapter 9

American Diabetes Association. "Glycemic Effects of Carbohydrates. A Policy Statement of the American Diabetes Association." *Diabetes Forecast* (May/June 1985):20–21; also in *Diabetes Care* (November/December 1984).

Case, R. B., et al. "Type A Behavior and Survival After Acute Myocardial Infarction." *New England Journal of Medicine* 312 (1985):737–41.

Food and Nutrition Board, National Research Council, National Academy of Sciences. *Recommended Dietary Allowances.* 9th edition. Washington, D.C., 1980.

Friedman, M., and R. Rosenman. *Type A Behavior and Your Heart.* New York: Alfred A. Knopf, 1974.

National Institutes of Health. *Exercise and Your Heart.* NIH Publication No. 81-1677, 1981. Available from the National Heart, Lung, and Blood Institute, Bethesda, MD 20205.

Ruberman, W., et al. "Psychosocial Influences on Mortality After Myocardial Infarction." *New England Journal of Medicine* 311 (1984):552–59.

The Sodium Content of Popular Prepared Food Items. Available from Consumer Affairs, Morton Salt Division, Morton Norwich Products, 110 Wacker Drive, Chicago, IL 60606

U.S. Department of Agriculture. *The Sodium Content of Your Food.* Home and Garden Bulletin No. 233. Washington, D.C.: Government Printing Office.

U.S. Department of Health and Human Services. "Health Implications of Obesity." *National Institutes of Health Consensus Development Conference Statement* 5, No. 9 (1985). National Institutes of Health, Office of Medical Applications of Research, Building 1, Room 216, Bethesda, MD 20205.

U.S. Department of Health and Human Services. *Sodium: Facts for Older Citizens.* HHS Publication No. 83-2169. Available from the U.S. Food and Drug Administration, 5600 Fishers Lane, Rockville, MD 20857

U.S. Department of Health and Human Services. "Treatment of Hypertriglyceridemia." *National Institutes of Health Consensus Development Conference Statement* 4, No. 8 (1983). National Institutes of Health, Office of Medical Applications of Research, Building 1, Room 216, Bethesda, MD 20205.

U.S. Department of Health and Human Services, Public Health Service, National Institutes of Health. *The 1984 Report of the Joint National Committee on Detection, Evaluation, and Treatment of High Blood Pressure.* NIH Publication No. 84-1088; also in *Archives of Internal Medicine* 144 (1984):1045–57.

U.S. Surgeon General. *The Health Consequences of Smoking: Cardiovascular Disease.* A Report of the Surgeon General, November 1983. Available from the Office on Smoking and Health, 5600 Fishers Lane, Parklawn Building, Room 110, Rockville, MD 20857.

INDEX

effect of dietary cholesterol
on, 36
receptors, 13–14
low-fat dairy products, 69–70,
71, 72
low-fat ingredients, cost of, 112;
substituting, 110–11
lunch
heart-healthy options, 89–90
menu changes to lower sat-
fat intake, 84–87
luncheon meats
calories (total and sat-fat),
Food Tables 382–86
sat-fat calories in, 68

Ma-Po Bean Curd, 186
Mandelbrot, 338
Marble Cake, 325
margarine, P/S ratio of, 73
Marinated Fish Steaks, 225
Marrakesh, Chicken, 200
Marsala, Turkey Scaloppine, 217
Marvelous Cookies, 340
Matzo Ball Soup, 155
mayonnaise, 75
meal plans (two weeks), 114–
30
meat(s). See also Chicken; Fish;
Turkey
calories (total and sat-fat),
Food Tables, 368–73
and dietary cholesterol, 36;
charts, 37, 67
nutritional value of, 145
red, sat-fat in, 35, 62
sat-fat content of, 61–68
men and HDL level, 15
men and heart disease, risk factor, 96–97
metabolism, 404
Mexicali Pasta, 273

Mexique Turkey, 220
milk
calcium in, 70
high-fat food, 69
low-fat, 69
low-fat, advertising claims,
109
products, nutritional value
of, 144–45
sat-fat content of, 69
skim milk, 69–70
Minestrone, 170
Mocha Cake, 329
modifying recipes, 110–11
Mongolian Hot Pot, 204
Monhegan Island Fish Chowder,
168
Monkfish Broiled with Orange
Sauce, 224
monounsaturated fat, 404. See
also fats
in animal fats, 74
effect on blood cholesterol,
36, 73
Mother's Oat Bran Muffins,
309
Mousse, Strawberry, 343
Muffins
Apple Oat, 308
Apricot Oat, 310
Banana-Carrot, 312
Bran, 311
as breakfast food, 88
Gingerbread, 313
Mother's Oat Bran, 309
Oat Bran, 308
Orange Oat, 310
as snack food, 80
Mulligatawny Soup, 168
Mushroom(s)
and Broccoli, 246
-Celery, 249
Oriental, Braised, 252

IF YOU USE A PERSONAL COMPUTER...

The complete EATER'S CHOICE system can be installed on your PC at an unbeatable price.

Crafted by the leading designers of culinary software, TAKE CONTROL! OF CHOLESTEROL is easy to use, but powerful enough to satisfy the creative home cook or the practicing professional who wants to apply the EATER'S CHOICE system to a variety of situations.

The program calculates a Sat-fat Budget for each Personal Worksheet. Then, you plan meals using the recipe database and a sophisticated indexing system. Dozens of selection criteria satisfy virtually all individual food preferences and needs.

As you add foods to your meal plan, sat-fat balances are calculated there and in a unique PERSONAL DIETARY LEDGER. This daily synopsis facilitates planning as you go. Pressing a single function key anywhere in the program "pops" the ledger from background memory onto your screen.

Making new plans is simple and fast, too. Add days, start fresh, or clone and adapt any existing plan. And since any meal plan can be linked to any worksheet, it's easy to make customized plans from generic types. This makes the system faster to use, the more you use it.

With all of your work neatly organized on floppy disks, hard drives, or tape, this is the most efficient cholesterol control system you can own.

Now available for IBM, TANDY, and other compatible computers. Requires 256K RAM and one or more disk drives. Future editions will be available for Apple Macintosh, Apple //e, and Atari ST computers.

To order TAKE CONTROL! OF CHOLESTEROL, send $39.95 plus $5.00 shipping and handling to:

> Concept Development Associates, Inc.
> 63 Orange Street
> St. Augustine, FL 32084

or phone (904) 825-0220 for VISA/MasterCard orders.

State computer type. If you are an Apple or Atari owner, send us your address and we will notify you when your program is ready to order.

EATER'S CHOICE

POCKET COMPANIONS

Finally at your fingertips — the pocket companions
that put EATER'S CHOICE® to work for you!

EATER'S CHOICE PASSBOOK

The key to lowering your blood cholesterol is to
stay within your sat-fat budget. This convenient,
pocket-sized passbook with a handsome, vinyl
cover contains everything you need to keep
track of your sat-fat intake:

▶ ABBREVIATED FOOD TABLES which list
the total and sat-fat calories for 562 foods
plus space for 46 of your favorites.
▶ BALANCE BOOK for keeping a two-week
record of the sat-fat calories and total
calories of the foods you eat.

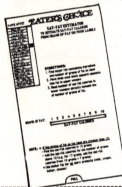

EATER'S CHOICE SAT-FAT ESTIMATOR

How much sat-fat is in Lean Cuisine Cheese Cannelloni or
Carnation Breakfast Bars? Or other convenience foods? This
durable, easy-to-use, pocket-sized slideguide helps you
estimate the sat-fat calories from the grams of fat listed on a
food label. Take it with you to the grocery store so you can
make intelligent food choices.

ORDER FORM

SHIP TO:

Name _____

Address _____

City _____ State _____ Zip _____

ITEM	QUANTITY	PRICE EACH	TOTAL PRICE
Sat-fat Estimator		$2.00	
Passbook		3.00	
Balance book refills		0.75	
Eater's Choice book		11.95	
		5% tax (MD residents)	
		Handling	.50
		TOTAL ORDER	$

Send check or money order to:
Eater's Choice
P.O. Box 2053
Rockville, MD 20852